Cultivating the City in Early Medieval Italy

Food-growing gardens first appeared in early medieval cities during a period of major social, economic, and political change in the Italian peninsula, and they quickly took on a critical role in city life. The popularity of urban gardens in the medieval city during this period has conventionally been understood as a sign of decline in the post-Roman world, signalling a move towards a subsistence economy. Caroline Goodson challenges this interpretation, demonstrating how urban gardens came to perform essential roles not only in the economy, but also in cultural, religious, and political developments in the emerging early medieval world. Observing changes in how people interacted with each other and their environments from the level of individual households to their neighbourhoods, and the wider countryside, Goodson draws on documentary, archival, and archaeological evidence to reveal how urban gardening reconfigured Roman ideas and economic structures into new, medieval values.

Caroline Goodson is Senior Lecturer in the Faculty of History at the University of Cambridge where her research interrogates material remains alongside archival and literary records to evaluate the rise of early medieval polities in the Western Mediterranean. In 2002–3, she was a Fellow of the American Academy at Rome for her doctoral research and subsequently has been funded by the British Academy and the Leverhulme Foundation. A Fellow of the Royal Historical Society since 2010, her previous publications include *The Rome of Pope Paschal I (817–824): Papal Power, Urban Renovation, Church Rebuilding and Relic Translation* (Cambridge University Press, 2010).

Cultivating the City in Early Medieval Italy

Caroline Goodson
University of Cambridge

CAMBRIDGE
UNIVERSITY PRESS

Shaftesbury Road, Cambridge CB2 8EA, United Kingdom

One Liberty Plaza, 20th Floor, New York, NY 10006, USA

477 Williamstown Road, Port Melbourne, VIC 3207, Australia

314–321, 3rd Floor, Plot 3, Splendor Forum, Jasola District Centre, New Delhi – 110025, India

103 Penang Road, #05-06/07, Visioncrest Commercial, Singapore 238467

Cambridge University Press is part of Cambridge University Press & Assessment, a department of the University of Cambridge.

We share the University's mission to contribute to society through the pursuit of education, learning and research at the highest international levels of excellence.

www.cambridge.org
Information on this title: www.cambridge.org/9781108733458

DOI: 10.1017/9781108773966

© Caroline Goodson 2021

This publication is in copyright. Subject to statutory exception and to the provisions of relevant collective licensing agreements, no reproduction of any part may take place without the written permission of Cambridge University Press & Assessment.

First published 2021
First paperback edition 2024

A catalogue record for this publication is available from the British Library

ISBN 978-1-108-48911-9 Hardback
ISBN 978-1-108-73345-8 Paperback

Cambridge University Press & Assessment has no responsibility for the persistence or accuracy of URLs for external or third-party internet websites referred to in this publication and does not guarantee that any content on such websites is, or will remain, accurate or appropriate.

For MRP

Contents

	List of Figures and Tables	*page* viii
	Acknowledgements	xi
	Terms and Measurements	xiv
	List of Abbreviations	xv
1	Urban Gardens and Gardeners	1
2	Patterns and Changes	32
3	The Shape of the Phenomenon	76
4	Alliances and Exchanges	115
5	Values and Ideals	156
6	Conspicuous Cultivation	190
7	Conclusions	222
	Bibliography	238
	Index	291

Figures and Tables

Figures

1. Map of places discussed. *page* xxi
2. Plan of the area of the lower Forum Romanum, including the Temple of Venus and Rome in the Middle Ages. Plan based on Lanciani, *Forma Urbis*, tav. 29. 3
3. Graph of the preserved charters from tenth-century Rome and the proportion of these documents which relate to urban gardens. 6
4. House of the Vestals and House of the Surgeon, Pompeii, in the first century CE. Plan based on Jones and Robinson, 'Water, wealth, and social status at Pompeii' and Anderson and Robinson, *House of the Surgeon, Pompeii*, fig. 1.3. 40
5. Market Garden Orchard at Pompeii, Regio I, Insula XV. Plan based on Jashemski, 'The discovery of a market-garden orchard', fig. 4. 42
6. von Thünen's model of city and hinterland. Image based on Chisholm, *Rural settlement and land use*, fig. 4. 48
7. *Domus* under Piazza dei Cinquecento, Rome. Plan after Meneghini and Santangeli Valenzani, 'Fasi tarde di occupazione', fig. 5. 52
8. Buildings along the via T. Grossi, Milan. A portico of the early fifth century was transformed in the fifth and sixth centuries to houses next to open areas of thick organic soil (Dark Earth). Plan after Caporusso, ed., *Scavi MM3*, fig. 225. 54
9. Plan of the Roman *domus* along the *decumanus maximus* at Brescia, and the residential buildings of the sixth or early seventh century. Plan after Brogiolo, 'The control of public space', fig. 2A. 55
10. Buildings at vico Carminiello ai Mannesi, Naples. Top: rooms on the upper terrace. Below: rooms on the lower terrace. Plan

List of Figures and Tables   ix

     after Arthur, 'Il complesso archeologico di Carminiello
     ai Mannesi', figs. 2 and 52.   56
11. Plan of early medieval Naples with areas of Dark Earth,
     and the location of Maru and Barbaria's garden and other
     gardens known from tenth-century documents.   59
12. Plan of Lucca in the eighth and ninth centuries.   78
13. Map showing density of the sites of properties transacted
     in the preserved tenth-century documents of Naples.   79
14. Map of the locations of *horti* in Rome, and property
     transfers pertaining to gardens, before 800. The large light
     grey areas are the late antique Horti, private ornamental
     gardens which were used as pleasure gardens until late
     antiquity, the squares are domestic gardens or urban garden
     plots identified through property documents from the late
     sixth to late eighth century.   87
15. Map of Crescentius' properties in Rome on the Caelian hill,
     based on documents from the *RS*.   90
16. Houses, gardens, and fields at the Porta Maggiore, Rome, in
     the tenth century, based on documents
     from the *RS* 14 (973), 17 (936), 27 (924), 122 (952).
     Plan after Coates-Stephens, *The Porta Maggiore*, fig. 92.   93
17. Image of the Genoard, Palermo, depicted in twelfth-century
     illustration of the city of Palermo in mourning for the death
     of William II, in Pietro da Eboli, *Liber ad honorem Augusti*,
     Palermo, 1195–7. Bern, Burgerbibliothek, Codex 120 II,
     f. 98 recto. Photograph © Codices Electronici AG,
     www.e-codices.ch.   102
18. Proportions of carpological remains from a Roman rural site
     (left) and a sixth- to seventh-century urban site (right). Data
     from Castelletti et al., 'L'agricoltura dell'Italia settentrionale'.   105
19. Reconstruction of two phases of gardens: vegetables on the
     right, in the early ninth century; and on the left imported soils
     for an orchard and vineyard of the later ninth century. Image
     from Meneghini and Santangeli Valenzani, *Roma
     nell'altomedioevo*, fig. 99.   109
20. Plan of site and samples of the Corso Porta Reno/via
     Vaspergolo, Ferrara. Plan based on Guarnieri and Librenti,
     'Ferrara, sequenza insediativa pluristratificata', figs. 3 and 4
     with additional information from G. Bosi.   111
21. Funerary relief of a vegetable seller, terracotta, h. 432 mm,
     dating from second half of second century CE. Ostia Antica,
     Museo Ostiense inv, no. 198. Photo © Eric Lessing.   117

22. Graph of market concessions in northern Italy. Data from Rapone, Il mercato nel Regno d'Italia. 129
23. Pavement of Forum Romanum, with signs of medieval market stalls. Plan based on Giuliani, 'Una rilettura dell'area centrale del Foro Romano', fig. 211 and Giuliani and Verduchi, *L'area centrale del Foro romano*, tav. III. 133
24. Plan of excavated pits inside the site of the Cassa di Risparmio, Piazza Garibaldi, Parma. Plan based on Bosi et al., 'Seeds/fruits, pollen and parasite remains', fig. 1. 135
25. BAV pal. lat. 187, f. 7r. Photo © Biblioteca Apostolica Vaticana, reproduced by permission of Biblioteca Apostolica Vaticana, with all rights reserved. 186
26. The gardens of early medieval Verona. 214
27. Diploma of Berengar I concerning a garden in Verona, 913 (=*DBI* 89). Photo © The British Library Board, Add Ch. 37631. 215

Tables

1. Property documents and references to urban gardens at Rome. 37
2. Selection of the food crops recovered from Corso Porto Reno, Ferrara, in 950–1050. 112
3. SS. Sergius and Bacchus, Naples, stocks its larder. 150
4. Recipes of BAV, pal. lat. 187, f. 7r, transcription C. Burridge. 184
5. Letters to Fulrad in Paris, BnF, MS lat. 2777. 209

Acknowledgements

Like gardens, books flourish in fertile ground. This project began in Berkeley and was transplanted to London and finally brought to fruit at Cambridge. At home with a small baby, on maternity leave in California, I read Novella Carpenter's *Farm City: The Education of an Urban Farmer* (New York, 2010), an account of her transformation of an empty lot near her house in Oakland into a food-producing garden for her neighbourhood. As a Visiting Scholar in the Department of History, University of California, Berkeley in 2012–13 (with the baby in Cal's amazing Haste Street Child Development Center) I surveyed the charters of early medieval Italian cities and kept seeing gardens and orchards. The parallels between the Bay Area's urban deserts and alternative foodways and the transformations of early medieval Italian cities were striking to me then, and the research carried out at Berkeley and elsewhere in the USA on urban ecology and community agriculture was – and continues to be – very exciting. I remain enormously indebted to Maureen Miller for her friendship and intellectual support at Berkeley and to the Department for making available the resources of the University to me as a Visiting Scholar. My garden project was put to one side when I returned to London and teaching at Birkbeck, but my colleagues there in the department of History, Classics, and Archaeology asked so many good questions about the subject and provided such helpful answers to my questions as they arose that with their stimulus and encouragement I applied for a Research Fellowship from the Leverhulme Trust to concentrate on the project. I am very grateful to my colleagues at Birkbeck for encouragement, solidarity, and for always having a moment to answer a question, especially Fred Anscombe, Jen Baird, Christy Constantakopoulou, Serafina Cuomo, Rebecca Darley, Filippo de Vivo, Catharine Edwards, Vanessa Harding, John Henderson, Lesley McFadyen, Jessica Reinisch, Jan Rüger, and Frank Trentmann. The Leverhulme Trust has been generous in awarding me the grant, which afforded me a year away from teaching to develop interdisciplinary and unconventional research. This research fellowship coincided with another period of maternity leave and then my move to Cambridge in 2017. I am fortunate to have been welcomed into a place filled with outstanding library resources, brilliant, enthusiastic colleagues, administrative support, and students with lots of very good questions. Cambridge has been an invigorating place to finish it, and my colleagues there have turned my eyes to new ways of thinking about cities, economies, and gardens. I would like to thank John Arnold, Gareth Austin, Matthew Gandy, Susanne Hakenbeck, Catherine Hills, Carrie Humphrey, Henry Hurst, Mary Laven, Rosamond McKitterick, Robin Osborne, Peter Sarris, and Andrew Wallace-Hadrill for sharing their ideas and research, asking unexpected questions, and helping me to find my feet in Cambridge. I am grateful to the Faculty of History and the Research Committee of King's College for financial support for the final phases of completing the book, and the King's Work in Progress group for pushing me to revise Chapter 1. I am also very grateful to the staff of the Interlibrary Loan office at University of California, Berkeley, the libraries of the École Française de Rome, the American Academy of Rome, Princeton's Firestone Library, the University Library, Cambridge, and the Rare Books and Music Reading Room at the British Library.

I am very thankful to many other friends and colleagues who have listened to my thoughts, encouraging and challenging me along the way, especially Anthony Bale, Dorigen Caldwell, Wendy Davies, Isabel Davis, Paul Fouracre, Jamie Kreiner, Margaret Meserve, Molly Murray, Jinty Nelson, and Emma Stirrup. I owe a particular debt of gratitude to Lisa Fentress, who has helped me to think through this project over many years and has kept me right on the Roman period, and to Ian Wood, whose belief that this subject might be worth a book sustained its slow gestation. Chris Wickham exhorted me, many times, to just write the book; when I did, finally, he read all of it with exactitude, making extensive comments and further provocations. The two anonymous readers for the press gave many suggestions which have improved the book significantly, I hope they will agree. Many other friends and colleagues have offered help in sharing unpublished material, suggesting sources or approaches and pointing out errors, especially Ross Balzaretti, Giulia Bellato, Giovanna Bosi, Sandro Carocci, Marios Costambeys, Laurent Feller, Clemens Gantner, Patrick Geary, Cristina La Rocca, Cristiano Nicosia, James Norrie, Paolo Squatriti, Riccardo Santangeli Valenzani, and Jack Watkins. At Cambridge University Press, Liz Friend-Smith has been an enthusiastic and thoughtful editor, shepherding it into production with grace and acuity. Denitsa Nenova took my scrappy plans and made consistent and coherent images out of them.

Acknowledgements xiii

As this project has developed, I have tried out my ideas in seminars, and this book benefits greatly from those audiences and their questions at Sheffield (2013), Birkbeck (2015), Oxford Patristics (2015), All Souls, Oxford (2016), Byzantine Worlds (Cambridge) (2018), AIA Clayburgh Lecture, Princeton (2018), AIA Jashemski Lecture, Spokane (2018), University of Colorado, Boulder (2018), CLANS (Cambridge, 2018), Birmingham (2019), Medieval Diet Group (Oxford, 2019), Cambridge Italian Research Network (2019), and Kent Centre for Medieval & Early Modern Studies (2019). The Earlier Medieval Seminar at the IHR, London, heard and commented on it before it was submitted to press, in January 2020, giving me several final nudges in the right directions.

In writing this book I have been reminded of how much of what we do – and what we believe is possible or what we ought to do – is shaped by what our families did. In my family there is a habitus of urban gardening. My father was a top-notch urban gardener in South Texas, growing sweetcorn, green beans, tomatoes, and excellent jalapeño peppers behind the garage, and oranges, lemons, and bananas in the yard. My maternal grandmother had been a farmer and when she retired to the city, she converted the yard of her house to an extraordinarily productive food garden with the best peas, carrots, and rhubarb in Calgary, Canada. My own efforts have never matched their successes, but from childhood I understood not only that it was possible to have a place to grow fresh food next to your house, but also that it was a very good thing. Wendy Davies, Lisa Fentress, and Marina Hamilton-Baillie have provided admirable examples of vegetable gardens and given me advice on planting, pruning, pea-sticks, and purslane. My family has been very forbearing about this project. This project began with my daughter's infancy and has been around for all of my son's life thus far. At various times they both have made toy computers to play with as too often they have seen me typing away on mine. John and Mary Pinkerton have countless times gracefully stepped in to look after babies while I've been away or in the library; my research life would hardly exist without their help. My partner, Mark, has heard too much and too often about the vexations of early medieval charters, the gaps in the archaeobotanical record, my perennial problem of needing books which are in a different city or another country, and many other laments about research and book-writing. With gratitude, appreciation, and love, I dedicate this to him.

Terms and Measurements

Pertica (measure of length): either 5.25 m (12 piedi of 43.75 cm each)[1] or 2.057 m (6 piedi).[2] For the documents discussed in this volume, I believe that Ruggini's measures are more likely and have used 5.25 m (see 'Berengar', p. 212, note 147).

Tavola (measure of area): in (modern) Milan is 0.273 acres (4 sq. *trabucchi*)[3]

Iugerus (measure of area): 2,500 sq. m. 1 *culleus* (50 L) of wine can be made from each 2,500 sq. m[4]

Decimata (liquid measure): used in late antique and early medieval sources from central Italy, uncertain capacity

Salma: a measure or load (as in saddle-pack) of liquid, grain, or salt, in Southern Italy = 270 L[4]

Libra (measure of weight): Roman period = 328.9 g; Carolingian *libra* : 489.6 g

Modius (variable unit of capacity and also of area):

Capacity: a volumetric dry measure, about 8.7 L (6.7 kg) of wheat.[5] As a point of comparison, the ration from late Roman *annona* was 5 *modii* per month (33 kg of wheat, equalling 1.1 kg per day) per citizen.[6]

Area: the amount of land which could be sown with one *modius* of grain. Dimensions varied from region to region, Pierre Toubert calculated that in Lazio in the central Middle Ages, 1 *modius* : 2,300 sq. m.[7]

---

[1] Cracco Ruggini, *Economia e società nell'Italia annonaria*, p. 505.
[2] Zupko, *Italian weights and measures*, p. 189.
[3] Zupko, *Italian weights and measures*, p. 306.
[4] Zupko, *Italian weights and measures*, p. 252.
[5] Carandini, *Schiavi in Italia*, pp. 249–50. See Montanari, *L'alimentazione contadina*, pp. 167–9. In this context the *modius* is probably equivalent to 8.75 L.
[6] Durliat, *De la ville antique*, p. 113, note 195.   [7] Toubert, *Les structures*, p. 459, note 1.

Abbreviations

c.	circa
ch.	chapter
d.	deceased
reg.	ruled
s.	century
AG	*Alfabetum Galieni*, ed. N. Everett as *The Alphabet of Galen: pharmacy from antiquity to the Middle Ages. A critical edition of the Latin text with English translation and commentary* (Toronto, 2012). References given to the numbers and names of substances used in the critical edition.
AGCS	*Il Regesto del monastero dei SS. Andrea e Gregorio ad clivum scauri*, ed. A. Bartola (Rome, 2003).
ARF	'Annales regni Francorum inde ab a. 741 usque ad a. 829, qui dicuntur Annales Laurissenses maiores et Einhardi,' ed. F. Kurze, *MGH, SS RG* 6 (Hanover, 1895).
ASRSP	*Archivio della Società Romana della Storia Patria.*
Benevento	*Le più antiche carte del capitolo della cattedrale di Benevento: 668–1200*, ed. A. Ciaralli, V. De Donato, V. Matera (Rome, 2002).
Cassiodorus, *Institutiones*	Cassiodorus, *Institutiones*, ed. R. A. B. Mynors (Oxford, 1937), translated as *Institutions of divine and secular learning and On the soul*, trans. J. Halporn, Translated texts for historians 42 (Liverpool, 2004).

Cassiodorus, *Variae*	Cassiodorus, *Variae*, ed. Th. Mommson, *MGH, AA* 12 (Berlin, 1894), translated as *The Variae of Magnus Aurelius Cassiodorus Senator*, trans. S. J. B. Barnish, Translated Texts for Historians 12 (Liverpool, 1992).
CDB	*Codice diplomatico barese*, 19 vols. (Bari, 1897–1971).
CDC	*Codex diplomaticus cavensis*, ed. Michele Morcaldi, Mauro Schiani, and Silvano De Stefano, 8 vols. (Naples, 1873–93).
CDL	*Codice diplomatico longobardo*, I-II, ed. L. Schiaparelli, FSI 62–3 (Rome, 1929–33); III, IV.1, ed. C. Brühl, FSI 64–5, IV.2 ed. H. Zielinski (Rome, 1973–83), V, ed. H. Zielinski, FSI 65bis (Rome, 1986).
CDLangobardiae	*Codex Diplomaticus Langobardiae*, ed. G. Porro Lambertenghi, Historiae patriae monumenta 13 (Turin, 1878).
CDMA	P. Fedele, 'Carte del monastero dei SS. Cosma e Damiano in Mica Aurea ab an. 982 ad an. 1200, pt 1, X-XI,' *ASRSP* 21 (1898), pp. 459–534; 22 (1899, pp. 25–107, and pp. 383–447), re-edited with index: P. Pavan: *Codice diplomatico di Roma e della Regione Romana*, 1 (Rome, 1981) (Pavan edition used).
CDP	*Codice diplomatico parmense*, ed. U. Benassi, 2 vols. (Parma, 1910).
CDV	*Codice diplomatico veronese*, ed. V. Fainelli, 2 vols. Monumenti storici ns 1, 17 (Venice, 1940).
ChLA	*Chartae Latinae Antiquiores. Facsimile editions of Latin charters*, First Series, eds. A. Bruckner and R. Marichal, Second Series, eds. G. Cavallo and G. Nicolaj, 118 vols. (Olten and Lausanne, 1954–2019), cited by vol. number.
CIL	*Corpus Inscriptionum Latinarum*, ed. Th. Mommsen et al., 17 vols. (Berlin: 1842–)

Cod.Per.	*Il Codice Perris: Cartulario Amalfitano*, ed. J. Mazzoleni and R. Orefice, 5 vols. (Amalfi, 1985–9).
CSS	*Chronicon Sanctae Sophiae: cod. Vat. Lat. 4939*, ed. J-M. Martin, 2 vols., Rerum Italicarum scriptores 3 (Rome, 2000).
DBI	*I diplomi di Berengario I*, ed. L. Schiaparelli, FSI 35 (Rome, 1903).
Dial.	Gregory I, *Dialogues*, ed. A. de Vogüé, in *Dialogues*, 3 vols., Sources Chrétiennes 251, 260, 265 (Paris, 1978–80).
Dionisi	Dionisi, Giovanni. *De duobus episcopis Aldone et Notingo Veronensi ecclesiae assertis et vindicatis* (Verona, 1758).
Dioscurides	Pedanius Dioscorides, *De materia medica libri quinque*, ed. M. Wellmann, 3 vols. (Berlin, 1907–14), trans. by L. Beck, in *De materia medica. Pedanius Dioscorides of Anazarbus*, rev. ed. (Hildesheim and New York, 2011).
DGL	*I diplomi di Guido e di Lamberto*, ed. L. Schiaparelli, FSI 36 (Rome, 1906).
DKar I	*MGH, DD, Karolinorum I, Pippini, Carlomanni, Caroli Magni Diplomata*, ed. E. Mühlbacher (Hanover, 1906), pp. 77–478.
DLoI	*MGH, DD Karolinorum II, Lothari I. et Lothari II. Diplomata*, ed. T. Schieffer (Berlin, 1966), pp. 1–365.
DLo	'*I diploma di Lotario,*' in *I diplomi di Ugo e di Lotario, di Berengario II e di Adalberto*, FSI 22 (Rome, 1924) pp. 249–88.
DMLBS	*Dictionary of medieval Latin from British sources*, ed. R. E. Latham (Oxford, 1975–2013).
DOI	'Otto I', *MGH DD, Regum et Imperatorum Germaniae I. Diplomata Conradis I, Henrici I et Ottonis I*, ed. T. Sickel (Hanover, 1879–84), pp. 80–638.
DOIII	'Otto III', *MGH DD, Regum et Imperatorum Germaniae II. Diplomata Ottonis II et III*, ed. T. Sickel, 2 vols. (Hanover, 1893), vol. I.

DUL	*I diplomi di Ugo e di Lotario, di Berengario II e Adalberto*, ed. L. Schiaparelli, FSI 38 (Rome, 1924).
ILS	*Inscriptiones latinae selectae*, ed. H. Dessau, 3 vols. (Berlin, 1892–1916).
Jaffé	*Regesta pontificum romanorum ab condita ecclesia ad annum post Christum natum MCXCVIII*, ed. Ph. Jaffé, rev. ed. (Leipzig, 1885).
LP	*Le Liber Pontificalis. Texte, introduction et commentaire*, ed. L. Duchesne, rev. ed., 3 vols. (Paris, 1955–7), translated as *Book of pontiffs (Liber pontificalis): ancient biographies of the first ninety Roman bishops to AD 715*, trans. R. Davis, Translated texts for historians 6, rev. ed. (Liverpool, 2010); *The lives of the eighth-century popes (Liber pontificalis): the ancient biographies of nine popes from AD 715 to AD 817*, trans. R. Davis, Translated texts for historians 13, rev. ed. (rev. ed. Liverpool, 2007), *The lives of the ninth-century popes: the ancient biographies of ten popes from AD 817–891*, trans. R. Davis, Translated texts for historians 20 (Liverpool, 1996).
LSA	*Last Statues of Antiquity*, http://laststatues.classics.ox.ac.uk
LTUR	*Lexicon Topographicum Urbis Romae*, ed. E. Margareta Steinby, 6 vols. (Rome, 1993–2000).
LTUR Suburbium	*Lexicon Topographicum Urbis Romae, Suburbium*, ed. A. La Regina, 5 vols. (Rome, 2001–8).
Manaresi	*I placiti del Regnum Italiae*, ed. C. Manaresi, 3 vols., FSI 91, 96, 97 (Rome:1955–60).
MEC 1	*Medieval European Coinage with a catalogue of coins in the Fitzwilliam Museum, Vol. 1: The Early Middle Ages (5th–10th Centuries)*, ed. P. Grierson, M. Blackburn (Cambridge, 1986).
MEC 14	*Medieval European Coinage with a catalogue of the coins in the Fitzwilliam Museum, Vol.*

	14: *Italy (III) South Italy, Sicily, Sardinia*, ed. P. Grierson, L. Travaini (Cambridge, 1998).
MÉFR	*Mélanges de l'École Française de Rome*
MGH	*Monumenta Germaniae Historica*
AA	*Auctores antiquissimi*
Capit.	*Capitularia regum Francorum*
Conc.	*Concilia*
DD	*Diplomata*
EE	*Epistulae*
Form.	*Formulae Merowingici et Karolini aevi*
LL	*Leges*
SS RG	*Scriptores rerum Germanicum in usum scholarum*
SS RL	*Scriptores rerum Langobardum*
SS RM	*Scriptores rerum Merovingicarum*
Poet.	*Poetae Latini*
MNDHP	*Monumenta ad Neapolitani Ducatus Historiam Pertinentia*, ed. B. Capasso, vol. I (Naples, 1881).
Museo	*Il museo diplomatico dell'Archivio di Stato di Milano*, ed. A. R. Natale (Milan, 1970).
Niermeyer	Jan Frederik Niermeyer, ed., *Mediae Latinitatis lexicon minus* (Leiden, 2004).
Papsturkunden	*Papsturkunden, 869–1046*, ed. H. Zimmermann, 3 vols. (Vienna, 1984).
PG	*Patrologiae cursus completus: series graeca*
P.Ital	*Die nichtliterarischen lateinischen Papyri Italiens aus der Zeit 445–700*, ed. Jan Olof Tjäder, Skrifter utgivna av Svenska Institutet i Rom, 8o XIX, 1, 2, 3, 3 vols. (Lund and Stockholm, 1954–82). Transcriptions have been given from *ChLA*.
PL	*Patrologiae cursus completus: series latina*, ed. J. P. Migne (Paris, 1844–55).
RE	Gregory I, *Registrum epistularum*, in *S. Gregorii Magni Registrum epistularum*, ed. D. L. Norberg. Corpus Christianorum, Series Latina 140, 140A (Turnhout, 1982). Translated as *The letters of Gregory the Great*, trans. J. C. Martyn, *Mediaeval*

	sources in translation 40, 3 vols. (Toronto, 2004).
RF	*Il Regesto di Farfa*, ed. I Giorgi and U. Balzani, 5 vols. (Rome, 1879–1914).
RN	'Regesta Neapolitana,' in *Monumenta ad Neapolitani Ducatus Historiam Pertinentia*, ed. B. Capasso, vol. II, I (Naples, 1885).
Rossini	E. Rossini, 'Documenti per un nuovo codice diplomatico veronese (dai fondi di S. Giorgio in Braida e di S. Pietro in Castello (803–994)', *Atti dell'Accademia di Agricoltura Scienze e Lettere di Verona* 18 (1966–7), 1–72.
RS	*Il Regesto sublacense dell'undecimo secolo*, eds. L. Allodi and G. Levi (Rome, 1885).
SMCM	*Cartario di S. Maria in Campo Marzio*, ed. Enrico Carusi (Rome, 1948).
SMVL	*Ecclesiae s. Mariae in Via Lata tabularium: partem vetustiorem quae complectitur chartas inde ab anno 921 usque ad a. 1045*, ed. L. M. Hartmann, 2 vols. (Vienna, 1895); ed. M. Merores, vol. III (Vienna, 1913).
TSMN	P. Fedele, 'Tabularium S. Maria Novae,' *ASRSP* 23 (1900), pp. 171–237; 24 (1901), pp. 159–196; 25 (1902), pp. 169–209; 26 (1903), pp. 21–141.

Figure 1 Map of places discussed.

1   Urban Gardens and Gardeners

Growing your own food in early medieval Italy was both a necessity and a luxury. To feed a family, you needed land to grow things on. Sometimes you found that land in the ruins or abandoned lots next to you. And sometimes those ruins and that garden plot were prestigious and highly valued. Property documents from tenth-century Rome reveal a bustling city, living and working around its past. In 965, Leo, a priest of the church of SS. Quattro Coronati, located on the Caelian hill, and Helena, daughter of Petrus and Ursa, sold to Crescentius, son of Petrus:

a whole two-story house roofed with tiles,[1] with a courtyard in front of it, in which there is a pergola and a well and a marble stair. And also a large garden next to it and behind it. Wholly planted with vine. With different fruiting trees, and likewise the ruins[2] with use of water, and with all of the things pertaining to them, located in Rome, Regio 2, next to the *Decennias* [i.e. marshland in the southeast of the city]. And between the boundaries on two sides are public roads, one to the Porta Metrovia, the other to the Lateran Palace next to *Decennias*. On the third and fourth sides ... and prepared ground of the monastery of the holy martyr of Christ Erasmus, and a vineyard, in which is the slope of the heirs of Ursa, of good memory.[3]

---

[1] On the terminology of Rome's houses, see Hubert, *Espace urbain et habitat à Rome*, pp. 172–9, and for Italy in general, see also La Rocca [Hudson], '"Dark Ages" a Verona', p. 67, note 149.

[2] On *crypta/cripta* as ruins, presumably with some functional use, see Wickham, *Medieval Rome*, p. 119.

[3] 'me leone religioso presbytero uenerabilis tituli sanctorum quattuor coronatorum. Seu Helena honesta femina filia quoddam petrus. Seu ursa quoddam iugalibus. Sub usufructu dierum uite nostrae do donamus. Cedimus. Tradimus et inreuocabiliter largimur atque offerimus. Nullo nobis cogente. Neque contradicente. Aut uim faciente. Sed propria spontaneque nostre uoluntatis. Post discessum nostrum donamus et largimus tibi crescentio dulcissimo atque dilecto filio petrus. ... Idest domus integram tiguliciam solaratum cum inferioribus et superioribus suis. A solo et usque ad summum tectum. Cum curte ante se in quo est pergola atque puteum et scala marmorea. Et cum introito suo. Nec non et ortuo maiore iuxta se et de post se. in integro uineato. Cum diuersis arboribus pomarum simulque et criptis cum usu aquae. Et cum omnibus ad eas pertinentibus posita rome regione secunda iuxta decennias; Et inter affines a duobus lateribus uie publice. Unam que ducit ad portam mitrobi. Et aliam que ducit a lateranensis sacri palatii iuxta suprascripta decennias. Et a tertio uel a quarto latere [lacuna] seu pastino de monasterio sancti martyris Christi herasmi et uinea in quo est pentoma de heredes quoddam ursa bone memoria. Iuris uestri [uenerabilis?] maioris sacri palatii.' *RS* 90 (965), pp. 135–6. For a map of the area, see Figure 15.

This house, garden, vineyard, and orchard were sold along with a number of suburban properties located outside the walls in Campanino, others at S. Lorenzo, and others outside the Porta Nomentana in a transaction recorded by a charter of 965, which was subsequently transcribed into the eleventh-century *Register* of Subiaco. The description of the properties conveys a rather fine urban parcel, including a substantial house and a range of cultivated land within the circuit of late antique walls around Rome. In this corner of the Caelian hill, the neighbouring lots were also cultivated properties, as the charter makes clear when describing the boundaries, so we might imagine this neighbourhood to have been a rather leafy patchwork of large houses, cultivated lots, and a couple of monasteries.[4] After the sale, the vendors retained use of the possessions for their lifetimes, a typical arrangement in cessions of early medieval Italian properties. The text of the transaction, at least the text as it has been passed down to us by the copy in the *Register* from the monastery at Subiaco, is very much in keeping with contemporary transactions concerning rural properties, as we shall see, and suggests that the buyers and sellers were of relatively high status, doing business within their same social horizon. Their cultivated lands were integral parts of their households, and the lots with houses and gardens were surrounded by other cultivated properties.

There were many types of food cultivation within the city of Rome, even within a single property. This is clear from another document dating to 982, according to which Iohannes, the archdeacon of the church of S. Maria Nova, Rome, rented out for three generations a house in Regio 4, near the Colosseum, to another Leo, this one a priest from SS. Cosma e Damiano (Fig. 2):

It is one two-storied house with roof tiles; the whole thing with lower and upper floor, up to its roof, with a small courtyard and pergola and marble staircase in front of it, with its garden behind it in which there are olive trees or other fruiting trees, with entrance and exit and with all that pertains to it. It is located in Rome, Regio 4, not far from the Colosseum, in the temple which is called the Romuleum [scil. the Temple of Venus and Rome], between the boundaries from one side, the house of Romanus, a smith, and the house of Franco and Sergio, brothers, and the garden of the heirs of Kalopetrus (deceased), and on the second side the garden on Constantinus the priest, and his associates, and on the third side the garden of Anna, most noble girl, and house of Stephen, a bronze-worker, and on the fourth side a public road.[5]

---

[4] On the Caelian Hill and other cultivated properties there, see p. 88, Chapter 3.

[5] 'inter Iohannem ... archidiaconum summae sanctae Apostolicae Sedis et praepositum venerabili diaconiae sanctae Dei genitricis Mariae domin[ae nostrae] quae appellatur Noba, consentientem sibi cuncto clero et serbitores eidem venerabili diaconiae, et te diverso Leonem humilem religiosumque presbiterum venerabili diaconiae sanctorum martirum Cosme et Damiani quae ponitur in Via Sacra ... condutionis titulo. Idest domum solarata

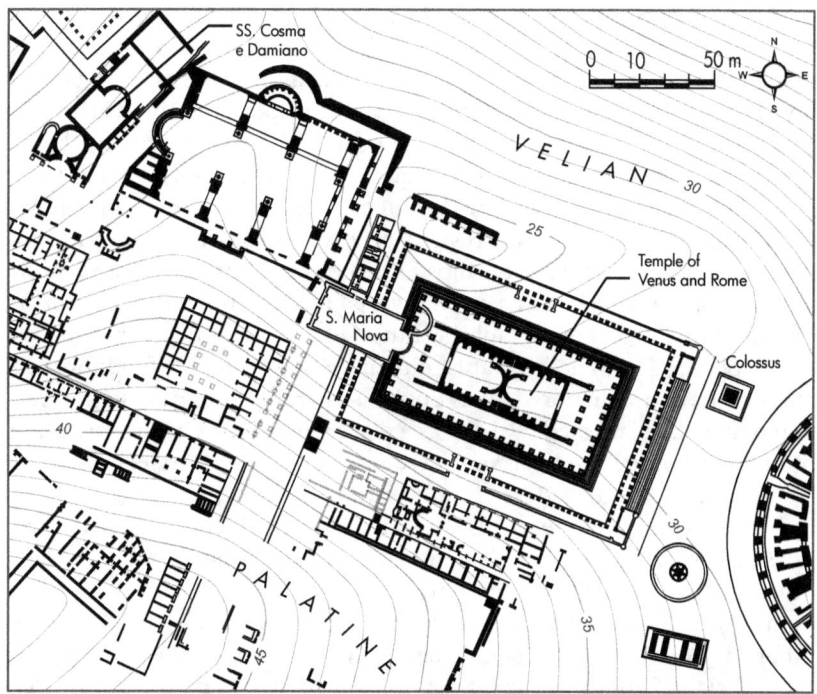

Figure 2 Plan of the area of the lower Forum Romanum, including the Temple of Venus and Rome in the Middle Ages. Plan based on Lanciani, *Forma Urbis*, tav. 29.

Here, on the Roman Forum, a house located within the precinct of an ancient temple is a sizeable structure with different kinds of cultivated land around it. Neighbouring properties were similar holdings, though these may not have been as lavish. A marble staircase and pergola are mentioned specifically in the charter; they may have been particularly

tegulicia et scandolicia una in integrum cum inferiora et superiora sua a solo et usque a summo tecto, cum corticella sua et pergula atque scala marmorea ante se, cum hortuo suo post se in qua sunt arbores olibarum seu ceteras arbores pomarum, cum introito et exoito suo vel cum omnibus ad eam pertinentibus. Posita Romae re[gi]one quarta non longe a Colossus in templum quod vocatur Romuleum, inter affines ab uno latere domum de Romano ferrario, atque domum de Franco et Sergio germanis, sive hortuo de heredes quondam Kalopetro, et a secundo latere hortuo de Constantio presbitero et de suis consortibus, et a tertio latere hortuo de Anna nobilissima puella et domum de Stephano herario, et a quarto latere via publica', *TSMN* 1 (982), pp. 182–4. On the neighbourhood around S. Maria Nova and the temple, see Augenti, *Il Palatino nel medioevo*, pp. 102–3; on the bronze-workers there, see Wickham, *Medieval Rome*, p. 143.

prestigious aspects of this house. The actors in the transaction are neighbours in some sense: S. Maria Nova is located between SS. Cosma and Damiano and the former Temple of Venus and Rome, so the people involved in this rental agreement worked and prayed very nearby this property in the centre of town, where Leo lived. These documents sketch for us the look and feel of the early medieval city, as well as a peek at the lives of its inhabitants, revealing the integral role played by urban cultivation in the life of Romans. Previous scholarship has paid considerable attention to the social relationships forged through property transactions and the ways in which status was conveyed through the re-use of ancient buildings and urban topographies. But the gardens and orchards, which linked people's houses and status to their ability to provide food for their families, have been ignored. This book takes urban gardens as its subject, to redefine the early medieval city as a place where households were often productive, where food gardens were desirable assets, strategically protected, and where new ideas about wealth and welfare emerged.

The survey of the early medieval property documents from the seventh to the mid eleventh century reveals gardens, orchards, and other cultivated lands located both on the edges of the city, as well as in the more densely built-up centre. In early medieval Rome, as in every other city of the Italian peninsula, people organised themselves and their social relations around their food gardens. Many of the people who appear in these Roman documents were attached to a Roman church in one way or another, as clerics, lay officials, or lessees. We see also a tradesman, the smith, and women with allotments; we can see families organising their possessions and inheritances with a view to safeguarding houses – and their gardens and orchards – for subsequent generations.

References to kitchen gardens at houses in Rome appear in letters and contracts from the late sixth century, the mid seventh century at Ravenna, and with increasing frequency as the documentary record expands in the early Middle Ages. The episcopal city of Lucca in the eighth century has been described as 'a garden city' based upon the frequency of '*horti*' among the houses in the preserved property documents.[6] Gardens have been taken as a ubiquitous part of early medieval cities.[7] Food gardens in the medieval city are generally taken by historians as clear signs of the

---

[6] Belli Barsali, 'La topografia di Lucca', p. 488.
[7] 'Avec une belle unanimité, les actes mentionnent tout au long de la période, et bien au-delà, la présence de jardins derrière les maisons. À cela rien d'original: dans toutes les villes, même les plus peuplées, espaces non bâtis et cultivés aéraient le tissu urbain ... Omniprésence des jardinets donc, du Xe au XIIIe siècle, quel que soit le quartier [of Rome]', Hubert, *Espace urbain et habitat à Rome*, pp. 164–5.

decline of the post-Roman world. Once their ubiquity is noted, their causes identified as the economic collapse of the Roman empire, urban gardens are not explored further. Such a summary view overlooks the confluence of many social, economic, and political forces which created the need and the possibility of gardening, and misses the vigorous efforts of people to make and secure their access to gardens, and the values they accorded to self-sufficiency.

In this book I examine the creation of urban spaces for cultivation, their use, by whom and how, and ideas about productive horticulture in the early Middle Ages. The primary place of food-growing in early medieval Italy was certainly in the countryside, in fields, orchards, and gardens that were either owned outright, rented, or worked by obligation or servitude.[8] A geographic division between rural production and urban consumption is nearly universal for urbanised pre-modern cities from antiquity on, but in Italy the distinction became fuzzy for a period between about 500 and 1050 CE, and it is in this period that urban food gardening emerged across the cities of Italy. In the early Middle Ages, much urban property was cultivated for food.

My study of urban gardens, through their textual and archaeological records, provides us with a window onto shifting social structures within the city, the presence or absence of markets in perishable foodstuffs, and emerging ideas of charity. The combined analysis of property documents with letters, narrative chronicles, and new urban archaeology make it now possible to observe urban food provisioning in early medieval Italy and to relate the phenomenon of urban gardening with wider economic patterns, cultural and social contexts, and shifting power structures in the city. The centrality of household economies emerges clearly from this study, as do the rich and sophisticated new ideas about cultivation and Christian charity; these ideas gave colour and value to the economic and ecological transformations of urban landscapes.

A significant proportion of early medieval Italian documents which refer to agricultural land growing fruits, vegetables, grapes, olives, and sometimes nuts describe these cultivated lands as being within cities. A graphic representation of all of the edited property documents, more or less, from tenth-century Rome is provided here (Fig. 3). Out of 186, three-quarters pertain to suburban and rural farmlands owned by people or institutions based in the city, the rest to urban properties; of these, four-fifths are, or include, cultivated spaces. As at Rome, so too at Salerno the majority of the documents which pertain to urban houses include references to cultivated spaces. Paolo

---

[8] Montanari, *L'alimentazione contadina*, pp. 309–36; and on domestic-scale food production in villages, see Petracco-Sicardi, 'La casa rurale nell'alto medioevo', pp. 364–5.

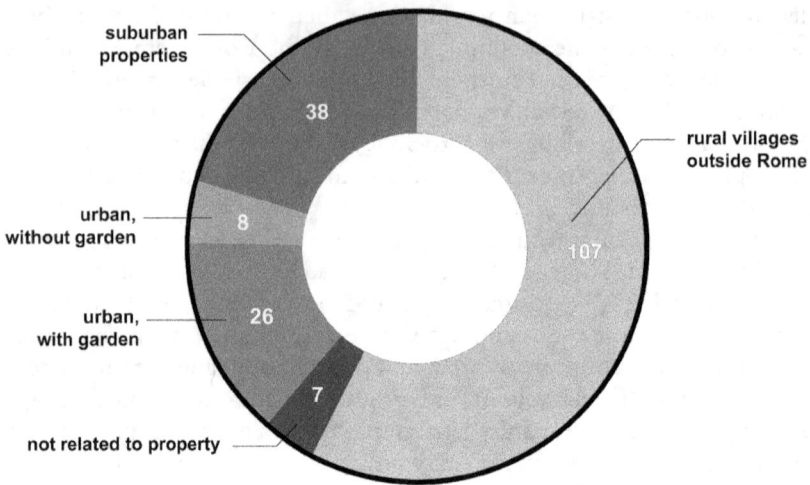

Figure 3 Graph of the preserved charters from tenth-century Rome and the proportion of these documents which relate to urban gardens.

Delogu surveyed property documents from Salerno preserved in the Abbazia di Cava, identifying 105 houses at or around Salerno in the period between 853 and 946 CE. Of these, 10 are urban townhouses, 8 of which have plots of land joined to them.[9] Documents recording property transactions such as these constitute a significant body of evidence for the phenomenon of urban agriculture and reveal, sometimes, not only where there was cultivation within cities but also who owned a garden, and to whom they passed it on.

Through my survey of the property documents from the seventh to the mid eleventh century, I can find gardens, orchards, and other cultivated lands located both on the edges of the city as well as in the more densely built up centre. In early medieval Rome, people organised themselves and their social relations around their food gardens. Many of the people who appear in these documents were attached to a Roman church in one way or another, as clerics, lay officials, or lessees. We see also a tradesman, the smith, and women with allotments; we can see families organising their possessions and inheritances with a view to safeguarding houses – and their gardens and orchards – for subsequent generations.

---

[9] Delogu, *Mito di una città meridionale*, pp. 118–19, notes 23–4. Later in the tenth and eleventh centuries, there are fewer documents recording houses with parcels of land: between 962 and 1064 there are 95 houses, with *curte* or *terra vacua* pertaining to only 10 of them, but 78 are without; 7 are unclear or pertain to houses already tallied.

Ubiquity of Urban Cultivation

Rome was the largest city in Italy in this period and in all of Latin Europe until the eleventh century; it was the most complex city but was in many ways a scaled-up version of other Italian cities. The picture of a city filled with houses next to gardens which emerges from this sample of the documentary record is borne out when compared to Naples and its documents, and across Italy, both in the north and in the south. As in Rome, it was common for wealthy families and monasteries based in Naples to own rural properties outside the city, extending beyond the immediate suburbs to rural villages in the periphery, as well as their houses with gardens inside the city. For example, a family of smiths owned a number of townhouses on the Vico S. Giorgio, within the walls, as well as concentrations of property at the villages of Marano, 6 km to the northwest, and Miano, 3 km to the north.[10] One document describes a property parcel including a 'terra', a term which usually refers to a grain field, within the city and a vegetable garden outside the Porta Capuana.[11] It is unlikely that there were fields of wheat within the city of Naples, which was a relatively small area enclosed by walls, so there was some fluidity to the terminology of cultivated spaces both within the walls and beyond, as we will discuss. Neapolitan documents of the tenth and early eleventh centuries give some sense of the wide range of crops grown in and around the city.[12] These include greens (*folia*),[13] onions and leeks,[14] wheat and millet,[15] grapes for wine, made into young wine (*saccapanna*),[16] fruit and nuts,[17] chestnuts and acorns,[18] white beans,[19] small fava beans,[20] red beans,[21] and barley.[22] There is an occasional reference to citron trees at Naples; citrus trees, such as they were in the

---

[10] Skinner, 'Urban communities in Naples', pp. 291–4.   [11] *RN* 5 (917), pp. 20–1.
[12] For discussion of the products grown in Italian cities, see Montanari, 'I prodotti e l'alimentazione'; Skinner, *Health and medicine*, pp. 4–7; Vitolo, 'I prodotti della terra'. Note that Skinner, *Health and medicine*, p. 7, identified cucumbers in two Neapolitan documents. This identification is a mistranslation of *caucumenas*, which refers to young plants or vine propagations and appears in many documents from Naples and elsewhere. See Libertini, *Documenti del regio archivio napoletano*, p. 70.
[13] *CDC* vol. II, 336 (982), pp. 162–4. It has been suggested that greens were exclusive to Neapolitan documents, *Health and medicine*, p. 7, but they also appear elsewhere, if infrequently, cf. *SMCM* 16 (1072).
[14] *RN* 443 (1033), p. 277 for the monastery of S. Gregorio, grown in Fullotani.
[15] Among many examples, see *RN* 379 (1019), pp. 236–7, from the monastery of SS. Sergio and Bacchus, grown in Paterno.
[16] There are dozens of records specifying payment in kind (wine) for the area of Naples.
[17] *RN* 379 (1019), pp. 236–7.   [18] *RN* 399 (1023), p. 250; *RN* 396 (1022), p. 247.
[19] *RN* 395 (1022), p. 247.   [20] *RN* 3 (915), p. 19; *RN* 281 (993), p. 174.
[21] *RN* 267 (990), pp. 165–6 in Casaferro; *RN* 275 (992), p. 170 in the area of the Porta Romana; *RN* 277 (992), pp. 171–2; *RN* 391 (1021), pp. 244–5.
[22] *RN* 392 (1021) pp. 245–6, in this case for the horses working the vintage.

early Middle Ages, were mostly grown in the south.[23] Through the documentary record, Neapolitan urban cultivation and the people who grew food and received agricultural products in rental payments emerge in fine detail. They are one part of a larger picture of agriculture and its sociopolitical context in early medieval Italy, a part which warrants, I argue, special consideration.

In selecting urban cultivation as the focus of special consideration, I aim to reveal the interrelationships of economies, ideas, and material realities. While on the one hand urban production related to the wider agronomics of medieval Italy, on the other hand it reveals in fine detail how some people negotiated the changed circumstances of urban life in the centuries after the fall of Rome. In focussing on urban farming, we can observe other broad changes, too, such as the church – both the people within the institution and the ideas which they developed and put forward – becoming a major force within society and economies becoming increasingly simplified, local, and centred on households. In this sense, a history of urban gardening serves as a sort of microhistory, a spyhole into urban relationships, household strategies, and the practicalities of getting food on the table, daily, in the profoundly unpredictable world created at the end of empire.

Despite the presumed ubiquity of food gardens, and the abundant evidence provided by property documents, no study has yet attempted to explain when and how the spaces for food horticulture – vegetable gardens, orchards, vineyards, and grain fields – appeared in the urban fabric and how these changes respond to, or provoke other changes in medieval cities. Nor has the significance of urban cultivation as it evolved over time been the focus of research. This absence of study prevails despite, or perhaps because of, the fact that scholars have long noted the omnipresence of cultivated spaces within early medieval cities. Given the intense focus in recent years on the early medieval city as a centre of production and a landscape of power, the extent and nature of early medieval urban horticulture still remain unclear. Does the presence of domestic gardens indicate a shift in landholding patterns or expectations about the nature of the urban landscape? Did they appear in certain sectors of a city more than others? Is there evidence for change over time in their appearance and use, or geographical variation? Early medieval archaeologists, while noting the presence of areas which might have been cultivated, have not examined the ways in which gardens changed

---

[23] 'portionem de domum et de curte et horticello, ubi est cetrarius', *RN* 67 (949), p. 57. On citrus, see Vitolo, 'I prodotti della terra', p. 18 and now *AGRUMED. Archaeology and history of citrus fruit.*

not only the urban profile of the city but also the social and economic landscape. Domestic food production and market gardens in early medieval cities have rarely been analysed at all, despite their widely recognised ubiquity.

Urban gardening was hardly unique to Italy among other parts of the post-Roman world, but there are two reasons for which Italy is a compelling focus of this study.[24] First, the cities of the Italian peninsula were emblematic of the processes of Roman urbanisation across western Eurasia. The legacy of ancient cities – and many of Italy's cities were very ancient by the Middle Ages – was both material and cultural. Roman cities had been the principal places of governance, administration, much commerce, as well as the performance of civilising cultural values and status within imperial hierarchies. A dense network of cities, linked by roads and rivers, had developed across the peninsula during the Roman Republic and became richer and more vibrant in the imperial period, up to about 350.[25] The fabric and built environment of Italian cities endured as a resource to be exploited and re-exploited in subsequent centuries, and the idea of a city as a social and political entity, a machine for the performance of social prestige and power, and an economic condition generated by residential density, underpinned much of Italian society through the Middle Ages.[26] Thus, because Italian cities had been more numerous and more sophisticated than elsewhere and because they provided such central pillars in the structure of early medieval society, the study of urban gardens in Italy is critical to our understanding of how cities and society worked.

The second reason that Italy is a suitable subject for the study of urban cultivation is the availability of evidence. We know more about cities in Italy than about cities nearly anywhere else in early medieval Western Eurasia thanks to documentary archives and well-preserved (and well-excavated) city centres. Documentary records of the properties of early medieval Italy and intensive urban archaeology over several decades of the twentieth century provide ample and diverse angles from which to view urban food production. Using charters, letters, and inscriptions, this book plots the emerging phenomenon of cultivated land inside the medieval Italian city, from domestic vegetable patches, orchards, and

---

[24] Compare Constantinople; see Maguire, 'Gardens and parks in Constantinople'; Koder, *Gemüse in Byzanz*. On Byzantine gardens (broadly defined), see Littlewood et al., *Byzantine garden culture*; Brubaker and Littlewood, 'Byzantinische Gärten'.
[25] On the cities of Roman Italy, Cracco Ruggini, 'La città nel mondo antico: realtà e idea'; Crawford, 'Italy and Rome from Sulla to Augustus'.
[26] Cantino Wataghin, 'Quadri urbani'; La Rocca, 'Public buildings and urban change'; Marazzi, 'Cadavera urbium'; Goodson, 'Urbanism in the politics of power'.

vineyards between houses, to arable fields cleared within city walls. References to these kinds of plots begin to appear in documents of the late sixth century and increase in frequency up to the late eleventh or twelfth centuries, when population pressures began to drive most cultivation outside the city again, as gardens were built over for new houses and suburban areas were developed for commercial agriculture. Urban archaeology provides some additional insights into these changes. The centres of most Italian cities have been excavated, whether in the nineteenth century, after the Second World War, or in modern commercial excavations. Some very recent excavations have included palaeobotanical analysis of pollens and plant remains. The archaeological identification of gardens remains challenging, but excavations have revealed late antique townhouses partially backfilled with earth where deposits of Dark Earth (thick accumulations of dark-coloured sediments) formed. The material realities of early medieval cities, when considered holistically, make newly clear the chronology and extent of the change in structures of townhouses, and the presence of urban agriculture within residential complexes and household economies and the possible roles that urban gardening played in the evolution of new ideas about early medieval societies. Further, by drawing on such textual and archaeological resources, this book also attempts to reconstruct the *un*built environment, revealing the range and intensity of urban cultivation in early medieval Italy and its economic and its social value. Consideration of the interplay between ancient buildings, residential architecture, and cultivated areas provides a new context to examine how people interacted in medieval cities through their urban spaces.

Urbanism

The intense urbanism of Italy is relatively unusual compared with the rest of the Western medieval world, where cities – such as there were – were small central places within territories filled with villages, rural monasteries, and elite country residences.[27] In Carolingian Europe, political ritual and social mobility were often tied to rural lands and their management. The Frankish kingdom (and later the empire), was ruled by the central authority of the king, but also through an extensive web of administrative forces, down to the county level.[28] By contrast, in post-Roman Italy, and in central and southern Italy in particular, cities persisted from antiquity

---

[27] On the unique qualities of Italian urbanism and its historiography, see La Rocca, 'Perceptions of an early medieval urban landscape', pp. 427–8; Wickham, *Framing the early Middle Ages*, pp. 644–56.

[28] Ganshof, *Frankish institutions under Charlemagne*, pp. 71–97.

through the Middle Ages as the key localities of power, politics, and economic activity.[29] Rome was, in many ways, the early medieval city par excellence. It was atypical in its scale but we might consider it the most successful urbanistic effort of the early Middle Ages, the most sophisticated expression of contemporary tendencies: a diversely populated city, with different social groups competing within the urban landscape to achieve and project status, a concentration of population which could both produce goods for exchange and demanded goods from beyond its region, and an elite which drove a market for luxuries. Other cities were less significant in their built fabric but nonetheless effective as tools for political and social mobility: from the period of the Lombard invasions of the mid sixth century onwards, several cities such as Pavia, Milan, Verona, and Benevento became residences of the new rulers and strategic positions in the military efforts against the Byzantines, while Naples, Rome, and Ravenna preserved official residences and administrative centres for the Byzantines.[30]

Much scholarly effort over the past forty years has gone into establishing and arguing over the qualities and characteristics of these cities in their transition to the early Middle Ages. Historians and archaeologists, depending on the countries in which they work, or the kind of evidence with which they work, have argued about what constitutes a city in the early Middle Ages, given the obvious decline (or devolution) of early medieval society and economy with respect to the Roman period.[31] Some emphasised the preservation of street grids and toponyms, or the maintenance of urban fortifications as testimony to the continuity of early medieval cities with their ancient past; others claimed that the fragmentation of urban fabric, the abandonment of much monumental architecture of antiquity and its replacement by timber buildings or open spaces, attests a radical rupture with the ancient pasts of Italian cities, and there could hardly be a claim of urban continuity.[32] The presence of cultivated spaces within urban areas was a charged wire within these discussions about definitions, as cultivation has been held to be a key marker of the ruralisation – and thus decline – of cities:

---

[29] Goodson, 'Urbanism in the politics of power', and discussion in Chapter 4.
[30] Goodson, 'Urbanism in the politics of power'; Brogiolo, 'Capitali e residenze regie'.
[31] For collections of essays related to this debate, see Brogiolo and Ward-Perkins (eds.), *Idea and ideal of the town*; Brogiolo et al., *Towns and their territories*; Christie and Loseby (eds.), *Towns in transition*; Hobley and Hodges (eds.), *The rebirth of towns in the West*. For a summary of the debate from the trenches, see Wickham, 'La città altomedievale'; for a retrospective view looking back on the debate, see Ward-Perkins, 'Continuitists, catastrophists'.
[32] For a summary, see Ward-Perkins, 'Continuitists, catastrophists'.

12   Urban Gardens and Gardeners

The countryside penetrated the city: fields, gardens, vineyards, and empty spaces were also on the insides of cities; whenever reference is made to a house, it is always surrounded by a plot of land; [the urban house] is presented to us as an element added to the land.[33]

In 1984, Gian Pietro Brogiolo described an overall picture of early medieval cities in Italy that was 'not very far from the rural model', and for him this was a loss, a negative trajectory of early medieval society.[34] An English archaeologist working in Verona, Peter Hudson, identified evidence for urban cultivation in the area around the Cortile del Tribunale in the heart of ancient Verona, and described this as 'an image of desolation and ruralisation of the early medieval city'.[35] The presence of cultivated spaces within Italian cities has similarly been described as 'an invasion'[36] or a 'descent into rurality'[37] and urban transformation has been cast as a social failing. Thus, for Andrea Carandini, the *eminence grise* of Roman archaeology, early medieval cities were ignoble social failures:

A nobleman who has become a bum is a nobleman only in spirit and a pauper in reality. Thus, an early medieval centre can continue to be considered the city that once it had been by who looks after souls and goods, even if it now it is little more than a squalid village. By efforts of misery and degradation, the nobleman looks more and more like a real bum and the city sheds its noble urban mantle, looking more and more like a village.[38]

These ideas have had a long life. Jean-Marie Martin, in his consideration of early medieval 'cultivated space' in southern Italy, excludes urban cultivated space as something aberrant, even while he acknowledges that agriculture was able 'to insinuate itself even inside towns'.[39] There have been alternative voices. Cristina La Rocca made the most optimistic case, already in 1986, also based on Verona. She argued that the changes to the early medieval city were not a worsening of conditions, but rather a new model: migrations into Italy and the reconfiguration of a new political class with the Lombards enabled the reconceptualisation of

---

[33] Galetti, 'Struttura materiale e funzioni', pp. 112–13, with reference to Piacenza.
[34] Brogiolo, 'La città tra tarda antichità e medioevo', pp. 48–55, quote on p. 53.
[35] Hudson, 'La dinamica dell'insediamento urbano', p. 289.
[36] Brogiolo, 'Capitali e residenze regie', p. 14.
[37] Gelichi, 'The cities', esp. pp. 181–2; Montanari, *L'alimentazione contadina*, p. 25; Montanari, 'Structures de production', p. 283.
[38] '... un nobile decaduto a barbone è un nobile solo nello spirito e un povero nella realtà. Cosí un centro altomedievale può continuare a essere considerato la città che un tempo era stata da chi amministra anime e beni, anche se ormai si tratta solo piú di uno squallido borgo. A forza di miseria e di degradazione il nobile somiglierà sempre piú a un vero barbone e la città si spoglierà gradualmente dell'aulico manto urbano, somigliando sempre piú a un villaggio', Carandini, 'L'ultima civiltà sepolta', p. 27.
[39] Martin, 'L'espace cultivé', p. 238.

ancient cities. While there was a strong interest in certain aspects of the cities of antiquity, the changes to cities, both in their ideals and in their realities, were part of the transformation of 'cultural values and of the exigencies of political affirmation'.[40] The weakening of boundaries between the activities in the countryside and those in the city had implications for society, too.[41]

If some scholars have insisted on the usefulness of urbanism as a line of inquiry in the early Middle Ages, whether they insist on the breakdown of urbanism or the perseverance of it, others have advocated abandoning it altogether. In their study of the pre-modern Mediterranean, Peregrine Horden and Nicholas Purcell argued for abandoning urbanism as an analytical category. 'Neither route nor town is a particularly helpful category. Both can be dissolved into less readily mappable kinds of microecological functioning and interaction'.[42] They cast out towns/cities and investment in them as a heuristic and replaced it with 'microecologies'. Horden and Purcell are indeed correct in the sense that a town never existed independently of its countryside; the agricultural hinterland of the city fed it, supported its economy. But a fundamental element of medieval Italian culture was its cities, and to negate the relevance of urbanism to medieval societies is to reject a category that was of principal interest to the people we are examining here. In this book, my interest is not in the city per se, but in the city as a particular form of cultural behaviour, of investment and effort with particular conditions and qualities of population density and political centrality.[43] Examining cultivation within cities both helps us to understand systems of food provisioning as well as it reveals hierarchies and values within cities, which were central to early medieval life in Italy.

The urban contexts of early middle Italy were defined and set apart in our medieval sources long ago, not just by modern scholars. For medieval perspectives, the first distinction to be drawn between urban and rural was whether something was located within the walls, or without. Early medieval communities invested heavily in the creation of urban defences,

---

[40] La Rocca [Hudson], 'Città altomedievali', p. 733; La Rocca [Hudson], '"Dark Ages" a Verona', p. 77. Her arguments evolved and became more complex with time and in response to the debate. See La Rocca, 'Lo spazio urbano', esp. p. 399; La Rocca and Majocchi, *Urban identities in northern Italy*. See also Zanini, *Le Italie bizantine*, pp. 200–2, who distinguished between the physical ruralisation and the social ruralisation of cities.
[41] Galasso, 'Le città campane nell'alto medioevo', esp. pp. 83–4; Arthur, 'La città in Italia meridionale in età tardoantica'.
[42] Horden and Purcell, *The corrupting sea*, pp. 89–108, quotation at p. 90.
[43] Chris Wickham asserted the value of a Weberian *Kriterienbundel* of different aspects of city-ness which usefully constitute a heuristic for the early Middle Ages, *Framing the early Middle Ages*, p. 592; see also Loseby, 'Gregory's cities'.

in Italy as well as elsewhere.[44] Sometimes, these circuits of walls included larger areas than ancient ones had done (this is the case, for example, at Milan, Ravenna, and Verona); in other cases and usually earlier, walls were simply rebuilt and repaired, leaving certain major elements of urban landscape without the walls. City walls in late antique and early medieval Italy served to delineate the areas that were explicitly under the care of the public authority of the city, whatever or whomever that might be.[45] This delineation sometimes excluded parts of the city which were integral to the collective identity and life of a city, such as cult centres and saints' shrines, or (less often) rulers' residences.[46] Processions moved inside and outside the walls, and the practice of civic and religious ritual knitted together the buildings and spaces inside the walls and outside.[47] Thus, we might imagine that in the early Middle Ages there was a certain degree of fluidity between the city inside the walls and immediately adjacent suburbs; the latter, though extramural, were nonetheless functionally integrated into the urban centre.

The authors of early medieval property documents made very clear whether a parcel of property is located within a city's walls. The documents specify whether a plot is in the city where the document was recorded (using phrases such as *in hanc urbem* or *hic infra civitate*) or next to the walls of the city, *prope muris civitatis*; otherwise, it may name the village or territory where the land is found. 'Urban' thus existed as a category for early medieval Italy, separate from everything that was not within the city, and this distinction was emphasised and reiterated by notarial practice.[48] The documents of early medieval Italy placed great emphasis on the city as a fixed topographic and socio-geographic entity, with clear boundaries between what happened inside the walls and immediately outside, and what happened beyond the city. We must therefore uphold the heuristic of our sources.

In leaving aside the debates about continuity or rupture, vibrancy or decline, we can also set aside these debates regarding ruralisation as a characteristic of Lombards or any other ethnic category.[49] As has

---

[44] Tracy, *City walls*; Wickham, 'Bounding the city'; Christie, *From Constantine to Charlemagne*, pp. 319–24; Christie, 'War and order'.
[45] La Rocca, 'Lo spazio urbano', p. 417.
[46] Carver, *Arguments in stone*, p. 33; Goodson, 'Urbanism in the politics of power'.
[47] On urban processions, see Andrews, 'The Laetaniae Septiformes'; Lønstrup Dal Santo, 'Rite of passage'; Flanigan, 'Moving subjects'; Dey, *The afterlife of the Roman city*.
[48] Mengozzi, *La città italiana*, pp. 93–4; La Rocca, 'Lo spazio urbano', pp. 426–7. For Milan in particular, see Balzaretti, *The lands of Saint Ambrose*, pp. 280–2. For an argument to contextualise the terminological distinctions made in property documents, see Settia, 'Identification et ventilation'.
[49] Fumagalli, 'Langobardia e Romania'.

been clearly shown by La Rocca, the arguments made by Michelangelo Cagiano de Azevedo and others that there existed ethnically distinct forms of urbanisation which centred on types of housing, approaches to ancient public monuments, and degree of ruralisation, are not supported by critical examination of evidence.[50] Across the whole of Italy – Lombard, Roman, and Byzantine – there is evidence for cultivation within urban contexts. Some areas had greater or lesser frequency of urban gardens, and across Italy, different terms were used for the spaces, and the means by which people owned them varied, too; people of 'ethnicity' or cultural identities of the owners had urban gardens.

Sources: Documents

Urban food-cultivating lands are referred to in the documentary record by numerous different terms that make clear the horticultural purpose of the plot and which can be treated as synonyms for our purposes: *(h)ortus, orticellus, ortalis, hortalicium, gardinus, iardinellus*.[51] The language of the medieval documents follows the usage of antiquity: *hortus* and derivations of it referred to a cultivated space, usually dedicated to the cultivation of fruits, flowers, and vegetables for consumption or sale, what we might now in English call by a range of different names: vegetable patch, vineyard, orchard, or garden.[52] In antiquity, a *hortus* (or *ortus*, or *ortalis*) was most often attached to a house or a tomb and was differentiated from a field (*ager*) or monumental parks (the named *horti* of Rome, discussed in Chapter 2, Rome, p. 47). In the early Middle Ages, horticultural terminology became much more fluid, following regional variations in vocabulary more than variations in practice. Occasionally there is a reference to a *uiridarium*, which for Italian documents referred to an ornamental pleasure garden, not a productive one.[53] In medieval property documents, a *hortus, orticellus, ortalis,* or *iardinus* were all cultivated with vegetables or fruits, including fruiting trees; a *vinea* or *pergola vineata* was planted with grapevines, most probably for making wine. Sometimes the plots were independent, such as a 'garden which is surrounded by a pergola, perhaps of grapevines, to be used as a courtyard, in

---

[50] La Rocca, 'Lo spazio urbano', pp. 429–31.
[51] On terminology see Vitolo, 'I prodotti della terra', p. 164; Niermeyer, s.v. 'hortale', 'hortalicium', 'hortellus', 'horticellus', 'hortifer', 'hortilis', 'hortivus', 'gardinus', using examples principally from Italian sources. For comparison with documents from Northern Iberia, where there were productive gardens, see Davies, 'Gardens and gardening in early medieval Spain', pp. 332–3.
[52] Lugli, s.v. 'Hortus'.
[53] On *uiridaria*, see Chapter 3 on pleasure gardens and Goodson, 'Admirable and delectable gardens'.

addition to a well[54] or a 'small piece of land in the city of Piacenza' measuring 6 *tabulas* and 10 feet.[55] Most often, however, cultivated areas appear in our documents as part of the urban residential plot with a house. Houses (*domus*) in the early medieval documents of Italy may have had one or two stories (*terrinea* or *solarata*), and some were roofed with tiles (*teguliciam*). Some *domus* had walled yards or courtyards (*clusura, corta, curta, curtis*) around them or within them. *Terra* (land) appears often in our documents; *terra vacua* was not cultivated, and *terrae* in the countryside were fields planted with grain, yet *terra* was clearly often used in an urban context to refer to a cultivated lot in cities, especially Milan.[56]

Scholars have rather boldly claimed that some terms certainly indicated cultivated spaces while others certainly did not. Cagiano De Azevedo saw the *corte* or *corticellae* in the documents of many cities as communal spaces for many families or courtyards in which a well was placed, not necessarily cultivated.[57] At Rome, some of them clearly were, as shown in a document from the early eleventh century recording a house in Trastevere with a garden (*ortua*) behind and a courtyard (*corta*) in front in which there are fruiting trees.[58] Arthur takes the view that many *curtes* in documents from Naples were 'back gardens or orchards' and the *curte commune* was cultivated communally.[59] By contrast, Delogu considered the phrase *casa et curticella qui est coniuncta* in the documents from Salerno to be a house with a 'verzière', a kitchen garden or domestic orchard; by contrast, he did not believe a *terra cum casa* was necessarily cultivated, but rather the *terra* was the curtilage (the land immediately surrounding a house) and thus not cultivated.[60] I do not believe that the people making these documents were consistent up and down the peninsula in their usage of terms such as *curta*; these may or may not have been cultivated,

---

[54] 'hor[tus] [in integr]o, qui est in pergulis exornatus, cum usu curtis et putei', ChLA.29.865 (=P.Ital I, 24, pp. 371–4 (s. vii). Square brackets refer to lacunae in the papyrus, round brackets provide the full text of words abbreviated in the document.

[55] 'peciola una de terra inter civitatem Placencia, per mensura tabulas sex et pedes decem', *Le carte più antiche di S. Antonino* 23 (855).

[56] See, for example, a dispute of 863 between Peter, abbot of S. Ambrogio, and Peter the priest over 'terra ipsius monasterii ... intra ipsa civitate', *CDLangobardiae* 226 (863). On the word *terra* in the documents of Milan, see Balzaretti, *The lands of Saint Ambrose*, pp. 253–4.

[57] Cagiano De Azevedo, 'Aspetti urbanistici delle città altomedievale', p. 668. Paul Arthur wants these to grow out of Roman peristyles, as a sort of reversal of the Republican-period *hortus* to imperial-period peristyle, but given the changes to residential architecture in Late Antiquity it would be improbable that such a direct connection could be made; Arthur, *Naples. From Roman town*, pp. 48–9; see my discussion of late antique residential architecture in Chapter 2, Townhouse Transformation, Archaeology.

[58] 'Idest terram in qua domus nostre construire edificate esse videtur, cum ortua post se et cortae ante se, cum arboribus pomatum infra se', *CDMA* 30 (?1026, ?1027).

[59] Arthur, *Naples. From Roman town*, p. 48.

[60] Delogu, *Mito di una città meridionale*, p. 119, note 26.

some or all or none of the time. In this book, I have based my analysis on documents which were clear about cultivated space, usually with terms that are unambiguous in their context, both productive and urban, such as this one from 1004 at Rome: 'It is a garden in which there are fig trees together with stones and column in it, and all inside it, which measures 40 feet in length, and 30 feet in width, surrounded by walls ... Located in Regio 6, Rome'.[61]

There are thousands of original Latin property documents from Italian cities which date from the seventh to the eleventh centuries, many of which are preserved in the original, others of which are transcribed in registers or cartularies. There might be about 7,500 documents issued by individuals and ecclesiastical institutions (that is to say, documents not issued by public authorities) from northern and central Italy (between the years 680 and 1000), and considerably fewer from the South;[62] but we could probably guesstimate a total of about 10,000 preserved documents, and perhaps another 5,000 for the first half of the eleventh century.[63] There are no significant archives of lay figures for this period, and the overwhelming majority of the documents preserved have been transmitted down to the present day because of the involvement of a church or monastery.[64] The societies of medieval Italy, like those of other parts of the post-Roman world, bought and sold properties. In doing so they forged relationships through the exchanges of property and cultivated moral and social values of generosity, reciprocal obligations, and the preservation of history, memory, and interpersonal bonds formed by land transactions and shared property boundaries.[65] Also, owning land was a means to exert power over other people; it was not only treated as an exercise in efficiently extracting surplus for profit.[66] Given the economic and social benefits arising from property transactions, the market of agricultural properties was generally brisk in most parts of medieval Italy.[67]

---

[61] 'Idest hortuo in quo sunt arbores ficulneis una cum petras et columna infra se et omnibus intro se habentes, quod est in longitudo ad pedes semissales mensuratum numero quadraginta et in latitudo triginta, a parietinis eundem ortuo circumdatum una cum introitu exoitu suo a via publica et cum omnibus [ad eunde]m hortuo generaliter et in integro pertinentibus. Posito Romae regione sexta', *SMVL* 26 (1004) pp. 33–4.

[62] A full list of preserved documents to 899 is in Martin et al., *Regesti dei documenti dell' Italia meridionale*.

[63] Bougard, 'Actes privés et transferts patrimoniaux', and discussion in Costambeys, 'The laity, the clergy, the scribes and their archives', pp. 236–7; Bartoli Langeli, 'Private charters'.

[64] Innes, 'Framing the Carolingian economy'; Bougard et al., *Sauver son âme*; Costambeys, 'The laity, the clergy, the scribes and their archives'.

[65] See Lagazzi, *Segni sulla terra*. [66] Wickham, *The mountains and the city*, ch. 3.

[67] On the land market in Italy, see Feller and Wickham, *Le marché de la terre*; Wickham, 'Land sales and land market'; and especially Feller et al., *La fortune de Karol*.

Through charters, the economic and social relationships around property are visible to us, and property documents constitute a major source for the history of the early Middle Ages, both how people related to each other and how people lived and worked in their environments. In the broadest sense, charters preserve the terms and key elements of a transaction in a consistent format, usually composed by a professional. For early medieval Italy, whether in Lombard, Roman, or Byzantine areas, these documents follow certain patterns of composition: they include the date, often the ruler, the names and sometimes parents of the actors in the transaction, the details and boundaries of the property or properties being sold, donated, exchanged, or rented, and the terms of the agreement. There is a sanction clause against possible violations of the agreement, and then the document was signed by witnesses. The properties are often described in some detail, as the examples above make clear; boundaries are specified in relation to neighbouring properties or geographical features, permitting us to see clusters of neighbours and sometimes family members living in proximity to each other. Sometimes they specify the surface area of the properties – this is especially true of Milanese documents – and they give a price or a rent of the land, usually specified in local currency.

Property documents for rural and urban residences often assume the presence of cultivated areas alongside houses. Many documents recording the transfer of property use formulae; notaries had collections of model documents which could form the skeleton of a new document, and the formats and phrases which were used and reused in these formulae speak to the assumptions and expectations of those who commissioned and used these documents in their transactions.[68] Documents used formulae which mention gardens, such as a gift from Radualdo of Antraccoli to the church of S. Prospero, Gurgite, near Lucca, of half of 'all his possessions, whether house or house-structure, foundation, courtyard, garden, vineyard, lands, cultivated or uncultivated, trees whether fruit-bearing or not, and movable, immovable, and semimovable goods'.[69] The formulae used in Milan covered properties 'whether houses, buildings, areas, farms, gardens, the use of wells, enclosures,

---

[68] Rio, *Legal practice*. On medieval charters in Italy and their composition, see Petrucci, *Writers and readers in medieval Italy*; Everett, *Literacy in Lombard Italy*; *Les transferts patrimoniaux*; Amelotti and Costamagna, *Alle origini del notariato italiano*.

[69] 'omnes res mea medietatem, tam casa cum structura case, fundamento, curte, orto, uineas, terris, cultum uel incultum, arboribus fructiferas uel infructiferas, mobile uel inmouile seo seomouentibis', *CDL* vol. II, 133 (759) pp. 21–3. For other examples of formulae including gardens, see *CDL* vol. I, 134 (759), 136 (759), 139 (759), 140 (759), 148 (761), 175 (764), and many others. For examples from Southern Italy, see Benevento: *CDC* vol. I, 26 (845); Salerno: *CDC* vol. I, 207 (960); Rome: *AGCS* 78 (974?), 79 (991).

fields, meadows, pasture land, vineyards and woods, houses and all things, and houses and all farmsteads'.[70] Documents and the formulae by which they were created speak to the prevalence of gardens among estates and in urban contexts as well. In the minds of those who used property documents, urban properties could be expected to have productive land with them. These productive lands contributed to the household's food resources and also permitted their owners to interact with other owners including institutions of the church.

The rate of preservation of property documents from early medieval Italy inevitably has conditioned the geography and detail of our discussion of urban horticulture. I have considered the textual record of property documents from the major cities of Italy, both the largest (Rome, Naples, Milan) and the politically central (Pavia, Parma, Verona, Ravenna, Bari, Benevento, Amalfi, Salerno, Lucca). Within these cities there are some major gaps: the archiepiscopal archive of Milan has been lost, central Italy (Lazio and Tuscany) is by far better represented by preserved documents than the south and even parts of the north, and Bari has very few Latin documents prior to the eleventh century.[71] There are no Arabic property documents from this period which provide the kind of detailed accounts of land use, buildings, and cultivated areas for Italy that the Latin documents do.[72] Likewise, there are few Greek documents preserved which include detailed information of urban properties; the Brebion of Reggio (c. 1050) lists properties and their values from Reggio Calabria, and small collections of charters are preserved from Basilicata and Calabria, though they too pertain to rural properties.[73] The disparity in preservation of documents makes it challenging to assess regional variation across the diverse geography of the Italian peninsula. There is also a risk that the expansion of the documentary record from the mid tenth century onwards might lead us to perceive an increase in gardens where we simply see an increase in documents.[74] I have tried to account

---

[70] 'casis, edificiis, areis, curteficiis ortis usum puteis clausuris campis, pratis, pascuis, vineis et silvis'; 'casis et omnibus rebus'; and 'casis et rebus illis masariciis', Balzaretti, 'The politics of property in ninth-century Milan', p. 760. For discussion of charter production at Milan, see Balzaretti, *The lands of Saint Ambrose*, pp. 57–9.

[71] Brown et al., *Documentary culture*, especially Costambeys, 'The laity, the clergy, the scribes, and their archives'; Martin et al., *Regesti dei documenti dell' Italia meridionale*.

[72] Chris Wickham has pointed me to one Arabic document about a residential building (قاعة, qāʿa) in Palermo, dating from after 998, recently edited in Mouton et al., *Propriétés rurales et urbaines à Damas*, 7 (998), pp. 130–3, but it is surely the exception which proves the rule.

[73] *Syllabus Graecarum Membranarum* includes about thirty-five documents from our period, all rural; Robinson, *History and cartulary of the Greek monastery of SS Elias and Anastasius of Carbone* has a couple of wills including rural properties.

[74] On the chronological shifts in the documentary record, see Cammarosano, *Italia medievale*; Maire-Vigueur, 'Révolution documentaire'.

for this in my analysis and by considering the proportions of documents in a given place which pertain to urban cultivation.

I have privileged documents preserved in the original or in authentic copies, and I have eliminated many dozens of documents that refer to urban cultivation but which exist only as later copies and which use language or formulae reflecting periods later than the focus of this study. Some of the Latin documents are known to us only in cartulary transcriptions or in contemporary or subsequent copies. The reliability of these copies varies enormously, and some editors have been more interested than others in rooting out anachronisms which point to forgeries. Early on in my research, Cristina La Rocca reminded me of the forgeries of Pacificus of Verona, which she has shown to be products of later invention of a Carolingian past; and thus the purported ninth-century donations of Ratoldus, bishop of Verona, of five townhouses including one with a garden and a small garden nearby to form a *scola* for the training of priests of the cathedral, cannot be held as evidence for the creation of a *scola*, as the document is a forgery of the eleventh or twelfth century, as is the purported will of Pacificus which describes the dispensation of fresh food from his house and garden in a village outside Verona to the poor.[75] The general lines of what these documents claim may well have been true. But in order to explore questions about changes over time within the period considered by this book, I have tried to keep to documents which are original, or as close to original as possible. For Naples, this is practically impossible, given the destruction of the Archivio di Stato in 1943, though the main nineteenth-century editor of Neapolitan documents, Bartolomeo Capasso, recorded some information about copies.[76]

Charters rarely tell us what was grown on land that is being exchanged, however. Sometimes they describe the property in words that make clear that they grew wine grapes, fruit, or nut trees; some documents specify rental payment in kind, such as the Neapolitan crops mentioned in the section 'Ubiquity of Urban Cultivation'. The specification of a product in a document might sometimes suggest that on the land, the growers specialised in a certain crop with the aim to sell at markets. The majority of the documents considered in this book, however, do not specify crops, because they pertain to household-level cultivation as opposed to market production. In nearly every city of early medieval Italy, a significant

---

[75] *Scola: CDV* vol. I, 101 (813), La Rocca, *Pacifico di Verona*, pp. 54–81; will: *CDV* vol. I, 176 (844), on which see La Rocca, *Pacifico di Verona*, pp. 105–20; Costambeys, 'The laity, the clergy, the scribes, and their archives', pp. 256–7.

[76] *RN*. More work with the inventories of the Archivio di Stato, especially the *Pergamene dei monasteri soppressi*, would probably be advantageous.

proportion of residences had lots for cultivation, and gardens appear in different phrasing in the documents, as well as in the archaeological record, as we shall see.

Massimo Montanari's work on the agricultural properties in northern Italian documents has shown that gardens attached to houses on plots for extensive farming were, apparently, exempt from dues owed to landlords; while a portion of the proceeds of the field were extracted as payment, proceeds of the garden were fully for the use of those who planted them.[77] While these exemptions are not often stipulated in the documents from southern Italy, where payment in kind was possibly less frequent than in Montanari's northern documents, they may very well have nonetheless been practiced. Exemptions for gardens were, according to Montanari, the most relevant factor in the increased importance of the garden in the domestic economy in the early Middle Ages because they permitted the occupant to invest freely and reap the benefits of intensive farming without fear that the proceeds might be taken or that the value of the produce might fluctuate with the market.[78] While the return on planting of grains was, he calculates, one to three in the early Middle Ages, the return on garden sowing was surely much higher than that.[79] The value of the vegetable garden lay in its continual production of intensive crops. Through investment in fertiliser, irrigation, and labour, the soil of a garden could produce different crops nearly year-round. An oft-cited definition of a garden, from Isidore of Seville's witty *Etymologiae*, is that 'a Garden is so called because something always springs up there, for in other land something will grow once a year, but a garden is never without produce'.[80] The appearance of specific mentions of domestic gardens in property documents occurs before mentions of their exemption, however. The appeal of intensively cultivated fruit and vegetable crops adjacent to the household was probably more than their tax exemption, if indeed they were consistently exempt. The value of household crops in the context of widely variable crop yields and inconsistent marketing conditions,

---

[77] Montanari, *L'alimentazione contadina*, pp. 310–11, cites sixteen documents, out of his total of forty-nine ninth-century documents from northern Italy with payment in kind; eighteen documents out of sixty-seven tenth-century documents similarly exempt the garden with phrases such as 'anteposito orto ... unde non retdatis'. See also Vitolo, 'I prodotti della terra', p. 172; Andreolli, 'Il ruolo dell'orticultura'.

[78] Montanari, *L'alimentazione contadina*, p. 310. See also Squatriti, *Water and society*, pp. 80–1.

[79] Montanari, *L'alimentazione contadina*, pp. 176, 314.

[80] 'Ortus nominatus quod semper ibi aliquid oriatur. Nam cum alia terra semel in anno creet, ortus numquam sine fructu est', *De Agricultura Liber XVII*, 10.1 (ed. André, p. 227), trans. Barney et al., *The etymologies*, p. 355. For Isidore's source, see Varro, 'De sono vocum, 280 [57]' in *Grammaticae romanae fragmenta*, ed. G. Funaioli, p. 297.

discussed in Chapter 4, means that gardens attached to houses provided a certain amount of cushion for household consumption.

The houses in the Roman documents discussed above had not only gardens but also olive and fruit trees and vineyards, and all of these might have been recorded in documents with the word *hortus*. Like vegetable gardens, orchards of fruiting trees appear to have been common in the cities of Italy. Unlike vegetable gardens, which could, in the right circumstances, produce a continuous supply of different fresh foods, fruit trees had annual cycles of crops. It sometimes takes years for young trees to produce fruit regularly, perhaps ten years after planting, so cultivating fruit and nut trees in an urban plot was an investment towards the medium and long term.[81] The documents from Italian cities tended to refer to fruit trees in a general way as *arbores pomarum*; in medieval Italy, people did indeed grow apples as well as pears, figs, hazelnuts, chestnuts, citrons (*Citrus medica*), cherries, and peaches as food crops, though our sources rarely mention fruit *taxa* by name.[82] Grape vines were planted on pergolas around houses and also between trees (*arbustis*), common in areas which produced wine; and vegetables could grow between rows of vines, as archaeological evidence sometimes makes clear.[83] Polyculture seems to have been normal for urban cultivation; space was at a premium. *Coltura promiscua*, a strategy of planting trees, grape vines, and vegetables together, has been traditional for Italian agriculture since the Roman period and seems to have been used in the early Middle Ages.[84]

Sources: Archaeology

Food-cultivation and production were among the most common activities of past societies, but just as with sleep and sex, the archaeological evidence for the most common and essential activities of life is exiguous. The excavation of ancient and medieval gardens and fields has thus far concentrated mostly on boundaries, not usage.[85] Sown fields and the crops which grew there are challenging to recognise in the archaeological record without careful analysis of soils: the constant turning of soils prevents the formation of substantial archaeological stratification, the preservation of seeds depends on either waterlogged

---

[81] Squatriti, *Landscape and change*, p. 24. On olives, see Graham, 'Profile of a plant'.
[82] Vitolo, 'I prodotti della terra', pp. 174–84. On the produce revealed through archaeobotany, see Chapter 3.
[83] See the garden excavated in Rome, discussed in Chapter 3.
[84] Desplanques, 'Il paesaggio rurale della coltura promiscua', and Barbera and Cullotta, 'The traditional Mediterranean polycultural landscape'.
[85] Gleason, 'To bound and to cultivate', p. 13; Beaudry, 'Why gardens?'.

contexts or carbonised remains, and the collection of these requires sieving or flotation, which are time-consuming recovery techniques, not always adopted.[86]

In Baldini Lippoli's survey of dozens of excavated urban *domus* in late antiquity, not a single house had an identifiable kitchen garden.[87] Her study examined urban contexts of a wide range in size, from Rome and Constantinople to smaller episcopal centres, like Djemila (Cuicul) in what is now Algeria; but in no cases could she identify areas for food-growing. It is, of course, possible that excavation strategies and the emphasis on architecture in the study of late antique houses might have neglected areas given over to cultivation. As we shall see in Chapter 3, direct archaeological evidence of garden planting is difficult to discern. But it remains nonetheless generally true that in the imperial and late antique periods, Roman cities had active markets of foodstuffs, grown on estates outside the city, and while they had planted porticos and pleasure gardens, *uiridaria* – these later attested at least until the third century – there were not usually kitchen gardens at or around townhouses.[88]

The horticultural products best studied by archaeologists are wheat, oil, and wine; this is perhaps related to the recognisability of the structures which their processing left in the archaeological record or the traces left of oil and wine containers attesting the distribution of processed crops. It is perhaps also because of the central roles those crops played in the Roman economy, especially through the *annona*.[89] Archaeological analysis of vegetable gardens has depended upon very exceptional conditions of preservation and very attentive excavations; a few examples are discussed in Chapter 2. Urban archaeology in Italy has been extensive in many cities of the north, somewhat less in the south. There have been some impressive recent excavations in Milan, Rome, Naples, Palermo, and Salerno which cast new light on the early medieval period in those cities. While medieval archaeologists have long noted the presence of Dark Earth in late Roman and early medieval urban contexts, this dark-coloured deposit has conventionally been interpreted as decomposed timber and thatch from structures in organic materials, decomposing rubbish left in

---

[86] For a broad summary of the techniques and processes, see Campbell et al., *Environmental archaeology*.
[87] Baldini Lippolis, *La domus tardoantica*. She includes one garden of the fourth century at the Casa di Amore e Psiche, Ostia, p. 233, but this is a very small area, open to the sky, which had a nymphaeum. It appears to have been an ornamental planted area; it was clearly not for food production; Shepherd et al., 'Giardini ostiensi'.
[88] On gardens in the imperial period, see Grimal, *Les jardins romains*; Farrar, *Gardens of Italy and the western provinces of the Roman Empire*; and now Jashemski et al., *Gardens of the Roman Empire*; see Chapter 2.
[89] Carandini, 'Hortensia', p. 71.

abandoned areas, colluvial/alluvial sediment collected in abandoned areas, and/or sometimes spaces of urban cultivation. Such deposits are analysed in Chapter 2, where it is argued that Dark Earth might attest to horticulture; but more to the point, it attests to conditions which provided opportunities for horticulture in cities.

My study of urban gardens, through their textual and archaeological records, provides us with a small window onto shifting social structures within the city, the presence or absence of markets in perishable foodstuffs, and emerging ideas of charity. The analysis of property documents combined with letters, narrative chronicles, and a new urban archaeology make it now possible to observe urban food provisioning in early medieval Italy and to relate the phenomenon of urban gardening with shifting power structures in the city, cultural and social contexts, and wider economic patterns. The centrality of household economies emerges clearly from this study, as do the rich and sophisticated new ideas about cultivation and Christian charity; these ideas gave colour and value to the economic and ecological transformations of urban landscapes.

Urban food gardens of early medieval Italy were not simply ubiquitous symptoms of the decline of urban fabric, as they have often been treated by historians and archaeologists.[90] They were planted because certain consumers wanted fruits and vegetables and made space among their houses to grow them. Urban gardening developed in direct relation to changes in economy, society, and the urban environment; they created new realities and prompted new relationships and new ideas, which in turn changed other parts of life in the Middle Ages. And the vegetable patches examined in this book were more than simple patches scratched out of abandoned space for the subsistence of individuals. Rather, they were strategic investments, undertaken by the highest and the lowest landholders; far from being a sign of ruralisation and therefore decline of the quality and sophistication fabric of medieval city, they attest to the reorganisation of urban economies and power structures. When considered in detail, the evidence for urban gardening in Italy is substantial; the many historians who assumed that medieval cities were filled with kitchen gardens were indeed correct. The phenomenon was not consistent, however, across all Italian cities nor throughout the Middle Ages. Understanding which consumers created urban cultivated space, by what means, and for which reasons, where, and when is the subject of what follows. The answers to these questions reveal a new sense of the urban household which emerges over the period between approximately 500

---

[90] Emblematic of this approach is Montanari, *L'alimentazione contadina*, p. 25; see also references in note 102.

and 1050 and a new vision of how the household might serve as a model and even a constituent element in political structures.

This book is an urban history examining the changes and consistencies in the ways in which people organised themselves in and around cities. I am seeking to explore an urban phenomenon, agriculture, which is typically rural, and this exploration challenges some of the key principles of urbanism in the post-Roman world. Food gardening was part of urban life in the early medieval Italy, and exploring its forms and variations makes clear that gardens do not simply reflect wider changes in politics. Rather urban cultivation changed the ways in which people interacted with each other as well as with their environment, in terms of new views on the ways in which land related to power and households cared for themselves and the needy.

My research methods have been necessarily multiple and diverse in order to disentangle the structures and significances of this aspect of urban life. What would an environmental urban history of the early medieval city reveal? How can we characterise the experience of the unbuilt? Must we use the tools of analysis of the built environment? Was the cultivation of food an unspoken part of the daily grind of getting by, or was it culturally noble? I have deliberately juxtaposed evidence which is not always complementary: the documentary record provides altogether different data from the archaeological one, and both of these are unsatisfactorily incomplete for the period considered here. In considering the ways in which people organised their houses and the cultivation within cities holistically in the panorama of economic patterns we can see urban cultivation take on prominence when large-scale trading networks and opportunities for market exchange are few. Because of the importance of household-scale production in this economic sense, for the period between approximately 500 to 1050, urban cultivation also played a part in changing constructions of power in the urban landscape. When the overall scale of economic activity is reduced, as it was in this period, small-scale contributions can make large differences. Similarly, the consideration of cultivated areas within the city should prompt us to analyse changes on the timescales of plants and trees and the ways in which gardens might prompt novel human interactions.

Early medieval history has embraced the material turn, perhaps even more successfully than other subfields of history, and most early medieval historians now eagerly engage with archaeological evidence, art, and imagery alongside texts.[91] As I will show in subsequent chapters, the built environment – while obviously not capable of sentient choice or

---

[91] See, for instance, Deliyannis et al. *Fifty early medieval things*.

biological preservation – nonetheless provoked responses from the people who lived in it, prompting them to change their behaviours. One strand of material culture studies, which engaged with actor-network theory (ANT), has sought to blur the Cartesian divide between the dead, material elements of the world and the conscious thinking parts of the world. ANT has provoked reconsideration of the role which objects play in people's lives by thinking about machines, or microorganisms, as provoking humans to do things differently. Andrew Pickering has suggested the metaphor of a dance to convey shared, reflective negotiations between people and things, including rivers/flood gates/engineers/levees.[92] I suggest that thinking about the built environment as a changing and evolving reality, with buildings standing and collapsing, being built and decomposing, and parts of the city growing and dying might help to push our thinking about the ways in which material forms manipulate our interactions. Architectural historians and archaeologists have long recognised that buildings, by restricting or inviting certain behaviours, delimit what happens in them.[93] Geographers and urban ecologists recognise the ways in which unintentional landscapes, or wastelands, decentre and disrupt webs of modernity and public urban space, and can even provide footholds for new plant species.[94] By thinking about interactions between people and their cities as co-productive and involving the intensive cultivation of useful plants, I suggest that we will see the domestic garden as a force which prompted new means of thinking about how people lived in early medieval cities: by forging and developing social networks around the household.

New Directions

Through this work I seek to build upon three intersecting discourses in early medieval studies: the social interactions facilitated by the property market and its records, the co-productive nature of human relations with their environment, and material culture as an agent in human interactions. For most early medievalists the first discourse is easily recognisable. An enormous body of scholarship has developed in the past 100 years investigating how people in the early Middle Ages used agricultural land, identifying patterns of ownerships at the end of the Roman Empire,

---

[92] Pickering, 'Material culture and the dance of agency'. I thank Tina Sessa and Lucy Grig for their invitation to discuss Pickering and the agency of late antique Rome at the Oxford Patristics Conference (2015).

[93] Hillier and Hansen, *The social logic of space* remains foundational along with de Certeau, *The practice of everyday life*.

[94] Gandy, 'Unintentional landscapes'.

exploring how tenacious these patterns were, and discovering by which means new practices of land-holding and farming supplanted old systems. Early medieval land was not a commodity, though it was bought, sold, and also donated and bequeathed. Land in early medieval Europe was worked to make useful things – food, material for clothing, and firewood – and it was pastureland for useful animals. Land was also a means of status; it was given, conserved, and exchanged with others, and in the nature of these exchanges, we can see individuals, families, and institutions strategising for their well-being, their food, and their status. The documents which record these transactions, of which we have seen some excerpts above, are narratives of alliances and ambitions in men's and women's relationships with their landscape.

The second discourse which informs this book has emerged recently in environmental history. Recent studies of early medieval plant- and animal-use have revealed not only the complex exploitation of natural resources in the early medieval period, but also that the natural world changed and responded to this use and prompted further interaction. Jamie Kreiner's analysis of pigs in early medieval Europe has shown the ubiquity of the pig as a food resource, and critically, she has revealed the correlation between pig biology and agricultural strategies as they changed along with Merovingian farming. Because of their flexibility, pigs thrived in post-Roman landscapes of what is now France, and Merovingian Franks ate considerably more pork than Britain in the same period, in particular at certain sites where micro ecologies encouraged the beech and oak woods that pigs liked to eat in.[95] Kreiner has shown through the study of pigs that Merovingian society 'was "thinking with" ecologies' in the ways in which new legal codes, taxation structures, and foodways evolved in relation to changes in lived environments and the resources that could be extracted from them. Similarly drawing upon methods from ecology and biology, Paolo Squatriti has shown that early medieval cultivation of chestnuts in Italy developed in relation not only to the changing needs of post-Roman society (fewer people, less interregional trade of foodstuffs) but also in relation to the qualities of the trees as they grew and spread in the benign neglect of post-Roman forestry management.[96] For Squatriti it is not sufficient to chart the rise in documentary references to chestnut groves in eighth-century Italy. Alongside this work, Squatriti points out the biological qualities of the genus *Castanea* which permitted the groves to thrive and the people in villages

---

[95] Kreiner, 'Pigs in the flesh and fisc', p. 27; Kreiner, *Legions of pigs*.
[96] Squatriti, *Landscape and change*; Squatriti, 'Trees, nuts, and woods at the end of the first millennium'.

around Lucca and Salerno to eat. The species of chestnut which is edible grows well where wheat does not; the shade it produces repels pigs but not goats and sheep, animals which were consumed in greater frequency in these parts of Italy than they had been in the Roman period and than they were in Frankish Gaul, for instance. Chestnuts reproduce by seed, without much assistance.

Some animals and plant species capitalised on the emerging conditions of late antique and early medieval settlements. In the post-Roman world some Roman fruits and vegetables endured, such as apples, pears, cherries, and plums. But everywhere we have comparative data from the archaeobotany, 'wild' fruits increased within the panorama of food stuffs; dogberry and blackberry grew more commonly in the early medieval Middle Ages than in the Roman period, taking advantage of less regular maintenance and abandoned space. Blackberries (*Rubus fruticosus*) and raspberries (*Rubus ideaus*) were known in antiquity; Pompey apparently brought the first raspberry canes from what is now Turkey to Rome about 65 BCE.[97] However, they rarely featured prominently in the archaeobotanical record and are often taken as things that animals ate. When the seeds appear in a dump, as at Roman sites from Modena, they are interpreted as animal dung, not human food.[98] But blackberry brambles, which are vigorous fruiting canes, grew in the suburban fields around Roman cities which had been cleared but cropped less intensively than in antiquity, if at all. Brambles have a propensity to increase in height and density when not cut back, as new canes grow over old dead ones. Blackberries, currants, dogberry, sloeberries, alongside the stalwarts of fig, olive, and grape: these all appear among the food waste of early medieval settlements and cities with greater frequency than they did in earlier periods. This change was not simply a subsistence move by hungry people to forage for food, but it was also an aggressive takeover by an opportunistic plant.

The Shape of This Study

Having laid out the parameters of the study and the motivations for carrying it out, the following chapter, Chapter 2, juxtaposes the urban and agricultural patterns of antiquity with those of the early Middle Ages. A picture of food-cultivation and urban density of the cities of

---

[97] For the self-fertilising qualities and tip layering propagation, see s.v. Blackberries, Raspberries, and Rubus L., *New RHS dictionary of gardening*, ed. Huxley; Blamey and Grey-Wilson, *Flora of Britain and Northern Europe*, p. 176 on wasteland growth.

[98] Bosi et al., 'The life of a Roman colony'.

Roman Italy is sketched in order to gauge the transformations of late antiquity, which included the populations in Italian cities and the fragmentation of urban density, especially with regard to high-status townhouses. The changed urban landscape created possible spaces for food cultivation where there had not been any before. These are apparent in the archaeological record as early as the fifth century and in the textual record in the later sixth century. A key piece of evidence for the transformation of cities is the presence of Dark Earth, dark-coloured sediments formed in urban contexts after the end of the Roman Empire. Dark Earth in Italy is shown here to have been transformations of deposits which were formed deliberately and which underwent a number of different, related processes of waterlogging, accretion, and weathering. These changes, like the deposit and accumulation of soil and rubbish, which grew into open earthy areas in the formerly dense Roman city, are explained in summary, invoking two contrasting views of the changes of ancient to medieval society: one stressing the overall indebtedness of the early medieval city to its ancient precedents, the other stressing the dramatic breaks between the past and the early medieval present. New scientific analyses provide new data on the formation of Dark Earth, tipping the scales to recognise the deliberate efforts involved in making Dark Earth and making clear that such urban contexts reflect conscious decisions and collective efforts. The broader economic shape of early medieval Italy, in terms of both regional networks as well as Mediterranean connections, provides a sense of how strategically important urban cultivation became in post-Roman Italy.

Chapter 3 surveys the overall shape of the phenomenon, situating urban food cultivation against the backdrop of rural agriculture which characterised the majority, though not the totality, of Italian agronomics. If the majority of food production for cities was rural, what prompted urban cultivation? What political, social, and economic benefits might be derived from farming in cities? Examples from Lucca reveal how the documents which attest to urban cultivation can reveal urban topography, relations between neighbours, and relations to larger institutions, such as churches. In small cities such as Lucca, we can see some tightly controlled cultivated spaces within the walls. Archaeobotanical evidence is providing new evidence for the extent and nature of this cultivation. Here I use it to demonstrate the radically changed cerealiculture in Italy for the fifth to seventh centuries, and then analyse in detail the floral remains of two urban gardens, one from ninth-century Rome and one from tenth- to eleventh-century Ferrara. These case studies reveal the wide range of foodstuffs cultivated in cities and the prevalence of polyculture, that is, growing many different things for household consumption rather than single crops for market production.

Observations and arguments about the political value of cultivated spaces in cities must take into account the economic context of urban food production of the Middle Ages. Chapter 4 explores the emergence of evidence for urban markets for foodstuffs and suggests ways in which we might understand the absence of that evidence for the period prior to the eleventh century. In the absence of commercial-scale farming of foodstuffs, household-level cultivation was the principal means of acquiring food for most city dwellers. The possession of food gardens and their exchange through horizontal networks of families or social groups allow us to see the prominence of family links and *consortes* or associates in the management of urban property and the control of urban food production.

In Chapter 5, I consider cultural attitudes towards cultivation and gardening in the early Middle Ages to understand how new ideas interacted with emerging economic conditions. From antiquity, land management was nested in several different clusters of ideas and values: the ancient Roman cultural esteem that was placed upon effective estate management; emerging ideas about self-sufficiency of religious households, such as monasteries; and ideas about health and medicine. Some of these ideas were rooted in different genres of literature from antiquity, from agronomic treatises to medical theory; and new, early medieval writing on monastic communities and recipe books for medicines emerged. Both sets of writings are considered here for the light they shed on agricultural practices and consumption of urban produce. This chapter also considers the movement of cultivated urban spaces into ecclesiastical hands and explores whether the new cultural values attached to food provisioning for certain groups, such as the dedicated religious, might have informed habits of charitable or pro anima donations of cultivated land.

Chapter 6 examines how urban cultivation worked in relation to traditional and emerging strategies of social power. Patronage and commissioning of public events and buildings was a key tool in the attainment and replication of social status in antiquity. In the early Middle Ages, new ideals emerged around Christian forms of wealth and support, and different values were attached to the acquisition of agricultural land. Urban properties took on new relevance, and agricultural property became socially valuable in new ways. Cultivated spaces within cities thereby were newly prestigious. This chapter charts three examples of this development from the mid eighth century to the early tenth century.

To conclude, we will consider the cities of early medieval Italy and the role of urbanism in social and political forms. We end with a glimpse of how the phenomenon of urban gardening for household consumption changes over time in the eleventh and twelfth centuries with the rise of commercial production, markets, and communes, a changed world, in which the social and moral value of self-sufficiency endures.

2 Patterns and Changes

The widespread use of urban areas for food cultivation was a new development in the cities of early medieval Italy, and it accompanied a reconfiguration of individual houses. Residential properties took new forms: houses tended to be surrounded by open, unbuilt areas, including cultivated spaces growing food. A picture of this new kind of townhouse emerges clearly from the letters of Pope Gregory the Great at the end of the sixth century, and it marks a real change in the character of urban housing in Italy as well as a change in its system of food production. Five of Gregory's letters refer to urban gardens at Rome, all of them parcels of property owned by clerics or religious communities. These provide a window into the phenomenon of urban cultivation at an early stage, and we will consider them in some detail later.

Two centuries before Gregory wrote, urban garden plots and houses with gardens such as he describes would have been entirely unknown in a large Italian city – and in Rome in particular – as the townhouses of the late Empire dedicated rather little space to food cultivation, and fresh foodstuffs were readily available in regular markets. In the small towns of Republican Italy, house plots had come with back gardens. An example comes from the town of Cosa, where second-century BCE houses all had substantial kitchen gardens at the back.[1] At Cosa, some of these kitchen gardens subsequently were filled in with new houses, but productive back gardens survived into the imperial period in some smaller places; Juvenal's second-century critique of crowded Rome celebrates that in small cities one could buy a pleasingly modest house with a garden and well.[2] In cities such as Pompeii, Naples, Rome, and Ostia, however, the crush of buildings and the price of land seem to have eliminated small domestic vegetable gardens from the urban landscape in correspondence with the rise of foodstuffs available in city markets in the first century BCE

---

[1] Bruno and Scott, *Cosa IV: The houses,* esp. 'The Houses of the Second Century B.C.', pp. 13–78, and for general discussion of the design, p. 30, note 24.
[2] Juvenal, *Satire III*, lines 223–9, ed. and trans. pp. 184–5.

and the first century CE.[3] The typical Roman townhouse, the *domus*, often had an atrium or courtyard at the centre, open to the sky and paved to facilitate water collection, sometimes with a fountain. Pompeii has key examples of these houses, but they are also typical across Italy. Some included open unpaved areas that were gardens planted with ornamental trees and plants but not productive ones.[4] Tenement buildings, *insulae*, may have included open areas for the use of residents, containing shrines and sometimes planted with ornamental plants, but they were not food-producing, as examples from Ostia make clear.[5]

The shift from the Roman townhouse to the new configuration of urban house with kitchen garden reflects larger shifts in both economies and social values at the end of the Roman Empire. Both textual sources and archaeological work provide information about the changes that Italian cities underwent in late antiquity. Documenting these changes can be challenging, given the sporadic material evidence that exists for early medieval townhouses, paltry in comparison to earlier evidence. In what follows, I will attempt to provide a general picture of imperial-period urban Italian houses and their gardens, and the changes they underwent in the early Middle Ages. Some of the changes discussed here are structural, to do with the sophistication and shapes of late antique and early medieval houses. Other changes occurred in relation to the material conditions and deposits across the urban landscape, reflecting shifting which took place in relation to shifting economic strategies and political structures, altering urban environments and ecologies.

Gregory the Great

The *Register* of the letters of Pope Gregory (d. 604), an incomplete record of his official correspondence, includes five letters relating to four gardens within the city of Rome, all of which were located within the walls and all owned by ecclesiastics:[6] (Tab. 1). In Letter II, 46 (September 591–August 592), the subdeacon Sabinus is instructed to give a garden (*hortus*) that had been owned by the priest Felicianus (deceased) to a convent of Euprepria and her community of nuns. We do not know where the

---

[3] For a summary of this chronology, see Morvillez, 'The garden in the *domus*', pp. 18–19. I thank Lisa Fentress and Andrew Wallace-Hadrill for their thoughts on urban gardens in the Roman period.
[4] See discussion on pp. 39–44, Ancient Roman Horticulture.
[5] See discussion on p. 44; Shepherd et al. 'Giardini ostiensi', esp. p. 70.
[6] On the *Register*, see, Norberg, 'Praefatio' and Martyn, 'Introduction', esp. pp. 13–14. Robert Markus estimated the total number of entries in the *Register*, which bore an uncertain relationship to the full correspondence of Gregory as pope, at over 850, *Gregory the Great and his world*, pp. 15, 206–8.

convent was located, but the garden was in the first *regio*, near S. Sabina on the Aventine, an area which was not densely built up in antiquity.[7] The nuns were to own the plot outright; we are not told whether there were gardeners to work it, or whether the nuns were expected to do so. We are also not told whether the garden was a market plot, planted with certain crops to be sold for a profit, or whether the plot was a sort of allotment for growing food for the community of nuns. The aim of the property transfer is clear, however; it was to aid the nuns in their commitments to God:

> We are compelled by our duty of piety to make a decision for the monasteries, with prudent consideration, so that those who are known to have allotted themselves to the service of God, may not endure any need. And for that reason we order your Experience with this authority to hand over quickly and without uncertainty the garden of the dead priest Felicianus. It lies in the first region before the steps of S. Sabina. Leaving aside any excuse, give it to the convent of Euprepia, in which a community of nuns are known to live, for them to possess with a proprietary right, so that aided by the benefit of our generosity, they may persevere in serving God, with his support also, with secure minds.[8]

In Letter III, 17 (January 593), Pope Gregory instructed the subdeacon Gratiosus to transfer a *domus* that the Roman Church had inherited from a patrician woman to a community of nuns. The nuns should own the house outright, along with its garden (*hortus*) and a second lodging within the property.

> For those choosing a religious vocation we should take care, with suitable consideration, that the occurrence of some hardship neither makes them inactive, nor undermines the strength (Heaven forbid!) of their holy way of life. For that reason we order with the present authority that you should hand over the following property to the Abbess Flora, with the right of possession for her indubitable ownership. The house is located in this city in the fourth region, next to a place called the 'White Hens', the property of the Holy Church of Rome, over which we preside with God's authority, and in which a patrician lady, Campana, is known to have once lived. Hand it over with the garden also and the lodgings, which a doorway encloses within the same house. Thus with Christ's help, the abbess can construct a convent in this house, where she can live with her community, so that she, and also her successors in status and position, can possess the abovementioned house and garden and all things belonging to them, as we have said, with a peaceful and inalienable right, as granted by us, due to our respect for her piety.[9]

---

[7] On the *regiones*, see Frézouls, 'Rome, ville ouverte'.
[8] *RE* II, 46, vol. I, p. 138, trans. Martyn, *Letters*, I, p. 227. On the monastery, see Ferrari, *Early Roman monasteries*, p. 136.
[9] *RE* III, 17, vol. I, pp. 163–4, trans. Martyn, *Letters*, vol. I, pp. 247–8. On the monastery, see Ferrari, *Early Roman monasteries*, pp. 11–12; on the toponym 'Gallinas albas', see Platner, *A topographical dictionary*, p. 246.

Gregory does not specify whether the garden of the property is food producing, but the use of the word *hortus* certainly implies it. The garden lies within the residential complex and is meant for the use of the nuns.

In Letter VI, 44 (July 596), Pope Gregory attempted to move an established community of monks to a house next to an oratory, set up by a priest, now deceased, who had left his house, the oratory, and a garden as well as the rest of his property, including a suburban estate with its appendages, a tavern, and a pickled-food storage building, to the Roman Church.[10] The monks were instructed to move because their present residence was in danger of collapse. The move apparently did not happen, because in 599, three years later, Gregory instructs Bona, an abbess, to move her community to this same house, garden, and oratory, which the Roman Church had maintained over the previous years at its expense.[11] Gregory clarified that not only should the nuns take over the property because their existing house was in need of repair, but they should receive other properties as well, which seem intended to supply income to the community, not to foster self-sufficiency by providing fresh food directly to the women. Gregory's concern in this letter is that the religious women should leave their current, dangerously decrepit residence for better quarters and that the wishes of the house's previous owner, the priest, should be honoured where they had not yet been. The abbess is instructed to make sure that divine offices are celebrated at the convent and the donation is made permanently for future successors to honour.

The last reference to urban gardens at Rome from the *Register* comes from Letter XIV, 3 (September 603), in which Iohannes, Bishop of Palermo, is given permission to sell off a property in Rome that his church has inherited from a patrician.[12] The house included a bath (*balnea*) and a garden (*hortus*), but was in ruinous state and costing the Palermitan church money rather than turning an income as, presumably, the original donation had intended it to do. Again, it is not clear whether the garden in this letter is intended to be an ornamental garden or a productive one, but as we shall see, the wider context certainly suggests it.

There are also other gardens referred to in the letters, such as the two gardens located outside the walls in the plain between the Tiber and the portico of S. Paolo fuori le mura, next to other monasteries' gardens and vineyards. These were added to the endowment of the church of

---

[10] *RE* VI, 44, vol. I, pp. 416–7, trans. Martyn, *Letters*, vol. II, pp. 433–4.
[11] *RE* IX, 138, vol. II, pp. 688–9, trans. Martyn, *Letters*, vol. II, pp. 624–5.
[12] *RE* XIV, 3, vol. II, pp. 1069–70, trans. Martyn, *Letters*, vol. III, p. 870.

S. Paolo.[13] There are also gardens which Pope Gregory confirmed to be among the possessions of the monastery of S. Martinus, in Campania, and those of the Milanese church, at Como.[14] Thus, there is evidence in the *Register* of gardens within Rome as well as outside the walls, in other towns, and in the countryside. Most of those that Pope Gregory refers to were owned by the church; this is because his correspondence relates to his responsibilities as bishop to manage the properties of the church, not necessarily because of any special or exclusive link between churchmen and domestic gardens at this point.[15] Indeed, two of the gardens had come to the church, apparently recently, from laymen and laywomen.

This *Register* of letters reveals the pope's concerns for the economic affairs of his clergy as well as his duty to provide for religious communities. The *horti* referred to in these letters are kitchen gardens, not the elite pleasure parks called 'horti' within Rome.[16] The productive quality of the garden in Pope Gregory's letters is suggested by the general context of Letters II, 46 and III, 17, where the communities of women were to have the gardens and residences as a means of support for their community. It is possible that they were specialised market gardens in the city; however, since three of the letters refer to gardens located adjacent to or within a residential complex in relatively dense parts of Rome, it seems unlikely that they were enormous in size. They were probably not the kind of fields that were farmed for profit in the hinterlands of ancient Rome in previous centuries.

Other documents, including the very earliest preserved property documents, give the impression that Italian cities were increasingly filled with green spaces within the walls, sometimes attached to houses, in the seventh century. Two papyri from Ravenna record donations of urban properties by churchmen to the church of Ravenna. In 625, the subdeacon Deusdedit of Ravenna gave 'a house with a little garden next to it', along with a mill and two lodgings also within the complex, to his church.[17] In the mid seventh century, Gaudiosus, *defensor*, gave to the church of Ravenna a garden surrounded by a pergola, perhaps of grapevines, with the use of a courtyard and a well[18] (Table 1).

[13] *RE* XIV, 14, vol. II, p. 1086, trans. Martyn, *Letters*, vol. III, pp. 880–1.
[14] *RE* IX, 187, vol. II, pp. 743–4; *RE* III, 23, trans. Martyn, *Letters*, vol. I, p. 51.
[15] These transfers of property are discussed in Lenzi, 'Forme e funzioni', pp. 776–9. They are identified because they attest to the Roman church's responsibility to provide economic means to churches and monasteries and to oversee their management (p. 779).
[16] On these, see p. 47.
[17] '[hor]ticellum in integro positum iuxta domum eius, sed et pistrino atque duo hospitia intra se cum curticla sua, in s(an)c(t)a Ravennate [eccl(esia)]', *ChLA* 22.720 (=*P.Ital* I, 21, p. 356),(625). In this and the following note, square brackets refer to lacunae in the papyrus, round brackets provide the full text of words abbreviated in the document.
[18] 'hor[tus] [in integr]o, qui est in pergulis exornatus, cum usu curtis et putei', *ChLA*.29.865 (=*P.Ital* I, 24, p. 374 (s. vii).

Table 1 *Property documents and references to urban gardens at Rome*

Property	Source	Text, Date	Location
garden of Felicianus the priest, deceased, located in Region 1, in front of the steps of S. Sabina	*RE* II, 46 (Sept. 591–Aug 592)	hortum Feliciani quondam presbiteri, positum regione prima ante grados sanctae sabinae, 591/2	Regio 1
house located in this city, in Regio 4, next the place called White Chickens, and garden	*RE* III, 17 (Jan. 593)	domum positam in hac urbe regione quarta, iuxta locum qui appellatur Gallinas albas ... et hortum, 593	Regio 4, Viminal Hill
house with garden located in this city, next to the Baths of Agrippa	*RE* VI, 44 (July 596), *RE* IX, 138 (April 599)	domo ... [cum horto] posita in hac urbem Roma iuxta thermas Agrippianas, 596; 599	Regio 9, in the Campus Martius
house with garden and its bath and everything pertaining to it, in this city	*RE* XIV, 3 (Sept. 603)	domum cum horto et balneo suo et omnibus ad eam pertinentibus, 603	At Rome, no specific location
house with its garden, located in this city of Rome, next to the Baths of Diocletian, Regio 4	Ep. 117, Register of Honorius I, Deusdedit, Collectio Canonum[19]	domum cum horto suo positam in hac urbe Roma iuxta thermas Diocletianas regione Δ, in the time of Honorius I (625–38)	Regio 4
house and garden which is called after Catellus, the silkweaver	Inscription from time of Pope Sergius I (687–701)[20]	intra hac urbem Romam domum et hortum quae appellatur quondam Catelli siricarii ... positum regione quarta	All Regio 4
a portion of a house with garden which has vines, located in Regio 4		portione domus juris sui cum horto vineato posito in regione quarta	
also in Regio 4, house and garden of the Anniboni (Regio 4)		Item in regione quarta domum et hortum cata quondam Annibonium	
garden with vines next to S. Susanna (Regio 4)		hortum vineatum juxta s. Susannam quem tenet Cyriacum.	

[19] Deusdedit, *Collectio Canonum* 117 (ed. Martinucci, pp. 293–4).
[20] Inscription now lost; see text and analysis in De Rossi, 'Un'insigne epigrafe'.

Table 1 (cont.)

Property	Source	Text, Date	Location
vineyards which are in the Pincio	Mid eighth-century inscription of donations to S. Maria in Cosmedin[21]	bineas qui sun<t> in Pincis bersur(arum) III . . . bineas tabul(arum) II s(emis) qui sunt in Testacio	
vineyards . . . which are in Testaccio			

Pope Gregory's letters and these charters from a few years later attest to a new urban landscape where private food-producing gardens sat within residential complexes and among other buildings and even ruins within the city centre. The change from densely built-up cities with private planted courtyards, public spaces, and periurban farmlands, to less dense cities with intermixing of ornamental and productive horticulture, and ecclesiastical and private ownership, was fully underway by the turn of the seventh century, and so Gregory and his colleagues may not have considered these parcels of urban agricultural property as novel in any way. However, they were markedly different from the gardens of the imperial period, both the atria and porticos that had graced urban townhouses with their splashing fountains and ornamental plants and the large suburban or rural estates with gardens and fields that supplied food for the markets of Roman cities. Turning to consider a general picture of urban landscapes and their cultivation, we can examine the wealth of evidence from Pompeii, other Italian cities, and Rome itself, first in antiquity and then in late antiquity, from the fourth to seventh centuries.

Ancient Roman Horticulture

Scholarship on Roman gardens is prolific, given the extensive sources available in both literature and archaeology and the prominence Roman authors accorded to the pleasures of cultivated landscapes in houses, villas, temples, and public monuments.[22] Kitchen and market gardens in the Roman world have received significantly less scholarly attention than ornamental gardens; nonetheless, they were essential and integrated

---

[21] De Rubeis, 'Epigrafi a Roma', pp. 119–20; Meneghini and Santangeli Valenzani, *Roma nell'altomedioevo*, p. 127.

[22] von Stackelberg, *The Roman garden*. On the terminology of *hortus, horti, holerarium*, and related things, see Lugli, see 'Hortus', and Purcell, 'Dialectical gardening'.

components of many Roman settlements.[23] In the towns and cities of Italy, however, gardens were predominantly ornamental. At Pompeii, a regionally important town on the Tyrrhenian coast which was decimated by a volcanic eruption in 79 CE, as soon as excavations began in the late eighteenth century, remains of ancient wood and traces of plantings were recovered.[24] In the twentieth century, Wilhelmina Jashemski developed new techniques to analyse and identify the remains of plants that were in the ground at the time of the eruption, adding considerably to our knowledge of what was grown, where, and in what density.[25] Her research, as well as analysis of painted representations of gardens, and more recent archaeobotanical study of the unpaved, open areas in and around many of the townhouses at Pompeii and their drains and wells have permitted reconstructions of the variety of plants cultivated in Pompeian gardens. In general, the evidence for planting attests to ornamental gardens, with deciduous and coniferous trees, fruiting vines, and flowering plants, sometimes set into pots (*ollae perforatae*). These planted areas often provided decorative frames through symmetrical plantings intended to be visible through the social spaces of townhouses, across an atrium or tablinum.[26] To create formal gardens in Pompeian townhouses of the first century, garden soil seems to have been imported to the houses, to raise the levels of the area for planting, as excavation at the House of the Surgeon made clear (Fig. 4).[27]

Marina Ciaraldi has recently analysed the archaeobotanical remains from two Pompeian houses, the House of the Vestals and the House of Hercules' Wedding, both excavated stratigraphically using modern, single-context excavation techniques.[28] The remains recovered are both carbonised and mineralised; they mostly represent items that were cooked and eaten in the houses, or used in rituals, though there are also preserved macro-remains from plants that may have been grown at or near the house rather than acquired as semi-prepared products and brought to the site. This research gives us very detailed information, in clear chronological phases, about the flora of Pompeii in domestic contexts. Analysis of plant remains from an entire insula, Regio VI, insula 1, has made clear that food plants, including wheat, olives, grapes, and nuts, were mostly brought to

---

[23] Jashemski et al., *Gardens of the Roman Empire*. See also Richardson et al., 'New directions'.
[24] Borgongino, *Archeobotanica*.   [25] Jashemski, *The gardens of Pompeii*.
[26] Morvillez, 'The garden in the *domus*'.
[27] Anderson and Robinson, 'Room by room discussion', pp. 350–1. On the two townhouses in this insula, see Jones, 'Urbanisation of Insula VI,1'.
[28] VI, 1, 1–6 and VII, 9, 47; Ciaraldi, *People and plants in ancient Pompeii*, pp. 88–151.

Figure 4 House of the Vestals and House of the Surgeon, Pompeii, in the first century CE. Plan based on Jones and Robinson, 'Water, wealth, and social status at Pompeii' and Anderson and Robinson, *House of the Surgeon, Pompeii*, fig. 1.3.

the townhouses already processed rather than grown and processed at home.[29] In the first century BCE and first century CE, several of the species identified in macro-remains and seeds were ornamentals, including cypresses (*Cupressus sempervirens*), viburnum (*V. lantana*), bay (*Laurus nobilis*), and violets (*Viola sp.*), but they may also have been consumed for medicinal purposes; they include purple gromwell (Lithospermum), opium poppy (*Papaver somniferum*), forget-me-not (*Myosotis*), pimpernels

---

[29] Murphy et al., 'Roman food refuse'.

(*Anagallis*), and Viper's bugloss (*Echium vulgare*).[30] Thus Pompeian domestic gardens may have grown both decorative and useful plants, but they were not the principal source of foodstuffs for urban dwellers.

It may be that the destruction or abandonment of some Pompeian properties after the earthquake of 62 CE permitted their use for agriculture in ways that may not have been typical for other Roman cities. Jashemski identified an area in the south-eastern part of the city where there was intensive cultivation of foodstuffs – both orchards and gardens as well as commercial-scale production of flowers for perfume and garlands.[31] In Regio I, Insula XV, for example, two damaged houses appear to have been joined to a single property. One of the houses was perhaps converted to a dormitory for labourers; and the common area behind both houses, at the centre of the insula, was used for a garden. There was a sunken area with large holes (Jashemski guessed perhaps autumn onions or cabbage), and grapevines surrounded the field. Along the walls were twenty-eight pots, perhaps for citron trees. Among the carbonised foodstuffs recovered in the garden were filberts (*Corylus avellana*), grapes (*Vitis vinifera*), almonds (*Prunus dulcis*), dates (*Phoenix dactylifera*), and beans (*Vicia faba minor*);[32] most of these were probably produced in the plot, though the date may have been eaten there and its stone discarded (Fig. 5). Jashemski's interpretation of this and several other sites as market or commercial gardens has been challenged recently by Ciaraldi, who argues that the shape of the planting holes provided too little evidence to determine what was planted in it and for what purposes.[33] Jashemski had estimated that market gardens and kitchen gardens, including vineyards and orchards, occupied 9.7 per cent of the excavated area of Pompeii, while ornamental gardens took up less than that, only 5.4 per cent of the excavated area.[34] Pompeii has been excavated only partially, and given the ambivalence of some of the archaeological information in the earliest-excavated areas, it is doubtful that we could arrive at any meaningful quantification of the cultivated space of Pompeii. A further complication is the fact that despite or because of its extraordinary state of preservation, it is very difficult to know how

---

[30] Ciaraldi, *People and plants in ancient Pompeii*, pp. 118–51.
[31] Jashemski, 'The garden of Hercules at Pompeii'. For a review of the research on Pompeian flora, see Ciaraldi, *People and plants in ancient Pompeii*, pp. 38–43. See also the general discussion of Ciarallo, *Flora pompeiana*, pp. 122–4.
[32] Jashemski, *The gardens of Pompeii*, pp. 235–40, Appendix I, no. 106. I.xv.3, vol. II, pp. 61–3; Jashemski, 'The discovery of a market-garden orchard'.
[33] Ciaraldi, *People and plants in ancient Pompeii*, p. 41; see also Moorman, 'Giardini al piede del Vesuvio'.
[34] Jashemski, *The gardens of Pompeii*, p. 24.

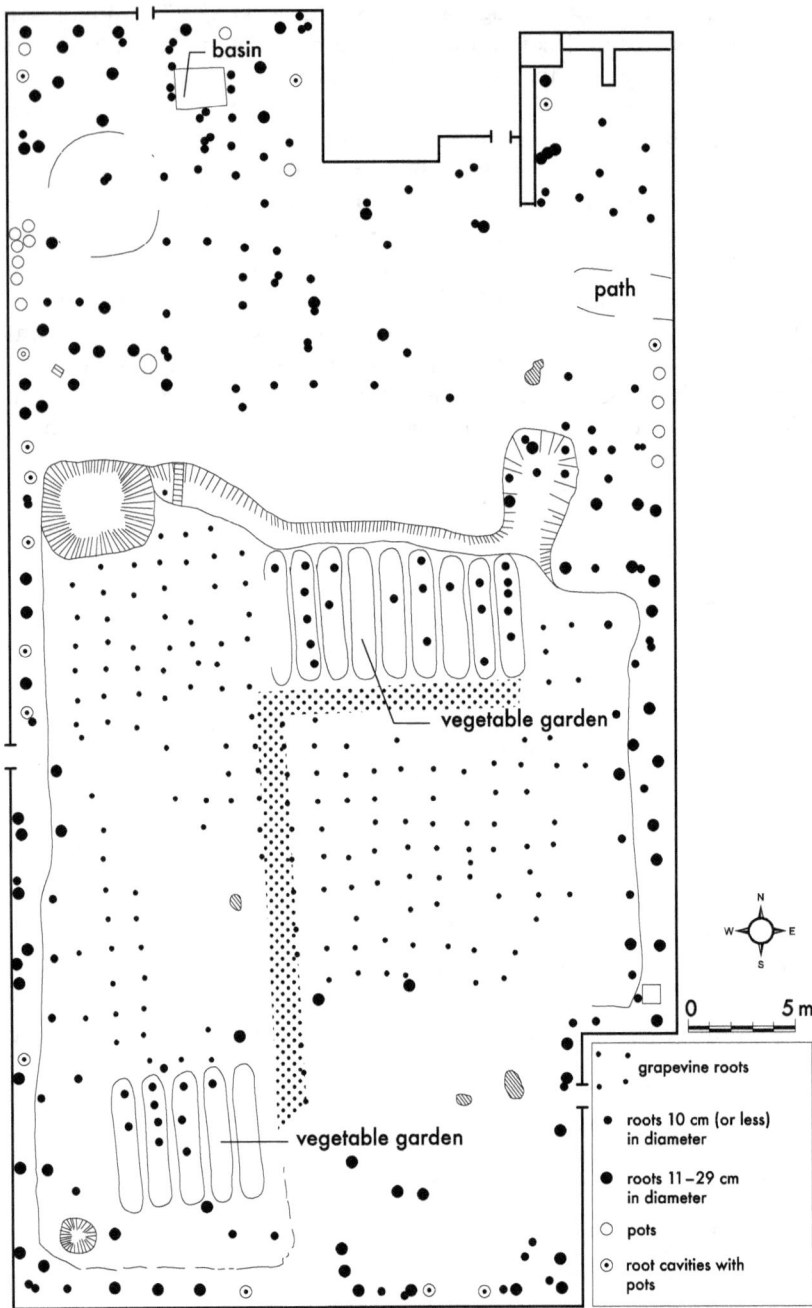

Figure 5 Market Garden Orchard at Pompeii, Regio I, Insula XV. Plan based on Jashemski, 'The discovery of a market-garden orchard', fig. 4.

representative Pompeii is among Roman large towns or small cities.[35] Indeed, the destruction wrought by the earlier earthquake may have opened up an unusually large amount of space within the city for intensive cultivation when compared to other comparably urbanised centres. Generalisations about Pompeii's gardens are difficult to make and impossible to extrapolate beyond Pompeii itself, but in their particulars the gardens of Pompeii show cultivation of ornamental plants in houses and some intensive horticulture of foodstuffs in reclaimed lots after the destruction and abandonment brought about by the earthquake of 62.

Beyond Pompeii, our understanding of the spatial organisation of Roman townhouses depends on identification of *domus* in urban excavations or in towns that were subsequently abandoned, such as Ostia or Herdonia.[36] As the town at Rome's main port, Ostia, expanded in the second century and its population increased, some individual family townhouses (*domus*) were replaced in the second century with large tenements with multiple residential units (*insulae*). Some of these, such as the ones south of the Cardo degli Aurighi, named the Garden Houses (Case a Giardino) by their excavators, were designed to face onto areas open to the sky, possibly gardens. These, like most of the earlier gardens at Pompeii, seem to have included shrines and fountains and were probably ornamental leafy spaces, pleasure gardens not meant for the production of food.[37] These open areas may not have been distinctly private or public. They provided pleasurable places of *amoenitas*, a certain kind of pleasurable, cultured leisure for aspiring Romans.[38]

The same is true for housing of the later Roman period. As the population of Ostia fell in the third and fourth centuries, space opened up for larger sprawling houses, often incorporating parts of earlier *insulae*.[39] In the fourth century, as in the late Republic and early Empire, gardens could be found growing within and between residential buildings, and though these may have been intensively cultivated, available evidence suggests that they were not principally designed for food production.[40]

Rome

The city of Rome itself shows very few signs of productive horticulture within the walls during the imperial period; for the early Middle Ages, the

---

[35] Lomas, 'Introduction', esp. p. 4; Parkins, 'The "consumer city" domesticated?'
[36] Jashemski, 'Produce gardens'.
[37] On the Case a Giardino, dated to *c.* 128 in a period of expansion of the city, see Calza et al., *Scavi di Ostia* I, pp. 136–7. They had a collective garden for the buildings' inhabitants. See now Shepherd et al., 'Giardini ostiensi'.
[38] Purcell, 'The Roman garden as a domestic building', p. 123.
[39] Becatti, *Case ostiensi del tardo impero*, pp. 44–6.
[40] On houses at Ostia, see Hermansen, *Ostia: Aspects of Roman city life*, pp. 17–54.

evidence is very rich and is analysed in Chapter 3. In antiquity, Rome was, of course, much bigger and more densely populated than anywhere else on the peninsula and for that matter in the Mediterranean world. From the first century BCE onwards it enjoyed the benefit of a huge population that could buy goods from throughout the Roman world, both as private consumers and as recipients of state-sponsored benefits. Research into the Roman economy is currently a lively field, with major disagreements among scholars about the mechanics of trade, disparity of wealth and the means by which it should be measured, though the general picture of how food was put on the table at Rome is fairly uncontroversial.[41] Most food for Imperial-period Rome (first to the fourth centuries) came from sub-urban areas around the city and specialist farms slightly further afield.[42] Strikingly detailed new evidence for market gardens at the margins of the city has emerged from recent excavations for the Metropolitana Linea C, which has revealed extensive agricultural zones of the Republican, Augustan, and Flavian periods on the eastern side of the Caelian where Aurelian's Wall was later built. In the Augustan and early Imperial periods, a field with a large rainwater cistern was planted with fruiting trees (*Prunus* roots were recovered; these were probably peach trees), fig trees, grapevines, and nut trees, and perforated plant pots were used for transplanting trees or planting hedges.[43] The system of provisioning the city from beyond the urban centre, of which the first- and second-century orchard was a typical example, represents one of the many ways in which city dwellers were fed: through agricultural work on the margins of the city.

The populace of Rome, usually estimated at around one million in the first century BCE, including everyone from the imperial household down to slaves, ate agricultural products that came to the city through one of three main routes. First, wealthy Romans owned rural estates which directly supplied their townhouses when they were in residence; estates may have been far away from Rome or nearby in Central Italy, but in both cases there appears to have been a lot of movement of privately produced foodstuffs between country estate and urban house.[44] The relationship between rural allotment or estate and urban dwelling is very ancient in Greco-Roman society, and in the Roman imagination it related to deep and old ideas about citizenship and the edifying virtues of husbandry for

---

[41] Scheidel, *The Cambridge companion to the Roman economy*.
[42] See Morley, *Metropolis and hinterland*, p. 104, map 2.
[43] Rea, 'Archeologia nel suburbio di Roma', pp. 438–9; Rea and Saviane, 'At the foot of the Lateran Hill'. My thanks go to Ian Haynes for discussion.
[44] Purcell, 'Town in country and country in town'; Purcell, 'The Roman garden as domestic building'.

even the city-dweller.[45] Imperial-period urban elites may have been very removed from tilling the soil on their estates, but they were keenly interested in the moral value of proper estate management. Roman elites also saw profit potential in intensive agriculture within easy access to the city, for sale at markets. Second, urban Romans who had means to prepare food at home – not all did – bought ingredients at markets and small shops located throughout the city. There were specialist markets which sold mostly wholesale, such as the Forum Holitorium for vegetables and the Horrea Piperataria which offered storage and probably sale of spices and pepper.[46] There were *macella* for retail purchase of meats, fish, fruit, and vegetables, perhaps specialising in delicacies, as well as smaller shops and street hawkers throughout the city.[47] Third, Roman male citizens received the grain dole, which evolved over time from a certain measure of wheat, to wheat plus oil in the early second century, to bread plus wine and pork in the later third century.[48] The grain dole was a major administrative effort, which involved harvesting, processing, transporting, and then distributing products in the city, but the amount of food given was never enough to feed a family and thus must always have been supplemented with food acquired by other means.[49]

Staples such as oil, wine, and grain arrived in Rome through the *annona* system and also through private sources; processed foods, both luxury and common, were shipped to Rome from different corners of the empire and thence redistributed within the city as well as to other urban and rural centres. Perishable fresh vegetables like asparagus, lettuce, cabbages, onions, and garlic, as well as tree-fruits, berries, and fresh flowers for decorations and temple use, were grown in the periphery.[50] Peri-urban farming was most intensive over about a 7 km radius, or an hour's brisk walk for man or pack animal, from the centre.[51] Perishable products were high value in that they could return high profit for a small area of cultivation, and they required only a short journey to arrive at market still fresh.

---

[45] Purcell, 'The *horti* of Rome and the landscape of property'; Purcell, 'The Roman garden as domestic building'; Giardina, 'Aristocrazie terriere e piccola mercatura'; Vera: 'Strutture agrarie e strutture patrimoniali' and discussion in Chapter 4.

[46] See 'Forum Holitorium' in *LTUR*, vol. II, p. 299; see 'Horrea Piperataria' in *LTUR*, vol. III, pp. 45–6.

[47] Holleran, *Shopping in ancient Rome*.

[48] On the system, see Durliat, *De la ville antique*, esp. pp. 237–65; Tengström, *Bread for the people* and Chapter 4, 'Marketing in Late Antiquity', and Chapter 6, 'Conspicuous Cultivation'.

[49] Garnsey and Whittaker, 'Trade, industry and the urban economy'; Garnsey, *Food and society in classical antiquity*; Papi, *Supplying Rome and the empire*.

[50] See Cato, *De agri cultura*, 7, 8; Carandini, 'Hortensia'.

[51] On the customs imposed at the Aurelianic walls (and the earlier customs line which the Aurelianic walls traced), see Palmer, 'Customs on market goods'.

Mapping the locations of cisterns and water supplies, Andrew Wilson has shown that the greatest demand for irrigation in the area around Rome came from the fruit trees, vegetable gardens, and flowers that were grown there for the urban market.[52] Some market gardens and estates were farmed by urban dwellers as day workers, both those urban poor who might have received the grain dole, as well as non-citizen freedmen who lived in the city and were not entitled to grain supplies.[53] Refuse from the city – rubbish, spoiled food, and human and animal excrement – provided fertilizer for suburban fields.[54]

In the immediate environs of Rome, several different activities competed for suburban land, especially along arterial roads and along the Tiber and Anio rivers. In the periphery of the city were villas, estates developed for a particularly Roman kind of country residence and agricultural production, as well as plots of market gardens developed as investments, and tombs, the land around which was also sometimes cultivated as gardens.[55] The particular combination of religious observances and property law fostered a very particular intensification of agriculture around the city: lots immediately outside the city for the dead owned by the living and existing structures of regular markets and a concentration of consumers with coins in their pockets to buy small batches of flowers, fruits, and vegetables.

These same economic strategies also led to the deliberate absence of food agriculture and productive gardening from urban cultivated areas. Along the edges of Rome's walls, both just inside and just outside them, were the famous *Horti*. The name of these residential estates for the senatorial elites suggests vegetable gardens, but these were anything but.[56] They were pleasure gardens, with planted groves, shrines, fountains, pergolas, topiary, and other ornamental plants cultivated for the

---

[52] Wilson, 'Villas, horticulture and irrigation infrastructure'.
[53] Carandini, 'Hortensia', p. 72; Park and Maxey, *Two studies on the Roman lower classes*, p. 73.
[54] Scobie, 'Slums, sanitation and mortality', p. 413; Flohr and Wilson, 'The economy of ordure'; Miller and Gleason, 'Fertilizer in identification and analysis of cultivated soil', p. 38.
[55] On 'villas' and their agricultural production, see Purcell, 'The Roman villa', esp. pp. 162–6. On tomb gardens, see Purcell, 'Tomb and suburb', esp. pp. 35–6; Purcell, 'The Roman villa', p. 157; Lugli, see 'Hortus', esp. p. 1043, and now Bodell, 'Roman tomb gardens'. Lugli argued that if the tomb had been declared a *locus religiosus* it was inviolable and inalienable, but the majority were common gardens with vegetables, fruiting trees, and grape vines. Sometimes the crops of these gardens were intended for the dead, as argued by Toynbee, *Death and burial in the Roman World*, pp. 97–8, but in other cases they were used for commercial production; Bodell, 'Roman tomb gardens', pp. 201, 222.
[56] On these, see the conference at Rome, Cima and La Rocca, *Horti romani*, and a review, Purcell, 'Dialectical gardening'.

enjoyment of the owner and his guests, more like the *vigne* of Renaissance Rome than anything economically productive. In his analysis of the *Horti* of Rome, Nicholas Purcell claims that 'the truly ornamental garden was born from the excitement of being able to show off water, rich soil, a location near the market, and abundant labour force – and deliberately chosen and soignée sterility'.[57] Their value to Roman (elite) society was in their distinctly *un*productive nature. Even legal discourse maintained a clear distinction between gardens that were productive and planted with crops for market and ornamental gardens, which were expected to be in urban contexts. The legal collection compiled by the emperor Justinian in the sixth century includes a ruling from the third-century jurist Ulpian which identifies as 'urban' any garden surrounded by buildings, unless it is primarily for profit; then it should not be considered urban.[58]

The preservation of clear distinctions between urban built environment and rural horticulture in ancient Rome adheres to a pattern of urban food production in the pre-modern world theorised by J. von Thünen, *Der Isolierte Staat* (Fig. 6).[59] In von Thünen's model, the city itself consumed products from outside its walls. The areas around the city were given over to somewhat specialised food production, in concentric rings. The most perishable and costly to transport, such as fresh milk and vegetables, came from the nearest city; beyond this zone were forests for wood and fields for grains and so on, increasingly distant from the city. Profit was maximised by increasing intensification where transport costs were less, immediately nearest to the centre, and this intensification was facilitated by the availability in the city of fertiliser, workers, and staples to feed them. Two concepts of the model, crop location and intensification based on proximity to urban market, have been invoked to explain the agricultural supply to Rome by ancient historians and economists such as Carandini,[60] Morley,[61] and others.[62] This model of urban consumption

---

[57] Purcell, in 'The Roman garden as a domestic building', p. 135. For more on *Horti*, see Hartswick, *The gardens of Sallust*, and Carroll, 'Contextualising art and nature'.
[58] 'Idem [Ulpianus] libro secundo de omnibus tribunalibus ... proinde hortos quoque, si qui sunt in aedificiis constituti, dicendum est urbanorum appellatione contineri. plane si plurimum horti in reditu sunt, uinearii forte uel etiam holitorii, magis haec non sunt urbana'. (Ulpian, All Seats of Judgment, book 2 ... So it must be said that gardens also, if there are any among buildings, are included in the designation 'urban'. Clearly, if the gardens are for the most part productive, as, for instance, vineyards or vegetable patches, these are for the most part not urban.) Justinian, *Digest* 50.16.198 (ed. Mommsen, trans. Watson, vol. IV, p. 950).
[59] von Thünen, *Der isolierte Staat*, trans. as von Thünen, *Isolated state*.
[60] Carandini, 'Hortensia', p. 66.   [61] Morley, *Metropolis and hinterland*, pp. 62–3.
[62] Wilson, 'Villas, horticulture'. For late antiquity, see Santangeli Valenzani, 'Vecchie e nuove forme'.

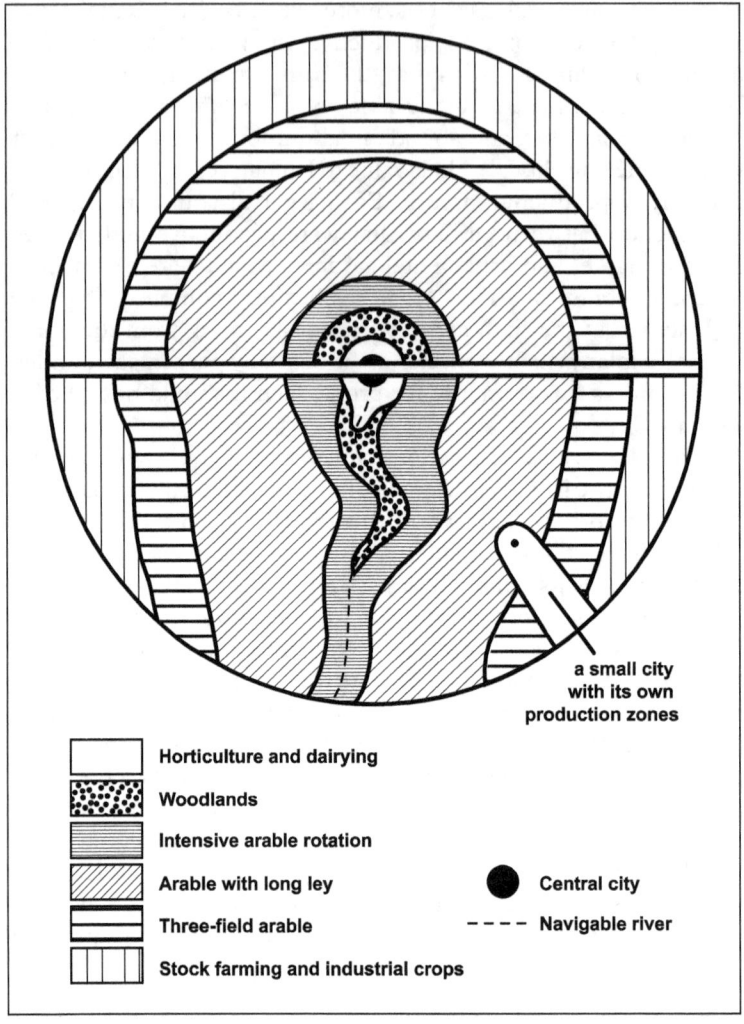

Figure 6 von Thünen's model of city and hinterland. Image based on Chisholm, *Rural settlement and land use*, fig. 4.

of rural produce has been the subject of debates about the nature of the Roman consumer city, or productive city, but it begins to lose relevance for understanding the economies and societies of urban centres and Rome, after the fifth century, because the cities themselves become productive.

Late Antiquity

Domestic architecture played a central role in the presentation and performance of social status among Romans of the imperial period, both rural villas and urban townhouses. In the capital of Rome, senatorial families built and rebuilt in their homes employing new fashions in decoration and architecture; in other cities, urban elites followed suit. Aristocrats' attention to their townhouses, their decoration, and their gardens was essential to showing the social status of the owner to clients who visited each morning to greet their patron in the *salutatio*. Ammianus Marcellinus, writing in the mid fourth century, scathingly described the clients attending aristocrats in their townhouses: chatty flatterers 'admiring the rows of columns hanging in the air in a high façade or walls gleaming with the remarkable colours of stone, raise these noble men above mortals'.[63] Through the house, homeowners established their position in relation to other elites who visited the house as guests, often to dine; to their clients, who came to the house to greet and to do business with the owner; and to the rest of people in their city, who may not have entered the home, but might pass it. Elite houses were, as Carlos Machado argued particularly with regard to Rome, strongly connected with their owner, his family, and its history.[64]

Townhouse Transformation, Textual Evidence

In Rome as well as in other Italian cities, the urban landscape changed significantly in late antiquity, losing density and complexity. In the fourth century there had been a small boom in the construction of townhouses in major Italian cities, but this diminished at the end of the century, and the great peristyle *domus* of the imperial period were not built anywhere in Italy or beyond after the fifth century.[65] Broad demographic and economic changes affected the cities of Italy, as we will consider in Chapter 4; these changes were destructive to the density of townhouses in Italian cities.[66] In the fifth century, there

---

[63] 'ita hi quoque columnarum constructiones alta fronte suspensas mirando, atque parietes lapidum circumspectis coloribus nitidos, ultra mortalitatem nobiles uiros extollunt', Ammianus Marcellinus, *Rerum gestarum libri*, 28.4.12, ed. Rowe, p. 145. See Ellis, 'Power, architecture and decor'; Lawrence and Wallace-Hadrill, eds., *Domestic space in the Roman world*.

[64] Machado, 'The aristocratic *domus*'; Machado, 'Aristocratic houses'; Machado, *Urban space and aristocratic power*, pp. 219–28. See also the views of Hilner, '*Domus*, family, and inheritance'.

[65] In 1988 Ellis cited the House of the Falconer in Argos, Greece as the last peristyle house of antiquity, built 530–50 CE; Ellis, 'The end of the Roman house', p. 565.

[66] Guidobaldi, 'Le domus tardoantiche'.

were still luxurious houses at Rome, which included ornamental gardens, called *uiridaria* in the poetry that continued to celebrate them, but gardens and indeed well-maintained houses were increasingly rare.[67] Some of the elite of Rome went to Constantinople, others retreated to provincial rural estates. Some elites were targeted when the city was besieged and were held for ransom, their houses sacked and destroyed.[68] In the fifth century, senators living in the provinces were exempted from previously obligatory trips back to Rome, and this must have meant that elite townhouses at Rome were less valuable in the construction of social capital among Rome's elites.[69]

The destructive effects of war in the early fifth century caused the abandonment of some townhouses and the radical reordering of others. New troops in Italian cities sometimes seized houses and subdivided them for billeting soldiers, as at Pavia in 489 under Theodoric: 'You would have seen the city teeming with vast thongs of troops, and huge townhouses cut up into the narrowest of huts. You would have seen even the largest buildings disappear from their foundations, nor was the ground itself sufficient to take such a dense mass of people.'[70]

Legal structures existed to compel building owners to rebuild property that was damaged or to distribute abandoned property, after a time, to other private owners or, with the consent of local magistrates and neighbours, to convert unredeemable ruins to a garden (*hortus*):

8.10.3. The same Augustus [Alexander] to Aper, a veteran.

Whether, after a house collapses, it is permitted not entirely to restore the same urban exterior but to change it to a garden, and whether this was done with the consent of magistrates who did not prohibit it and (with that) of neighbors, after it is shown what has often been done in a city in this sort of dispute, the provincial governor will hear the case and decide. Promulgated March 26, in the consulship of Julian and Crispinus (224)[71]

---

[67] See Flavius Merobaudes, *Carmen* III, p. 4, trans. Clover, 'Flavius Merobaudes', pp. 28–9; for a walled garden in a palace at Rome, cf. Rutilius Namatianus, *De reditu suo*, I.111–12; Goodson, 'Admirable and delectable gardens'.

[68] Machado, 'Between memory and oblivion', p. 123.

[69] See discussion in Machado, 'Between memory and oblivion', p. 123; Barnish, 'Transformation and survival'.

[70] 'domorum inmanium culmina in angustissimis resecata tuguriis', Ennodius, 'Vita beatissimi Epiphani', c. 15, p. 98. See discussion in Brogiolo, 'Ideas of the town in Italy', p. 104; Machado, 'Between memory and oblivion', p. 122.

[71] '*Idem A. Apro evocato*. An in totum ex ruina domus licuerit non eandem faciem in civitate restituere, sed in hortum convertere, et an hoc consensu tunc magistratuum non prohibentium, item vicinorum factum sit, praeses, probatis his quae in oppido frequenter in eodem genere controversiarum servata sunt, causa cognita statuet.' PP. vn k. April.

Just as they had been after the earthquake in Pompeii, so too in late antiquity, some residential lots seem to have been converted to market gardens. This law suggests that the same conversion took place in the third century, and perhaps even the sixth century, when this law was included in Justinian's compilation. The *horti* created in Italian cities of the later fifth and sixth centuries by converting ruinous residential buildings may have been the first steps towards the plots of individual houses with urban gardens that came to characterise early medieval cities.

Townhouse Transformation, Archaeology

The material transformations of urban residential buildings and their surroundings in late antiquity made possible the space for urban cultivation. There is unambiguous archaeological evidence for the partial abandonment of large townhouses, usually the most luxurious reception rooms, which were stripped of marbles and building materials and buried under earth. Much of this evidence comes from Rome, where families restored the service rooms of several fifth-century houses to more modest homes, sometimes recreating the traditional courtyard- or atrium-centred *domus* of the past.[72] One clear case of this transformation comes from the house at Piazza dei Cinquecento in the fifth century (Fig. 7). This house was excavated in 1947–9 when Linea B of the Metropolitana was built. Though it was not carried out stratigraphically, the documentation from that twentieth-century excavation has permitted modern archaeologists to reconstruct phases of construction and use for the building, including its late antique phases.[73] The original *domus*, dating from the second century, with its frescoed rooms and private bath building, was partially abandoned in the second half of the fifth century or the early sixth century. A masonry wall was built between the abandoned rooms and those which continued to be used, the 'piccola domus', and excavation records make clear that it was constructed against earth, so the abandoned part of the house was filled with earth at that time.[74] The rooms of the bath complex were partly used, as was a small trapezoidal courtyard opening on to two vaulted rooms. The latrine of the *domus* was given a new wall and door out to the exterior (not excavated) for keeping animals, perhaps. It is not known what purpose the rooms to the east of the 'piccola domus' served, either in antiquity or this later phase, and the whole complex now sits underneath the Stazione Termini.

Iuliano et Crispino conss. [a. 224]', *Codex Iustianianus*, VIII, 10, 3 (p. 334), trans. vol. III, p. 2041.
[72] Machado, 'Between memory and oblivion'.   [73] Barbera and Paris, *Antiche stanze*.
[74] Meneghini and Santangeli Valenzani, 'Fasi tarde di occupazione'.

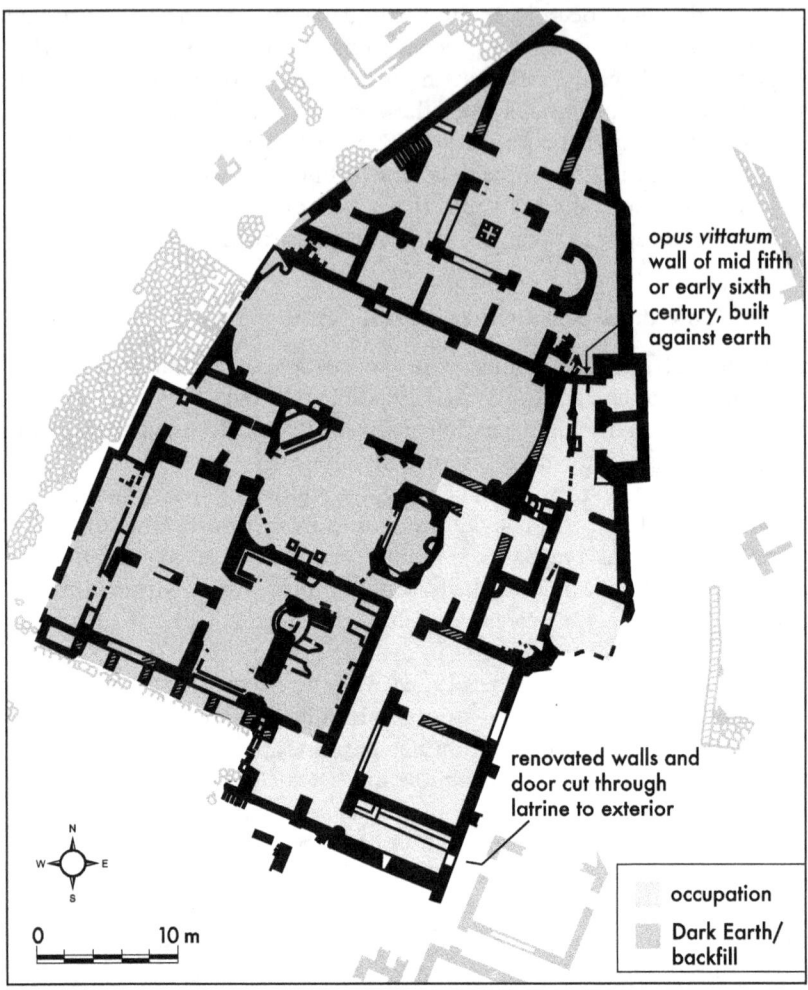

Figure 7 *Domus* under Piazza dei Cinquecento, Rome. Plan after Meneghini and Santangeli Valenzani, 'Fasi tarde di occupazione', fig. 5.

This example, recovered from the archaeological archive, gives us a compelling model for the transformation of the urban landscape. The exterior frames of buildings were preserved as property boundaries, as were roads which continued to be used, while the interiors of Roman townhouses were transformed from articulated complex buildings into simpler clusters of rooms and open areas. These open areas, then, may have taken on a productive role. Roberto Meneghini claimed that backfilling structures was one of the quickest and most common ways to obliterate or to rehabilitate an area or buildings. It can be recognised at many sites at Rome, where structures were filled with earth and then built over, or the lowest levels of buildings were filled with earth, either for stability or to create areas for planting, or both.[75]

We can see many other examples of the formation of cultivated or cultivatable spaces between and around houses across the cities of Italy, especially in so-called Dark Earth, a term which has been often used to describe archaeological deposits of thick, dark soil with few inclusions, found between contexts of the Roman period and medieval structures and deposits of the twelfth century (see Archaeology for further discussion of the term):

In Milan (Fig. 8), in the area northwest of Piazza Duomo, at via Tommaso Grossi/via Santa Margherita (what had been the *cardo maximus* of the Roman city), a late antique portico was dismantled and the area was covered by a layer of Dark Earth 35 cm thick in the period 425–600; a series of buildings with wells were built atop the foundations for the portico adjacent to the Dark Earth.[76] Also at Milan, at S. Maria alla Porta, a collapsed late antique building was covered in one area by a metre of Dark Earth, while in the other area it was covered by layers of pavements in beaten earth and *cocciopesto* with post holes from the uprights for structures.[77] This last example suggests that the deposit of Dark Earth was formed deliberately by backfilling and that the unbuilt area of humic soil stood next to structures. The centre of the late Roman city was covered by deposits, some of which were Dark Earth.

At Brescia (Fig. 9), a *domus* on the *decumanus maximus* (now the via dei Musei) was restructured in the sixth century, with partial demolition and backfilling with rubble to create a few small-scale houses with open areas in between. These new houses of the sixth century and later maintained, more or less, the orientation of the earlier Roman houses, sometimes reusing their walls, and, perhaps, respecting their property boundaries, though the organisation of the houses was fundamentally different, being smaller single- or double-room houses, perhaps of double stories, facing onto courtyards that were either private or shared.[78]

---

[75] Meneghini and Santangeli Valenzani, 'Fasi tarde di occupazione', p. 176, citing as other similar efforts the levelling and filling of the cemetery of the Vatican, the mithraeum under S. Prisca, Tiber-side wharf buildings, and the substructures of the Colosseum, all of which were backfilled in the fourth or fifth centuries.

[76] Perring, 'Lo scavo di via Tommaso Grossi', p. 223, interpreted the dark grey soil as a garden or Dark Earth.

[77] Ceresa Mori, 'Milano via del Lauro 1', p. 94.

[78] Brogiolo, 'The control of public space'.

54 Patterns and Changes

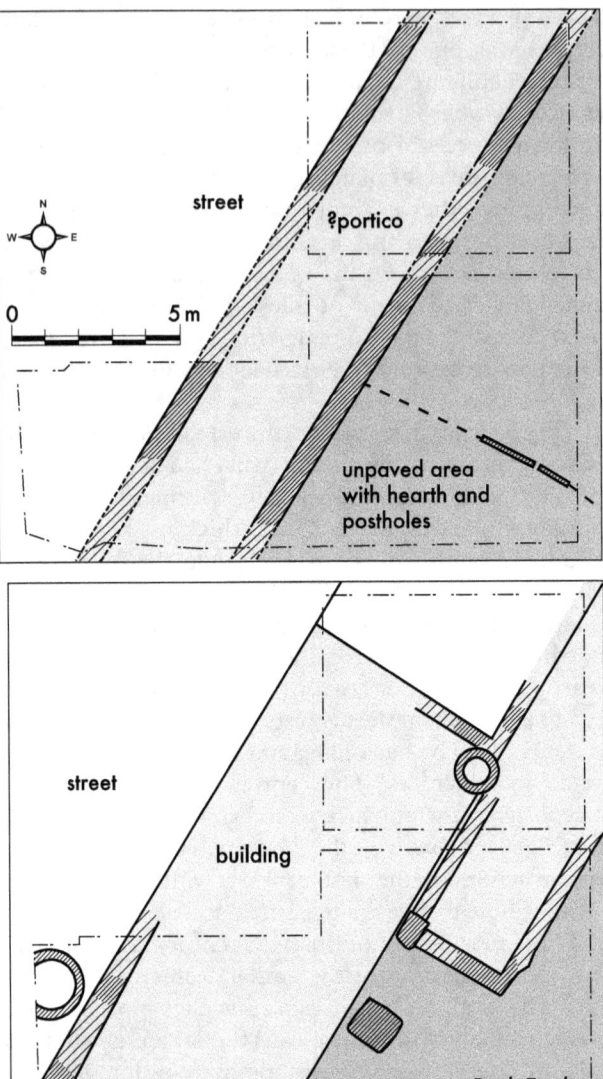

Figure 8 Buildings along the via T. Grossi, Milan. A portico of the early fifth century was transformed in the fifth and sixth centuries to houses next to open areas of thick organic soil (Dark Earth). Plan after Caporusso, ed., *Scavi MM3*, fig. 225.

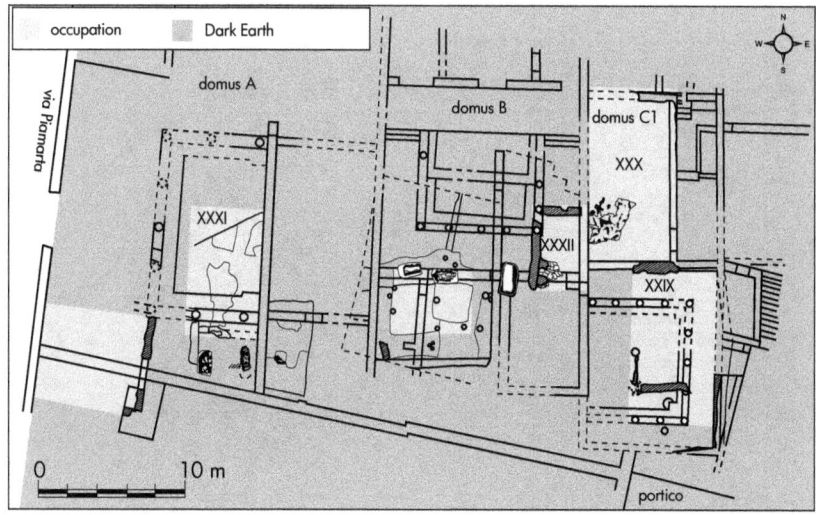

Figure 9 Plan of the Roman *domus* along the *decumanus maximus* at Brescia, and the residential buildings of the sixth or early seventh century. Plan after Brogiolo, 'The control of public space', fig. 2A.

Naples (Fig. 10): Excavation at the urban site of vico Carminiello ai Mannesi revealed earth and rubble blocking up an entire city street, accumulating from the sixth to the seventh century; by the eighth century, the insula block was split into a lower set of rooms and an upper set of rooms, both of which opened on to a flat earthen terrace, which, the excavators believe, was intended for intensive cultivation.[79] The habitation envisaged for the early medieval period comprised a series of rooms carved out from the Roman-period structure with earthen terraces and some quite deep deposits of Dark Earth.

These examples, alongside many others which could be provided, paint a picture of late antique and early medieval residential complexes in Italian cities as small suites of rooms or single-room houses, set within open unpaved areas, unlike the densely infilled blocks of housing that characterised imperial-period urban architecture. This pattern of reuse/remodelling affected high-status townhouses as well as *insulae* in northern cities and southern ones, too. Other sectors of Italian cities were also closed off, as they were designated rubbish tips, and parts of public buildings became obsolete.

---

[79] Arthur, *Naples. From Roman town*, p. 52; Arthur, *Il complesso archeologico di Carminiello ai Mannesi*, p. 74.

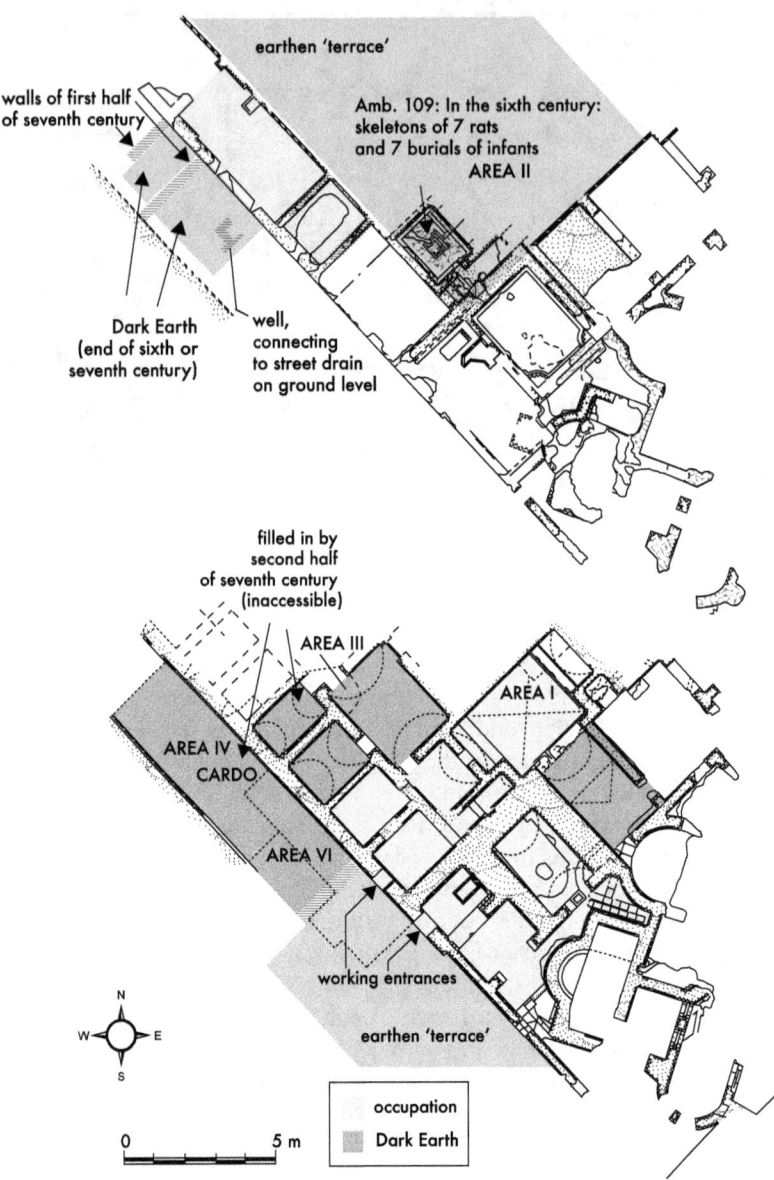

Figure 10 Buildings at vico Carminiello ai Mannesi, Naples. Top: rooms on the upper terrace. Below: rooms on the lower terrace. Plan after Arthur, 'Il complesso archeologico di Carminiello ai Mannesi', figs. 2 and 52.

Large-scale rubbish tips seem to have been a feature of late antique urban landscapes. Recent research on Milan and Rome has used amphorae deposits as indices of urban rubbish tips, analysing these in relation to the uses and abandonment of the urban landscape in late antiquity. At Rome in the fifth century, piles of broken amphorae, transport containers which had held large quantities of wine, oil, or other liquids, formed in areas of the Forum, within high-status late antique housing on the Aventine, and even in parts of the imperial residence on the Palatine; at Milan, rubbish was dumped along transport routes in the same period.[80] Paul Johnson has argued that these deposits formed not necessarily in abandoned areas, but rather as deliberate dumps in partially blocked-off buildings or areas that continued to be used. Given the quantities of waste involved, it is unlikely that they formed through individual rubbish habits, but rather, Johnson suggests, they may have been deposited in the context of a communal strategy on the part of civic authorities to maintain some monumental open areas by consolidating dumping in areas that were being cut off.[81] Such urban interventions happened even earlier in some cities. At Lucca, dumps of earth rich in organic material and some residual pottery have been identified in the area of the Forum, at the centre of the walled town, as well as in suburban areas. Dumps in the Forum began to form already in the third century.[82]

Late antique urban dumps were often found near markets. At Naples, one of the roads by the *macellum* beneath the later church of S. Lorenzo Maggiore was filled in the end of the fifth century with deposits of soil and waste, effectively blocking access to the substructures of the *macellum*.[83] Along the river bank running through the city of Pescara, a street-fronting *taberna* and *horreum* of the second century were partially dismantled and a number of timber huts were built there in the eighth century, after a continual deposition of Dark Earth had raised the ground level progressively higher.[84] The *macellum* at Alife, a town in Campania, filled up between the second and sixth centuries.[85] These deposits, filled with

---

[80] Johnson, 'Investigating urban change', pp. 177–85.
[81] Johnson also points out that at Rome, churches tended to be built in the abandoned parts of the urban fabric, not where the rubbish tips were forming, while at Milan, rubbish accumulations seem to have been cyclical.
[82] Ciampoltrini, 'Città "frammentate" e città-fortezza', esp. pp. 615–20.
[83] De Simone, 'Il complesso monumentale', p. 195, n. 26; De Simone, 'San Lorenzo Maggiore', p. 252, where the filling of the substructures of the macellum is dated to a flood of alluvial mud. Cf. comments by Arthur, 'Naples: a case of urban survival', p. 770, note 36.
[84] Staffa, 'Scavi nel centro storico di Pescara', esp. pp. 217–19. Other deposits of Dark Earth, filled with materials, in other parts of the city were identified as eleventh-century phases, p. 249.
[85] Marazzi et al., 'I ritmi e le stagioni di una città'.

organic material including food waste and broken transport containers, were not suitable for cultivation, but there are some cases where rubbish dumps may have served as the initial deposit on top of which humic soil was deposited. At Palazzo Giusso, Naples, the deposit of Dark Earth had more pottery inclusions at the bottom, while towards the top the fragments were fewer and more abraded.[86] It appears that here, over an initial deposit of rubbish, more humic and loose soil formed and was eventually cultivated – excavators suggested that the garden area which was eventually formed was as large as 5 × 20 m.

Across Naples in the late fifth and early sixth centuries, a number of urban buildings were abandoned, and parts of the city accumulated significant quantities of Dark Earth.[87] Five sites excavated within the town have yielded accumulations of Dark Earth, up to 1.5 m in thickness, over demolished Roman buildings: Palazzo Giusso, just mentioned, and via San Paolo, vico della Serpe, S. Patrizia, and S. Marcellino (Fig. 11).[88] The upper walls of the Roman buildings had collapsed or were partially razed and organic material and soils had been brought in. The excavator of Carminiello ai Mannesi argues that at least in that case, if not also the others, the accumulations of Dark Earth did not form naturally but were deliberately backfilled, an effort that was perhaps organised by the administration of the city in the Ostrogothic period (490–536).[89] Samples from via San Paolo, Naples, yielded carbonized and mineralized plums, nuts, and cereals, admittedly in small quantities.[90] These indicate what may have been grown and processed there, or grown nearby and consumed by people who dumped their refuse, or their ordure, at this site.

The formation of Dark Earth and its characteristics will be discussed in Archaeology. For the moment, the relevant points to be made are two. First, some townhouses in Italian cities changed in nature and form over late antiquity, from lots which stretched from street to street with built courtyards and rooms, to lots which comprised built rooms and unroofed open areas filled with building materials and Dark Earth. Second, within Italian cities, some public buildings and areas of the city came to be designated as rubbish tips or dumps. These were not abandoned per se, as they were deliberately earmarked for the collection of refuse. The

---

[86] Carsana, 'Napoli: uno scavo archeologico', p. 145.
[87] Arthur, *Naples. From Roman town*, p. 52.
[88] Arthur, *Naples, From Roman town*, p. 53; for the former three, see Arthur, 'Naples: a case of urban survival', pp. 769–70; for the latter two, see Carsana, 'Napoli: uno scavo archeologico'.
[89] Arthur, *Il complesso archeologico di Carminiello ai Mannesi*, p. 437.
[90] Arthur, *Naples. From Roman town*, p. 54.

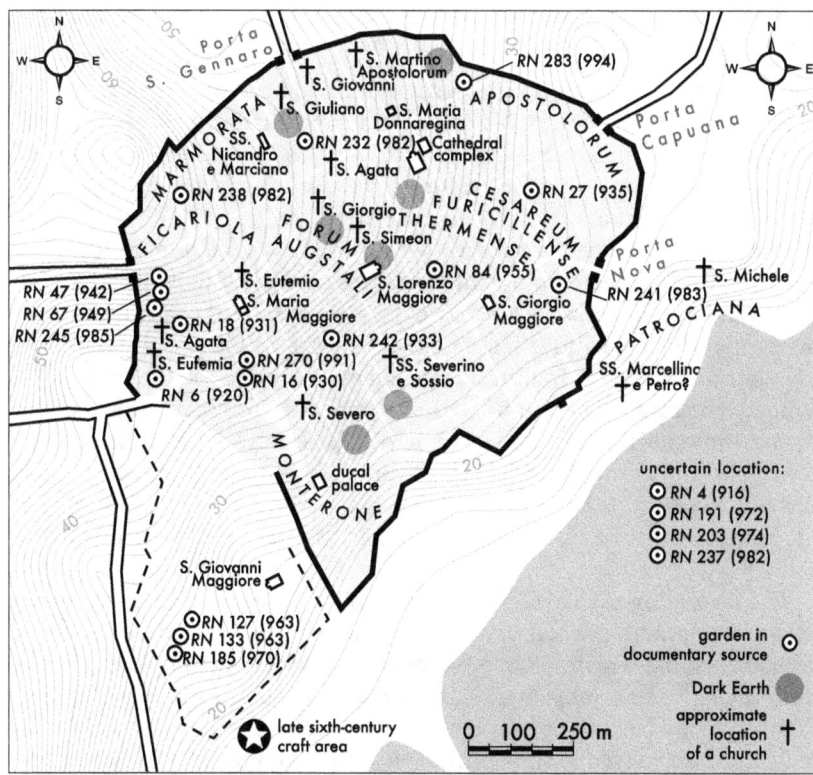

Figure 11 Plan of early medieval Naples with areas of Dark Earth, and the location of Maru and Barbaria's garden and other gardens known from tenth-century documents.

arrival of accumulated refuse changed somewhat the aesthetic and physical appearance of late Roman homes and cities as well as marked shifts from the administrative habits and maintenance regimes of the ancient city.

In the early sixth century, the retired statesman Cassiodorus lamented the breakdown of civic order he saw at Rome, another shift in administration and maintenance of urban structure. The letter he drafted for Theodoric in 510/11 notes in particular the abuse of the public water supply of Rome for private gardening:

Now, it is said that the water of the aqueducts, which should be protected with the greatest attention, has been diverted to power water-mills and irrigate gardens, through concern for private profit. This practice should hardly be adopted in the countryside; its occurrence in that city is a lamentable disgrace.[91]

Cassiodorus objected to the private infringement of what had before been a public, state-controlled good, and in particular that water should be used for profit-bearing agriculture, that is, a market garden. His concerns were probably not entirely new, as infringement of public water had been the subject of legislation at the time of Theodosius.[92] His letter suggests that in a century of major transformation of the urban fabric of Rome, when city townhouses were being partially backfilled to leave smaller, more manageable dwellings, there were those at Rome who attempted to create and irrigate market gardens within the city walls.

In late antiquity, the hundreds of small market plots outside the walls of Rome were gradually consolidated into larger latifundia which were part of the imperial fisc, or owned or leased privately.[93] Later these were owned by the church and leased out in relatively small parcels; within the city, small-scale producers may have been able to take advantage of the transformations of the city's fabric to create small plots inside the walls.[94]

The breakdown that Cassiodorus laments, between categories and activities – public/private, urban/rural – previously held to be relatively separate, is that which made possible urban gardening in medieval Italy, both the kinds of arrangements described in the letters of Pope Gregory, with which we began this chapter, and the further developments of urban cultivation in subsequent centuries, to which we now turn. It was these changes that brought about the so-called ruralisation of the city and urban agriculture, not just at Rome but elsewhere. Throughout cities, the appearance, density, and quality of architectural integrity and degree of decorative order would have changed over time, through the introduction of a designated rubbish dump in one place, a gleaming new church elsewhere, a cemetery over in another place, and the repair or restoration of an ancient monument in another. The qualities and experiences of urban contexts changed further with the incorporation of small-scale agriculture. In these changes, we will also begin to see new strategies of legitimisation and topographies of power.

---

[91] 'Dicitur ergo commodi cura priuati aquam formarum, quam summo deceret studio communiri, ad aquae molas exercendas uel hortos rigandos fuisse deriuatam turpe et miserabile hoc in illa urbe fieri, quod per agros uix deceret assumi.' Cassiodorus, *Variae*, III. 31 (ed. Fridh, p. 119), trans. Barnish, pp. 62–3.

[92] See *Codex Theodosianus* XV.2, 'De aquaeductu' (pp. 814–7); Alföldy, 'Urban life, inscriptions'.

[93] Carandini, 'Hortensia', p. 68. [94] Barnish, 'Pigs, plebians and potentes'.

Archaeology

The identification of areas of concentrated dirt and earth within the fabric of late antique cities has not always been seen as a mark of administrative organisation, as we have seen.[95] Some scholars see the accumulation of urban refuse as proof of a drastic decline in living standards and social complexity, while others see it as the evolution of proactive strategies for new ways of living. Beyond issues of interpretation of the changes to early medieval cities, the very means by which urban deposits of earth formed, a long-term process which eventually permitted the kind of urban cultivation under analysis here, has been the subject of a lot of debate within the archaeological community. New strategies for the analysis of this material, along with new evidence for cultivation emerging from archaeobotanical study, are shedding new light on the phenomenon and make it clearer than ever before that the cultivation of food-gardens in Italian cities was a deliberate and even desired activity. In the following section I will discuss the evolution of thinking about Dark Earth and its relationship to urban cultivation, and then I will address the emerging data from archaeobotany, which indicate firstly the prevalence of cultivation in early medieval cities, and secondly the utility (for food and maybe for medicine) of the plants grown.

For decades, archaeologists excavating medieval cities have found 'Dark Earth'. The term 'dark earth' or 'dark made-earth' was used in English as early as 1912 to describe the deposits which sat on top of the remains of Roman London and beneath medieval London structures.[96] 'Terres noires' had been recognised in early medieval layers in French cities in the mid nineteenth century. In the 1970s, when the skyscrapers going up in the City of London prompted many separate excavations, archaeologists repeatedly encountered deposits covering Roman layers which they identified as 'Dark Earth' and the term became common usage. Italian archaeologists, often aided by English diggers, found very similar types of contexts when excavating city centres in Italy in the 1980s. They were also found in France and Belgium at the same time in similar city-centre excavations. In European archaeology, especially urban archaeology, the term 'Dark Earth' has historically connoted deposits that were dark in colour, with little obvious internal stratification, and few inclusions or inclusions that were highly abraded, including brick, tile, charcoal, bone, and pottery. The term was often used to characterise deposits between ancient contexts (up to about the fifth century) and

---
[95] On p. 56.
[96] Norman and Reader, 'Further discoveries relating to Roman London, 1906–12', pp. 276, 278, 290.

medieval structures and deposits of the twelfth century onwards.[97] The term filled an interpretative void for understanding late antique and early medieval sites, because once late Roman pottery disappears, by 600 at the latest (by 400 in Britain), very good chronological indicators of early medieval use and occupation are hard to find – this was especially true in the 1980s, and it remains true now though to a lesser degree. In the 1980s and 1990s, Dark Earth became an important marker of early medieval phases in the absence of material culture, from either the Roman or later medieval periods, sitting between these two highly recognisable phases. It was long believed that Dark Earth layers were colluvial or alluvial deposits of earth sealing the Roman layers by natural accumulation over a site left undisturbed by use, after the Romans had gone and before migration-period settlements became substantial. (By way of comparison, sites in London abandoned after the Second World War have accumulated significantly thick deposits in half a century, just as parts of Berlin have accumulated 20–25 cm-thick silty and humic deposits in the same amount of time.[98]) Comparing the stratigraphy of various medieval sites revealed that while Dark Earth occurred consistently in chronological phases – that is, after Roman buildings – it appeared at different absolute layers; which is to say the Dark Earth was not a uniform horizon over abandoned Roman layers but appeared in different contexts in relation to the previous buildings, suggesting that the process was not singular but occurred over time.[99]

Italian Dark Earth

Deposits of Dark Earth very similar to those in Britain have been recognised in early medieval Italian cities. Their significance has likewise been debated, though the shape of the argument is different from the British discourse.[100] In Italian cities, Dark Earth deposits have ranged in thickness from 0.70 to 3.0 m and have often been found in the centres of Roman cities, over *fora* and also within Roman housing blocks.[101] At Verona, for example, the paving of the Roman Forum and the steps of the Capitolium on its northern side were covered by deposits of domestic

---

[97] Nicosia et al., 'The contribution of geosciences'; Macphail et al., 'A future for Dark Earth?'; Nicosia and Devos, 'Urban Dark Earth'.
[98] Yule, 'The "dark earth"'; Blume and Rung, 'Genese und Ökologie'.
[99] Sheldon, 'The 1972–74 excavations', p. 40. See discussion in Yule, 'The "dark earth"', where he argued then that the Dark Earth in London was formed as a depositional process after abandonment, not a deposit as such.
[100] See a summary in Christie, *From Constantine to Charlemagne*, p. 261.
[101] Brogiolo, 'A proposito dell'organizzazione urbana', citing Dark Earth in Cremona, Mantua, Verona, and Brescia.

waste, and the cryptoporticus of the Capitolium was filled to layers over 3 m thick after the second half of the seventh century.[102] Some scholars have claimed that these were formed by abandonment, as was previously believed to have been the case for similar contexts in England, while others have held that they were deliberate deposits of rubbish and waste.[103]

For some, especially archaeologists working on urbanism in Italy in the 1980s, Dark Earth, however it may have been created, pointed to a major break with the ancient city. It made entirely apparent the comprehensive abandonment and restructuring of houses and of whole areas of the city. For some scholars, it meant the breakdown of civic maintenance, organised rubbish collection, and other markers of the organised urban communities of the late Roman past, but for others it signified a degree of effort and coordination of resources.[104] By virtue of the sources different scholars concentrated on, historians of the period may have had less trouble imagining the new configurations of houses, churches, and open areas of brown/green space than archaeologists. The documents describe houses with lots and annexes, bounded by neighbours, along roads and within urban quarters. The archaeology, by contrast, looks significantly different from the order of Roman-period cities. Further, the inheritance of British archaeological terms and concepts, such as 'Dark Earth', came into conflict with Italian cultural values or assumptions about cities. A small freestanding house with a thatched roof, next to an open field, may have seemed less primitive to someone living in England (where thatched roofs and village greens are highly prized) than to someone living in modern Padua or Milan, where houses are rarely free-standing and cities are paved.[105] And, as Paul Arthur pointed out, the interpretative model that suits post-Roman Britain may not be particularly suitable to Italy; for instance, the building materials used in many late antique Italian cities – Naples served as his principal example – were probably more robust than in early medieval London, and thus the idea that Dark Earth might be decomposed thatch, wood, and other organic building

---

[102] Cavalieri Manasse, *L'area del Capitolium di Verona*, pp. 134–5, includes a lot of butchery waste. For depths of post-Roman deposits across the city, see La Rocca [Hudson], '"Dark Ages" a Verona', tav. 11. These latter data were taken by Brogiolo as strong indicators of the degradation of the city of Verona in the early Middle Ages, 'A proposito dell'organizzazione urbana', p. 39.

[103] Cavalieri Manasse, *L'area del Capitolium di Verona*, p. 135, for the deposit.

[104] For the *loci classici* of the two diverging opinions on the interpretation of Dark Earth in Italy, see Brogiolo, 'A proposito dell'organizzazione urbana', p. 35, contra La Rocca [Hudson], '"Dark Ages" a Verona', p. 71. See also Chapter 1; Brogiolo et al., 'Processi di stratificazione'; Carver, *Arguments in stone*, p. 50.

[105] Ward Perkins, 'Continuitists, catastrophists', and Chapter 1.

materials is not entirely convincing as an explanation for Dark Earth in urban Italy.[106]

Archaeological analysis of Dark Earth in the early medieval cities of Italy developed in the hothouse of debates about how to characterise the changes that cities underwent in the early medieval period, wider arguments about whether the early Middle Ages constituted continuity with the past or rupture from ancient ways of life. Until new methods of analysis came to be used, Dark Earth remained a key sparring point in the debate over the nature of early medieval cities. The value of soil analysis in reconstructing past human and environmental actions has therefore become increasingly apparent. New techniques reveal what had previously been invisible. Earlier archaeological field reports characterised Dark Earth as homogenous humic soils, with (few) anthropogenic inclusions, but since the 1990s, petrological and chemical analysis of the components of the soils, including minerals and archaeobotanical elements, has revealed the diversity of the contexts and attested to different formation processes. Sampling deposits and analysing them through various means helps to identify different elements which make up a soil and the composition of the sediments of the grains.[107] Soil studies usually begin with description of visible elements, measurement of water content and total organic matter, reading of pH (to assess leaching), consideration of organic carbon and nitrogen (to understand bioactivity and bio-decay), assessment of organic and inorganic phosphates (as a marker of intensity of human occupation or animal stabling), and other methods.[108] Components, whether geological, man-made materials or plant remains, can be identified through thin section analysis, which aids in petrological identification of sediments as well as the study of phytoliths and pollens which might be mineralised or vitrified and preserved in a soil. These various sources of information, analysed in conjunction with a growing body of published soil studies, have now made clear that numerous and varied transformations which occurred successively or concurrently contributed to the formation of Dark Earth.[109] These can be understood in relation to specific examples, discussed briefly below.

Decay of Buildings Made of Perishable Materials: The destruction of buildings and the decomposition of building materials certainly

---

[106] Arthur, *Naples. From Roman town*, p. 53. Nicosia has pointed out that the idea of Dark Earth formed from decomposition of building materials departed from Macphail's early publications on the subject: *Geoarcheologia delle stratificazioni urbane*, p. 14.
[107] On principles and methods, see Goldberg and Macphail, *Practical and theoretical geoarchaeology*, pp. 336–67; Goldberg and Macphail, *Applied soils and micromorphology*.
[108] See the brief technical overview in Nicosia et al., 'The contribution of geosciences'.
[109] Goldberg and Macphail, *Applied soils and micromorphology*, esp. section 12.3, European Dark Earth.

leave traces in archaeological soils which are sometimes recoverable in soil analysis. Thus vegetable fibres, fragments of wood tissue, and charcoal are recognisable in some contexts, and the holes, trenches, and bits of a building, its uses, and its destruction form part of a wider archaeological context. At Ferrara, which was not a Roman city but was created anew in the seventh century, waterlogging of some contexts meant that some vegetal material such as wood was preserved in the deposits.[110] Occupation layers at the Corso Porta Reno site were interleaved with deposits of ashy midden and manure. The silty alluvial deposits and waterlogging prevented the bioturbation that occurs in many archaeological contexts, but the river water caused some weathering and reworking. Archaeological research revealed the timbers to be associated with the earliest phases of wooden construction at Ferrara, in the eighth century, though what earlier archaeologists had considered to be flooring was recognised as alluvial sediment.[111] After the wooden structures and midden deposits interleaved with alluvial silt, a brick building of the thirteenth century sealed the entire context. Unlike many Dark Earth deposits, these appeared stratified, because the reworking typically caused by animals and plants did not occur in the sometimes waterlogged and then sealed deposits, and the tendency towards homogenisation and soil formation was limited.[112] This site, among others, made very clear the importance of repeated flooding in the formation of this Dark Earth. Similar conditions have been revealed archaeologically, though without detailed soil analysis. For instance, at Piazza Ferrari, Rimini, an aristocratic residence of late antiquity built next to the city walls was abandoned and razed, replaced in the eighth century by a small hut, which after a few decades decomposed and was replaced by what was interpreted as a large vegetable garden.[113] Decomposing building material may have added fertility to soils.

Dumping Waste: At Ferrara, the accumulation of domestic waste from human occupation also aided in forming Dark Earth deposits. So too at Castelletto di Brenzone, a small settlement on the Lago di Garda, thin section analysis of the Dark Earth deposits reveals accumulations of domestic waste, including ash, charcoal, small bones, and fragments of building rubble sitting directly over the top of the floor surfaces of a Roman villa.[114] These Dark Earth deposits date from the sixth and

---

[110] Cremaschi and Nicosia, 'Corso Porta Reno, Ferrara'.
[111] Gadd and Ward Perkins, 'The development of urban domestic housing'.
[112] Nicosia would indeed avoid calling the deposits at Corso Porta Reno 'Dark Earth' because the original aspects of the urban deposits there are recognizable. Pers. comm. 2020.
[113] Ortalli, 'Formazione e trasformazioni'.
[114] Nicosia et al., 'The contribution of geosciences', pp. 158–60.

seventh centuries and represent the vertical accumulation of trampled waste deposits, reworked by processes of soil formation. Similarly, at Florence, excavations carried out between the Uffizi gallery and the Arno river revealed a deposit of Dark Earth which formed over about 400 years, from the seventh century onwards.[115] Within this profile, there were several different recognisable components, including abundant manure of an omnivore (pig? human?), towards the bottom as well as layers of ash, such as from domestic hearths (see Manuring). These elements were well mixed by active bioturbation by plants and animals in the soil. The second main phase, dating from the tenth century, similarly comprised dumped material, more in the way of kitchen waste than manure. Here the rate of dumping exceeded the rate of mixing from animals and weathering, creating a certain kind of internal stratification, and this sequence was sealed by a silty alluvial deposit. The deposits of manure and domestic waste associated with human occupation, laid down in a site which became repeatedly wet, assisted in forming the Dark Earth. Wood ash was a very common waste product at sites occupied by humans in the past, and its alkaline nature may have inhibited bacterial contributions towards soil formation.[116] In the example from Florence, the layers of ash were distinct within the Dark Earth deposits. Soil analysis has revealed that high proportion of charcoal contributes to the colour and appearance of Dark Earth, and thus it may not have such a high humic content as once assumed.[117]

Manuring: Soil analysis can sometimes reveal evidence of manuring. Herbivore dung has a lot of embedded plant materials which can endure in Dark Earth soils, both as mineralised carpological remains or vitrified phytoliths visible through a microscope.[118] Under blue light, calcium phosphate materials fluoresce, and Fe-Ca-P nodules appear in X-ray as well; both are indicators of carnivore or omnivore excrement, human waste or pig manure.[119] Excavations at Prosper-Mérimée Square, Tours, revealed a sequence of Dark Earth deposits, the formation of which was aided by the inclusion of night-soil (human faecal matter) and manure. In the fourth century, a ruined aqueduct was backfilled

---

[115] Nicosia et al., 'Medieval Dark Earth'.
[116] Bang-Andreasen, 'Wood ash induced pH changes'; Nicosia, *Geoarcheologia delle stratificazioni urbane*, p. 49 (at Padua), 61 (at Verona).
[117] Goldberg and Macphail, *Applied soils and micromorphology*, section 12.3.3.
[118] There is some controversy around the degree to which soil analysis can confirm the agricultural practice of manuring. See Carter and Davidson, 'An evaluation of the contribution'; Macphail, 'A reply to Carter and Davidson's "An evaluation"'; Carter and Davidson, 'A reply to Macphail's comments'; and now Lancelotti and Madella, 'The "invisible" product'.
[119] Goldberg and Macphail, *Applied soils and micromorphology*, section 12.3.6.

with deposits of ash middens and fills from human latrines.[120] From the fourth to sixth centuries, these were covered by further ashy deposits and midden waste, interspersed with gravel and surfaces trampled by traffic, and in the seventh to eighth centuries there were large new deposits of human latrine waste. In the eighth century the upper layers of Dark Earth were used for gardening and eventual viticulture for a population living nearby in the city. Of the six examples of Dark Earth from early medieval Italian cities analysed by Cristiano Nicosia (Florence, Ferrara, Padua, Verona, Castelletto di Brenzone, and Aquilea) all included human/pig or herbivore fecal matter.[121] Deposits of manure and the dark soils created as they aged may have been used elsewhere for horticulture; at the Uffizi site, Florence, just discussed, the first (seventh-century) phase of Dark Earth, which includes a lot of manure and ash, was interpreted as a deposit deliberately accumulated and aged with the intention of moving it for eventual cultivation elsewhere.[122]

Late medieval statutes from Lazio address the agricultural use of animal manuring, sometimes stipulating the quantity to be used per annum.[123] Night-soil, collected and dumped, is a common traditional fertilizer for domestic gardens along with animal manure in some cultures.[124] Human excrement from ancient Roman cities had been collected and sold as fertilizer, and it follows that similar practices may have been in place in early medieval cities.[125]

Cultivation: Cultivation for food crops by its very nature limits the amount of pollen which may accumulate in situ: annuals are usually picked before going to seed, for instance.[126] Thin section analysis can reveal phytoliths, microscopic silica 'fossils' in some plant matter, which permits the reconstruction of (some of) what was grown in situ. Thus several Dark Earth deposits from Brussels have been analysed and shown to date from tenth- to thirteenth-century phases of grassy growth, with manure and compost added to garden soil, with some crop weeds present.[127] Turning soil with a spade or a plough contributed to the

---

[120] Summary in Macphail and Goldberg, *Applied soils and micromorphology*, section 12.3.6; Macphail, 'Dark Earth and insights into changing', esp. pp. 158–9.
[121] Nicosia, *Geoarcheologia delle stratificazioni urbane*.
[122] Nicosia et al., 'Medieval Dark Earth', pp. 118, 119.
[123] Toubert, *Les structures*, p. 235.   [124] McGarry, 'The taboo resource'.
[125] Scobie, 'Slums, sanitation, and mortality'. See also Flohr and Wilson, 'The economy of ordure'; Miller and Gleason, 'Fertilizer in identification and analysis of soil', p. 38. Cf. Jones, 'Manure and the medieval social order', a study of medieval fertilizing which finds little evidence for human manure in medieval documents and suggests that it 'may have been taboo', p. 219.
[126] For other problems in using in situ pollen analysis, see Fish, 'Archaeological palynology of gardens and fields'.
[127] Devos et al., 'Studying urban stratigraphy'.

breaking down of stratified deposits and facilitated bioturbation, though it is impossible to know from the soil which methods were used.[128] Indeed, the activity of tilling, planting, and sowing facilitated mixing and biological reworking, rendering soils' appearances homogenous, and helping to form Dark Earth.[129]

Bioturbation and Soil Weathering: The processes of soil formation rework sediments over time, and these can be encouraged through other forces. The reworking of sediments by earthworms and other insects, rodents, and plant roots (bioturbation) and the breaking down of surface sediments exposed to sun, heat, and weather mix sediments and make soils increasingly homogenous. The shrinking and swelling caused by wetting and drying can also break down and churn soil elements and cause the reorganisation of soil particles. These increase porosity and then aid in further reworking. In deposits with high organic content (refuse, ash, charcoal, manure), natural processes of soil formation can readily form Dark Earth.

In sum, Dark Earth is a label for apparently similar but structurally often different early medieval deposits. Some scholars advocate continuing to use the term as a 'concept d'attente', a term that serves as a holding-place for a range of concepts.[130] The term continues to be used regularly in the field of medieval archaeology and history, like many other terms (such as feudalism) which have been shown to be problematic but have, nonetheless, such wide usage and encompass so many different meanings that to avoid using the term altogether seems defeatist. As it is used now, it reflects several different types of archaeological contexts, created through different though sometimes related and overlapping conditions and processes. Soil analysis, which has revealed the relationships between these transformations, emerged as a field strongly pertinent and related to archaeology in the decades after Dark Earth became widely recognised. Improved methods within the field of applied soil analysis have led to refinements in our understanding of the material of Dark Earth itself, showing the term to be inadequate.[131] Dark Earth is a product of several interrelated processes always related to human settlement.[132] In Italian early medieval urban contexts, Dark Earth is consistently produced

---

[128] Bryant and Davidson, 'The use of image analysis'.
[129] Macphail, 'The reworking of urban stratigraphy', esp. pp. 36–7.
[130] Galinié, 'L'expression terres noires'. See also Nicosia, *Geoarcheologia delle stratificazioni urbane*, pp. 103–4.
[131] See Macphail and Goldberg, *Applied soils and micromorphology*, section 12.3.2 and pp. 490–516; Nicosia et al., 'The contribution of geosciences'; Macphail, 'Dark Earth and insights'. See also Rogers, *Late Roman towns in Britain*, p. 10.
[132] Nicosia, *Geoarcheologia delle stratificazione urbane*, summary at pp. 104–5.

through dumping household waste and manure, and it is always an indicator of human occupation. It is not necessarily produced through cultivation, but Dark Earth may in fact have been created for purposes of cultivation (the activities of cultivation creating different kinds of archaeological contexts through regular tiling). In sum, the formation of Dark Earth was peculiar to late antiquity, but this kind of urban soil was produced through a set of related processes, and some of the conditions in which these deposits formed were more common after about 400.

Broader Economic and Social Context

The varied processes that created different Dark Earths are, of course, related to the cultural and urbanistic transformations of Italian cities in late antiquity and the early Middle Ages. The breaking up of houses and the formation of Dark Earth deposits are changes which occur in the conditions established by broader shifts in the economies of late antiquity, and it is worth situating the transformations that have been discussed within current research on late antique and early medieval economies.

Accompanying a decline in population across Italy (and elsewhere in the western Empire), the economy of Italy went from being empire-wide and complex around 400 to being regional and rather narrow with the exception of Rome itself around 700.[133] The factors which caused this demographic and economic involution are numerous and have been much discussed in recent literature.[134] Opinions range from a starkly negative view of the situation, stressing the cessation of long-distance trade, specialisation, and markets, to a more optimistic view pointing to the continued movement of certain goods to Italy and the persistence of building works of some scale, especially churches, suggesting money to spare and paid artisans to do the work. In recent years a lot of attention, analysis, and debate has been directed at understanding the reasons behind these transformations, integrating familiar and well-studied data with emerging or hitherto ignored evidence. These will be discussed more fully in Chapters 4 and 6. For purposes of the present discussion, it is

---

[133] On population decline in Italy, see the following efforts to quantify the change by using field survey: Patterson et al., 'Three south Etrurian "crises"' (though note the wariness about such efforts, p. 5); Valenti, 'La formazione dell'insediamento'; Librenti, 'Ricognizione di superficie'.

[134] See Halsall, 'Movers and shakers'; Zanini, *Le Italie bizantine*, pp. 320–32 and the special issue of *Journal of Agrarian Studies* 9.1 (Jan. 2009) (= Special Issue: *Aristocrats, Peasants and the Transformation of Rural Society, c. 400–800*).

sufficient to stress the degree to which both economic contractions and political reconfigurations created the urban landscapes of late antique Italy, and the possibilities for as well as the need for urban cultivation.

Changes in both economies and imperial politics are apparent to us in the contraction in the number of urban settlements in Italy, the reduction in their dimensions, and diminished architectural investment in them. For instance, in the late Roman cities of Italy, the *domus* was, as we have seen, a key tool in the social representation of senatorial classes, an expression of status as well as a means to further that status.[135] As the political structures which supported those classes, such as the Roman Senate based in Rome, changed, so too the relevance of the *domus* changed, becoming less important an investment, less directly implicated in the performance of status. This is not to say that houses ceased to be meaningful tools with which to express and negotiate status. As I will explain, in urban contexts the location of one's house, the materials with which it was constructed, and whether it included space for food cultivation all continued to serve as potent markers of the owner's status and social position in late antiquity and the early Middle Ages. Starting from the fifth century, however, the broader patterns of political change and deeper economic downturns meant that restoration of houses and public buildings damaged by age, war, or neglect was no longer either necessary or, sometimes, possible. Areas of cities became designated rubbish tips, and structures made in perishable materials decayed in situ. Reductions in population, even if difficult to quantify with any degree of precision, assisted in this pattern of abandonment, neglect, and accumulation of waste in Italian cities.[136] So too, the reduction in scale of elite residences: even the largest high-status residences, often two-story at least in part, were smaller than imperial-period townhouses.

What role might change in the climate have played in changes to the cities of late antiquity? As early as the eighteenth century, both Edward Gibbon and Ludovico Muratori argued that changes in climate had contributed to the decline and fall of the Roman Empire.[137] Since the 1990s, and especially since the early 2000s, a wide range of entirely new evidence has emerged for the average temperature, rates of precipitation, and wildlife in Western Eurasia in the last 3,000 years, compelling historians and archaeologists even more to consider the role played by the

---

[135] Guidobaldi, 'L'edilizia abitativa' and further references in note 64.
[136] For a discussion of the reduction in population, see Cheyette, 'The disappearance of the ancient landscape', pp. 132–6.
[137] Gibbon, *The history of the decline*, ch. 9; on Muratori, see Traina, 'Muratori e la "barbarie" palustre'.

Broader Economic and Social Context

environment in the broad changes of late antiquity. Most scholars are reluctant to attribute major cultural changes exclusively to environmental factors, but increasingly studies of environmental proxies from natural sciences, such as tree rings, speleothems, growth of certain plants or plankton, ice cores, and lake sediments, permit the reconstruction of past environments, making the scale of changes demonstrable and quantifiable. There is still no established model for understanding the relationship between environment and historical change. Indeed, there is considerable division in the ways in which arguments are constructed and the degree to which climate variability, including changes in temperature and precipitation, can be understood to have affected society, politics, culture, and economy.[138] One line of argument holds that changes in climate prevented resilience to political upheaval, wars, and disease; sometimes weather catastrophes, such as major volcanos and floods, brought about a thermal shock for decades or longer, and these were tipping points in complex webs of concurrent events.[139]

The evidence for changes in the environment may be pertinent to the conditions in which Dark Earth formed, as the wider economic context just discussed. Specifically, in many of the processes which contribute to the formation of Dark Earth, wetness plays a contributing role. And in the period in which Dark Earths of Europe formed, the climate of parts of Italy may have indeed been, on the whole, rather wetter. It is increasingly apparent that in late antique and early medieval Europe there was a general downturn in average temperatures from around 400–50 until 600–50 CE and, in some parts of Western Eurasia, an increase in annual precipitation.[140] It has long been claimed that northern and central Italy in the later sixth century was wetter and more prone to floods than in previous centuries.[141] Gregory the Great, Gregory of Tours, and the author of the Life of Pelagius II in the *Liber Pontificalis* all refer to flooding of the Tiber (and the Adige) in 589.[142] Paolo Squatriti has shown clearly

---

[138] Sessa, 'The new environmental fall of Rome'.
[139] The literature on this topic is large and growing annually. Cheyette, 'The disappearance of the ancient landscape'; McCormick et al., 'Climate change during and after'; Manning, 'The Roman world and climate'; and Haldon et al., 'History meets palaeoscience'. See now Harper, *The fate of Rome*, and a critique of his approach and the findings in Sessa, 'The new environmental fall of Rome'; Haldon et al., 'Plagues, climate change, and the end of an empire: A response to Kyle Harper's *The Fate of Rome* (1) Climate', and Erdkamp, 'War, food, climate change'.
[140] Büntgen et al., 'Cooling and societal change', p. 231; Squatriti, 'Il clima dei Longobardi'.
[141] Squatriti, 'The floods'.
[142] *Dial.* 3.19.2 (pp. 346–50); Gregory of Tours, *Historia Francorum*, Book 10, 1 (p. 477); *LP* 65, ch. 1 (vol. I, p. 309). For discussion of these texts and their subsequent use by later medieval authors, see Squatriti, 'The floods', pp. 804–5.

that references to post-Roman flooding, and those floods in particular, took on a colourful literary life distinct from the historical reality of the climate in Italy in that period. He has also pointed to varying and conflicting climatological data emerging from natural science research and the challenges facing historians who engage with them. For instance, tree-ring data from the Alps and the Altai mountains suggesting a northern hemispheric period of summer cooling after the 530s have been, on the one hand, taken by some historians as broad widespread downturns in temperature, and on the other hand refined by some earth scientists to reflect only a period in the 530s to 570s.[143] Looking at a number of sources of evidence, however, shows that the rivers of the Italian peninsula do seem to have flooded more in the sixth and seventh centuries than in prior and subsequent centuries.[144] As the literary accounts suggested, environmental data point to Tiber flooding and alluvial deposits throughout its network.[145] The movement of the fluvial channel of the Arno near Pisa suggests that it too was subject to repeated flooding in the fourth to sixth centuries;[146] at Florence, the Arno left alluvial deposits which have been dated to the later sixth century.[147] Using multiple types of environmental data from Italy, including expansion of an Apennine glacier (Ghiacciaio del Calderone), lake sediments, and archaeological pollens, a team has recently confirmed an increased period of wetness from about 450 and 720 for southern Italy.[148] It should be noted that there has also been evidence of precisely the opposite. Changes in microscopic sea life, taken as a proxy for climatic conditions, from the Bay of Salerno point to a dry period between about 500 and 950 and species associated with warm waters.[149] While historians remain uncertain whether or how much

---

[143] See also Squatriti, 'The floods', pp. 810–11; Büntgen et al., 'Cooling and societal change'; Helama et al., 'Dark Ages cold period: A literature review and directions for future research'; Büntgen et al., 'Reply to "Limited late antique cooling"'; Haldon et al., 'Plagues, climate change, and the end of an empire: A response to Kyle Harper's *The Fate of Rome* (1) Climate', pp. 4–5.

[144] Camuffo and Enzi, 'The analysis of two bi-millennial series'; Keenan-Jones, 'Large-scale water management projects'.

[145] Buried alluvial deposits have been recognised in a scarp along the Grand Sasso Massif and dated by carbon-14 and internal stratigraphy to the sixth and seventh centuries: Giraudi, 'Late-Holocene alluvial events'. Squatriti is skeptical of Giraudi's use of the evidence: Squatriti, 'The floods of 589', p. 814, note 61.

[146] Benvenuti et al., 'Late-Holocene catastrophic floods'.

[147] Nicosia et al., 'Medieval Dark Earth', p. 109.

[148] Sadori et al., 'Climate, environment and society in southern Italy'. See Chapter 3 for concerns around using archaeobotanical evidence.

[149] Margaritelli et al., 'Marine response', p. 66; Lirer et al., 'Planktonic foraminifera as bio-indicators', pp. 547, 550. Frustratingly, these studies use proxy data from the Alboran sea (the far Western Mediterranean) and the Jura to contexualise the findings from the Bays of Salerno and Gaeta. As Haldon, Izdebski, and others have pointed out, the

Conclusions 73

explanation of social and economic change should be attributed to climatic change, earth scientists are not ambivalent: 'Our data provide independent evidence that agrarian wealth and overall economic growth might be related to climate change on high- to mid-frequency (interannual to decadal) time scales'.[150] Very recent research on the arrival of iron-rich Saharan dust in the Colle Gnifetti Alpine glacier deposit point to a series of dust events between 370 and 450, which then remained infrequent until about 870, when they increased substantially, at the same time as the onset of the Medieval Climatic Anomaly of greater warmth between 900 and 1000 CE.[151] The coincidence of evidence for these Dust Events with other periods of climate forcing point to broad overall patterns of increased warmth towards the end of our period, with mineral-rich deposits of Saharan dust arriving on European fields annually.

For purposes of the current study, a fundamental difficulty in attributing the rise of Dark Earth or changes in agriculture to widespread changes in climate is that Italy is geographically very diverse and is affected by microregional patterns which differ greatly from one another and may have been affected by climatic variation differently.[152] Without more data clearly linked to the specific localities explored, it will be difficult to explain the rise of urban gardening in relation to climate change. All the same, the possibility remains that wetter cities aided the formation of Dark Earth.

Conclusions

Economic and social factors, perhaps also environmental ones, contributed to make the cities of Italy more earthy, with more accumulations of dirt in the fifth and sixth centuries than there had been before. As large ancient houses and some public buildings were divided into smaller spaces and partially backfilled, the accumulation of waste in those areas

---

geography of the Mediterranean varies enormously, and small-scale local or regional case studies are the soundest way to examine relations between climate, environment, and society. Haldon et al., 'Plagues, climate change, and the end of an empire: A response to Kyle Harper's *The Fate of Rome* (1) Climate', p. 4; Izdebski and Mulryan, *Environment and society in the long late antiquity*.

[150] Büntgen et al., '2500 years of European climate variability', p. 582.
[151] Clifford et al., 'A 2000 year Saharan dust event proxy'. I thank Chris Loveluck for sharing his thoughts on this research. On the Medieval Climatic Anomaly, see Diaz et al., 'Spatial and temporal characteristics of climate in medieval times revisited', Xoplaki et al. (eds.), 'Medieval climate anomaly', and Ljungqvist et al., 'European warm-season temperature'.
[152] For demonstration of this point, see Labuhn et al., 'Climatic changes and their impacts', esp. p. 267.

and the decomposition of structures no longer in use contributed to the formation of Dark Earth, making the cities of Italy fundamentally browner, with areas of soils accumulating where they rarely existed in antiquity. Large townhouses, which had been constructed as complexes of rooms around decorative courtyards and which had been central to the performance of social status in imperial-period society, changed in nature, becoming increasingly fragmented lots with individual rooms and areas backfilled by rubble and earth. Similarly, whole areas within ancient cities were abandoned or designated as rubble or rubbish dumps. In these areas, a number of biological and geological transformations occurred, permitting the formation of earth which was suitable for cultivation. Some of these areas were indeed used for cultivation. When the documents of the late sixth century and later report on houses in Rome and elsewhere, they often describe houses with outbuildings and cultivated areas. Over the course of the eighth and ninth centuries, as the number of documents produced increased and the rate of preservation improved, throughout Italy we can see cities filled with personal gardens attached to houses or free standing.

Some archaeological deposits of Dark Earth from Italian cities have been interpreted as cultivated spaces or areas for possible cultivation. Finding areas that were cultivated or cultivatable has led some scholars to lament the 'ruralisation' of the city and others to celebrate the creative opportunism of its early medieval inhabitants.[153] There are those who see humic soils as the product of effort and as elements which permit productivity, and there are those who see humic soils as evidence of wreck and ruin. Based on the organised accumulation of agricultural soils within the city of Naples, Arthur suggests that under royal (Gothic) and then ducal (Lombard) administration, Naples had better sanitation than some contemporary cities, thanks to the more efficient and centralized efforts this accumulation represents.[154] He points to the collection and movement of manure to fixed places in the city as evidence for the creation of urban gardens and the complex social organisation that such an operation required. Macphail, looking at the English evidence, has taken the opposite view, suggesting that the presence of human waste, butchery refuse, and grazing areas should be understood as 'a breakdown in local organisation and management of human waste'.[155] In the case of Italian cities, Arthur is, I believe, correct that the organisation of urban waste was

---

[153] See p. 64.
[154] Arthur, 'Archeologia urbana a Napoli', p. 521; Arthur, *Il complesso archeologico di Carminiello ai Mannesi*, p. 433.
[155] Macphail, 'Dark Earth and insights', p. 152.

Conclusions

centrally organized, and as La Rocca suggested thirty years ago, the accumulation of Dark Earth is hardly 'disordered and indiscriminate'.[156] As will become clear in Chapter 3, urban cultivation constituted a significant and deliberate shift in food production, and as we shall see, this shift permitted new social strategies in the urban landscape.

[156] La Rocca [Hudson], '"Dark Ages" a Verona', p. 71.

3 The Shape of the Phenomenon

By the eighth century, a significant proportion of properties in and around the cities of Italy included cultivated land; not all, but many and sometimes most. We see gardens and fields most clearly in the property documents, but there is some evidence for them in urban excavations, as well. Analysis of property documents alongside narrative chronicles and a lot of recent urban archaeology now make it possible to observe the place of cultivated lands within the early medieval urban landscape and to relate the phenomenon of urban cultivation to shifting power structures in the city. In all of the cities of Italy there were many areas given over to growing food. Some of these were lots attached to houses, as kitchen gardens within the residential complex or adjacent to it. Others were separate gardens, orchards, or fields, sometimes found in clusters in a certain region. Some ancient monuments, such as theatres and baths, had been subdivided into houses with gardens or fields. There were also cultivated plots throughout the suburbs of cities, and these may sometimes have been larger, more extensive fields rather than intensively cultivated vegetable gardens or orchards (we often find more *horti* in cities and *terrae* outside the walls); but the terminology of the documents is not fixed, and some cities had open fields and vineyards as well as vegetable plots within their walls.

A characteristic example of cultivated land within a city is preserved in a document from eighth-century Lucca:

It is established by me, Aurepert the cleric, son of Autus, on this day, that I have sold, have transferred to you Iordanus, venerable man, priest, my house which I am seen to have inside this city, with its lot, garden and well, located near S. Giorgio. One side is held by Radual the notary, with a hedge, and at the far end is the lot of Berucionus Belongonus, and on the other side is Mamarianus's garden. As I said, a house with lot, land, garden or well, and everything which is seen in them, wholly; to me no authority is retained.[1]

---

[1] 'Constat me Aurepert clerico filio quondam Auti hac die uindedisse et uindedi, tradedisse et tradedi tibi Iordanni uiro uenerabili presbitero casa mea quem hauire uideor hic infra

The price that Iordanus paid was 25 gold solidi and a piece of land which had belonged to his servant Agnichis and which had been sown, located in Flexo (now Montuolo, fraz. Lucca).[2] The document stresses that the house was located inside the city, as many documents from Italian cities do. While the city's population was expanding outside the ancient Roman walls in these centuries, the documents make clear that for the people living there, there was still a meaningful distinction between what was inside the walls and outside. The house included a lot with a garden and a well located in a cluster of similar cultivated properties next to the church of S. Giorgio (now S. Paolino, on the via S. Paolino, one of the *decumani* of the Roman city; Fig. 12). This document does not specify the dimension of the house, lot, or garden; it may have been minuscule, but it was deemed worthy of mention. The house is not described in any way; some other documents specify the roofing materials, or the number of storeys, and occasionally the dimensions of the plots. The notary adjusted a formula to enumerate the elements; the full formula ran something like 'everything, whether house, with the structure of the house, lot, land, garden, vines, lands cultivated or uncultivated, trees fruiting or non-fruiting, [goods] movable or immovable, or semi-movable.[3] (The phrasing could have been equally useful for urban and rural properties, and was tailored to fit.) That Aurepert had a household well and complete control of it speaks perhaps to his status and the value of the property. Wells were associated with high-status properties, and their use was highly structured.[4] Sometimes rights to the water of a well were subdivided and sold, or donated, but in this case Aurepert held control of all of the well and ceded it with the rest of the property. This parcel of a house and its lot, in the centre of town, with a garden with a source of water for the house and irrigation, must have been valuable. It served Iordanus well, as he became rector of the church, which acquired donations of properties in 747.[5]

This is but one of numerous cultivated plots recorded at Lucca in the eighth century. Among the 126 Lucchese documents dating from 700 to

---

ciuitatem, cum fundamento, orto, seo puteo; et posita est prope Sancto Georgio: uno latere tenet in sepe Radauld notarii, et caput tene in fondamento Barucioni Belongoni, et alio latere tene in orto Mamarian[i]; ut dixi, casa cum fundamento, curte, orte, uel puteo, omnia quem iniui hauir[e] uisus sum in integro; unde mihi nihil reseruaui potestatem,' *CDL* vol. I, 65 (738) (=*ChLA* XXX, 913, pp. 96–7).

[2] On the location, see *Inventari altomedievali*, p. 212, n. 4.

[3] 'omnes res mea ... tam casa cum structura case, fundamento, curte, orto, uineas, terris, cultum uel incultum, arboribus fructiferas uel infructiferas, mobile uel inmouile seo seomouentibus', *CDL* vol. II, 133 (759) pp. 21–3.

[4] Squatriti, *Water and society*, pp. 26–31; Squatriti, 'Water, nature, and culture'.

[5] *CDL* vol. I, 90 (747) pp. 260–3.

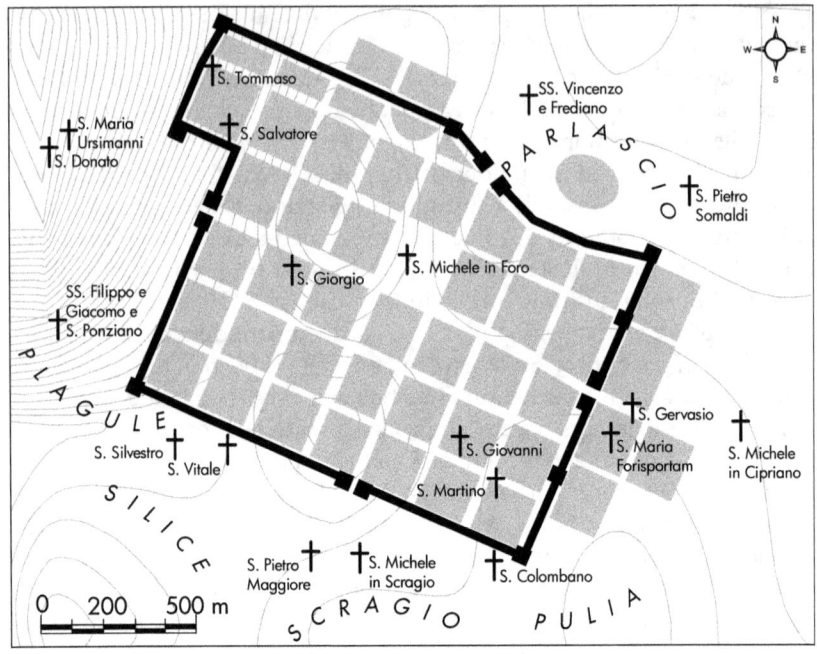

Figure 12 Plan of Lucca in the eighth and ninth centuries.

774 preserved in the archiepiscopal archive, there are about a dozen documents referring to cultivated lands within the city (*hic infra ciuitatem*, or similar) and the same again in suburban lands (*propre murum*, or near some other identifiably suburban monument).[6] So about 20 per cent of the documents preserved in this archive relate to urban or suburban cultivation; the rest refer to rural properties, some in villages as far as 20 km away or even farther.

Variation across Cities

Across the Italian peninsula, wherever documents are preserved from early medieval cities, there are always property documents recording cultivated spaces within and immediately adjacent to the cities. There are some variations in the density of urban cultivation across different cities. At Naples, there are relatively few documents pertaining to urban

---

[6] On Lombard-period Lucca, see De Conno, 'L'insediamento longobardo a Lucca'.

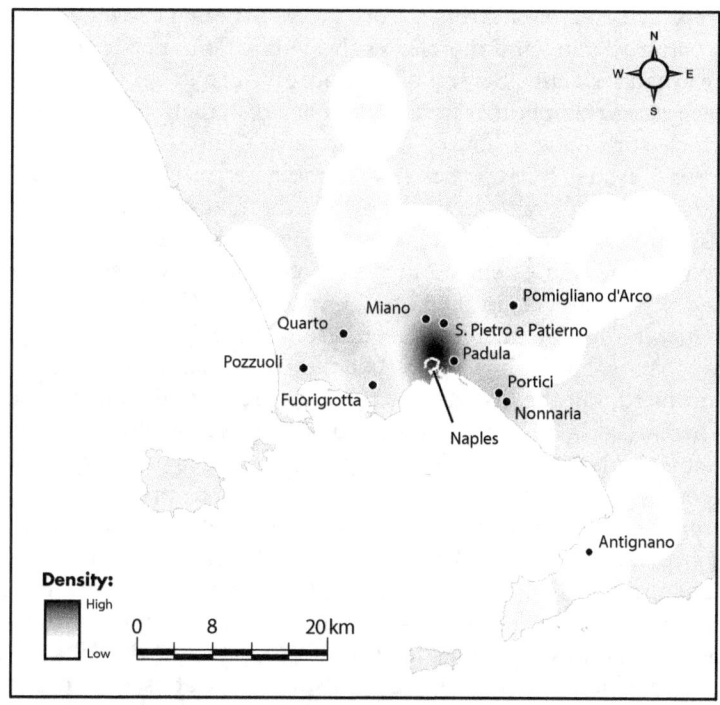

Figure 13 Map showing density of the sites of properties transacted in the preserved tenth-century documents of Naples.

properties compared to those in the immediate hinterlands or countryside around the city. Of 325 documents that have been preserved from the tenth century, 64 pertain to urban properties, and of those, only 26 mention cultivated plots. There is certainly evidence of urban cultivation at Naples, both in terms of these property transfers and the archaeological evidence for Dark Earth, as we have seen. However, the overall picture of agricultural properties at Naples shows the vast majority of its cultivation just outside the walls. Indeed, plotting the locations of all the preserved documents of tenth century makes clear that the suburban lands just outside of the walls and the natural boundaries formed by the hills which encircle the urban centre were most exploited for urban cultivation (Fig. 13).

Some early medieval cities had relatively little in the way of urban gardening, perhaps because of the confines of the geography or perhaps because of local habits of land use. For example, at Bari, the dozen or so preserved documents from the pre-Norman period convey a sense of little urban gardening and more extensive cultivation outside the city, owned by urban residents. Several of the houses which appear in the documents have a *curtis* (sometimes written *curta* or *curte*), that is, a curtilage (the land which surrounds a house) or courtyard. (The word *curtis* also means a rural estate, but there is never ambiguity in sources about whether a document refers to an urban plot or a rural estate.) A court case from Bari in 988 regarding a door built in a neighbour's property describes both of the houses surrounded by a curtilage and resolves that Falco, *iudex*, should wall up the door he made into Caloiohannes' courtyard (*curte*, in this document). (The house was previously owned by his relative, Maria, and he believed he had right of entrance and exit through that courtyard, but the dispute was resolved such that the door was closed.)[7] These curtilages, lots, or courtyards may have been planted with useful plants, infiltrated by weeds, or they may have been paved; the sense of this document is that they were not considered to be productive parts of the property. Some urban residents, such as Gualprandus, a priest, owned houses in the city of Bari and also land outside it which was clearly agricultural; Gualprandus sold to his daughter Tamfinita for 10 *solidi* two houses, one in the city which had a *curte* and abutted several other *curtes* of houses as well as land in Cilaro, which included a 'courtyard, garden, vines, vineyards, lands, fields, woods, waters, olive orchards, and other cultivated and uncultivated lands'.[8]

Like Bari, Amalfi was geographically limited in scale and it also had very few gardens in the city. Among the exceptionally few documents pertaining to gardens is an order from 1023 of Sergius *dux* and his son Iohannes ordering two brothers to respect the terms of a charter they made with the archbishop regarding 'the land of the garden' (*de ipsa terra de ipsum ortum*) of the episcopal palace of Amalfi from the early eleventh century.[9] The few gardens that there were within the city appear to have been controlled by aristocrats. Some of the produce consumed by Amalfitans came from the island of Capri, which served as part of the agricultural hinterland for the city; Amalfi itself had very little farmland in the canyons immediately surrounding it. In 998 the duke of Amalfi

---

[7] *CDB* vol. IV, 3 (988).
[8] *CDB* vol. IV, Framm. 1 (942). The document is fragmentary, but in what is preserved of the text there is a clear distinction between the urban property 'intus civitate bari quem ego per cartam hemptionis... abunt finis de prima parte fine curte et case Maioni magistri... de secunda fine casa Theodori magistro, et Alberti clerici, et curte commune, de tertia parte fine casa cu... casa Amatdi ferrarii, de quarta vero parte cucurrit via publica' and the rural one: 'curtis, ortalis, vine, vinealis, terries, campis, silbis, aquis, olibetis... fructiferis, cultum incultisque'.
[9] *Cod. Per.* LIV (1023).

designated specific parcels of land, including a few houses and gardens, on Capri to be farmed, and ordered that 20 *modii* of legumes (a mix of mostly *favino* beans, plus *mauci* and *cicercle* which perhaps is grass peas (Ital. *cicerchie*)) per annum should be brought to Amalfi, and this pattern of provision continued into the eleventh century.[10]

Despite its small size, at Lucca there was a significant area of cultivation within and immediately without the city walls. Pertuald, *uir deuotus*, a major early eighth-century aristocrat, offered a number of properties to the suburban church of S. Michael the Archangel, Lucca (beyond the eastern gates; Fig. 13), which he had founded near his house. First among these is the house and garden of the church:

> The courtyard with the lot where the church and monastery are located, bounded by a ditch [perhaps a canal ditch] and across the western ditch, to the old well and the public road. The land is one *modius*, where the abbot and monks have their [kitchen] garden and medicinal garden (*pigmentarium*) ... to you, the above-named church of S. Archangel, I give.[11]

He also gave rural properties and tithes of the produce of other properties. Pertuald was surely a wealthy man, having founded a church in his house just outside the gates of Lucca, as well as owning seven houses in villages in the area, one of which had been a royal gift, and lands throughout the region, producing grain, wine, olives, and oil, with pastures and pens for animals.[12] The document specifies that pertaining to the suburban property where the church had been built, there was the house with a field, where the monks presently had a kitchen garden and medicinal garden, measuring 1 *modius*. In the Middle Ages a *modius*, originally a unit of volume, became also a measure of area equal to the amount of land which could be sown with one *modius* of grain. Dimensions of a *modius* varied greatly from region to region. Pierre Toubert calculated that in Lazio in the central Middle Ages, 1 *modius* equalled 2300 sq metres.[13] If we use this figure to approximate the dimensions of the plot next to the church, it would have been a sizeable suburban plot. Given the rest of the

---

[10] *Cod. Per.* LXXX (998); Cf. *Cod. Per.* XLIX (1067) and XCI (1098).

[11] 'idcirco ego Pertuald uir deuotus offero Deo et tibi ecclesie Beati Sancti arcangeli Michaeli, quem a fundamentis fabricis uestibulis in honore Christi Domini constitui prope domus cellula mea ubi cummanire uideor ... Id est: curte cum fundamento ubi ipse ecclesia uel monasterio sitas sunt per loca designata, fini fossato et trans fossato da occasum solis, finis puteo antiquo et strata publica; terra p(er)tenente modilocu(m) unum, ubi sibi abbas uel monachi iniui consistentis ortum uel pigmentarium hauire debeat ... tibi predicte ecclesie Sancti Ancargeli ... trado'. *CDL* vol. I, 28 (720). On the location of the church, see Belli Barsali, 'La topografia di Lucca', p. 532.

[12] His son went on to be bishop, and the family can be seen through a number of Lucchesi charters; see Schwarzmaier, *Lucca und das Reich*, pp. 78–85.

[13] Toubert, *Les structures*, p. 459, note 1.

endowment, the gardens at the church were hardly the sole source of produce for the ecclesiastical community. Goods came to the church and its dependents through other means, and the houses located across the region, with cultivated and uncultivated lands, were rented out for income in kind or in cash which would have provided the institution an income of food and the means to acquire agricultural products such as wool, wax, and firewood for the community. Pertuald's donation, the charter makes explicit, was intended to redeem his soul and to support the ecclesiastical institution in its diverse functions, both the religious offices and its support of pilgrims, widows, orphans, and paupers:

for the redemption of my soul, through a title gift I am seen to offer, from this day, I give all possession, such that the priest, who has been or will be set up there, through my deeds, he should give to the Lord what is owed, that the office to God should be conducted, the widow, orphan, and pauper consoled, pauper and pilgrims received, aid of all precepts should not cease to be given next to God.[14]

Two elements of this arrangement, the allowance for medicinal cultivation and the charitable aspects of this suburban church, will be addressed in Chapter 5 for what they tell us about the motivations behind and attitudes towards urban cultivation. For the present purposes, however, it is relevant to consider how the urban landscape of this small Roman city, with Aurepert's house with garden and well and Pertuald's suburban house and garden, had changed with respect to the past.

As had been the case with other Roman cities of Italy, the hinterlands of ancient Lucca provided the majority of the food and much of the income of the city and its inhabitants, and it was also a central point on a regional and interregional network of commerce and communication. Lucca was joined to the Garfagnana by the Val di Serchio, and, south and east of the city, the Lucchese plain extended to the valley of the Arno; the city was on the via Cassia, one of the ancient consular roadways, which connected Lucca to Florence and Rome.[15] These lands around the Roman city had been centuriated in antiquity with plots of 20 × 20 *actus* (about 705 m on each side) and had been intensively cultivated since then.[16] Depending on the geography,

---

[14] 'pro anime me remedium per dotis titulo offerre uisus sum, ab hodierna die trado in integrum possedendum, ita ut sacerdus, qui iniui constitutes est aut fueri, pro meis facinorib(us) D(omi)n(u)m deprecari debeat, officium D(ei) p(er)agendum, uiduam, orfanum et pauperem consulandum, eginum et peregrinum recipiend(um), iuxta D(e)i preceptum omnium opem ferre non desinat', *CDL* vol. I, 28 (720).
[15] On the geography, see Wickham, *The mountains and the city*, pp. 15–39.
[16] On centuriation, see Sommella and Giuliani, *La pianta di Lucca romana*, p. 10. On the hinterlands of Lucca in the early Middle Ages, see Ciampoltrini et al., 'Materiali tardoantichi ed altomedievali'.

olive, vine, wheat, or spelt was grown; in the Middle Ages, there were also extensive chestnut groves. In the Roman period, the owners of these lands were mostly urban, and though they lived in the city their wealth was based on their ability to sell their agricultural produce not only there but also across larger empire-wide networks. Ancient Lucca had been a densely built, monumental urban landscape, with temples, a paved Forum, public buildings, baths, and streets lined with townhouses, with very little or no productive gardening, as we have seen in other Roman cities of Italy.[17] Its walls formed a strong delineation between the city inside and the suburbium outside. In the plain outside the walls leading to the river there was an amphitheatre, an addition to the urban framework in the imperial period.[18] In all other directions were roads leading out to the countryside, lined with tombs and apparently villas and *horti*, luxurious residences with productive farms.[19] The plot where Pertuald's house had been, and the church now stood, had been close to the gates, about 100 m east of the walls themselves. In the early Middle Ages, both the intramural core of the ancient city and the suburbium of Lucca had developed into neighbourhoods where people lived in houses with some land, among religious institutions. The documentary record attests some 24 churches in Lucca in the eighth century, and 17 in the suburbium.[20] From the eighth century, the ducal palace was located just outside the walls, the bishop and the king were inside the walls, and the location of the mint is uncertain; the distinction drawn in the documents between inside and outside the walls was not firmly one between monumental and agrarian, but rather an urban nucleus and a nearly equally dense suburban zone.[21]

One example of a rural estate is attested by a document signed at Pistoia and relating to the sale of property from Filipert, a cleric, to Gaidualt, *uir magnificus* and royal *medicus*.

Filipert the cleric, son of Filimarus, metalworker and vendor, now deceased, here accepts the price of Gaidualt, *uir magnificus*, royal *medicus*, of 100 new gold solidi, the price for one-half of a single-story hall (*sala*) on the ground floor, with enclosing wall and tiled roof, along with half of the courtyard (*corte*), and half of the meadow where the building is located, and his portion of the mill built on the Braina [Brana River], and his portion of the vacant lands over Gora [or over the

---

[17] On Roman Lucca, see Mencacci et al., *Lucca romana*.
[18] Ciampoltrini, 'Ricerche nell area dell'anfiteatro'.
[19] On the urban and suburban transformations of Lucca, see Ciampoltrini, 'Città "frammentate" e città-fortezza', pp. 615–20; Ciampoltrini, 'Lucca tardoantica e altomedievale'; Quirós Castillo, *Modi di costruire*, pp. 13–14.
[20] Belli Barsali, *Lucca. Guida alla citta*, p. 10.
[21] Belli Barsali, 'La topografia di Lucca'; Wickham, 'Bounding the city'.

canal?], bounded by the garden (*orto*) of Gumfulonus and a public road and up to the Braina on the eastern side.[22]

Gaiduald paid 100 gold solidi for the collection of properties, which comprised subdivided plots which were not contiguous. The countryside around Pistoia, indeed most of the hinterlands around Italian cities, was dappled with villages of several houses and agricultural buildings, cultivated fields and fields laying fallow, as well as intensively cultivated gardens of people who lived in the countryside. These lands had many different owners and were owned in a wide variety of arrangements, as we will see. The format of this rural property transfer, indicating location by proximity to natural features as well as to neighbours, is just like documents of urban properties. In both cases, the laying out of boundaries by reference to geography, topography, and adjoining landowners gives an indication of the intensity with which these lands were worked; each owner was known, and the limits of the parcels were recognised by the people who lived there. This document in particular includes a '*corte*', a curtilage or courtyard. Gaiduald later donates many *curtes* (in this case, estates) in the area of Pistoia and Lucca to the monastery of S. Bartolomeo which he founded near Pistoia, and the sense of that later document is that these were agricultural lots without houses.[23] Gaiduald, who bought the urban property from the cleric, was presumably attached to the royal court at Pavia at least until 774 and did not live in any of the rural properties he acquired.[24] Gaiduald was a high-ranking landowner, and the scale of his holdings, and his donation of them to a proprietary church, is probably very typical of the cycle of land acquisition and transfers of upwardly mobile and aristocratic laity in early medieval Italy.[25] As noted, cities were central to social and political interaction in Italy. It is also the case that around cities, agricultural land was strongly tied to

---

[22] 'Filipert clirico filio quondam F[i]l[imari] fabro et uenditore, qui [pr]etium accepit ad Gaiduald uiro magnifico medico regiae potestatis auri solidus nobus nomero [c]ent[um], pre[tium pro medietate] de sala iuri sui, pedeplana, mura cercumdata, scandula cooperta, una cum medietate de [cu]rt[e, et medietate] de prato ubi ipsa sala edificata est pertenire nuscetur, adque omnem portionem eius de [mulino qui] edificatus est in flubio qui dicitur Braina, seo super Gora portio sua de terra uac[ua] qu[e posita est inter] fine: orto Gumfuloni et uia pubblica seo a partibus orientali usque in flubio Brai[na]', *CDL* vol. I, 38 (726) = *ChLA* 25, pp. 70–3.
[23] *CDL* vol. I, 203 (767).
[24] On him, see Pilsworth, 'Could you just sign this for me John?', pp. 378–9; Wickham, 'Rural society and economy', p. 123; Rauty, *Storia di Pistoia I*, p. 116.
[25] See another example of such a type and the long-term strategies employed by his family in Wickham, *The mountains and the city*, pp. 40–67.

urban owners, such as Gaiduald. Ross Balzaretti has shown a similar picture for Milan.[26]

Rome

The evidence of urban gardening from Rome warrants special consideration. Early medieval Rome was utterly unlike anywhere else in the early medieval West, though by its very nature it was influential upon nearly everywhere else. In our period, it was bigger and it enjoyed more commercial activity (at least of luxury goods, probably of everything) than any other city; it also had many houses with gardens. The available evidence for Rome, its urban fabric, and its inhabitants is also denser than for other cities, at least for the late tenth century onwards; comparatively there are more charters for the city itself than elsewhere. Also, there has been extensive excavation over the past two centuries (see Rome, Forum of Caesar later in this chapter). These different kinds of sources speak to a significant amount of urban gardening, both adjacent to houses and cultivated lots, starting in the late sixth century and then continuing through the eleventh century and beyond.

On the one hand, the property documents of Rome follow broadly patterns observed in major cities elsewhere in Italy in that they report on individuals, their social relationships, and the houses in which they lived and the lands they worked; on the other hand, the nature of landholding around Rome was different from elsewhere in Italy because the Church preserved ownership and permitted extended rents. Land in and around Rome was not bought and sold in the same way as it usually was elsewhere in Italy; rather, it was rented for one or more generations (usually three) and then returned to the owner, an ecclesiastical institution in the city. A renter would make a profit on the crops of the land; indeed, agricultural work on rented lands was one means of improving one's economic condition, but this operated slightly differently from elsewhere in Italy.[27] Beyond Rome's differences in economy, space, and landholding, there were greater numbers of pilgrims, dedicated religious, and poor at Rome than elsewhere in Italy, and therefore, so too the need to provide food for them was greater. Some of the urban gardens we see in

---

[26] 'Milanese residents owned property in Milan itself (by definition), in villages quite close to the city (rarely more than 20 km away) but not further afield. While it is likely that many of these people had recently moved into the city from nearby villages and that is why they still had land there, the pattern may also suggest that urban land and land near town were more desirable', Balzaretti, 'Women, property and urban space', p. 564.

[27] For the market of land in Tuscany, for instance, see Wickham, 'Land sales and land market'; for the area around Rome, see Wickham, 'La struttura della proprietà fondiaria'.

the documents of Rome were used to feed religious households, such as the earliest gardens which appear in our textual record.

Among the episcopal letters from early medieval Rome which attest to papal property interests, the letters of Gregory the Great give us the first glimpses of food gardens attached to houses at Rome among the properties which he managed, as we have seen in Chapter 2, Table 1. Other seventh- and eighth-century texts mention houses with gardens and vineyards among the properties endowed to ecclesiastical institutions, and these were located both inside the city and in the suburbs. In the mid eighth century, inscriptions recording the donations from Giorgio and Eustacio, *dux* and *dispensator* of S. Maria in Cosmedin, to that church's *diaconia* (charitable assistance centre) record several properties, urban and rural, including vineyards in the city on the Pincian hill and in the Testaccio region.[28] Though none of these gardens or vineyard sites can now be located with precision, it is nonetheless clear that they were mostly located on high ground; the Viminal, the Aventine, and the area around the baths of Diocletian and S. Susanna, in the upper part of Regio 4, were higher than the parts of the city around the Forum or along the rivers, and the vineyards were mostly on hills on the outer edges of the city (Fig. 14). Cultivated spaces which appear in our documents were also often located near water sources. The houses near the baths, both up in Regio 4 and down on the Campus Martius in Regio 1, may have taken advantage of aqueducts which ran to the baths in antiquity and which probably still ran in the early Middle Ages, or to the tanks which provided water for the Baths of Diocletian in late antiquity.[29] These were not isolated references to unusual urban kitchen gardens and vineyards but glimpses of what was clearly a wider phenomenon; many houses included parcels of land for fruit and vegetable growing. There are extremely few property records at all for Rome in the sixth to eighth centuries, thus ten references among only a few dozen known urban residential properties suggest that kitchen gardens were common if not frequent at Rome in the late sixth to eighth centuries.

Descriptions of cultivated properties at Rome from donations, sales, or rental agreements increase in number in the ninth and tenth centuries and, like the earlier ones, these indicate that cultivated areas were interspersed throughout the city inside the walls. Ninth- and tenth-century property documents make clear that there were kitchen gardens and

---

[28] Arena, *Roma dall'antichità*, pp. 119–20.
[29] For the Aqua Marcia and the Aqua Virgo, which fed the Baths of Diocletian and Agrippa, respectively, and their continued use in the Middle Ages, see Coates-Stephens, 'The walls and aqueducts of Rome'. On the tanks, see Thermae Diocletiani, *LTUR* vol. V, pp. 55.

Variation across Cities

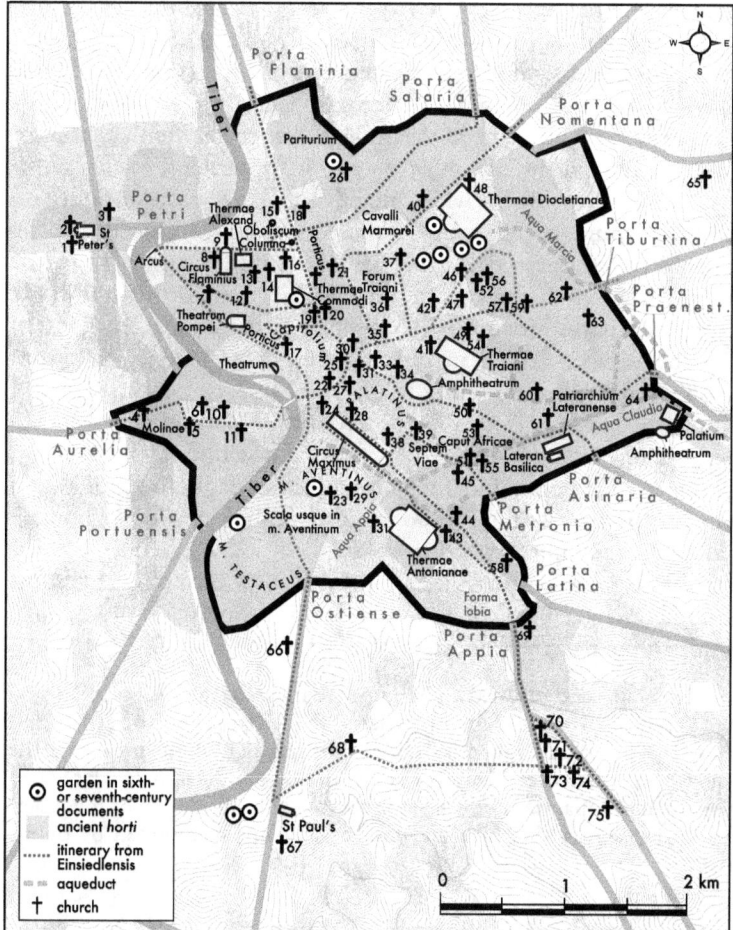

1. S. Martino; 2. S. Stefano; 3. S. Pellegrino; 4. SS. Giovanni e Paolo; 5. SS. Cosma e Damiano (S. Cosimato); 6. S. Maria; 7. S. Lorenzo in Damaso; 8. S. Agnese; 9. S. Apollinare; 10. S. Crisogono; 11. S. Cecilia; 12. S. Stefano; 13. S. Eustachio; 14. S. Maria in Aquiro; 15. S. Lorenzo in Lucina; 15. S. Maria ai Martiri; 17. S. Angelo; 18. S. Silvestro; 19. S. Marco; 20. S. Marcello; 21. S. Sergio 22. S. Giorgio 'in Velabro'; 23. S. Sabina; 24. SS. Apostoli; 25. S. Maria 'in Cosmedin'; 26. S. Felice; 76. S. Teodoro; 28. S. Anastasia; 29. S. Prisca; 30. S. Adriano; 31. S. Maria 'Antiqua'; 32. S. Saba; 33. SS. Cosma e Damiano; 34. S. Maria 'Nova'; 35. S. Quirico; 36. S. Agata; 37. S. Vitale; 38. S. Lucia; 39. SS. Giovanni e Paolo; 40. S. Susanna; 41. S. Pietro in Vincoli; 42. S. Lorenzo in Lucina; 43. SS. Nereo ed Achilleo; 44. S. Sisto; 45. S. Maria in Domnica; 46. S. Pudenziana; 47. S. Eufemia; 48. S. Ciriaco; 49. S. Lucia in Selcis; 50. S. Clemente; 51. S. Stefano Rotondo; 52. S. Prassede; 53. SS. Quattro Coronati; 54. S. Martino ai Monti; 55. S. Erasmo; 56. S. Maria Maggiore; 57. S. Vito; 58. S. Giovanni 'a Porta Latina'; 59. S. Eusebio; 60. SS. Marcellino e Pietro; 61. Mon. Honorii; 62. S. Isidore; 63. S. Bibiana; 64. S. Croce in Gerusalemme; 65. S. Lorenzo 'fuori le mura'; 66. S. Menna; 67. S. Anastasio (Tre Fontane); 68. SS. Felice, Aduacto e Emerita; 69. S. Sisto; 70. S. Sotero; 71. SS. Marco e Marcelliano; 72. S. Sisto; 73. SS. Nereo ed Achilleo; 74. S. Cornelio; 75. S. Sebastiano

Figure 14 Map of the locations of *horti* in Rome, and property transfers pertaining to gardens, before 800. The large light grey areas are the late antique *Horti*, private ornamental gardens which were used as pleasure gardens until late antiquity, the squares are domestic gardens or urban garden plots identified through property documents from the late sixth to late eighth century.

cultivated areas on the hills and even in the very densely built-up parts of the city and the low-lying areas in the centre of town, along the via Lata (now the via del Corso), and in the Forum of Trajan.[30] A portrait of one neighbourhood on the Caelian hill emerges from the property documents of the *Subiaco Register* dating from the mid ninth to the eleventh centuries. It describes perhaps a dozen houses, some with gardens, orchards, or vineyards, on the hill inside the walls, mixed among a few late antique and early medieval churches, chapels, monasteries, and a charity centre. Roads ran north from the Porta Metronia, a southeastern gate in the walls, into town across the crest of the Caelian hill, and northeast towards the Lateran; a Roman aqueduct, still functioning, came across the crest of the hill.[31] The *Subiaco Register* includes sixteen documents, dating from between 857 and 1035, pertaining to properties in the neighbourhood, both inside the gate and outside the Porta Metronia; several sales relate to properties which included parcels within and without the walls.[32] Between these documents and their descriptions of the boundaries of the relevant properties, we have a good picture of the city's mix of houses, kitchen gardens, and more extensive fields.[33]

A document from 1003 provides a representative example. The 'most humble monk' Crescentius Murcapullo gave his property on the Caelian hill in Rome to the nearby monastery of S. Erasmo:

It is a one-story house entirely tiled and shingled, with an oven inside it and a yard and a vined pergola in front of it. Also a garden with fruit trees next to it, with right of passage to a public road, and with all things pertaining to these, located in the region called 'porta metrovia'. Where I Crescentius up to now have lived. On one side is the garden of Iohannes Folle. On the other side is the garden of Iohannes, priest and cardinal. And the third and fourth sides are surrounded by public roads.[34]

---

[30] *SMVL* 29 (1008) for the via Lata; *SMVL* 17 (989) for upper via Lata at S. Silvestro; *SMVL* 26 (1004) for Forum of Trajan.

[31] On the neighbourhood, see Goodson, *The Rome of Pope Paschal I*, pp. 103–4 and Wickham, *Medieval Rome*, pp. 116–17.

[32] *RS* 83 (866); *RS* 87 (857); *RS* 9 (926); *Papsturkunden* vol. I, 57 (926); *Papsturkunden* vol. I, 85 (938); *RS* 103 (943); *RS* 89 (953); *RS* 88 (967); *RS* 80 (968); *RS* 90 (965); *RS* 59 (978); *RS* 82 (1003); *RS* 86 (1008); *RS* 85 (1011); *RS* 100 (1021); *RS* 102 (1024); *RS* 106 (1024); *RS* 101 (1034); *RS* 98 (1035); *RS* 99 (1035).

[33] For discussion of a comparable neighbourhood of houses and gardens at the Porta Maggiore, see p. 92 and Coates-Stephens, *Porta Maggiore*, pp. 120–1.

[34] 'Idest domus terrinea una in integra tigulicia et scandolicia cum clibano intra se cum corte et pergola uineata ante se. Seu ortuo iuxta se cum arboribus pomarum cum introito et exoito suo a uia publica. et cum omnibus ad eas pertinentibus posita in regione qui dicitur porta mitrobi. Ubi ego crescentius usque actenus resedi; Et inter affines ab huno latere ortuo de iohannes folle. A secundo latere ortuo de iohannes presbyter et cardinalis. Et a tertio et a quarto latere uie publice circundate', *RS* 82 (1003) pp. 126–7.

In the same document he also bequeathed a grain-field measuring 13 *modii* outside the nearby Porta Metronia, in the Prata Deci (Decenniae),[35] which was surrounded by four other grain fields (Fig. 15). Crescentius himself appeared as neighbour to other properties which ended up at S. Erasmo, as renter of other parcels, and then as donor of this land.[36] This seems a rather plush package, comprising an urban residence with gardens and nearby fields; it clearly included land for growing grain, vine, fruit trees, and vegetables. The total measure of the combined property is 16 *modii*. Using Toubert's conversion of 1 *modius*: 2,300 sq metres,[37] the urban plot would have been 6,900 sq metres, and the extramural piece over 4 times that. The land inside the walls was obviously smaller than that outside, but the entire parcel permitted a range of horticulture for those who lived there, as well as a fairly urban lifestyle, in proximity to neighbours and several churches, all joined together by major roads laid out in antiquity.[38]

The gardens of Crescentius and the dozens of others which appear in the documentary record were key means to supply food to the people of Rome. A look at food supply to Rome in the Middle Ages, and the politics which shaped it, helps to clarify the significance of these gardens and their changes over time in response to shifting demography. A significant portion of the food for the city came from within its walls. The author of the Life of Pope Hadrian I describes a flood in 791 which caused 'a great struggle' for the greater part of Romans who 'were not able to sow', and enumerates the parts of the city which were flooded and in which 'houses were overturned and fields laid waste, trees and crops uprooted and swept away'.[39] The destruction in and around the city by the river's flooding was clearly related by the author to agricultural destruction and hindrance to future crops. In addition to what was farmed in gardens and orchards attached to houses and sitting independently within the city, Romans also clearly had suburban and rural cultivated lands for wheat, olives, and large-scale vineyards. These are apparent in the sources as papal *domuscultae* (see below), but it is probable that there were analogous rural estates owned by other institutions and perhaps families.

---

[35] On the Decennia, see Decennia, in *LTUR Suburbium* vol. II, pp. 196–7.
[36] *RS* 59 (978) pp. 100–1 is 'terra ad vineam', neighbouring his *terra*; in *RS* 84 (1008) pp. 128–9, he rented parts of several 'cesinae' on the Celio and out on the via Appia; *RS* 91 (1003) pp. 137–8 describes a house with garden which neighboured his garden.
[37] Toubert, *Les structures*, p. 459, note 1.
[38] Santangeli Valenzani has also observed that parcels of cultivated land within the walls were often smaller than those outside the wall of Rome: Meneghini and Santangeli Valenzani, *Roma nell'altomedioevo*, p. 127.
[39] *LP*, Vita Hadriani, ch. 94 (vol. I, p. 513).

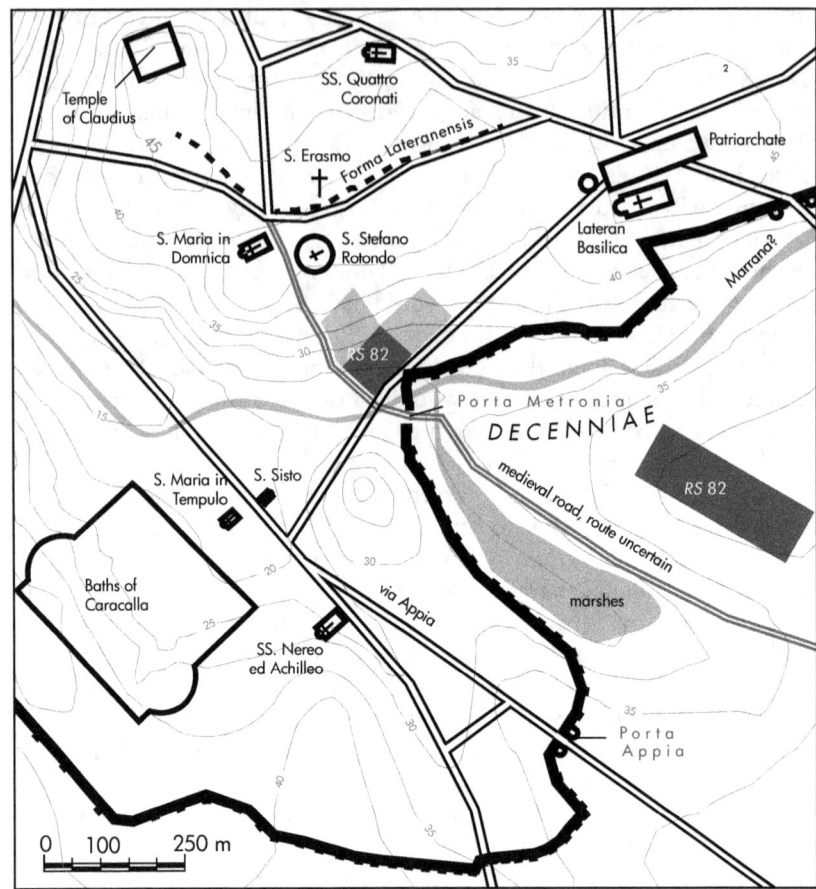

Figure 15 Map of Crescentius' properties in Rome on the Caelian hill, based on documents from the *RS*.

From the eighth to early ninth centuries, the papacy undertook extensive measures to provide food for the people of Rome, both the extensive household and dependents of the Roman church and the poor and pilgrims of Rome. Firstly, the papacy began a concerted effort of endowing the churches and monasteries of Rome with estates. The *Liber Pontificalis* charts the increase in donations of agricultural properties to different institutions in Rome in order to ensure self-sufficiency of monasteries and convents, as well as *diaconiae*, the charitable distribution centres administered by the papacy.[40] Secondly, a series of popes used lands acquired by inheritance or purchase to create the *domuscultae*, farms run by the Roman church, in the countryside around Rome.[41] The *domuscultae* were created out of lands that were not in the immediate suburbs of Rome, but were in the Agro Romano, the ancient zone of cultivated wheat fields, vineyards, and farms in the hinterland of Rome. Hadrian's four *domuscultae* were within about 20 km of Rome; another was as far away as Formia, some 140 km away.[42] The functions of the *domuscultae* were two. They were the estates where grain, vegetables, and animals were grown and raised and wine was made for the consumption of the papal household and the needy of Rome, in perpetuity. Wheat and barley from the farms were to be stored in the papal *horrea*, wine and various legumes (*diversa legumina*) were to be stored at the papal *paracellarium*, and 100 pigs were to be fed up on the farms, slaughtered, and brought to the same storage each year. These farms' foodstuffs were served at the papal household and were doled out at Rome to 100 needy a day on the Lateran steps (each receiving from the cellarer a portion of 50 two-pound loaves, two 60-pound *decimatae* of wine, and cauldrons of porridge (*pulmentaria*).[43] The dozens of *xenodochia*, hospitals, and *diaconiae* in the city, administered by the papacy or by separate monasteries and churches, similarly dispensed the produce of their estates in the Agro Romano and perhaps also their cultivated lands in the city.[44] The fact that urban cultivated lands did not factor in the creation of the *domuscultae* speaks to the scale of their operation; they were large farming enterprises, intended to provide food for hundreds of people daily. It also relates to the second function of the *domuscultae*: they marked the

---

[40] On this point, Delogu 'Rome in the ninth century' cites donations of *praedia* and olive groves from Gregory II to the basilicas of St Peter's and St Paul's (e.g. Jaffé 2184); Gregory III's donations of *praedia* to S. Crisogono 'for the sustenance of it' (*LP*, Vita Gregorii III, ch. 9, vol. I, pp. 418–19) and gifts to the *diaconia* of SS. Sergio e Bacco (*LP*, Vita Gregorii III, ch. 13, vol. I, p. 420); Hadrian's gifts of vineyards, olive groves, and servants to *diaconiae* (*LP*, Vita Hadriani, ch. 81, vol. I, pp. 509–10); Leo III's gifts of *praedia* to the hospice/hospital at Naumachia, which went to the monastery of S. Stefano Maggiore (*LP*, Vita Leonis III, ch. 90, vol. II, p. 28); Paschal donated *praedia* and rural and urban properties to S. Prassede, S. Cecilia, and S. Maria in Domnica, the latter a *diaconia*: *LP*, Vita Paschalis, ch. 10, 18, 22 (vol. II, p. 54; vol. II, p. 57; vol. II, p. 58).

[41] Marazzi, *I 'Patrimonia'*; Christie, *Three south Etrurian churches*; Christie, 'Popes, pilgrims and peasants'; Noble, *The republic*, pp. 247–8.

[42] *LP*, Vita Hadriani, 54 (vol. I, pp. 501–2), trans. pp. 147–8.

[43] *LP*, Vita Hadriani, 54 (vol. I, pp. 501–2), trans. pp. 147–9. My guess is that these loaves are approximately 980 g each, using a *libra* closer to a Carolingian weight than to an ancient Roman one.

[44] On these institutions, see Santangeli Valenzani, 'Pellegrini, senatori e papi'; Dey, 'Diaconiae, xenodochia', and Chapter 4.

territory of the papal state, including lands well beyond Rome and its walls. Reviewing the development of the Roman economy in the eighth and ninth centuries, Paolo Delogu has recognised parallels to the efforts of the papacy in other city churches and surmised that urban lay society, as well, was seeking to obtain large rural estates to provide food, firewood, and other goods for urban personnel and dependents.[45]

If in the ninth century churches were acquiring estates inside the city and in the countryside outside Rome, in the tenth century some of these urban gardens and suburban gardens immediately outside the city walls were split up into smaller plots for rental income for the churches which owned them. For example, in 924 private owners bequeathed to a priest the *domus maiore, cum ortuo maiore cum diuersis arboribus* just inside the Porta Maggiore near the aqueduct and a main road (Fig. 16).[46] It was clearly a sizable gift, as the house included a chapel of S. Teodoro, in addition to a courtyard, the garden, and the fruit trees. It was surrounded by the priest's own house and another garden. Fifty years later, that single plot of vineyard, orchard, and garden was broken up into smaller pieces and rented out to different owners.[47] Similarly, the large vineyard in the Forum of Caesar, traced in the archaeology (see Rome, Forum of Caesar), was replaced in the beginning of the tenth century with a neighbourhood of at least five houses lining a new road.[48] They were relatively small, one-room houses, surrounded by unbuilt lots probably used as gardens, as hypothesised by the excavators.[49] The laying out of these plots of land in the tenth century may have been the work of a property speculator; Santangeli Valenzani conjectures that in the tenth century, this area was under the control of Leo Protoscrinarius, a high-ranking member of the papal bureaucracy who in 963 became Pope Leo VIII.[50] He may have been responsible for reorganising the area, breaking up the vineyard, and renting out the little houses. The new neighbourhood taking over agricultural plots was not unique to the area of the Forum.[51] A few decades later, plots in an existing orchard owned by a monastery were rented out with the stipulation that houses be built upon them: in 1019 SS. Ciriaco and Nicola in via Lata conceded three parcels of orchards for the building of houses in Regio 9, on the Campus

---

[45] Delogu, 'Rome in the ninth century', p. 105. [46] *RS* 27 (924) pp. 67–8.
[47] Coates-Stephens, *Porta Maggiore*, pp. 117–20.
[48] Santangeli Valenzani et al., 'I fori imperiali nel medioevo', p. 278. [49] Ibid.
[50] Santangeli Valenzani et al., 'I fori imperiali nel medioevo', p. 280.
[51] In addition to what follows, see Hubert, 'Mobilité de la population'.

Variation across Cities 93

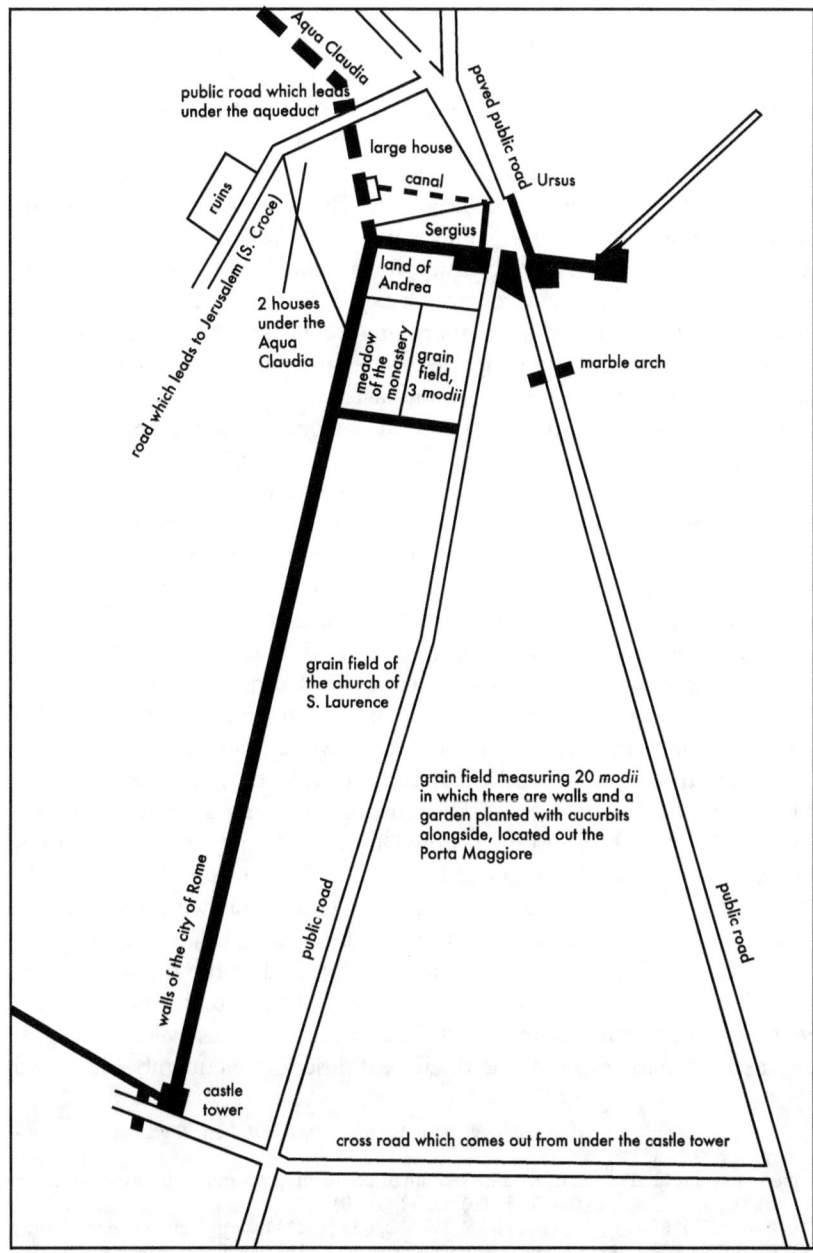

Figure 16 Houses, gardens, and fields at the Porta Maggiore, Rome, in the tenth century, based on documents from the *RS* 14 (973), 17 (936), 27 (924), 122 (952). Plan after Coates-Stephens, *The Porta Maggiore*, fig. 92.

Martius.[52] The orchard trees, however, remained as the annual rent for tenants was cash and half of the fruits and nuts grown.[53] Other similar clusters of houses with orchards and vegetable gardens appear in the early eleventh century: there was a neighbourhood on the Campus Martius near the baths of Alexander Severus, called ad Scorticlari (Tanners' (or Whores') Yard) with several houses with gardens and orchards and a church of SS. Benedict, Maria, and Biagio, a dependency of the Sabine monastery of Farfa.[54] The Aqua Alessandrina had been built to feed those baths in the third century; it was called the Forma Jovia in the Middle Ages and had been restored by several early medieval popes.[55] It may well have still served the tanners and orchards in this neighbourhood in our period, like the water supplies of the other ancient baths which may have fed the gardens in Gregory's monastery houses.

From the tenth century, there was an obvious rise in the population of Rome and increasing demand on urban space for residential needs. Some areas, such as the neighbourhood on the Caelian hill, may have stayed much as they had been in the ninth century with large residential complexes comprising houses, gardens, orchards and vineyards, and suburban plots, several neighbouring each other next to churches and monasteries. We do not know what the monastery of S. Erasmo did with these plots after Crescentius and his neighbours gave them to the monastery, a dependent of the abbey at Subiaco. The monastery of SS. Cosma e Damiano in Mica Aurea rented out houses with gardens in the area just outside the walls, Portuense, and vineyards in southern Trastevere. In either 1026 or 1027, Iohannes, the abbot of SS. Cosma e Damiano, rented a house in Trastevere with gardens to Domenicus, '*uir honestus*, swineherd', Petro, '*uir honestus, cervinus*', and the widow Demetria. It has a garden behind it, a courtyard in front of it with fruiting trees.[56] Elsewhere in the city, blocks of land which had previously been open cultivation were broken into numerous smaller parcels, for rent; these in some cases included gardens and orchards. With the increased demand for land within the walls, more agricultural activity moved outside the walls in the tenth and eleventh centuries, and some of these extramural garden plots were, it seems, destined for market use: A 966 document describes a cucumber or gourd

---

[52] On the toponym of S. Maria quae vocatur Isinicheo, see Halphen, *Études sur l'administration*, p. 9 note 3.

[53] 'terra bacante ad domum faciendum sedium unum in integrum cum arboribus pomarum infra se habentem', *SMVL* 41 (1019), cf. 43 (1019).

[54] *RF* vol. III, 426 (998), 506 (1017), vol. IV, 652, 653 (1011) have gardens and or orchards; *RF* vol. IV, 658 (1012) was a two-storey house with a tiled roof and marble stair.

[55] Coates-Stephens, 'The walls and aqueducts of Rome'.

[56] *CDMA* 30 (?1026/?1027?). See discussion of eleventh- and twelfth-century expansion, including in Trastevere, in Wickham, *Medieval Rome*, p. 129.

garden (*ortus cucummerarius*) near a grain field just outside the Porta Maggiore in an area which had other gardens and grain fields in earlier documents.[57] The specialisation in cucurbits suggests that this was a market garden – an early one; no others appear before 1000.[58] Monasteries used payment in kind to provide food for the urban communities. In 1035, the abbess of S. Maria in via Lata rented out a garden located 4 miles outside the Porta Portuense for the annual rents of one of every 8 *modii* of *purcule* [?], two phials of mustard greens, one basket of beans, one of coriander, and two bundles of dried gourds.[59] This plot was surrounded by gardens rented out to other tenants. The abbess who signed that 1035 document made several other contracts, not all of which required payment in kind, so there seems to have been some strategy for providing landlords with both cash and crops from their lands, perhaps to mitigate risk for the landowner. This strategy had the benefit of supplying the urban community of religious men and women with food stuffs. It was not unique to Rome, and we will see an example from Naples in Chapter 4. Whereas earlier monasteries may have used kitchen gardens to provide for themselves, as the letters and stories of Gregory indicate, in early eleventh-century Rome, religious communities owned parts of market gardens and fields outside of the city, and the profits of these brought fresh fruits and vegetables to the urban houses, as well as cash to permit the purchase of other foodstuffs and goods at a produce market which clearly existed by then. The dichotomy between personal, private food garden and large market-focussed specialist garden is perhaps too rigid to be accurate; there was surely opportunity to pass on surplus from one's garden in barter, sale, or donation. We might consider these two modes of food production to be the ends of a continuum.

The evidence for specialised market gardens becomes clear at Rome in the eleventh century, not least through a document from 1030 reporting that eight *ortulani* (gardeners) joined together to elect a prior and to ensure parity among their leases.[60] These were professional gardeners working in a zone of market gardens outside the city.[61] Their organisation

---

[57] *RS* 118 (966). On cucumbers and melons, see Peña-Chocarro and Pérez-Jordà, 'Garden plants in medieval Iberia', pp. 387–8. For a history of cucumbers and gourds in medieval Italy, see Paris, et al., 'Occidental diffusion of cucumber'.

[58] See discussion in Chapter 6.

[59] 'annis sine omni mora vel dilatione pensionis nomine dece purcule, de omni octo modia uno, de sinape fialas duas, de fasoli galato uno, de pitartima galato uno, de cocutias siccas manipu[lo]s duos', *SMVL* 50 (1025) pp. 62–3; note the corrections to the edition in Monaci, 'Per il Tabularium'.

[60] Hartmann, *Urkunde einer römischen Gärtnergenossenschaft*; for the text itself, see pp. 13–15. On the document, see now Wickham, *Medieval Rome*, p. 89, and Chapter 4, p. 1.

[61] For the identification of the gardeners in the *scola* with the gardens at Criptule, see Wickham, *Medieval Rome*, pp. 89–90.

and their specialisation in gardening attests a rise in the complexity of Rome's urban agriculture. It parallels an increase in monetization, implying the use of coinage for purchases and payment of tolls and rents in the city.[62]

Overall, the evidence for cultivated spaces attached to houses and lots which were cultivated within the city as well as just outside the city walls of Rome is clear, even if thinly spread. The pattern of early medieval urban gardening at Rome might be this: substantial houses had kitchen gardens in the sixth through eighth centuries – houses that were substantial enough to warrant the attention of the papal administration and which were often bequeathed to religious institutions as income-producing endowments as well as residences. Clerics, papal bureaucrats, monks, and abbots were the major landowners in Rome, especially of these kinds of substantial houses. This preponderance of urban gardens in religious hands might be a fault of the preserved documentation, which is overwhelmingly in monastic archives, but might also reflect the nature of landholding in Rome, which was consistently ecclesiastical.

The property market in Rome, and perhaps especially that of urban properties with gardens, was dominated by clerics and members of the ecclesiastical administration. In some cases, abbots and priests may have been acting on behalf of their church in the management of the church's properties; in other cases, they appear to have been acting as private owners. Alternatively, they may have been property agents, such as the priests from S. Stefano al Monte Celio, who sold to Leo, priest of SS. Quattro Coronati, and a laywoman and her son Crescentius use of vacant lands and a garden owned by the monastery of SS. Nereo ed Achilleo.[63] The lands were surrounded by public roads, and the house of one *vir magnificus* and the garden of another. The priest and the laywoman then sold to Crescentius the use of a house with a marble stair, and the large garden next to it, with grape vines and fruit trees and also numerous estates outside the walls.[64] Lay members of the ecclesiastical bureaucracy of Rome were also among the property owners with gardens. Pipino, *vestararius*, leased a plot with a spring to make a house and a garden on the Caelian to Romano, a subdeacon.[65] Another *vestararius* leased a newly planted vineyard with a house in Regio 1 from Iohannes, priest and monk, formerly the duke of Albano.[66] The priests, monks, and clerical bureaucrats were the aristocracy of early medieval Rome, and their control of properties with gardens meant that they controlled the urban means of fruit and vegetable production, at least insofar as it is visible to us through the documentary record. This

---

[62] Wickham, *Medieval Rome*, pp. 136–54, 168–72, though see also Chapter 4.
[63] *RS* 89 (953) pp. 134–5.   [64] *RS* 90 (965) pp. 135–6.
[65] *RS* 87 (857) pp. 132–3.   [66] *RS* 79 (976) pp. 122–3.

control, however, does not seem to be institutional; these clerics were not acting collectively for the good of their churches, but rather acting towards the advantage of their households, until the end of their lives, when they gave their properties to a monastery.

There was intensive agriculture of vegetable plots and orchards very close to the city, indeed inside the city walls, while cereals seem to have been grown in the fields outside the city, reflecting von Thünen's model of concentric rings of decreasing intensity moving away from the city (Fig. 7, Chapter 2).[67] Though von Thünen did not consider the city to be at all productive agriculturally, medieval Rome certainly was. Inside the city walls, intensive and mixed cultivation seems to have been more common, with gardens and grape vines, or fruit trees and vegetable gardens beneath the trees.

On Pleasure Gardens

Our broad sketch of the shape of the phenomenon of urban gardening in the early Middle Ages does not include anything which might resemble a pleasure garden, that is, a cultivated space of ornamental plants not intended for consumption or industry. As noted in Chapter 2, in the Roman period, cities and villas alike made extensive use of ornamental plants, such as evergreen hedges and trees (*Buxus, Cupressus sempervirens*, myrtles, and apricots) and flowering plants, such as violets and roses, or forced lily, or gladiolus.[68] Roman gardens, whether in townhouses, villas, or urban porticos, were planted mostly with trees and shrubs, bounded by fences, walls, basins, and animated with mosaics, sculpture, and sometimes exotic animals. The term *uiridarium* was used in antiquity for pleasure gardens, areas of greenery usually enclosed by architecture, either walls or porticos; they may have had flowers, shrubs, and trees, perhaps topiary.[69] Ancient examples were described by authors such as Pliny the Elder, Varro, and others for parts of imperial palaces or other prestigious places. There is some debate about the precise sense of the name in antiquity; it may mean 'collections or displays of plants' or simply a 'deliberately planned garden area' or both.[70] Some plants included in gardens identified as *uiridaria* were chosen for symbolic values, either to

---

[67] Santangeli Valenzani, 'Vecchie e nuove forme', and in Chapter 2.
[68] On the different plants grown, see Landgren, *Lauro, myrto et buxo frequentata*, and Jashemski et al., *Gardens of the Roman Empire*.
[69] On ornamental hedges and topiary, see Landgren, *Lauro, myrto et buxo frequentata*, pp. 104–18.
[70] Marzano, 'Roman gardens', p. 196, note 4 and discussion, p. 243; Landgren, *Lauro, myrto et buxo frequentata*, pp. 6, 154–5. On other definitions, see also *Oxford Latin Dictionary*, s.v.; Purcell, 'The Roman garden as a domestic building', p. 141.

connote conquered lands or to allude to historic or idealised models.[71] The few times that the term *uiridarium* appears in Italian early medieval texts (aside from descriptions of long-disappeared gardens, or when it is a toponym recalling a past garden at that site) it seems to denote a kind of garden space that was cultivated with trees or other plants, perhaps walled. The plants in medieval *uiridaria* were never described beyond an occasional reference to trees. Essentially this was a very privileged space in the cities of Italy, and it was most often owned and maintained by an imperial, royal, or very high-status cultivated owner.[72]

Historians of the decorative gardens of Europe trace the origins of geometrically planned ornamental parks and gardens back to the Middle Ages, through the symbolic functions of gardens in courtly literature of the twelfth century and later, and the development of planned parks in late eleventh-century France and England. This emergence has been attributed to contacts with the Islamicate world in and through Iberia and especially Sicily.

Pleasure gardens in the Christian west 'emerge as a distinct form in Western Europe by the twelfth century ... the cultural forces that made possible Gothic cathedrals, the first European universities, and the wheelbarrow also drove an aristocratic fashion for elaborate pleasure grounds'.[73] 'The recovery of the pleasure garden, as well as higher techniques in cultivation, went hand in hand with the general rediscovery of ancient science and technology through the scholars of Islam.'[74]

These claims that pleasure gardens firstly were a new cultural product in the twelfth century and secondly were influenced by transmission through the Muslim world need to be evaluated. Did the practice of distinctly ornamental cultivation come to Europe through contact with the Islamicate society and culture, and not through the very few high-status *viridaria* of the post-Roman provinces? The sophistication and comprehensiveness with which Italian – especially Sicilian – Norman court society embraced Arab courtly traditions, especially of ornamental gardens as places of politics and pleasure, has encouraged many to think of them as the agents, through the conduit of Italy, for the medieval garden in Europe.[75] One example oft-cited among garden historians of such encounters is the narrative of Amatus of Montecassino, writing of

---

[71] Marzano, 'Roman gardens'; Landgren, *Lauro, myrto et buxo frequentata*, esp. 194–5.
[72] Goodson, 'Admirable and delectable gardens'. [73] Howes, 'Use and reception', p. 92.
[74] Harvey, *Mediaeval gardens*, pp. 22 and 37–51. On the disappearance of gardens from early medieval Europe, see Cardini and Miglio, *Nostalgia del paradiso*, pp. 10–2; Harvey, *Mediaeval gardens*, pp. 25–51, and compare the relatively few references to ornamental gardens in Davies, 'Gardens and gardening in early medieval Spain', p. 333.
[75] Tronzo, 'Zisa and Cuba in Palermo'; Tronzo, *Petrarch's two gardens*, pp. 25–67 and references, note 86.

the Norman siege of Palermo in 1072. Amatus of Montecassino reported that the Norman troops seized a suburban palace on their approach to the city, which Roger I (d. 1101) and his men divided, giving the '[*prince*] the delightful gardens full of fruit and water, and the knights had the royal bounty and a terrestrial paradise for themselves.' He was writing this about 1080, some time after the event, and there were several themes which repeatedly appeared in his account about worthiness of the Normans to rule, the perfidy of the Italian Lombards, and the sanctity of Montecassino.[76] In this passage, the private gardens around 'Saracen' Palermo and their paradisiacal fruits and fountains were desirable and attractive, and within the conquered property, the gardens were suited to the nobleman, not his men.[77]

Amatus' Latin history has been lost; it is known only through an Old French translation which probably dates from the early fourteenth century.[78] It may be, then, that the later translator inflected a romantic ideal of courtly gardens onto the passage, which Amatus may not have intended originally. In later medieval literary imaginations, pleasure gardens played key roles in romance literature. They provided places of unexpected interactions, sensual pleasures, and earthly delights. In the twelfth-century vernacular literature of Europe, songs, poems, and stories of courtly love centre on walled gardens planted with trees. The example of Chrètien de Troyes's *Cligés*, in which lovers meet in an orchard, typifies an often used literary device: 'Enmi le vergier ... la sont a joie et a delit.'[79] These were places of pleasure, assignations, arrangements, and consumption of fruits, from the Biblical forbidden fruits of sexual pleasure to enchanted foods, only eaten inside a walled garden.[80] Amatus' translator may have interjected a significance to the account of conquest not intended by the original author, but we cannot know either what Amatus knew about gardens, nor what he thought about their pleasures.

---

[76] Loud, 'Introduction'; Wolf, *Making history*, esp. pp. 96–7.
[77] 'partirent lo palaiz et les chozes qu'il troverent fors de la cité; donnent a li prince [scil. count] li jardin delictoz pleins de frutte et de eaue, e par soi le chevaliers avoient le choses royals et paradis terrestre', Amatus of Montecassino, *Historia Normannorum*, Book VI, ch. 16, trans. Dunbar, p. 156; cf. Book V, ch. 3, in which a Beneventan monk dreamt of a garden with trees, a lady seated in a tree, and Robert Guiscard watching her (glossed as the Virgin) and drinking a stream of water.
[78] Loud, 'Introduction'.
[79] Chrétien de Troyes, *Cligés*, lines 6380–98; Biblolet, 'Jardins et vergers dans l'oeuvre de Chrétien de Troyes'.
[80] Cf. Diamond, 'Meeting grounds'; Curtius, *European literature and the Latin Middle Ages*, pp. 183–202; Fleming, 'The garden of the Roman De La Rose'; Augspach, 'Meaning'.

This is not to say that there were no gardens around Palermo in the eleventh century, or that they could not have been impressive to the Norman conquerors. Geographers writing in Arabic about Sicily often noted the richness of its irrigated cultivation in and around its cities, though given the nature of Arabic geographic traditions, not all geographers reporting on Sicily had seen gardens first-hand.[81] There were gardens for vegetables and orchards for fruits in the early Middle Ages, just as there were around and inside other cities of Italy. Just as the letters of Pope Gregory the Great attest townhouse gardens in the city of Rome, so too there were gardens in the city of Palermo in the sixth century.[82] Though there is a substantial gap in our evidence for land use in Sicily for the Byzantine and early Islamic periods, it seems very likely that gardens attached to houses, or to religious buildings such as those described by Gregory, continued as they did elsewhere in Italy. Ibn Ḥawqal, a traveller, merchant, and geographer, wrote in the tenth century about the whole of the Islamicate world, including Sicily.[83] He visited Palermo in 973 and wrote about, among other things, the city's markets, produce, and products for sale, describing as well kitchen gardens and orchards in Palermo. He mentioned streams and millstreams outside the city, the banks of which were lined with sugar cane, domestic gardens, and commercial plots of melons, papyrus, and flax.[84] Given the presumed greater degree of commercial activity between Sicily and other parts of the Muslim Mediterranean in the later ninth and tenth centuries, it follows that there may have been greater commercial farming in Sicily than

---

[81] Lorenzi, 'Parchi e verzieri nella Sicilia islamica e normana', and on the literature in particular, Cassarino, 'Palermo experienced, Palermo imagined'. Historians of gardens have claimed that 'in the ninth century Al-Wāqidī prompted Muslim conquerors on to Sicily, 'a fertile island that has many fountains and trees with stupendous fruits', Barbera, 'Parchi, frutteti, giardini e orti', p. 14. Arabists, however, have long recognised that this text of a pseudo-Al-Wāqidī was not written before the twelfth century, and thus this passage is hardly telling of the horticulture of ninth-century Sicily. On the authorship of this passage, see Amari, *Biblioteca Arabo-Sicula*, pp. xlv–xlvii. On the geographers in general, see De Simone, 'Palermo nei geografi e viaggiatori' and Cassarino, 'Palermo experienced, Palermo imagined'.

[82] 'synagogas in ciuitate Panormitana positas cum hospitiis suis ... uel earum parietibus cohaerent, atque hortis ibi coniunctis', *RE* IX, 38 (October 598), vol. II, pp. 597, trans. Martyn, *Letters*, vol. II, p. 569 about the bishop of Palermo's seizure of synagogues, with their hostels and gardens.

[83] On Ibn Ḥawqal, see Miquel, 'Ibn Ḥawḳal'.

[84] Ibn Ḥawqal, *Kitāb ṣūrat al-Arḍ*, ed. and trans. Kramers and Wiet, Arabic pp. 117, 122, and French pp. 118 and 121; discussion in Nef, 'Islamic Palermo and the Dār al Islām', p. 53. Kramers translated مقاثٍ as fields planted with cucumbers, but these were not grown in the Mediterranean in this period; see above, note 57. I am grateful to Ed Zychowicz-Coghill for his thoughts on the text.

elsewhere in early medieval Italy, but our evidence to analyse it further is limited.[85]

The Norman rulers of Sicily, especially the kings of the twelfth century, Roger II (d. 1154), William I (d. 1166), and William II (d. 1189), created ornamental gardens and fountains, the remains of which are only faint traces of what must have been extraordinary horticultural complexes. Many Arab authors of the court wrote to celebrate the Norman garden projects of the eleventh and twelfth centuries.[86] It is clear that these were distinguished spaces for the use of the court and courtiers, probably built with an effort to emulate some aspects of contemporary gardens of al-Andalusi rulers and the pleasure gardens of Fatimid cities, which combined planted trees, especially fruiting trees, with basins, fountains, and pavilions.[87] The Norman gardens of Sicily held exotic animals, identifiable in some images of the gardens, and perhaps also rare plants; certainly they were mostly ornamental in nature.[88] In the course of the twelfth century, the Norman gardens of Sicily evolved in line with other cultural influences and aspirations, such as forested areas, akin to the hunting grounds and preserves of eleventh-century Anglo-Norman courtly culture (Fig. 17). Yet, the craft of Norman courtly behaviour employing models of bureaucracy, imagery, woodworking, and gardens, developed over the course of Norman rule, not immediately upon the conquest of Sicily. And in the lands of southern Italy and Sicily that were conquered by the Normans, there was a long and rich tradition of urban gardens, including a few very high-status gardens associated with courts. There were some exceptional enclosed gardens in royal, imperial, and princely contexts set apart from the common productive gardens of Italian cities by their name, *uiridaria*, and the ways in which they were used by their owners.[89]

The horticulture of Islamicate and Norman Sicily was much more like the gardens and farms of al-Andalus than it was the rest of Italy, in large part because of the fundamentally different agricultural irrigation systems

---

[85] On trade, see Nef, 'Islamic Palermo and the Dār al Islām', pp. 52–6. For a document-based analysis of later medieval Palermo and its urban and suburban gardens, which were both productive for citrus fruits especially and valued for their artificial, constructed beauty, see Bresc, 'Les jardins de Palerme (1290–1460)' and Bresc, 'Palermo in the 14th–15th century: urban economy'.

[86] Barbera, 'Parchi, frutteti, giardini e orti'; Lorenzi, 'Parchi e verzieri nella Sicilia islamica e normana'.

[87] Leone et al., 'Royal art in the Norman age. The sollazzi and the royal park'. On Fatimid gardens, see Pradines and Khan, 'Fāṭimid gardens'. On Islamic gardens more generally, see Brookes, *Gardens of paradise*; Ruggles, *Islamic gardens and landscapes*.

[88] Masseti, 'In the gardens of Norman Palermo', stresses the diversity of animals in the Norman gardens.

[89] Goodson, 'Admirable and delectable gardens'.

Figure 17 Image of the Genoard, Palermo, depicted in twelfth-century illustration of the city of Palermo in mourning for the death of William II, in Pietro da Eboli, *Liber ad honorem Augusti*, Palermo, 1195–7. Bern, Burgerbibliothek, Codex 120 II, f. 98 recto, Photograph www.e-codices.ch. © Codices Electronici AG.

employed there. The rise of the caliphate brought many changes to the lands, including new species, new agricultural technologies to cultivate them, and new theories about agriculture, transmitted in Arabic, as well as new strategies of performing power in the Islamicate parts of Iberia.[90] Even in the Christian parts of Spain, there were gardens for household agriculture; some were even in cities. Wendy Davies has demonstrated that across Northern Iberia, the few urban centres that existed there, such as León, Burgos, Zamora, and Coimbra, were more likely to have documents which describe productive gardens as part of residential property parcels than documents from rural properties.[91] In Iberia, certain kinds of cultivated spaces were intensively farmed for food or textiles and associated with irrigation, the rural *ortos* of the Latin documents, and peri-urban *jannāt* or *basātīn* in Arabic.[92]

Archaeobotanical Research in Italy

The examples of urban gardening of the productive sort discussed in the previous pages have mostly come from textual evidence, and the documents which record them and the processes by which they were phrased and written were shaped by the broader structures of early medieval society, as we shall see. Archaeology has also provided evidence for the phenomenon of urban gardening, showing the transformations of townhouses, public buildings, and open areas of the city. To understand this aspect of our story, archaeobotany has been very valuable.

Archaeobotanical research in Italy has had a relatively slow start, compared to Britain and France, but since the 1990s it has become a really progressive, creative, and increasingly coherent field interested in climate change, the cultural aspects of changes in food products, and historical agronomic practices. Archaeobotanical evidence can speak both to broad backgrounds and detailed portraits, depending on what has been examined and where the material was recovered. Pollen preserved from archaeological layers can attest to changes in the environment over time; instead, plant macroremains provide a lot information on the human–plant relationship in the past. In any case, there are some plants that are very difficult to trace because their elements do not preserve well. Thus mineralised pollens which are recovered from sediments in the bottom of lakes, bogs, or bays attest to overall environment and changes at the rate of centuries or millennia. Pollens preserved from wells or in waterlogged

---

[90] For an introduction to Islamicate agriculture, see García Sánchez, 'Agriculture in Muslim Spain', and on Arabic agronomic literature in al-Andalus, see El Faïz, 'L'apport des traités agronomiques'. On irrigation in particular, see the review in Gutiérrez Lloret, 'The case of Tudmīr', pp. 395–7.

[91] Davies, 'Gardens and gardening in early medieval Spain', p. 337.

[92] On 'ortos', see Davies, 'Gardens and gardening in early medieval Spain', p. 336; on Arabic terminology, see García Sánchez, 'The gardens of al-Andalus', pp. 207, 215; García Sánchez, 'Cultivos y espacios agrícolas'.

soil contexts can attest to the general local environment. And preserved plant remains, like seeds, nuts, seed hulls, or rinds, attest to plants that were grown, prepared, consumed, or thrown away at a given site. In any case, there are some plants that are very difficult to trace, either because their pollens do not travel far or their plant remains do not preserve well.

Looking specifically at the remains of plants within contexts of late antiquity, there was a change in cereal consumption/cultivation starting in the fifth to seventh centuries, whereby the classic Roman combination of free-threshing wheats (*Triticum aestivum/durum*) and barley (*Hordeum vulgare*) became more diverse. Given that every site undergoes any number of different depositional processes and has varied conditions which affect the preservation and recovery of plant remains, the archaeobotany of one site can appear vastly different from that of another for reasons that may not be attributable to the nature of the site in antiquity. It is therefore difficult to make specific comparisons across sites. The data are emerging from new research very rapidly, so it is not uncommon to find that an article of five years ago is out of date. Archaeology is by its nature unpredictable, you never know what you are going to find. That said, there are some very big gaps in our evidence. So, for the Middle Ages, that is, the period between 600 and 1500, as of March 2018 there are sixty-one sites in Italy with published archaeobotanical remains, and most of these are rural.[93] There are essentially no published contexts of archaeobotanical remains of foodstuffs from Rome between the fourth and ninth centuries; only very partially published records from anywhere in Campania, including Naples. Nonetheless, comparison between sites of the Roman imperial period and late antiquity reveals a direction of change that was continued in subsequent centuries.

When considered proportionally, the carpological remains from an imperial-period rural site near Trento and late antique urban contexts from the urban domestic site of S. Giulia, Brescia provide an example of the kinds of changes we can observe, though they reflect the specific geographies of those two sites; no single site can represent all of the geographically varied peninsula (Fig. 18).[94] In the Roman period at Mezzocorona, cereals make up nearly half of the remains, while legumes are not quite one-tenth; fruits and other plant remains make up the rest. Of the cereals, barley and free-threshing wheat are by far the most common, though there are millets and hulled wheats as well. Of the legumes,

---

[93] See the website of Botanical Records of Archaeology Italian Network, https://brainplants.successoterra.net/

[94] The proportional comparison was produced by Castelletti, Castiglioni, and Rottoli from their research at these two sites. Their published analysis does not report the raw numbers. Castelletti et al., 'L'agricoltura dell'Italia settentrionale'.

Archaeobotanical Research in Italy

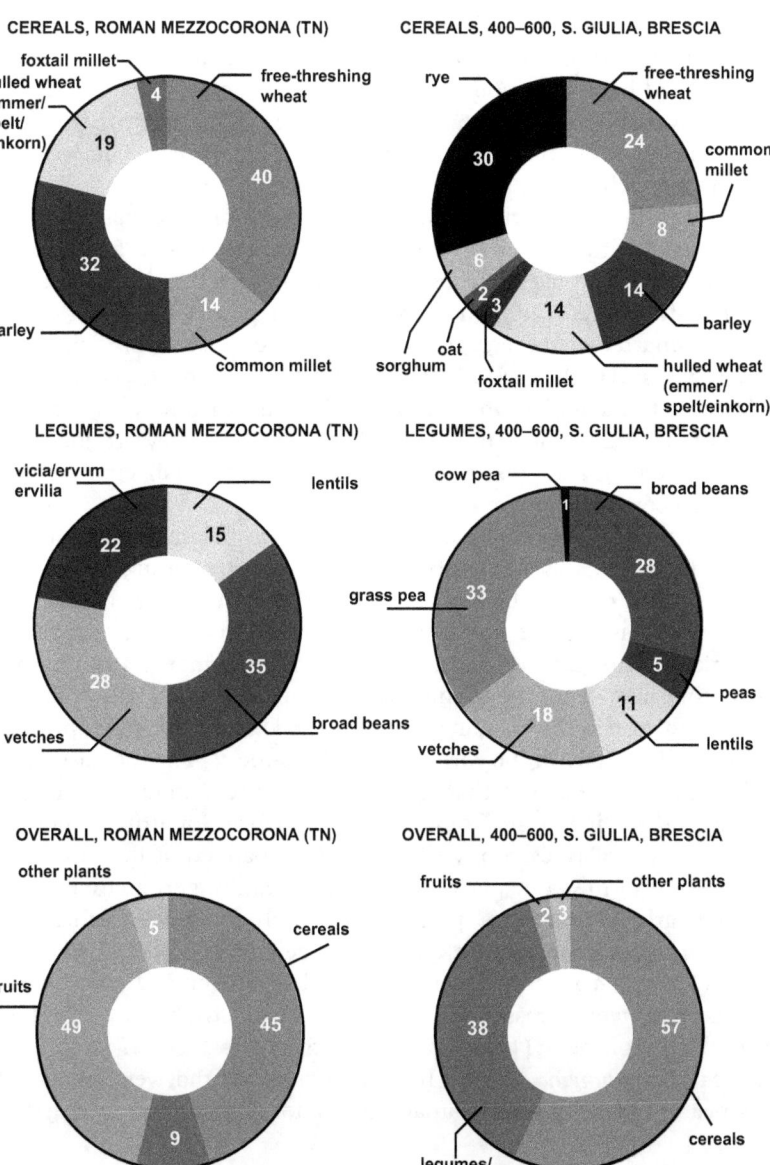

Figure 18 Proportions of carpological remains from a Roman rural site (left) and a sixth- to seventh-century urban site (right). Data from Castelletti et al., 'L'agricoltura dell'Italia settentrionale'.

half are for the table (broad bean and lentil), and the rest are vetches, which might have been animal fodder or human food. In the Roman period it had been common to alternate cereals and legumes annually; classical authors attest to the benefits for the soils, and broad bean or *favino* (*vicea faba* or *favino, v. f. var. minor*) and lentils (*lens culinaris*) were consumed widely and also given to animals as fodder.

By contrast, at the early medieval site of S. Giulia, cereals form well over one-half of the overall carpological remains recovered, and legumes over one-third. Among the cereals, barley and free-threshing wheat are certainly still present, though there is a much greater variety of grains. Nearly a quarter of the cereals recovered were rye, not present in the Roman site, and in the early medieval site there are also oats, sorghum, as well as millets and hulled wheats. The legumes have similarly increased in types; broad beans and lentils are still present, but they are joined by a range of vetches and grass pea (*Lathyrus sativus*), a small legume grown for human consumption or animals.

The changes to the cereals and legumes grown in late antiquity recognised here in S. Giulia are visible elsewhere in sites dating to the early Middle Ages. Free-threshing wheat and barley continued to be the most dominant grains at some sites but there was also more significantly more rye, einkorn, and oats than there had been in the Roman period. Emmer (spelt) continued from the Roman period as did sorghum, which had not been a food crop in the Roman period; both became much more prominent in northern Italy in the early Middle Ages too.[95] The increase in rye cultivation may be a shift that farmers made to counteract a period of drought and cooling in late Roman times, though as Squatriti has pointed out, while rye tolerates cool well, sorghum expanded at the same time (and in some of the same places) and it likes heat for germination.[96]

In the early Middle Ages, pulses increasingly formed the other main component of human diet, in addition to cereals. The field bean (*Ital. favino*) (*Vicia faba minor*) was very common but also lentil (*Lens culinaris*), pea (*Pisum sativum*), grass pea (*Lathyrus cicera/sativus*), bitter vetch (*Vicia ervilia*), common vetch (*Vicia sativa agg.*), chickpea (*Cicer arietinum*), and cow pea (*Vigna unguiculata*).[97] It is often assumed that vetches such as grass pea or chickling were animal fodder, not human food, but there is

---

[95] On sorghum, see Castiglioni and Rottoli, 'Broomcorn millet'; for a general view from the documentary record, see Montanari, *L'alimentazione contadina*, pp. 133–44.

[96] McCormick, 'What climate science, Ausonius', p. 84. For a cultural history of rye in the early Middle Ages, including discussion of the possible, though unclear relationship between climate and agricultural change, see Squatriti, 'Rye's rise and Rome's fall', esp. pp. 344–5.

[97] See summary in Rottoli, 'Reflections on early medieval resources', p. 23.

ample evidence from the developing world for the cultivation of some of these legumes for human food in times of uncertain food supply, and some archaeological sites from late antique Italy have identified grass pea alongside prepared grains in what really looks like a kitchen hearth.[98]

If we consider the archaeobotanical remains of fruits, it is clear that some of the main fruit crops of the Roman period remained constant from the Roman period to the Middle Ages, such as fig, walnut, grape, plum, cherry, and olive.[99] Other fruits common in Roman contexts, like peaches, decrease during the fifth to seventh centuries. Foraged berries or species which occurred naturally but might have been tended to encourage fruiting, such as blackberry, elderberry, sloe berry, *corniolo/ dogberry* and also raspberry and strawberry, are common; chestnuts appear as foodstuffs, with increasing frequency over the course of the early Middle Ages. These plants may have exploited the landscapes around post-Roman cities, which were no longer as regularly maintained as they had been in antiquity. Blackberry brambles (*Rubus fruticosus*) thrive in clear-felled sites and tolerate poor soils well. Unless they are cut back, they grow back over their canes to increase in height and density, while producing edible fruit.[100]

It is against this background of diversifying food resources and expanding native plant species that we must see the rise of urban food gardening. We see a diversification of cereal and legume production, which might reflect an effort to mitigate risk on crops, to compensate for increased climate variability and/or changes to the broader patterns of market production, grain subsidies, and commercial availability at the end of the Roman Empire. These same issues prompted the reconfiguration of households into homes set into open areas, or with earth-filled areas adjacent to them. The textual evidence for this kind of home in the major cities of Italy appears in the late sixth century, and, as we have seen, references to houses with gardens or cultivated areas rise in frequency in the documentary record in the eighth and ninth centuries as the documentary record itself expands. The archaeology might suggest that the change in houses surrounded by unbuilt lots occurred already in the sixth century. When we get robust archaeological evidence for cultivated spaces within cities, with well-preserved plant remains, they certainly point to urban gardens of some size, with diverse fruits, vegetables, and legumes. And because the available property documents very rarely

---

[98] Sadori and Susanna, 'Hints of economic change during the late Roman Empire'.
[99] Mercuri et al., 'Olea, Juglans and Castanea'.
[100] Deconchat and Balent, 'Effets des perturbations du sol'.

describe what it is that is grown in gardens or lots, it is exciting to find excavated contexts which reveal kitchen garden crops.

Rome, Forum of Caesar

The major excavations in Rome of the 1990s that revealed a previously unexcavated stretch of the Imperial Fora, with attention to all of their post-Roman phases, has brought to light a moderately sized garden, vineyard, and orchard not known from any preserved documents, but resembling in many ways the gardens interspersed between houses and roads that the documents describe. The area of the Fora remained open public spaces within the city in the earliest Middle Ages, and archaeological evidence suggests that many of the Imperial Fora, including the Forum of Trajan, were cleaned down to their paving stones regularly. However, in the eighth and ninth centuries these areas were taken over for different uses. The stone pavers of the Forum of Caesar were removed in the late eighth century, small trenches were cut in the earth underneath the pavement, and a garden was planted, with cabbages, lettuces, white mustard, mint, and aniseed.[101] New earth was brought to the area in the mid ninth century to level the area for another planting over a larger area (Fig. 19). The newly raised bed had trenches 5 m from one another for grape vines and then irregular circular pits for fruit trees. Palaeobotanical analysis identified cherries, yellow plums, hazelnuts, and especially figs. Among the grapevines there were probably also kitchen vegetables; coriander has been identified, and it is not difficult to imagine other greens.[102] The excavators hypothesized about the scale of production possible in these mixed fields, noting that this was larger than most of what appears in the documentary record: 'the area excavated measured about 1,000 sq m, and if the cultivated area included the entire area of the former Forum of Caesar, it could have covered a total of 2,000–2,500 sq. m, of which about 1,000 or a bit more was vine and the rest was orchard'.[103]

The range of different crops indicates that this was no market garden, but one aimed at covering the needs of a family or small community. The excavators hypothesized that the vineyard of the Forum of Caesar produced about 200–250 L per annum, sufficient for the needs of

---

[101] Meneghini and Santangeli Valenzani, *Roma nell'altomedioevo*, pp. 127–8. The archaeobotany is reported in this publication but has not been published in detail.

[102] Santangeli Valenzani, 'I fori imperiali nel Medioevo'; Santangeli Valenzani, *Edilizia residenziale*, pp. 80–6.

[103] Santangeli Valenzani and Meneghini, *Roma nell'altomedioevo*, pp. 127–8; Santangeli Valenzani, 'I fori imperiali nel Medioevo', pp. 274–5.

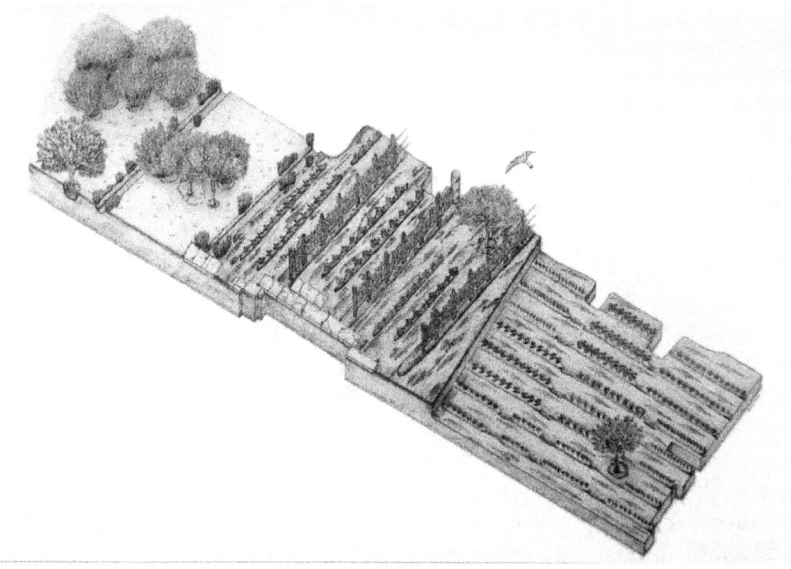

Figure 19 Reconstruction of two phases of gardens: vegetables on the right, in the early ninth century; and on the left imported soils for an orchard and vineyard of the later ninth century. Image from Meneghini and Santangeli Valenzani, *Roma nell'altomedioevo*, fig. 99.

a household, more or less. They envisioned this to be a substantial family or household plot, rather than one destined for commercial activity.[104]

Ferrara

Unlike most of the cities considered in this book, Ferrara was not a Roman city; it was newly founded in the seventh century, probably as a fortified settlement (*castrum*). As the site grew into a city in the Middle Ages it developed some of the same urban qualities as its counterparts with Roman foundations in that its streets were laid out in somewhat of a grid pattern and it had a dense centre with a mix of houses and monumental buildings, including a number of churches within the urban nucleus.[105] In the early Middle Ages it was not fortified with city walls, but one area seems to have been walled and surrounded by a ditch.

---

[104] Meneghini and Santangeli Valenzani, *Roma nell'altomedioevo*, pp. 127–8.
[105] On the urban form of Ferrara, see Uggeri Patitucci, 'Sviluppo topografico', and Uggeri Patitucci, 'Scavi nella Ferrara medioevale'.

South of the cathedral, on the modern Corso Porta Reno and via Vaspergolo, an extensive archaeological trench revealed a slice through the history of medieval Ferrara, including a number of wooden structures and pits of the tenth to the twelfth centuries (Fig. 20).[106] The structures resemble in some sense the kind of residential arrangements we have seen throughout our period: a house, single-room or double, on an earthen plot. These have some evidence of fencing which might have been property boundaries, and many pits dug for rubbish and soak-away latrine pits. The first phase of occupation is sporadic, but in the first half of the eleventh century, a number of wooden buildings were constructed, dividing the area into lots. There were four structures in this phase, running parallel to the dividing walls; the rubbish pits were in the west, apart from the structures.[107] The nature of the plant remains in the pits, both pollens and carpological remains, indicates that this or a site very near to this was cultivated with a wide range of food crops, and also attests to the hedges and ditches, very near to the site.[108]

Among the species recovered for the period of the tenth and eleventh centuries, there are a great number of cultivated fruits and vegetables (Table 2). The archaeobotany of the site points to a certain continuity with Roman-period cultivation in this part of Italy, as well as some notable differences reflecting the changed economies, cultures, and agriculture of Northern Italy in the early Middle Ages.[109]

Among cereals, the classic Roman crops of barley and free-threshing wheat were present, as were other 'minor' grains, including foxtail and common millet, oat, sorghum, and emmer wheat. Sorghum, as we have seen, was new to Northern Italy as a food cereal in the early Middle Ages, and common millet was the most frequent species in this period. These were probably not grown at this site but in fields further out from the centre.

---

[106] On the site, excavated in 1993–4, Guarnieri, 'Un indagine nel centro storico'; Guarnieri and Librenti, 'Ferrara, sequenza insediativa pluristratificata'. Note that another excavation, in a site immediately adjacent, was excavated in 1981–4, and it also produced timber houses and pits, though these were apparently not examined for botanical remains. The outlines of the late thirteenth-century and nineteenth-century brick buildings revealed in the excavations are marked on the current paving of the site. The results of those excavations have been published in Gadd and Ward-Perkins, 'The development of urban domestic housing', which anticipates a comprehensive publication, though it never appeared. The palaeosoils were also studied: Cremaschi and Nicosia, 'Corso Porta Reno, Ferrara'.

[107] Guarnieri, 'Un indagine nel centro storico'.

[108] Bosi, 'Flora e ambiente vegetale'; Cuoghi, 'L'orto alto-medievale di Ferrara' and unpublished data.

[109] Bosi et al. 'Archaeobotanical evidence of food plants'.

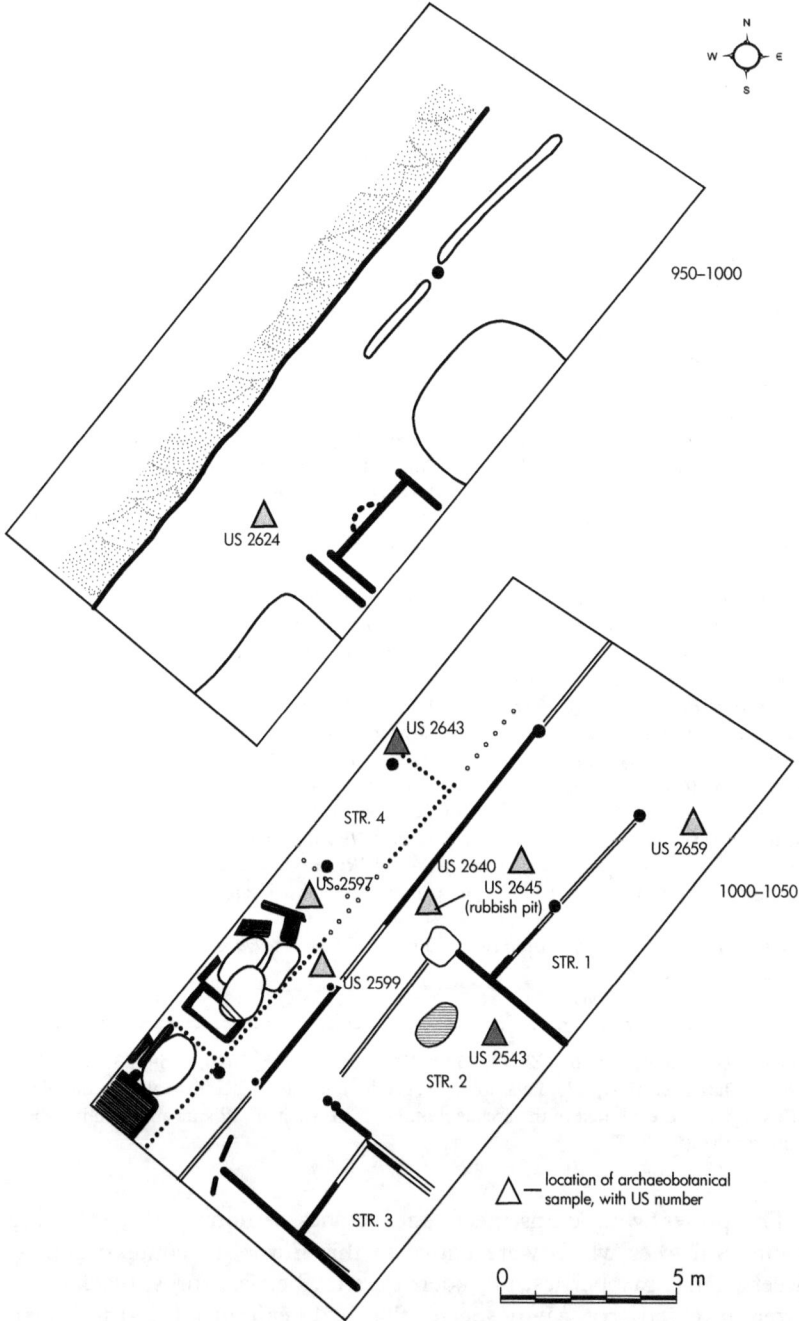

Figure 20 Plan of site and samples of the Corso Porta Reno/via Vaspergolo, Ferrara. Plan based on Guarnieri and Librenti, 'Ferrara, sequenza insediativa pluristratificata', figs. 3 and 4 with additional information from G. Bosi.

112   The Shape of the Phenomenon

Table 2 *Selection of the food crops recovered from Corso Porto Reno, Ferrara, in 950–1050**

Cereals	Legumes
Free-threshing wheat (*Triticum aestivum/ durum*)	Lentil (*Lens culinaris medicus*)
Emmer wheat (*Triticum dicoccum*)	Pea (*Pisum sativum*)
Sorghum (*Sorghum bicolor Moench*)	Slender vetch (*Vicia cf. tetrasperma* Schreb.)
Foxtail millet (*Setaria cf. italica* Beauv.)	Winter vetch (*Vicia villosa* Roth)
Common or Broom Corn Millet (*Panicum miliaceum.*)	
Barley (*Hordeum vulgare*)	
Oat (*Avena sp.*)	
Fruits	**Vegetables, aromatics, seasonings**
Grapes (*Vitis vinifera subsp. Vinifera*)	Aniseed (*Pimpinella anisum*)
Sweet cherry (*Prunus avium*)	Basil (*Ocimum basilicum*)
Raspberries (*Rubus idaeus*)	Beet (*Beta vulgaris*)
Dewberries (*Rubus caesius*)	Carrot (grown either for root or for carrot seed) (*Daucus carota*)
Blackberries (*Rubus fruticosus aggr.*)	Chicory (*Cichorium intybus*)
Sorbs (*Sorbus domestica* and wild)	Dill (*Anethum graveolens*)
Strawberries (*Fragaria vesca*)	Gourds (*Lagenaria siceraria*)
Blackthorn (sloe berries) (*Prunus spinosa*)	Hyssop (*Hyssopus officinalis*)
Dogberries (Ital. corniolo) (*Cornus mas*)	Lettuce (*Lactuca sativa*)
Hazelnut (*Corylus avellana*)	Oregano (*Origanum vulgare*)
Elderberry (*Sambucus nigra*)	Parsley (*Petroselinum sativum*)
Watermelon (*Citrullus lanatus*)	Parsnip (*Pastinaca sativa*)
Fig (*Ficus carica*)	Poppy seeds (*Papaver somniferum*)
Pinenut (*Pinus pinea*)	Rocket (*Eruca sativa*)
Sour cherry (*Prunus cerasus*)	Sorrell (*Rumex acetosella*)
Damask plum (*P. domestica subsp. domestica*)	Summer savory (*Satureja hortensis*)
Damson (*P. domestica subsp. insititia*)	Thyme (*Thymus vulgaris*)
Peach (*P. Persica*)	
Chestnut (*Castanea sativa*)	

* Phases I–III, contexts: 2624, 2643, 2543, 2597, 2599, 2645, 2640, 2659, 2395, 2122, 1703. Data from Bosi, 'Flora e ambienti vegetali', and Cuoghi, 'L'orto alto-medievale di Ferrara'. For the context of the archaeobotany, see Bosi et al., 'Plants and man in urban environment'.

The pulses were lentils, peas, and vetches. Among fruits, there are plants and trees which were native to this European context: grapes, sweet cherry, raspberries, blackberries, strawberries, sorbs, blackthorn, hazelnut, elderberry. Many species that had been introduced to Italian agriculture in the Roman period continued into the Middle Ages, such as pine nut, peach, and cherry. In Ferrara the cultivation of melon (*Cucumis melo*) increases considerably over the Middle Ages. In our period, there is the notable arrival of sour cherry (*Prunus cerasus*). Among vegetables, remains from parsnip and carrot were recovered, though it is not clear whether they were used for roots or aromatic seeds, or both. Purslane (*Portulaca oleracea*) was grown for the green leaves and the seeds as aromatics.[110] Leafy greens were present in lettuce, chicory, rocket, sorrel, and summer savory, and many herbs and seasonings: aniseed, hyssop, dill, oregano, basil, parsley, and thyme. The excavators pointed out the abundant presence of poppy seeds, which may have been used as a seasoning, or perhaps even for oil; they might have had a medicinal purpose.[111] There were also remains of textile plants, namely hemp (*Cannabis sativa*) and flax (*Linum usitatissimum*), with seeds/fruits used as food.

In this urban site in Ferrara, dating from the end of our period, we have strong evidence for the cultivation of many different crops on a given site, from fruits to legumes to seasoning herbs, and possibly the processing of other field crops. There are plants that were cultivated from indigenous wild species for food purposes, and the introduction of new crops and their refinement for better eating.

At the Corso Porta Reno, in the second half of the twelfth century the houses and buildings with this garden were replaced by houses with brick foundations and then, in subsequent phases, entirely of brick. Statutes of 1287 required the fencing in of 'gardens and courtyards' as streets were increasingly paved and drainage was increasingly organised centrally.[112] Across Italy we can see the contraction of domestic gardening, the laying out of new properties for rent overtop of cultivated spaces, and the return to market-scale production in suburban plots. This constitutes a shift in agricultural and economic systems that provides the bookend to the phenomenon we are discussing and the counterpart to the changes of the fifth century we considered previously. I do not mean to suggest that there were no urban gardens in later medieval contexts, because there certainly were. But they were not the norm, as tower-houses and stone-built houses on street frontage became the typical townhouse, and market-scale cultivation, including specialisation of crops, characterised the overall pattern of agricultural production for urban consumption.

This chapter has revealed the broad contours of urban gardening: most early cities in Italy (and probably larger towns, too) had houses with

---

[110] Bosi et al., 'Ethnobotany of purslane'.
[111] Bosi et al., 'Applicazioni morfobiometriche'.
[112] For statutes, see *Statuta Ferraria*, ed. Montorsi, XV, p. 287, and discussion in Guarnieri and Librenti, 'Ferrara, sequenza insediativa', p. 288.

cultivated areas adjacent to them. These appear to have been used for mixed cultivation of fruiting trees, grape vines, and fruits and vegetables for the table. Across the urban landscape, these gardens provided for household consumption and augmented what was grown in open rural fields, such as grain and cereals. Chapter 4 explores urban food markets and suggests ways in which we might understand the absence of evidence for food markets prior to the eleventh century. The possession of food gardens took on new relevance in the context of relatively low levels of market exchange, though just how low these levels were must be determined. The consideration of family networks of exchange reveals the key roles played by social ties in the distribution of foods in early medieval Italy.

4 Alliances and Exchanges

In the 880s, life in Salerno was difficult for the widow Wiletruda.

> I, Wiletruda, daughter of Winepert, widow of Maurus, son of Ermemarus, have declared that because we are surrounded by Saracens, and we think we will die from the dangers of hunger, and I have nothing of any aid by which to live, unless I want to sell my 1/8 portion of our things, which belongs to me, which Maurus, my husband, gave to me, in the day of our marriage, so that I may free myself of the hunger of necessity.... Thus for the above sale, presently I receive from you 6 *solidi* in *denari* from the Salernitan mint, at the rate of 12 *denari* per *solidus*; this is the final and total price.[1]

She sold her *Morgencap*, the property that was exclusively hers from her marriage, to a priest, Angilpert.[2] Other similar stories attest the famine during the Saracen siege of the city in the 880s, when, it was claimed, the wife of the ruler paced the walls and abstained from food, and the people were hungry to the point of eating cats and mice.[3] It is relatively easy to see how Salerno would suffer when besieged, located between a mountain and the sea. There were urban gardens among the properties of the city,

---

[1] 'Ego mulier nomine wiletruda filia wineperti, que uxor fuit mauri filii ermemari, declarata sum quod a sarracenis sumus circumdati et a periculis famis nos perire cogitamus, et nihil habeo aliquid remedium qualiter bibere possam, nisi ipsam octabam portionem meam de rebus bindere bolo, que mihi a supradicto mauro viro meo pertenuit quod in die nuptiarum mihi traditum habuit, ut mea famis necessitatis liberare possam. ... unde pro suprascripta mea binditione in presentes recepit a te qui supra hemtorem meum solidos numerum sex de dinari ex moneta salernitana et aba duodecim dinari per solidum; finitum vero abeo totum pretium eam rationem', *CDC* I, 97 (882), pp. 123–4.

[2] On the *Morgencap* in Lombard Italy, see Toubert, *Les structures*, pp. 736–49, Taviani-Carozzi, *La principauté lombarde*, pp. 385–9; Vismara, 'I rapporti patrimonali'. Angilpert was buying quite a lot of property, cf. *CDC* I, 84 (880), 88 (882), 91 (882), 95 (882), 96 (882), 97 (882). Barbara Kreuz reported that at this time property was sold for notably lower prices; *Before the Normans*, p. 177, note 34.

[3] 'Set dum famis valida predictam urbem consumeret, coniux Guaiferii principis per semet ipsam per muros civitatis gradiebat, alimentaque deferebat nimirum et confortabat ... valida fames attereret, in tantum ut cathos et mures commederent, decreverunt, ut si annus continuus misericordia Dei abesset, Agareni si subderent', *Chronicon Salernitanum*, ch. 115, p. 128.

so people did grow their own fruits and vegetables. But there was nowhere near enough area within the city walls for anyone to grow grain, the principal foodstuff of the Middle Ages. And the Saracens, it is reported, cut off access between the city and the fields of grain grown behind the coast and presumably took their livestock, too. We might imagine that the result of this document was that Wiletruda took her 72 *denari* and bought food somewhere – in a market, perhaps, there were still some cabbage, onions, dried chickpeas, and wine. After all, in the Roman period, the principal means by which people put food on the table was buying it in shops, stalls, or from street vendors. From the imperial and late antique periods, there are many depictions, both literary and visual, of food stalls in marketplaces, shops in *macella*, and food hawkers wandering the streets of Pompeii, Ostia, and other cities of the Empire (Fig. 21).[4] But in the ninth century, despite considerable evidence for the layout and functioning of the city, we have no information about marketplaces at Salerno; there was a market area outside of town, licensed by the dukes, though how frequently a market was held in normal circumstances and what happened to it during a siege is hard to guess.[5] And 72 silver *denari* would have been a considerable amount. Even in a crisis provoked by Saracen siege, 4 *denari nobi* (of Guaimar I, the major coin issued at the time) would purchase a chestnut grove, a young orchard, and a field prepared for planting outside of Salerno; her coin money was not even in denominations suitable for foodstuffs, even if she were paying a year's worth of groceries.[6] How then did people feed their families? What role did urban cultivation play in the economic systems of early medieval Italy? And to which other economic patterns of household-scale production did urban cultivation of the period circa 500–1050 relate?

Re-examination of the physical and regulatory structures of marketing, the patterns of coin finds, and other evidence for the ways in which goods moved between hands in early medieval Italy up to about 1050 makes clear the centrality of gardening to provide food for households and the deep structure of personal relationships and extended household economies (including ecclesiastical households). It also makes clear that interpersonal obligations and responsibilities, rather than commercial forces or state-like structures, governed the circulation of everyday objects and

---

[4] Holleran, "Representations of food hawkers'. For foodstuffs in the *macellum*, see Holleran, *Shopping in ancient Rome*, pp. 160–81; Ellis, *The Roman retail revolution*; De Ruyt, *Macellum: marché alimentaire*, esp. pp. 341–50. On diet in ancient Rome, see Garnsey, 'Mass diet and nutrition'; André, *L'alimentation et la cuisine à Rome*; Erdkamp, 'The food supply of the Capital'.

[5] For the location of the market, see *CDC* vol. I, 44 (856) and p. 128. On Salerno, see Peduto, 'Salerno nell'alto Medioevo'.

[6] *CDC* vol. I, 88 (882); *MEC* I, p. 73.

Figure 21 Funerary relief of a vegetable seller, terracotta, h. 432 mm, dating from second half of second century CE. Ostia Antica, Museo Ostiense inv, no. 198. Photo © Eric Lessing.

foodstuffs. This chapter provides the context for the rise in household-level cultivation within the cities of Italy, explaining why having cultivated spaces in cities became essential in the sixth century and less relevant in the eleventh. While the questions of this book are fundamental to cities and the people who lived in them, we must consider the wider panorama of field crops, which produced grains and animal fodder at scale. This is because when we observe the contraction of the structures of large-scale agriculture and circulation of goods, we can analyse the implications of those economic shifts for domestic consumption and domestic-scale horticulture.

Economic Patterns and Their Origins

Given the ambiguity of much of our evidence, analysis of early medieval economies in Italy and elsewhere has relied upon assumptions about the extent of economic activity which must have taken place below the threshold of the documentary record. Opinions vary considerably about the frequency and motors of exchange. At the first part of the twenty-first century, two major works in English each dedicated nearly 1,000 pages to the problem, with different inflections and results. Michael McCormick's major review of the economies of the early Middle Ages pointed to the end of the *annona*, the system of taxation in goods and circulation of grain to Roman citizens, which brought ships of wheat and other produce and products to Rome from North Africa, as one of key reasons why long-distance movement of goods declined in the fifth century. For the period from about 700, McCormick enumerated textual and numismatic evidence for movement of people and goods across the Mediterranean in the period between about 300 and 900.[7] He argued that a skeleton network of long-distance trade and travel for administrative purposes endured even through very lean times and that high-status goods continued to circulate in reduced quantity. He sought to show that long-distance trade was resuming along similar, if not identical networks as obtained in the late Roman period, alongside new networks such as the route through Venice. In his analysis, the Church emerges as a powerful motivator for long-distance movement and exchange, especially of luxury goods like silks, spices, and relics.[8] McCormick argues for the durability of certain kinds of commercial and political interaction across the Mediterranean in late antiquity through to the Middle Ages, and that while the motors changed, the rarefied commodities which continued to be exchanged, travelled along the same lines as in previous centuries.

In contrast, Chris Wickham's analysis of the early medieval 'Mediterranean world system' emphasizes the differences in patterns of long-distance trade between the Western half of the sea and the Eastern half and stresses that the overwhelming majority of exchange was local, not long-distance. Like McCormick, he stresses that tax collection was

---

[7] McCormick, *Origins of the European economy*.
[8] McCormick, *Origins of the European economy*, pp. 622–6. Monasteries also provided significant demand for resources, fueling a certain amount of exchange; ibid. pp. 633–4.

a key motor of the movement of goods, from Africa to Italy in particular up to the mid fifth century, and that these effects diminished and then ceased during the political fragmentation of the late Roman Empire, the Byzantine reconquest, and the Arab conquests.[9]

Wickham's attention to pottery production and consumption as proxy evidence for economic trends permits him to see the strongly regional character of late antique Italian commerce, a regionalism which only increased in the wake of broader changes and the weakening of the administrative structures of the empire. Wickham noted major shifts in the frequency and breadth of patterns of exchange: downward at the end of the *annona* with the Vandal conquest of Africa Proconsularis (439), downward again at the time of the Gothic War (535–54), and slowly upward from about 700 to 750, as separate regions became more coherent and consistently administered by regional kings and local rulers.[10] Wickham has argued that the fine threads formed by the trade of very high-status goods, so key to McCormick's economies, meant very little to the economies of the majority of the early medieval world and had no bearing on the trade of bulk goods like grain, livestock, oil and wine, quotidian textiles, skins, and animals.[11] Wickham's subsequent work has been analysing the commerce of the eleventh and twelfth centuries in Italy and elsewhere, in order to unpick assumptions around the European Commercial Revolution.[12] His research is again revealing the intensity of local trade in the eleventh century, whether by ancient routes established in the Roman period or newly created, and again suggests that the economies of the early Middle Ages were not shaped by long-distance commerce of luxury goods but rather by local circulation of local products – activities which became more complex and more lucrative over the course of the late tenth to eleventh centuries, at which point specialisation, market production, and monetised commercial exchange increased. Wickham's view of the predominance of very low levels of exchange provides the clearest immediate context for the gardens in Italian cities. Low-value goods, travelling not very far but perhaps across regions, such as wine from hilly areas exchanged for grain on plains, were typical across Italy. Similarly, home-grown fruits

---

[9] Wickham, *Framing the early Middle Ages*, pp. 709–13, 718–20.
[10] Wickham, *Framing the early Middle Ages*, pp. 728–42.
[11] Wickham, *Framing the early Middle Ages*, p. 733ff.
[12] Wickham, *Medieval Rome*; Wickham, 'The Donkey and the Boat: Rethinking Mediterranean Economic Expansion in the Eleventh Century' (public lecture: Padua, Kalamazoo, Birmingham, publication forthcoming); for the traditional view, see Violante, *La società milanese*.

and vegetables augmented crops grown at scale outside cities, in communities with very low levels of exchange.

Exploitation and Ownership

Land was worked, animals were fed, and field crops were grown for peasant farmers and for landlords. In Italy there was a vast range of ownership beneath the highest rank of individuals and institutions such as major monasteries, down to peasants who owned fragments of plots, and tenants who worked the land of others. Agricultural estates themselves, whatever their size, often comprised many different parcels of land, not all of which were contiguous and which were often relatively fluid, as pieces were sold off, given away, or acquired through purchase or swaps.[13] Over generations of partible inheritance as well as the diverse fortunes of individual landholders or institutions, the landscape of property in Italy was a patchwork of scattered plots and owners. In most parts of Italy, aristocrats and aristocratic institutions such as monasteries were regional figures, with landholdings which spread over a city and its hinterlands and not much beyond. It was relatively rare that people owned land portfolios beyond their region; some large monasteries did, but very few.[14] Land was a source of wealth as well as valuable as social capital and for forging new social bonds; the commercial value of crops, such as it might have been, was only of small benefit.

Estates (called manors, demesnes, *curtes*, or peasant holdings in the extensive scholarly literature which exists on the topic), farms, and smallholdings were worked in a number of ways. They could be farmed by individual owners, by renting tenants who paid in cash or in kind as well as performing regular service, or by unfree labourers, and most probably a combination of different labour systems.[15] One key to the durability of this system was its fluidity, encompassing a range of different landscapes and growing conditions within a region as well as a range of working conditions. Thus, one family's holdings may have comprised areas that were wooded, for nuts and pigs as well as timber and firewood, planted with orchards and vines, and ploughed for cereals. There were surely also crops of onions, cabbages, and fruits for everyone, and there were household gardens in the villages where the people who worked these lands

---

[13] Toubert, *Dalla terra ai castelli*; Andreolli and Montanari, *L'azienda curtense*.
[14] Wickham, *Framing the early Middle Ages*, pp. 216–17; Marazzi, 'San Vincenzo al Volturno tra VIII e IX secolo'.
[15] Wickham provides a very clear overview of the diverse practices and the complications of our evidence attesting to them: *Framing the early Middle Ages*, pp. 293–301, 387–92, with references to relevant literature; Balzaretti, 'The curtis, the archaeology of sites of power'.

lived. Compared to what had come before in antiquity (estates worked by slaves, tenants, or hired men for market sale) and what was to come later in the central Middle Ages (signorial estates worked for landlord consumption and market sale), early medieval estates were not particularly intensively farmed or controlled, perhaps because there was no large-scale, long-distance market for their produce, with perhaps the exception of wine in Francia.[16] This is not to say that major estates were closed, self-sufficient economic entities; the idea of closed estate units has been overturned. Recent research has pointed to the onward redistribution of produce for very large estates in Francia, undermining the rhetorical value of self-sufficiency that pervades those textual sources.[17] In Italy, only a few landlords controlled extensive agricultural enterprises; the royal monastery of Bobbio controlled a 'chestnut empire' by the late tenth century; the monastery was able to move the surplus of chestnuts on to market or to redistribute them by drying them. Chestnuts went firstly through their extensive network of dependents and secondly through outlets for onward sale in cities such as Genoa.[18] Beyond these networks of exceptionally large monasteries, however, there were relatively few mechanisms for marketisation of agricultural products, and hardly any for fresh, perishable fruits and vegetables. Over the later ninth and tenth centuries, concessions for markets increased, as intensification in estate management increased, as we shall see. However, cultivation for sale did not constitute the principal mode of working land.

Autonomy and Dependence

One of Wickham's arguments in *Framing the early Middle Ages* was that the seventh and eighth centuries were, in most parts of the West, marked by greater peasant autonomy than before, and this argument about autonomy speaks to the ways in which household food production fit into wider economic systems. Wickham's argument runs as follows: the end of the Roman taxation system, estate slavery, the weakening of major landowners, and the absence of any other entity to extract surplus so efficiently from working the lands and moving goods meant that those who controlled production, even just on their own patch, were better off.

---

[16] Wickham, *Framing the early Middle Ages*, p. 536; on the later period of reclamation and manorial systems, see Jones, 'Medieval agrarian society in its prime'.

[17] Wickham, *Framing the early Middle Ages*, p. 289; Verhulst, *The Carolingian economy*, esp. ch. 7; Devroey, *Économie rurale*.

[18] On chestnuts, see Squatriti, *Landscape and change*, pp. 183–5. Bobbio's early medieval estates and the immunities and advantages the monks enjoyed by royal concession were so large that the monastery probably always redistributed the surplus, even in the early Middle Ages.

Post-Roman territories, including and especially Italy, became 'a world of villages' which were organised by 'territorial forms of cooperation';[19] lands were worked by tenants who could keep the fruits of their labour after their rent was paid, and by people somewhere on the spectrum between free and unfree. The fragmentary landscape of properties allowed and perhaps even encouraged peasants without landlords (smallholders), and it also allowed kin groups (or other kinds of groups) to work together on plots of land, sharing risk and profit.[20] The models that Wickham develops for the simplification of structures for agricultural labour and extraction of surplus to a more autonomous means served as a 'springboard' to Peter Sarris and Jairus Banaji and others to reassess the social economies of peasants in a special volume of the *Journal of Agrarian History* in 2009. Sarris noted that when both tenant and landlord lived off the produce of an estate, the degree of exploitation of the tenant is practically invisible to us now in the material record, and Wickham's peasant autonomy may very well have been an intensely exploitative system.[21] Documents have been more helpful to us here than the material evidence. Alice Rio's recent work on slavery after Rome has shown that the contracts for work on estates in Italy, whether by free or unfree workers, do not align directly with the size of estates or the location of the lands. Nor is it the case that status distinctions along the spectrum between free and un-free become more fixed in the context of greater need for workers. In Italy, work obligations of tenants did not strictly correlate to the territory farmed; some small estates commanded huge numbers of working tenants. Rio suggests that greater insistence on workers' obligations on a given estate may have corresponded to greater need for agricultural work, as it did in Francia, or it may reflect a landowner's need to assert political dominance over a territory.[22] There probably was greater peasant autonomy in early medieval Italy than there had been previously, and the work that peasants did served in part to produce crops for consumption – obviously – but also to establish the status of the landowner. Equally, the 'cost' of land in a transaction did not relate to a fixed relationship between money and commodity, affected by market behaviours. Rather, prices and rents related to social relations between agents. Seventy years ago, Karl Polanyi and other substantivists argued for contextualising economic practices within social rather than market terms, and in particular, for separating the elite money economies of long-distance commerce from

---

[19] Wickham, *Framing the early Middle Ages*, pp. 514–18, 560.
[20] See Wickham, *Early medieval Italy*, pp. 119–22 on *consortes* and extended kin-groups.
[21] Sarris, 'Introduction', pp. 7–8.   [22] Rio, *Slavery after Rome*, pp. 200–6, esp. p. 202.

local economies.²³ These principles clearly describe the fluidity of work obligations and land value, and point to the factors governing the movement of goods being social rather than market.

For the most part, in early medieval Italy people lived near or on lands they worked, and the systems for marketizing or exploiting agricultural work were flexible but not particularly complicated. Marios Costambeys has argued that in central Italy, while dispersed settlement was indeed the most typical arrangement of peasant workers on the ground, there was nonetheless a strong hierarchical thrust to the movement of surplus. That is, the wealthy monastery of Farfa owned the lands that were rented or worked by dependents, and the monastery received cash or – more probably – its equivalent in agricultural produce as rent; the monastery then paid tribute or rent on some of its lands to the Roman church.²⁴ He explored the implications of this fact for the independence of the peasantry; I believe it also tells us about directions of exchange towards cities and its motors. The agglomerated 'villages' in which many Italian peasants lived after about 600, both in the areas later owned by Farfa and throughout the peninsula, were still strongly attached to urban centres or to one of the handful of major monasteries which acted as quasi-urban centres of consumption.

This system of working the land and feeding people, whether it was the independent peasants who thrived on their own surplus or the peasants left hungry by the extractions of their landlords, was by 800 the principal organisation of agrarian work. There was very little flow of agricultural goods towards markets, though there was redistribution of produce through networks of obligation and patronage. Only in the tenth century did established and regular markets emerge; these are visible to us in the increase for market concessions. From the mid tenth century onwards, new poles emerged in the form of rural castles and their lords; in the south this happened in the eleventh century with the Norman reorganisation of the landscape. These new rural centres acquired marketing rights and immunities from tolls and dues, which increased the mechanism for redistributions outside of the original household or estate networks. It is the expansion of rights of marketing and tolls beginning under Berengar, king of Italy from 888 to 915, and continuing throughout the tenth century, which signals the reorganisation of production towards marketing and – in the late tenth century – market specialisation of production.

---

[23] Polanyi et al., *Trade and market*; Hann and Hart, *Market and society*. See also Grierson, 'Commerce in the Dark Ages'. Richard Hodges, in particular, helped to make substantivism influential in the studies of early medieval economies. Hodges, *Dark Age economics*. See review of this discussion in *Dark Age economics: a new audit*, pp. 20–1.

[24] Costambeys, 'Settlement'; Costambeys, *Power and patronage*.

At that point, and really not before, were there agricultural specialisms which attest to market-scale production.[25] Up to that point, garden produce was always, whether in the countryside or in the city, a product for household consumption because of the relative infrequency or even absence of structures for marketing that were robust enough to permit the exchange of fresh food.

Markets

The change from a robust system of market-scale production (for the producer) and access to markets for purchasing goods (for the consumer) in the Roman period to their absence in the early Middle Ages constituted a major social and economic transformation in daily life for people in early medieval Italy. It had been typical of the whole of the Roman empire, and certainly of Italy, to have markets spread across rural and urban cycles and through temporal cycles, so that there were rural periodic markets distributing goods on a regional level and fixed, daily urban markets which met the quotidian needs of the urban populace and might have included, in cities, specialist products and luxury goods.[26] In antiquity, urban markets of foodstuffs necessarily depended on regional supply networks, and we have seen the evidence for zones of regional supply of agricultural products around Rome.[27] For the imperial period, creating a new market was a public right, just as the concession to levy sales from markets and other tolls associated with mercantile activity.[28] As anthropologists have long reminded us, markets were places not only for commercial exchange but also for interaction between communities, and they were tools of the state.[29] In the Roman empire, control of urban markets, from exaction of tolls to stabilising prices to regulating merchants, had been a key apparatus of the state; rural periodic markets similarly disseminated state regulations throughout a territory, and rural fairs were occasions for the convening of vendors and buyers from different regions and social groups.[30] How did these mercantile institutions weather the transformations of the early Middle Ages, and how does the urban cultivation

---

[25] For documentary evidence for crop specialization for market-scale production see Chapter 3, pp. 94, 100 (cucurbits at Rome and Palermo).
[26] Shaw, 'Rural markets' remains relevant; De Ligt, *Fairs and markets*.
[27] See Chapter 2, pp. 45 ('Urbs Roma').
[28] Gabba and Coarelli, *Mercati e fiere*, p. 153. On the emergence of tolls, see the Novel of Valentinian, 'De siliquarum exactionibus', *Codex Theodosianus* vol. II, pp. 99–100; De Ligt, *Fairs and markets*, pp. 167–74.
[29] For the Roman period, see Ker, 'Nundinae', p. 385; De Ligt, *Fairs and markets*, pp. 9–25.
[30] Shaw, 'Rural markets'; Gabba, *Mercati e fiere*; Lo Cascio, *Mercati permanenti*; De Ligt, *Fairs and markets*.

Marketing in Late Antiquity

Late antiquity brought significant changes to Italian agricultural markets. Some of these changes have been discussed, namely the shifts in the *annona* system and the enfeeblement of state-supported merchant networks in the fifth century.[31] While the *annona* system increasingly relied on contributions from within Italy to feed Rome, regional networks of exchange continued into late antiquity. It has been argued that late Roman commercial activity happened less and less in fixed daily markets in cities, shifting increasingly to weekly markets and rural fairs.[32] Markets and levies on their goods were sources of income; the larger the market and the higher the value of the goods exchanged, the more the income to the town, church, or private individual who held the concession. Cassiodorus describes the commerce at a rural fair near *Consilinum* (today, Padula in the province of Salerno). The market was held on the feast day of Saint Cyprian, 14 September, and on offer were slaves, livestock, and textiles, 'notable exports of industrious Campania, or wealthy Bruttium, or Calabria rich in cattle, or prosperous Apulia, [and] with the products of Lucania herself' in 'meadows gleaming with the loveliest of market-stalls', but apparently no permanent public buildings.[33] Sam Barnish has linked Cassidorus's description of the rural richness of southern Italy, Lucania in particular, to Cassiodorus's rhetorical flair on the one hand and a burst of wealth based on the rising value of pork in the fifth century on the other.[34] There were pigs being processed on vast scale at the villa of S. Giovanni di Ruoti, at a point when there was more coinage in circulation, and there were fluctuations in prices of pork, relating to needs of the cities of Rome and Naples and/or Ravenna.[35]

After this possible peak in the pork market, there was an overall decrease in the scale and diversity of commodities exchanged in Italy after the sixth century. All monetary systems – rents in cash, taxes in cash, gold and silver coinage, and credit – contracted.[36] Every kind of market system became increasingly geared towards relative self-

---

[31] See pp. 118–20.
[32] Cracco Ruggini, *Economia e società*, pp. 305–6; De Ligt, *Fairs and markets*, p. 64.
[33] Cassiodorus, *Variae* VIII. 33, pp. 340–2; Barnish, 'Pigs, plebeians and potentes', p. 171; Harper, *Slavery in the late Roman world*, p. 98.
[34] Barnish, 'Pigs, plebeians and potentes', pp. 172–4. See now Grey, 'Landowning and labour in the rural economy'.
[35] Barnish, 'Pigs, plebeians and potentes', pp. 172–4.
[36] For a bird's-eye view of the Roman economy, see Hopkins, 'Rent, taxes, trade and the city of Rome'.

sufficiency, cities from their immediate hinterlands, and institutions from their landholdings, and households from their gardens. The model of the ancient consumer city, drawing upon the produce of its hinterlands, remained somewhat relevant for the provisioning of cities with bulk staples such as grain, oil, and wine, yet without the robust and regular markets through which city-dwellers purchased fresh food, agricultural produce was distributed by other means.[37] New research has emphasised the roles played by courts and religious institutions in redistribution networks, pointing to monastic centres as drivers of both production and consumption, and the interest played by elites in controlling exchange.[38] This research has perhaps overemphasized the economic centrality of monasteries beyond the mega-institutions with royal immunities, and undervalued the resilience of cities and the roles played by household-level networks based in cities.

Rural Markets

If there was a move in the later Roman period towards commercial exchange in periodic regional markets in Italy, as suggested by Barnish and others, we might look there for evidence of early medieval commerce.[39] Evidence for regional markets only appears in our records in the mid eighth to ninth centuries, particularly visible when Carolingian rulers on the one hand consolidated regulations around pre-existing markets, and on the other hand created new markets in predominantly rural locations. Thus, for example, in 843 Lothar confirmed the possessions of the canons of Arezzo, including three *villae* (estates) and a market on the feast of Saint Ilariano (16 July), presumably near the rural estates.[40] The *villae* were given by a laywoman; perhaps the market had been a privately sponsored place of exchange previously, and then after the donation to the church any profits gained in terms of tolls for marketing were to be given to the church. Louis II confirmed several rights of the pieve (rural) church of S. Lorenzo (near Cremona) including the rights for boats to come and for markets to be held along the Delma and the

---

[37] Wickham, *The mountains and the city*, pp. 144–7, stressing that rural rents came into the city, in whatever form.
[38] For the state of the question in 1995: Balzaretti, 'Cities and markets'; see now Hodges, *Dark Age economics: a new audit*, chapter 4.
[39] See p. 125.
[40] 'per decretum suae sanccionis ditaverit villas scilicet tres, quae Durna, Speia, atque Plica nominantur quasque Burgundis matrona et Elbungus eidem ecclesiae contulerunt, nec non et mercatum annualem unum, qui in missa sancti Hilariani celebrator', *DLoI* 79 (843), discussion in Catini, 'Dall'economia complessa', p. 183.

Oglio rivers.[41] Place names also attest to villages or rural markets, so that in 745 we find mention of Uicomercado (i.e. *Vicus mercati*, now Vimercate, near Milan), the name indicating that it was a market village.[42] In 837, a document for the monastery of Monte Amiata was transacted at 'the market of S. Silvestro' in a very remote part of Tuscany, and in 892, another agreement was enacted 'in the market of Sesto Calende' near Milan.[43] New rural markets were also created, such as the markets of S. Silvestro and S. Ottaviano that Lothar I permitted the bishop of Volterra to build in a remote area in the mid ninth century.[44]

Over the early Middle Ages, the right to hold a market became less a public right of rulers and increasingly an asset, a source of income and authority for the person (or institution) who held the concession. King Berengar, who struggled to rule the late Carolingian kingdom of Italy in the late ninth and early tenth centuries, gave away rights that were traditionally a source of royal income.[45] He ceded rights to hold markets to dozens of bishops and abbots for markets at pieve churches or monasteries. Churches were awarded the tolls collected for circulation of goods at cities, and market tolls for ports on riverbanks, all in an effort to garner support.[46] Thus in 919 Berengar permitted Bishop Dagibertus of Novara to hold annual markets at S. Agabio on the first of September, a weekly market (on Saturday), and annually on 24 October at the pieve of Gozzano ('on the Feast of Saint Giuliano, when his bones, in that pieve, are known to vibrate').[47] Castles erected in the countryside could have markets, and bishops and abbots could hold markets annually, monthly, or weekly.[48] He assured the church of Bologna that transport between Po and Reno was safe and 'permitted all men and merchants with their boats and goods to come calmly and tranquilly'.[49] These concessions were clearly a desirable privilege and afforded income to the beneficiaries,

---

[41] *Le carte cremonesi*, ed. Falconi, vol. I, 14 (852).
[42] *CDL* vol. I, 82 (745). For a market at that place, see *DBI* 104 (911–15), pp. 269–70 and discussion in Settia, 'Per foros italiae'.
[43] 'Actum in mercato S. Silvestri', *Codex diplomaticus amiatinus* vol. I, 114 (837), p. 230; 'Actum in Sexto Mercado', *CDL* vol. III, 357 (892).
[44] *DLoI* 164 (822–5) (829–45); we know of these from a confirmation by Louis II.
[45] See further discussion of Berengar in Chapter 6.
[46] See, for example, *DBI* 52 (905), pp. 149–151 to the port of Treviso.
[47] 'ut eodem modo largiremur facultatem exequendi ebdomadalem mercatum, scilicet per omnem sabbatum, in quadam plebe [Gaudiano] memorati Novariensis episcopii et annuale [quoque in eodem loco] non kalendarum novembrium, it est per omnem festivitatem beatissimi Iuliani Christi confessoris cuius ossa in ipsa plebe miraculis coruscare dinoscuntur', *DBI* 123 (919), pp. 319–22.
[48] For example, *DBI* 43 (904), pp. 124–7, *DBI* 94 (902–13), pp. 249–50, *DBI* 102 (911–5) pp. 266–8, *DBI* 106 (912–5) pp. 273–4.
[49] 'sed liceat omnibus hominibus atque mercationibus cum suis navibus et supellectilibus quiete et tranquille venire', *DBI* 63 (905), pp. 172–3. For a broader picture of the

otherwise they would not have been a useful tool for Berengar. As we have seen in Chapter 3, Berengar's distribution of agricultural properties, mills, and these privileges for marketing were a strategy of his rule.

The strategic allocation of the rights of rural markets was exploited not only by Berengar nor only in the Po valley. Francesca Rapone assembled references to markets and their concessions in Northern Italy, identifying three in the eighth century, twenty-nine in the ninth, and eighty-three in the tenth.[50] These figures indicate an increased number of markets or, perhaps, an increased interest in bringing existing markets into regulations and an intensifying interest in documenting these practices; the evidence probably reflects both.

Cities and Their Markets

A central tenet of the historical narratives of the European Middle Ages is the rise of cities and interregional commerce in Europe, the formation of the European economy of the mid eleventh century and later.[51] Urban centres in Italy were greater in number and in scale than elsewhere in Europe and – it has been claimed – exerted a uniquely strong force on the agronomy of medieval Italy.[52] Despite a concentration of evidence from urban contexts, textual references to urban markets are exiguous before the ninth century. In Rapone's study of northern Italy, the 115 recorded concessions of market rights in northern Italy were predominantly for urban entities: bishops as individuals or the churches of a city; monasteries, both urban and rural, received concessions, too, and after 893, individuals (Fig. 22). As we have seen, the location of those markets was not urban, though it may have been suburban. Otto III gave to the bishop of Pistoia 'open land, where the market of this city is', presumably outside the city.[53] In ninth-century Salerno, markets and fairs were held at the suburban *Carbonarium* (where the charcoal was

---

commerce of the Po valley, see Gelichi, 'Dal delta del Po'; Gelichi et al., 'The history of a forgotten town'.

[50] Rapone, 'Il mercato nel Regno d'Italia'. Cf. the tables of Settia, who found references to rural markets in Northern Italy: eighth century, two; ninth century, nineteen; tenth century, fifty-eight; eleventh century, fifty-one. When considering only the evidence for newly established markets, he revealed a peak in the creation of new markets in the tenth century, pointing to greater support for – and control of – market activity among later Carolingian rulers of Italy: Settia, 'Per foros Italiae'.

[51] Lopez, *The commercial revolution*.

[52] Jones, 'Medieval agrarian society in its prime'; Toubert, 'La vita agraria nel medioevo'; Jones, 'Per la storia agraria italiana'.

[53] 'terram vacuam ubi mercatum est ipsius civitatis', *DOIII* 284 (998), pp. 709–10.

Cities and Their Markets

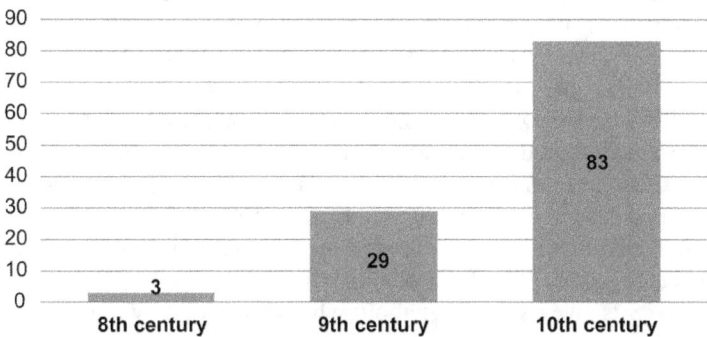

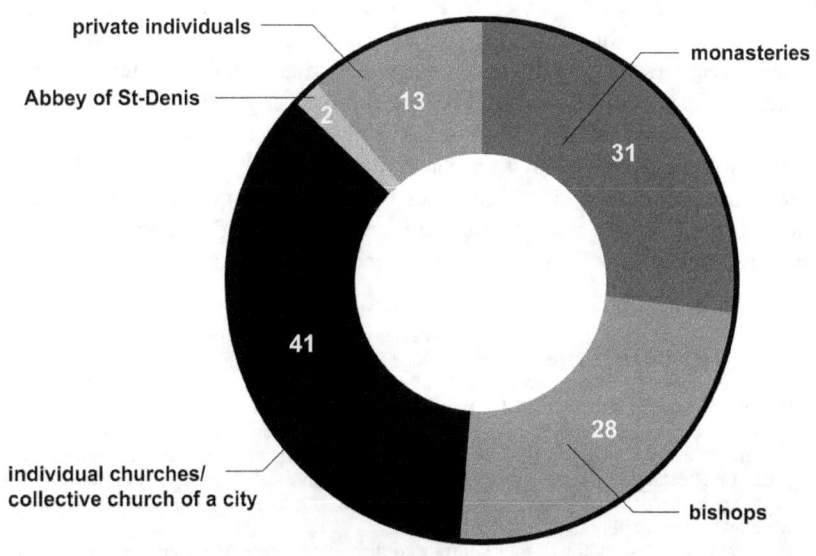

Figure 22 Graph of market concessions in northern Italy. Data from Rapone, Il mercato nel Regno d'Italia.

made), and these were confirmed by the Normans who held 'foire et marchié' outside the walls.[54]

Urban markets, though mentioned far less frequently in our early medieval sources than the rural ones just discussed, were also created or brought into regulation by the Carolingians. Charlemagne in 812 gave to Ratold, bishop of Verona, the forum and market where the celebrations of S. Zeno were typically held.[55] Charlemagne also authorised the bishop of Piacenza to create a new annual market, and that right was confirmed by Louis the Pious in 819: 'Like the instruction of [our] lord and father ... the market which is annually held in that place on the thirteenth day of the month of November, all *teloneum* however much is paid to the aforementioned church with all is to be handed over together.'[56] Post-Carolingian rulers confirmed these rights.[57]

Marketing rights give us no clues about what was sold, how often, or to whom. Occasionally, glimpses of markets appear in narrative histories, such as the tale of Charlemagne's courtiers wearing exotic Eastern outfits brought by Venetians to Pavia whence they were sold to the Franks, but this passage comes with a moral warning about luxury dress rather than clear details about trade of luxury goods up the Po valley.[58] According to the *Life* of Gerald of Aurillac, who passed by Pavia in the early tenth century, it was in the fields outside the walls to the south-east that Venetian merchants and other foreigners pitched their tents and did their trading of textiles and spices.[59] His account is not, in this case, a moralising episode, and it might report, more or less accurately, a suburban place of luxury trading; the author certainly characterised Italy as a place of exotic goods. Mentions of luxury trade such as these and the glimpses of cumin and pepper going to the monastery of Bobbio from Comacchio and Venice, and salt and spices for the Cremonesi, also coming from Comacchio, have garnered a significant

---

[54] *CDC* vol. I, 44 (856); Amatus of Montecassino, *Historia Normannorum*, Book VIII, ch. 14, discussed in Delogu, *Mito di una città meridionale*, p. 114.

[55] 'forum et mercatum que anniversario die ad sollepnitatem Sancti Zenonis conuenire solet terciam partem ad integrum', *CDV* vol. I, 96 (?812), pp. 117–8.

[56] 'dominus et genitor ... quoddam mercatum quod annuatim tercio decimo die mensis november in ipso loco fieret, videlicet omne toloneum quidquid exinde exigitur ad predictam ecclesiam cum omni integritate cumcessisse', *Le carte piu antiche di S. Antonino* 5 (819). A document of 896 refers to the 'mercato puplico' of Piacenza, which was presumably urban; *CDP* 39 (896).

[57] For example, in 948, King Lothar I of Italy confirmed to Count Manfred a donation from Louis the Pious to Manfred's father, Berengar: a *corte* in the city of Parma with two monasteries and markets and all things pertaining to them: 'et cortem in Parma civitate cum duobus monasteriis ibidem hedificatis uno in honore Sancti Bartholomei, altero sancte Mariae et sancti Alexandri cum mercatis et eorum omnibus pertinentis', Drei, *Le carte degli archivi parmensi* vol. I, 55 (948).

[58] Notker, *Gesta Karoli Magni imperatoris*, c. 17, ed. Haefele, pp. 21–2.

[59] *Vita sancti Geraldi aureliacensis*, I, 27; Bullough, 'Urban change', p. 111. See also Settia, 'Pavia carolingia e postcarolingia', esp. pp. 114–8.

amount of attention and have driven the narrative that Italy was the principal point of entry for Mediterranean goods into mainland Europe.[60] The Italian peninsula may indeed have been a source of these products and also may have had more people engaged in trade than elsewhere in early medieval Europe, but the scale of this commercial activity has been, I think, exaggerated as has its significance for the means by which people fed themselves and their families. There are fragments of exotic textiles in Italian treasuries, but exceptionally little in the way of imported luxury pottery, for instance. (In Constantinople and the major cities of the caliphate, where luxury silks were produced, exceptionally fine tablewares were produced, but these practically never arrived in Italy.)[61] Cities and major monasteries were not the principal places of exchange; until the tenth century and later, most textual evidence for markets attests to rural sites. Archaeological evidence is limited, but it does echo the chronology of textual references to markets increasing over the course of the early Middle Ages.

Physical Structures of Marketplaces

What forms did the markets for which these rights were awarded take? Markets, and urban markets in particular, might have been practically invisible in the archaeological record. To take a modern parallel, we might consider the physical traces of a modern market. In the Campo de' Fiori, Rome, every day of the week except Sunday, there is a bustling market. There are fruits and vegetables from Lazio or from Sicily, sometimes imported from South America; there are fish, cheese, cut flowers, and dried spices; some days there are t-shirts, hats, and crockery; every day there seem to be more tourist tchotchkes for sale. At the end of each day, all of the stalls are taken away, the rubbish is collected, and there is no physical trace of the day's trading. There is no reason to imagine that the markets described in the sources just analysed were any different from the modern Campo de' Fiori. Indeed, there have been very few archaeological contexts which have permitted the identification of market stalls in early medieval cities, and very few references in textual sources which permit us to recognise structures.

Milan: Excavations inside the Biblioteca Ambrosiana, at Milan, identified Roman paving which was interpreted by the excavators as the

---

[60] Bobbio Polyptych of 862 in *Inventari altomedievali*, ed. Castagnetti, pp. 130, 132; discussion in McCormick, *Origins of the European economy*, pp. 633–5. For the document, see now Laurent, 'Organisation de l'espace'.

[61] Three fragments of Egyptian lustre ware, dating from the mid eleventh century, were found at S. Vincenzo al Volturno, but these are too few and too late to suggest the travel of luxury goods in the early Middle Ages; Hodges and Patterson, 'San Vincenzo al Volturno and the origins of the medieval pottery industry in Italy', p. 23.

ancient forum. On its southern side, the paving bears signs of use in the early Middle Ages, perhaps wooden structures inserted into the stone pavement, as Giuliani suggested for Rome.[62] These finds are in the area of Quinquae viae; witness testimonies in early medieval documents suggest that merchants lived near the Quinquae viae, but as I have suggested, the high-status merchants who were identified as *mercatores* in our documents are probably not vendors running stalls but rather men brokering high-value sales.[63] References to the fixed location of a '*publicum mercatum*' appear in the documents from Milan of the mid tenth century: the emperor Otto gave to the monastery of S. Ambrogio five adjacent lots in the city of Milan 'in the place where the public market had been';[64] the same diploma includes a hall with its yard, in the market area, with stalls in it.[65]

Pavia: A merchant leased a structure for a shop in Pavia from the abbot of Nonantola: 'a shop with curtilage of the *ius* of S. Silvestro, Nonantula, inside Pavia in the Foro Cluso, with counter (or bench? *mensola*) in front and a common courtyard behind it, next to it on one side is the shop of the basilica S. Pietro *sita villa*, the other part, the shop of Ardenanus and Amalbertus, brothers, the third part the house of Leoninego and the above-mentioned common courtyard, the fourth side, the above-mentioned Foro Cluso, with use of the well'.[66] This description certainly suggests that there was an area for commercial activity at that point.

Rome: At Rome, cuts and holes in the travertine paving slabs of the Forum Romanum were interpreted by Giuliani as market stalls of the early Middle Ages, dated at some point between 608, when the Column of Phocas was renovated, and the eleventh century, when the entire

---

[62] Excavations reported in Ceresa Mori et al., 'Milano. Indagini'.

[63] Rapone, 'Il mercato nel Regno d'Italia', p. 77.

[64] 'concedimus, donamus atque largimur in coenobio beati Christi confessoris Ambrosii, ubi ejus venerabile corpus quiescit humatum, areas quinque terre juris regni nostri infra mediolanensem civitatem in loco, ubi publicum mercatum extat, conjacentes', *DOI* 145 (952) pp. 225–6.

[65] 'salam unam cum area in qua extat, similiter juris nostri regni infra prelibatam civitatem in pretaxato mercato sitam, cum stationibus in ibi banculas ante se habentibus', *DOI* 145 (952) pp. 225–6, discussion in Bocchi, 'Città e mercati', pp. 157–9.

[66] 'hoc est statione una cum area, in qua extat, juris predicti monasterii, quibus esse videntur intra hanc ticinensem civitatem in foro cluso, cum mensola de preposito ante se, et curticula comuna post se abente; ubi coerit ei de una parte staciona basilica sancti Petri sita Villa, de alia parte staciona Ardenani et Amalberti germanis, de tercia parte casa Leoninego et predicta curticula comuna, da quarta parte suprascripto foro cluso . . . cum usum putei', *CDLangobardiae* 393 (901). The editor of the document glosses *statione* as 'bottega', p. 658, note 1. On the Foro Cluso and the forum, see Bullough, 'Urban change', pp. 97, 110; Ward Perkins, *From classical antiquity*, p. 184; cf. Hudson, *Archeologia urbana*.

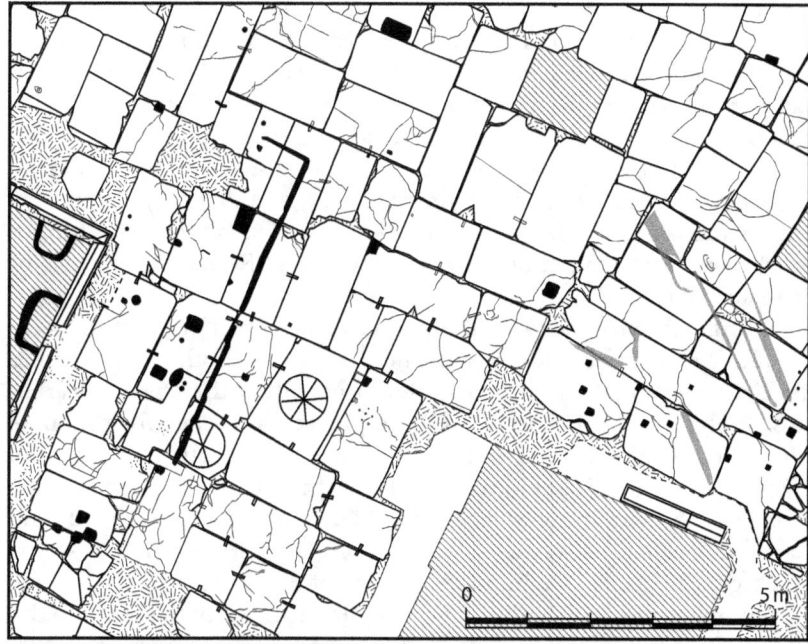

Figure 23 Pavement of Forum Romanum, with signs of medieval market stalls. Plan based on Giuliani, 'Una rilettura dell'area centrale del Foro Romano', fig. 211 and Giuliani and Verduchi, *L'area centrale del Foro romano*, tav. III.

pavement was covered by a thick colluvial deposit.[67] Given how difficult it is to find fixed-place urban markets anywhere in Italy before the tenth century, I would suggest that these structures on the Roman Forum should date from the later end of Giuliani's chronology (Fig. 23). One possible fixed selling place appeared in archaeology. Excavations at S. Angelo in Pescheria near the banks of the Tiber produced a tank and shells of mollusks, interpreted as a fishmonger's 'botteghina' prior to the eleventh century.[68] A famous story in Bede's *Ecclesiastical history* which recounts Gregory's encounter with 'English' slaves for sale is set in a forum, but it bears little concrete relation to mercantile activity in Rome.[69] In his 'Life of Gregory' (876), John the Deacon mentioned that the Jews selling their lovely wares remained outside of pontifical view, behind the curtain of a long portico, not on the stools/benches, as

---

[67] Giuliani, 'Una rilettura'.   [68] Ciancio Rossetto, 'Portico d'Ottavia', 421–2.
[69] Bede, *Historia ecclesiastica gentis Anglorum*, Book II, ch. 1, ed. and trans. Colgrave and Mynors, p. 132.

might have been normal, but on the marble pavement, not in view of the pope.[70] The passage continues with reference to the furs that Arsenius, then bishop of Orte (reg. 855–68), sought to wear in a procession. They had been purchased from Jews, and Pope Nicholas I (reg. 858–67) forbade his wearing them. The narrative context of the account of Jewish merchants in the portico at Rome might suggest that they should be understood as vendors of luxury merchandise, and that the Lateran was sort of marketplace within the city; but it is difficult to draw further conclusions about the structures of marketing at Rome on the basis of these accounts.

Parma: At Parma, in 948, there were markets run by the monasteries of S. Bartolomeo and SS. Maria e Alessandro, both located inside the city walls, and from the early eleventh century there was a market at S. Pietro.[71] For the latter, we have physical evidence for the marketing of fresh food. Excavations in Parma near S. Pietro *in foro* on the Piazza Garibaldi, at the site of the ancient forum of Parma, have revealed an urban marketplace (Fig. 24).[72] In excavations inside the Cassa di Risparmio (now Crédit Agricole), a long-running stratigraphic sequence cast light on the history of this Roman town, including a number of rubbish pits and a cess pit dating from the tenth to the eleventh century.[73] The plant remains from the medieval contexts were predominantly cultivated foodstuffs, including cereals, fruits, and leafy greens which were probably grown or foraged nearby. The pits provide a clear picture of what was available for purchase and what was consumed here at Parma. Some of the plant finds were waste products of processing, such as a high number of grape pips from wine production; others were fruit stones and seeds deposited in the latrine in faecal matter, or parts of plants discarded in eating or processing, such as cherry stones and peach pits; there were also animal bones and remains of meals. The mix of plants of different types strongly indicated to the excavators that they were dealing with a marketplace.

---

[70] 'omnes illius superstitionis homines quantumcunque pulcherrima mercimonia detulissent, numquam pontificalibus alloquiis fruerentur, numquam obtutibus apostolicis potirentur, sed extra velum longissimae porticus, non quidem in scamnis, sed in marmoreo pavimento sedentes, suscepta pretia numerabant, ne videlicet viderentur aliquid de manu pontificis accepisse', John the Deacon, 'Vita Gregorii', Book IV, *c.* 50, in *PL* 75, coll. 207C-D. I thank Shane Bobrycki for calling my attention to this passage and sharing his thoughts on the matter.

[71] 'de terra Santi Petri apostoli que est constructa ad honorem ipsius prope forum ubi mercationes sine cessatione agebitur', *Le carte degli archivi parmensi*, vol. II, 8 (*c.* 1005–15).

[72] Bosi et al., 'Seeds/fruits'.

[73] Bosi et al., 'Seeds/fruits'; Bosi et al., 'Indagini archeobotaniche'.

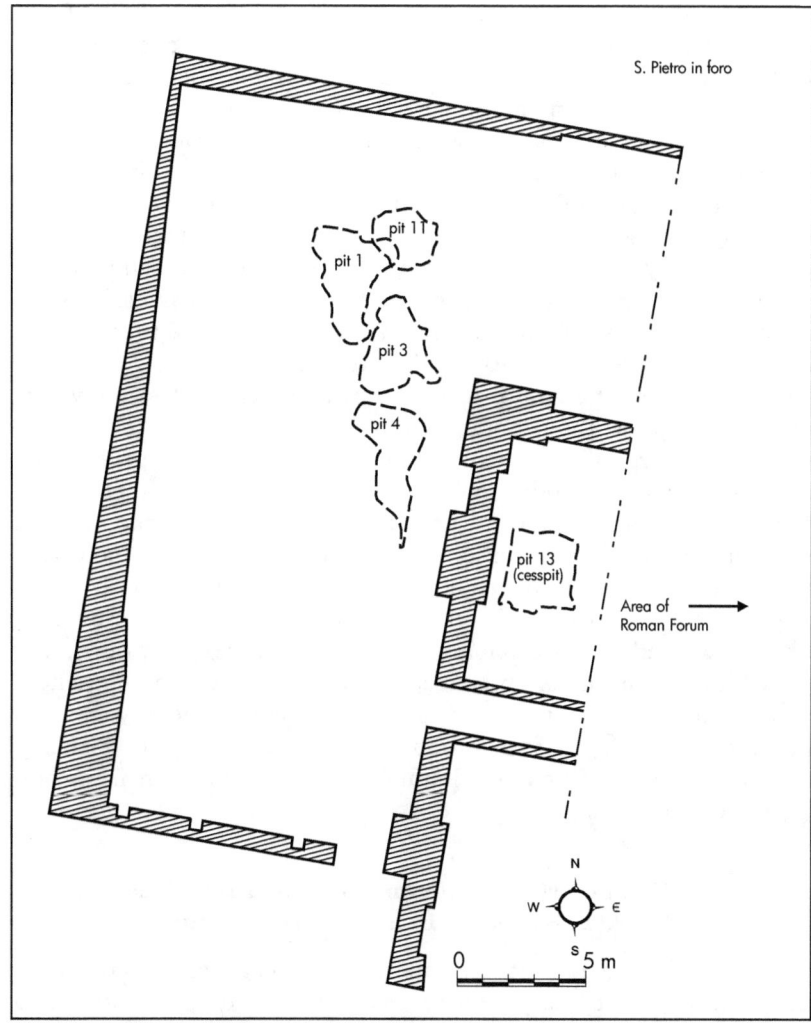

Figure 24 Plan of excavated pits inside the site of the Cassa di Risparmio, Piazza Garibaldi, Parma. Plan based on Bosi et al., 'Seeds/fruits, pollen and parasite remains', fig. 1.

Further excavation in the area revealed a wooden structure with a latrine, and the excavators suggested that perhaps this was the hut of the *brentatori*, the porters of wine *brente*, who were required by late medieval Parma statutes to stay next to the church of S. Pietro *in foro*, day and night.[74] The rubbish tips next to the hut included food, wooden cups, and some cooking pots, and that latrine again was full of seeds from easily acquired fresh fruits rather than dried fruits which might have been grown and processed elsewhere.

Examples of textual and archaeological sources from different parts of Italy suggest a relatively coherent picture of marketplaces within Italian cities from the beginning of the tenth century and later. There were designated places for commercial transactions before this, and these were temporary or ephemeral in terms of architecture, though they may have been fixed in terms of schedule. Urban stalls and marketplaces did not take the place of ones outside the city, which continued to increase in number over the tenth century, as we have seen.

When we view the rise of urban cultivation attached to individual households against the panorama of limited opportunities for marketing and little large-scale agriculture for market purposes, the centrality of household-scale production becomes clear. Unlike cities of the Roman period, and unlike cities of the eleventh century and later, as we shall see, people living in cities did not buy their fresh food from vendors in stalls or fixed markets. In a period of very low levels of exchange, in a place of relatively high density of urbanism, people were fed by an economy of gardens. There were, no doubt, many informal means of exchange; for instance, when one household had onions, and another had spinach. Clearly, there were also means of preserving garden produce by salting, drying, or pickling; but the centrality of household-scale production for fresh fruits and vegetables is obvious.

The End of Urban Gardening and the Rise of Markets and Market Gardening in the Eleventh Century

Scholars have long noticed the rapid pace of changes in agricultural activity in eleventh-century medieval Italy. This is traditionally attributed to a step-change in agricultural production, more efficient exploitation of labour, land, and water, as well as the introduction of some new crops. Urban consumers exerted a uniquely strong force on the agricultural economy of central and later medieval Italy, as Philip Jones and Pierre Toubert argued long ago.[75] In 1964, Jones made clear that from the tenth century, cities increasingly motivated agricultural production and

---

[74] Calvani, 'Iuxta Sanctum Petrum', pp. 209–11.
[75] Jones, 'Medieval agrarian society in its prime'; Toubert, 'La vita agraria nel medioevo'. On the eleventh century as a period of wider social and political change, see Violante and Fried, *Il secolo XI: una svolta?*

interregional exchange.[76] The model of increased rural productivity and concomitant increased exchange especially through urban networks is a key element of one of the principal historical narratives of the Middle Ages: the rise of cities and interregional commerce in Europe, the formation of the European economy of the twelfth century and later.[77] These changes, broadly speaking, brought an end to the phenomenon of household horticulture and urban gardening discussed in this book. Gardens did not disappear entirely; there continued to be cultivated spaces within city walls into the modern period. But there were fewer in the later Middle Ages, and what was there played a less critical role in urban food production as commercial gardening became more prevalent.

Professional gardeners are recognisable by their surnames in documents. The epithet or surname *hortulanus* appears infrequently before the eleventh century, compared to other surnames like smith or *medicus*.[78] A family group at Naples uses the name *hortulanus* in 935, suggesting that there were (at least a few) tradesman gardening in the city, and that the trade followed a family group.

Bonus *hortulanus* and his wife Eupraxia, son and daughter-in-law of Ursus *hortulanus*, called Pirindula, sold a house in Naples to Basilius, smith, and Marie his wife, son and daughter-in-law of Iohannes, smith and *maiorarius*(?), now a monk. The house, in the neighbourhood of Balnei nobi, had been acquired by a charter of sale from a certain Theodonanda, *honesta femina*, and Sergius, mother and son, widow and son of a certain Iohannes *militis*. And it touched in part [the property of] this couple and(?) that of Constantinus *hortulanus* and Maria, his wife, brother and sister-in-law of them, through division of a boundary, which the buyers replace.[79]

---

[76] See Jones, 'Per la storia agrarian italiana'; Cf. Toubert, 'La vita agraria nel medioevo', pp. 362–3 of the reprint edition.

[77] The classic expression of this position is Lopez, *The commercial revolution*; Hohenberg and Lees, *The making of urban Europe*, pp. 62–4, who argue that a medieval urban network system relied upon trading links between cities.

[78] In 721 Maurus *hortulanus* was a dependent of Wadulfus on a property at Ponticello (Benevento), and he and his family were ceded by Duke Romuald of Benevento to a monastery, *CSS* vol. II, 4 (721); Martin et al., *Regesti dei documenti dell'Italia meridionale* 234, p. 144. It might be significant that the *hortulanus* of the eighth century was a dependent or slave. On smiths at Naples, see Skinner, 'Urban communities in Naples,' pp. 291–5; on *medices*, see Pilsworth, 'Could you just sign this for me John?'.

[79] 'Bonus hortulanus et Eupraxia iugales, filius et nurua q. Ursi hortulani, qui nominatur Pirindula, vendunt et tradunt Basilio Ferrario et Marie iugalibus, filio et nurua q. d. Iohannis dudum Ferrarii et maiorarii, modo vero monachi, domum intus civitatem Neapolis in regione Balnei nobi ... que sibi obvenit per chartulas comparationis a q. Theodonanda h. f. et Sergio, genitricie et filio relicta et filio q. Iohannis militis, et ipsis iugalibus in portione tetigit a Constantino hortulano et maria, iugalibus, germano et cognata eorum per merissi divisionis, quam emptori remittunt', *RN* 27 (935), pp. 34–5.

None of the properties in this transaction specifically mention gardens, though Constantinus' neighbouring house has a *curticella* and there is a water pipe running down the public road. If they were professional gardeners they must have been living in the city but working land that was not simply the garden adjacent to their house. As with smiths in documents at Naples, it appears that the few men who were known as gardeners came to their trade through family relationships.

The clear and steady rise of what is recognisably market gardening in Italy starts at Rome around 1020. Crop specialisation emerges clearly in the documents as well as formal arrangements between professional *ortulani*, to be understood as fruit and vegetable farmers.[80] A remarkable document from 1030 records a private agreement among colleagues who established a *scola* of gardeners, its powers and terms of entry, its leader, and his powers.[81] The document attests the creation of a collective of eight men, none of them of aristocratic status (all *uiri honesti*), who agree to avoid actions which might be detrimental to each other's rights to do business as fruit and vegetable farmers. Other similar efforts to concentrate suburban cultivation for markets emerge elsewhere in the following decades. The island of Capri was intensively cultivated from the 1040s on to feed Amalfi and neighbouring towns, a day's sail away.[82] The value of suburban agricultural land increased in this period, where we can see it, and new lots were planted out. Contracts with tenants who bring land under cultivation were extremely common in Italy from the tenth century onwards.[83] Feniello notes a rise in the cost of, and the rates of acquisition of, agricultural lands in and around Naples (attested in the documents conserved at Naples) in the period from 1000 to 1040.[84] At Milan, the rise in land values begins in the late tenth century and continues to the mid eleventh.[85] The increase in value suggests a growing intensification of agriculture. In the countryside, the presence of castles in the eleventh century and the potential for production and processing in their networks increases, and this contributes to a reordering of regional systems of production and their specialisation, and thereby their trade.[86]

---

[80] Wickham, *Medieval Rome*, pp. 89–91; see also Moscati, *Alle origini del comune romano*.

[81] *SMVL* 57 (1030), pp. 72–4, see Hartmann, *Urkunde*; Moscati, *Alle origini del comune romano*, pp. 58–9; Wickham, *Medieval Rome*, p. 89.

[82] Skinner, *Medieval Amalfi*, p. 26.

[83] On *pastinatio* contracts, see Skinner, *Medieval Amalfi*, pp. 37–43; Andreolli, 'Contratti agrari'.

[84] Feniello, 'Alle origini di Napoli capitale'. Feniello did not consider agricultural properties within the walls among the data for prices listed on p. 575, note 45. It is worth noting that this change was not a steady rise; it sees a rise in the period 1000–40 and then a crash in both prices and acquisition circa 1050.

[85] Violante, *La società milanese*, pp. 129–37.

[86] Cantini and Grassi, 'Produzione, circolazione'.

Concurrently, the evidence for markets of all kinds, rural and urban, becomes much more abundant in the eleventh century. At Salerno, a diploma of Gisulf II for the archbishop Alfano, dated 1058, establishes a market on the *platea maior* in town.[87] While no earlier markets specialised in different kinds of products, in the eleventh century and subsequently, our sources refer not only to more markets but also separate markets for different products. At Rome there seems to have been a *macellum* at the Theatre of Marcellus already in 998, and a fish market a little further north certainly by the twelfth century if not before.[88] Rome was, of course, the largest city in Latin Europe in the tenth century, and its markets, when they begin to appear in the sources, stretched from the banks on the bend of the Tiber up to the Campidoglio.[89] In the late eleventh century there were market stalls in Amalfi, under control of the duke, 'where meats and fish are sold'.[90] A story in the Hebrew Chronicle of Ahimaaz (1054) seems to refer to a market at Venosa as the scene of a prank played upon a Jewish religious rabbinical teacher.[91] In several other Italian cities, it is possible to chart the rise of fixed markets, with stalls and eventually permanent structures sometimes under the control of the bishop, as at Pistoia, other times under the control of a monastery, as at Milan, starting in the eleventh century.[92]

At this point, urban gardening ceased to be such a critical source of fresh food for people in cities. Fixed markets became increasingly common, and market specialisation too. Urban gardens still existed, attached to some townhouses, but new stone forms of residential architecture in Italian cities, with street frontage and several stories, replaced the complexes of houses and gardens typical of the early Middle Ages. And the rise of fixed and regular marketing structures and systems brought about a change in the food provisioning of Italian cities, at which point the role of urban agriculture shifted, becoming less essential to urban foodways.

Having examined the radical changes in the ways in which fresh food, bulk goods, and other products moved from countryside to city in the early Middle Ages, the question of the role of money and coinage arises. If markets were annual or periodic, and they become robust and regular

---

[87] Delogu, *Mito di una città meridionale*, p. 123, note 41.
[88] 'macellum sub Templo Marcelli', Manaresi 236, discussion in Wickham, *Medieval Rome*, pp. 126–7.
[89] Wickham, *Medieval Rome*, p. 127; Moscati, *Alle origini del comune romano*, pp. 39–40 on multiple markets.
[90] Schwarz, 'Regesta amalfitana', p. 11; Skinner, *Medieval Amalfi*, p. 73.
[91] *Chronicle of Ahimaaz*, trans. Salzman, pp. 67–8.
[92] Alongside the evolution of marketplaces and their spatial signatures, there was a rising interest in the cultural and moral issues of exchange, recently analysed by Dennis Romano, *Markets and marketplaces*, and James Norrie for Milan, Norrie, 'Land and cult'.

only towards the end of our period, this might go some way to explaining the nature of the coins in use in early medieval Italy, such as they are; for the seventh to tenth centuries a *denarius*, or a *mancus*, might buy a sheep or a portion of an annual crop, rather than a chicken or a sack of onions.

Money and Its Circulation

Prior to 700, there was wide circulation of coins in a trimetallic system based on the late Roman denominations, decreasing in quantity and variety over that period, but circulating none the less. After about 700, in Italy, there is a stark contrast between the frequency of coins attested in written sources, suggesting highly monetised, economically vibrant societies, and the scarcity of coins in the archaeological record, whether as single finds or hoards.[93] Charters refer to rents, purchases of goods and slaves, or paying fines (or threatening them), and historians have been happy to believe that when charters mention coins, coins are what were used in transactions.[94] Archaeologists, however, are less inclined to believe in the pervasiveness of actual money. Urban and rural settlements of eighth- and ninth-century Italy are characterised by the rarity or, indeed, in some cases total absence of coin finds, whether as hoards or single coin finds. This picture is further complicated by the presence of coins from Italian mints, especially silver *denarii* from the *Regnum Italiae*, outside of Italy. Let us consider each of these issues in turn, in relation to the question of exchange of every-day goods.

The trimetallic system of the late Roman and early Byzantine empires limped along in Italy until the early to mid eighth century, with very debased coins being produced at Rome and coins from Byzantine mints arriving in Italy. Lombard and Byzantine Italy was bimetallic up to the 740s, and Byzantine coins from Constantinople, Carthage, Syracuse, and Rome arrived and circulated in parallel to Italian coins.[95] All of this is true up to the mid eighth century, and then there were practically none.[96]

Nonetheless documents of sale, exchange, and rent, as well as settlements of dispute and the occasional will, were produced in Italy by professional scribes or notaries from about 700 on, with increasing

---

[93] On hoards in particular, see Rovelli, 'I tesori monetali'.
[94] In an early article, Wickham claimed on the basis of one dispute, resolved to the effect that a document attested to payment in coin, and thus payment was in coin, that 'we can conclude that when Lombard charters mention coins, coins are what were used in transactions', 'Economic and social institutions', p. 28; his more recent work on the subject is less optimistic.
[95] Rovelli, 'Some considerations', p. 200 and passim; for the well-studied case of Luni, see Bertino, 'Monete attestate a Luni'.
[96] Rovelli, 'Some considerations', p. 205.

frequency over the course of the early Middle Ages. These documents use money as payment for purchases, rent, as value of items inventoried, and as sanctions for failing to honour the transaction and show considerable consistency regionally. And so Lombard and Byzantine documents refer to gold *tremisses/solidi*; documents in Carolingian areas refer to *denarii*, or *libri* of silver; throughout Italy, about 100 documents from the late eighth and ninth centuries refer to dinars *mancosi*, or Arab gold coins.[97] These documents all pertain to transactions of medium to high value, and while they reflect broad patterns of regional systems of coinage, they cannot inform about transactions of everyday goods, nor can we generalise from them about exchange.[98] They probably also do not refer to actual coins in our period.

The archaeological record reveals a perhaps startling lack of coins in Italy. At Farfa, a major early medieval monastery in central Italy, with documents attesting to use of *solidi* and *mancusi* in the eighth to tenth centuries, 178 coins were recovered, none of them dating from the eighth to tenth centuries.[99] At S. Vincenzo al Volturno, another huge monastery excavated over twenty years, with contracts citing payments in coins throughout the ninth century, 5 *denarii* were recovered.[100] In the extensive excavations at Milan for the new underground line, 500 coins have been recovered, none of them a Carolingian-period *denarius*; Milan was, it is worth recalling, one of the Carolingian mints of Italy.[101] One *denarius* of Milan was found at Brescia, none among the 1191 coins recovered in excavations at S. Giulia, a major royal monastery.[102] At Rome, among the 2,000 coins recovered in the excavations at the Crypta Balbi, 1 *denarius* minted by the papal mint was found.[103]

The situation is different in cities of the South, where a few coins from Constantinople circulated. At Otranto, in the area of Italy that was still notionally collecting taxes for Constantinople, there were 332 coins recovered in excavations from antiquity to the early modern period; 45 of them were bronze *folles* minted in Constantinople between 829 and 945.[104] While still relatively few, there are nonetheless more

---

[97] Rovelli, 'Circolazione monetaria e formulari notarili'; see now Prigent, 'Le *mythe du mancus*'.
[98] Rovelli, 'Some considerations', pp. 211–12. On coin finds in relation to coin usage, see Casey, *Understanding ancient coins* and now Burström, 'Money, coins, and archaeology'.
[99] The coins from the Farfa excavations were never published; Rovelli cites pers. comm. Hodges: 'Some considerations', p. 209.
[100] One of Salerno and four of Benevento; Arslan, *Repertorio dei ritrovamenti*, p. 89.
[101] Cited in Rovelli, 'Some considerations', p. 208.
[102] Arslan, *Repertorio dei ritrovamenti*, p. 70.
[103] Rovelli, 'Monete, tessere e gettoni'; see now Fusconi, *Gli antiquiores romani*.
[104] Travaglini, 'Le monete'.

bronze coins in Southern Italy than elsewhere and some sense of long-distance movement of people and money. At the Lombard shrine of Monte S. Angelo, upon the coast of the Adriatic, 120 ancient and medieval coins came from excavation and inventories of the shrine, of which 9 date from the ninth to eleventh centuries, all bronze coins from Constantinople.[105] Notably, political boundaries between Lombard, Byzantine, and Latin city-states do not correspond to circulation of coinage.

Few coins from Italy have been found beyond the peninsula. Scholars are divided about the relevance of those coins from Italian mints recovered outside of Italy. Some have argued that the relatively high proportion of Italian coins in some coin hoards points to extensive use of Italian money beyond its borders, evidence for interregional commerce across the Alps through Carolingian-controlled passes such as Aosta–Great St Bernard.[106] McCormick showed that several hoards in the Rhine-Meuse area (where he sees a new commercial route through Europe) contain high proportions of Italian coins, both Lombard and Byzantine gold productions, which clearly travelled alongside Arab coins.[107] Given issues around the reporting of metal-detectoring in countries where it is illegal (most of continental Europe), it is not useful to discuss single-coin finds or patterns of loss attested by single coins, though there are considerably more early medieval coin hoards north of the Alps in Francia than in Italy. There are high percentages of Italian coins in some hoards, but there are also a great many hoards with very few or no Italian coins. Alessia Rovelli has argued that in the broad panorama of coin hoards, the percentage of Italian coins found in Francia is probably only about 5 per cent of all recovered coins.[108]

Whichever way you look at it, there were relatively few coins made and used in Italy in the eighth, ninth, and tenth centuries, fewer than the period before 700, fewer than contemporary Francia, and fewer than contemporary Islamicate North Africa. Extensive and consistent production and use of Italian coinage is attested archaeologically only from the very late twelfth century, except for in the far south of the peninsula on the coast and Sicily.[109] Despite the almost complete absence of coin loss (single-coin finds) for the ninth to twelfth centuries across Italy, the documentary record, nonetheless, attests coinage as a system for

---

[105] Siciliano, 'Rinvenimenti monetali'.
[106] For example, Coupland, 'Charlemagne and his coinage', p. 449.
[107] Such as these (using his numbering): A 5 Biebrich (Germany); B 9 Colombier (France); A 35 Steckborn (Switzerland); A 23. McCormick, *Origins of the European economy*, p. 361. On these see now Rovelli, 'Some considerations'; Rovelli, 'Addenda and corrigenda', pp. 4–5.
[108] Rovelli, 'Addenda and corrigenda', p. 4. [109] Rovelli, 'La circolazione monetaria'.

Money and Its Circulation 143

medium- to high-value exchanges, with strong regional patterns for their use. Depending on the property, a few *denari* or *solidi* could pay rent for a year, and the purchasing power of the coins varied considerably based on the relationships and social status of the individuals involved in the transaction.

Economists and Roman historians alike tend to be snide about the economic viability of monometallic or single denominations. Michael Crawford remarked that 'a coinage-system which is only suitable for major transactions such as buying a house or paying over a dowry can hardly be regarded as a widely useful means of exchange'.[110] There is some truth to this; as Alessia Rovelli has pointed out, given the absence of fractional denominations of coins, any increase in the price of goods worth 1 *denarius* would have forced, effectively, a doubling of the price, if the transactions were tallied on the day with a coin.[111] But this is not how early medieval pricing worked. Based on the ninth-century documents of Lucca, Wickham showed that the prices of properties changed depending upon the relationships and social status of the actors in the exchange.[112] Properties and prices had rather less to do with market factors, or inherent value or earning potential of land, than status. Values of early medieval properties can be seen as sliding rates which moved alongside all kinds of other social values, especially kinship, friendship, and vassalage.

There might have been coins, non-coin proxies, or a combination of the two which facilitated transactions of scale.[113] There has been a long-running idea that late Roman bronze and silver coinage circulated in the Middle Ages as a fractional coinage for small-value items.[114] This theory was brilliantly tested by Rovelli against contemporary late Roman pottery in the large dumps of rubbish from the seventh and eighth centuries at the Crypta Balbi, in the centre of Rome.[115] Her analysis makes clear that

---

[110] Crawford, 'Money and exchange'; Rovelli, 'Introduction', p. xi. For Peter Spufford, bronze and small-denomination coins were never expected in rural contexts because the purchase of everyday goods was an urban phenomenon, *Money and its use*, p. 10.

[111] Rovelli, 'Introduction', p. xii.

[112] See discussion of sale and gifts to churches as expressions of social relationships in eleventh-century Tuscany in Wickham, *The mountains and the city*, pp. 210–15; cf. for Brittany, Davies, *Small worlds*, p. 57.

[113] Among the suggestions: 'late Roman small-coin survivals, the physical division of tremisses, leather, bread, silver weight, and so on'. Grierson, 'Problemi monetari'; Rovelli, 'Some considerations', pp. 200–1. The changes observed in Italy are not different from elsewhere in the post-Roman west, equally focusing on smaller scale, and contracting the production of coins; Hendy, 'From public to private'; Rovelli, 'Money and coinage'.

[114] Bognetti, 'Il problema monetario', esp. pp. 54–5.

[115] Rovelli and Saguì, 'Residualità, non residualità', p. 186.

earlier bronze coins were still in use into the early eighth century. This explanation is very compelling for Rome but does not hold true beyond the major city, and even at Rome it does not appear to continue into the later eighth, ninth, or tenth centuries.[116] Recently minted single-denomination coins might have been cut to make fractional denominations. It was common in Northern Europe to use half or quarter coins for smaller values, and very occasionally those appear in Italy, as in the case of the votive coins left at the altar of St Peter's at Rome, where fragments of foreign coins were left as gifts to Saint Peter.[117] Foreign money, however, and such an approach to fragmenting denominations to make smaller change do not appear to have been used elsewhere in Rome or in Italy.

Means of Exchange

Goods were used alongside or instead of money for transactions. One famous example of this comes from a Lombard document of 768, which specifies that Grasolf *munitario* (a moneyer) should pay for land outside Lucca, 15 solidi in gold and a house for the other 13 solidi; even the moneyer had insufficient cash for a big purchase.[118] This kind of arrangement appears often in our sources, where payment is to be delivered through a mix of currencies and payment in kind. Thus, a number of documents from ninth- and tenth-century Ravenna mix coins, rents in kind, and services: 'rent of one-tenth of each and every *modius*, a tenth of the [*manna*] of flax, a fourth of the [*arfora*] wine, and for the tribute and grazing fees and works to give we promise good *denarii*, and for the pasture we promise to give each year one *mancus*'.[119] Rovelli has shown that large livestock was the most common unit of exchange used alongside, or instead of, a coin payment.[120] The sources that she and others have gathered together are good evidence for the flexibility of the

---

[116] Rovelli, 'Some considerations', pp. 198–9.

[117] Arslan, *Repertorio dei ritrovamenti*, p. 61; Serafini, 'Appendice Numismatica'. In 2002, Verhulst noted that only 106 Carolingian coins have been recovered in Italy, *Carolingian economy*, p. 121.

[118] *CDL* vol. II, 220 (768), pp. 254–5, discussion in Wickham, 'Economic and social institutions', p. 27.

[119] For example, 'sub reddito de omnia et ex omnibus modio decimo, lino manna decima, vino arfora quarta, et pro exenio et herbatico et opere dare promittimus denareos bonos et pro glandatico dare promittimus omni annualiter mancoso uno', *Breviarium Ecclesiae Ravennatis*, no. 103 (pp. 56–7). Several other documents in the *Breviarium* combine these different mechanisms of payment, discussion in Rovelli, 'Circolazione monetaria', p. 128. See also Squatriti, *Water and society*, for payments of rent from mills in flour, p. 149 and Wickham, 'The Tivoli breve' for other mixed rents around Rome.

[120] Rovelli, 'La moneta nella documentazione altomedievale', p. 339.

monetary system, but such a system pertains only to medium- and high-value transactions.

Coins were not used for small-scale transactions and household-level needs; rather, people made and grew what they needed and exchanged or bartered their surplus. It is probably the case that this happened in nearly every community in late antiquity and the Middle Ages, alongside monetary transactions, though such practices are invisible in the historical record. In the absence of coins, anthropological models point to credit and bartering as conventional solutions in post-monetised societies.[121]

Legal structures supported sale between households without payment of the tolls which were usually charged of merchants. Thus, some Carolingian capitularies seem to permit the sale between neighbours and from owners without the charge of the *telonium*.[122] While these were Frankish regulations, some capitularies are preserved also in manuscripts written in Italy, and some were directed at Italy in particular.[123] However distant such regulations, there was a contemporary facilitation of exchange of everyday goods between neighbours and among the inhabitants of a city, without intermediaries of brokers.[124]

On balance, the evidence suggests to me that the coins in the documents of medieval Italy before the year 1050 were coins of account, but not necessarily actual coins. Sometimes actual metal coins were used in transactions, and the accounting systems of documents remained closely tied to whatever actual money was circulating in a given place. But between 800 and 1050, there are simply too few coins in circulation for them to have been in active use, and, as I have tried to suggest, beyond periodic markets for the sale of high-value items there were few spaces dedicated to economic exchange of goods. It appears that the majority of day-to-day objects including foodstuffs were made at home or circulated through non-commercial networks. Properties also moved along these lines, including properties with gardens. Archdeacon Heripertus and his nephew Rimpertus, a priest, rented half of two extramural oratories and their properties outside Parma in 853; in 860 Rimpertus, now an

---

[121] For instance, on post-Soviet Russia and Central Asia, see Humphrey, 'Barter and Economic Disintegration' and the essays in *The Unmaking of Soviet Life*. For early medieval credit systems, see Bougard, 'Le credit'.

[122] For example, 'De teloneis placet nobis, ut antiqua et iusta telonea a negotiatoribus exigantur, tam de pontis, quam et de navigiis seu mercatis, nova vero seu iniusta, ubi uel funes tenduntur... ut non exigantur. Similiter etiam nec de his qui sine negotiandi causa substantiam sua de una domo sua ad aliam ducunt, aut ad palatium, aut in exercitum', *Capit.* vol. I, 44, ch. 13 (p. 124).

[123] Davis, *Charlemagne's practice of empire*, pp. 278–89.

[124] Bocchi, 'Città e mercati', pp. 150–1.

archipriest, purchased the oratories and their properties, and Rimpertus sold some of them to his nephew, Stephanus subdeacon, including specifically a house with land and a garden in the city along with the oratories and their properties.[125] Stephanus does not get an advantageous rate for the property he purchases; indeed he pays more, suggesting that perhaps his uncle added more to the parcel of lands, including the townhouse with the garden.

Many wills created endowments supporting ecclesiastical institutions; some very explicitly furthered the aims of the institutions towards charity and the distribution of food to the poor. Two eighth-century wills from Monza provide an example. In 768, Thedoaldo endowed the church of S. Agata, of which he was custodian, all his possessions, leaving instructions for his niece and nephew to serve in the church upon his death. His nephew must feed twelve paupers with bread, wine, beans, and millet at Lent, the Ascension, and Epiphany; they received *lardo* apart from Lent. Another deacon, Grato, who had founded a *xenodochium* at Monza, left a will which provided for paupers' dinners each week feeding six paupers for three days.[126] The testament of Billongo, bishop of Verona, from 846, is useful to show the movement of goods and even food through networks of social obligation. Two vassals and their relations who received houses from Billongo were compelled by his testament to feed the poor at the first of every month on behalf of the soul of the bishop and to give 5 *solidi* each year to the *scola* of priests of Verona.[127] Through his will, and hundreds of others like it, the household of the deceased supported the poor and the dedicated religious in very direct material terms: they fed paupers directly, and they may have provided cash or kind to the religious house. We can see this structure working at its most comprehensive level at Rome where the portfolio of estates owned by the papacy (that is, the Roman episcopal fisc, not individual bishops) were worked in order to provide food directly to the paupers and pilgrims at Rome, to be distributed from the Lateran and through the numerous ecclesiastical distribution centres of the city.[128]

---

[125] 'Constat me Rimpertus, archipresbiter et filio bone memorie Lamperti, vindo et trado tibi Stephanoni, subdeacono et filio quondam Rimperti, nepote meo, emtori, idest casis cum terra sub se et edificiis suis muras vel parietibus circumdata una cum curte et orto uno tenenete, quae est positas infra civitat. Parmenses prop aqueducto', *CDP*, vol. I, 11 (860), p. 29.

[126] *CDL* vol. II, 218 (768), pp. 249–52, *CDL* vol. II, 231 (769), pp. 287–93, discussion in Gasparri, 'L'alto medioevo', pp. 66–9; Gasparri, 'I testamenti nell'Italia settentrionale'.

[127] *CDV* vol. I, 182 (846) pp. 272–8, discussion in Gasparri, 'I testamenti nell'Italia settentrionale'.

[128] On the *domuscultae*, see Marazzi *I 'Patrimonia'*; Stasolla, 'A proposito delle strutture assistenziali'; Delogu, 'Rome in the ninth century'; and Chapter 3, p. 91.

Wills and dowries, and this new conceptualisation of papal land acquisition as a household looking to feed dependents, all help us to see strategies and motives for the movement of household items, and show the household to have been an extended entity, united by kinship, social alliances, and even dependency, in the case of the poor. These extended households were the principal units of the economies of this period, and I argue that we ought to consider them key to the networks through which everyday goods moved.

Household-level needs were the principal motor of exchange in early medieval Italy. A household might have been an extended family, or men and their clients, vassals, dependents, and their families. Increasingly in the ninth and tenth centuries, we can see monasteries and churches as households with priests, monks or nuns, paupers, and pilgrims who needed to be fed. Perhaps the largest was the household of the Lateran, including the pope, his court, the priests of the papal churches, and the properties owned collectively by the papacy. Those properties, stretching around Rome and beyond, fed the members of the household in Rome as well as the poor and pilgrims in something of a closed network.[129] These same forces were at play at much smaller scales, too, such as in the case of the Neapolitan monastery, to be explored in 'An Urban Monastery Fills Its Larder', and down to less prominent social orders, who used property transactions to establish and reify social bonds from city to countryside and across regions. We can note that the emphasis placed on social bonds in the documentary record increases over the period of the eighth and ninth centuries, and this can contextualise, for instance, that Wiletruda, our widow in Salerno in 882, was in such a precarious position not simply because the entire city of Salerno was cut off from inland food supplies, but also because she would have been cut off from any wider social networks she may have enjoyed outside the city.

Food moved from field to table and household goods moved between men and women along social lines, motivated by the needs of households, and by contractual arrangements of rent and taxation. Urban landholders often received fresh produce as rent from tenants instead of or in addition to payment in money; this had been true in late antiquity and remained true through the Middle Ages.[130] It may be that some of these payments in kind were for storage and eventual sale by the landowner; the dried pulses, wheat, and wine which appear often in the documents would be

---

[129] The classic analysis remains Marazzi, *I 'Patrimonia'*.
[130] For a synthesis of the situation in late antiquity up to the seventh century, Vera, 'Forme e funzioni'; Garnsey, *Famine and food supply*, pp. 245–9.

ideal for this purpose. Some of the rental produce, however, must have been consumed directly by the landowners. In antiquity there was social capital for urban elites to dine in the city on produce from their rural villa estates, the *pastio villatica*.[131] In late antiquity, gifts of agricultural produce were made between landowners.[132] By the early Middle Ages, there is little sense of the prestige once accorded rural products for the city; they were simply needed for food. Landowners, including monasteries, received garden vegetables grown in town or nearby as part of their rent, sometimes stipulating that these should be paid regularly, each week or two. At Naples, urban laymen landlords were at times paid in beans, or in a portion of whatever their tenants decided to plant.[133] (At Rome there is another document with vegetable rents, from roughly the same period.[134]) The majority of property documents preserved from early medieval Naples record monasteries as landlords whose communities benefitted from the foodstuffs directly. There may have been sufficient surplus for subsequent sale or redistribution – certainly in the case of Bobbio in the ninth century, the quantities of agricultural produce paid into the monastery far exceeded the needs of the community.[135] The convent of SS. Marcellinus and Petrus ceded the land of an urban garden for a new bath for the nuns, to be managed by a lay couple; the annual payment was 100 eggs; perhaps the hens were cooped alongside the baths.[136] When the abbess of S. Gregorio Armeno, a major convent in the centre of Naples, leased out a mill with two gardens at *Fullotani*[137] in the suburban hinterlands to the *dispensator* of the monastery of SS. Apostoli, the rent due was part of grain milled plus part of the garden greens, onions, and leeks.[138] From lands at *Tertium* (Terzo), the convent received millet, beans, greens, onions, sesame, summer vegetables, gourds, and wine as well as linen (presumably as flax partially or fully

---

[131] Varro, *De re rustica*, Book III, ed. and trans. Hooper, pp. 422–529; Holleran, 'Representations of food hawkers'.

[132] Whittaker, 'Late Roman trade and traders'; Vera, 'Forme e funzioni'.

[133] Rent paid in kind: *RN* 395 (1022), p. 247: 7 quarts of white beans annually for people at S. Vitum *ad Padule*, near Pomigliano; *RN* 267 (990), pp. 165–6 = 1 *modius* red beans at Casaferrea *territorio padulano*; *RN* 212 (977), pp. 132–3 = payment of 8 *modii* of whatever has been planted at lands in Faragnano (now Marano).

[134] *SMVL* 50 (1025), pp. 62–3, discussion in Wickham, *Medieval Rome*, p. 91.

[135] *Inventari altomedievali*, ed. Castagnetti, pp. 122–44; pp. 145–65.

[136] *RN* 241 (983), pp. 150–1. Montanari suggests that chickens, eggs, and coins were compulsory gifts (*exenia*) whose value was mostly symbolic, *L'alimentazione contadina*, p. 312.

[137] Location unidentified by Capasso but in the suburban territory of Naples.

[138] 'Nunc convenient de quantitate frumenti macinandi in dicto Molino, et conciare debeant illum ad commune expendium et foleas et cepullas et porros ipsorum hortorum divider debeant', *RN* 443 (1033), pp. 277.

processed).[139] The urban monastery of SS. Sergius and Bacchus was paid in wheat, millet, wine, apples, and nuts from one parcel of their land and wheat and half the wine, chestnuts, acorns, and nuts from a property on the slopes of Vesuvius.[140] Their red beans and nuts came from properties near the Porta Romana and at Nola,[141] and 'well-dried' grain was to be brought directly to the monastery from their mills at *Tertium*[142] on the Feast of the Assumption in August, and baked bread at Saint Sebastian's day in December and Holy Thursday of Easter week, thus spacing out their grain and bread; a later document from the monastery for this or another mill at *Tertium* specifies a *modius* of grain to be paid to the monastery each month in addition to the rest, an arrangement which would have permitted a steady supply of a modest amount of fresh grain throughout the year.[143] (Given the variables of milling, humidity of flour, and baking, it is impossible to determine how much bread 1 *modius* of wheat would produce, though we can estimate to determine roughly the order of magnitude: 1 *modius* of wheat (6.7 L or 5.4 kg weight) at 100 per cent extraction will make 9.8 kg of bread, about eighteen 500 g loaves.[144]

An Urban Monastery Fills Its Larder

The contracts arranged by Pancratius, the higumen of the Neapolitan urban monastery of SS. Sergius and Bacchus between 1016 and 1023, attest an organised programme to bring in agricultural products to his urban monastery and one of its local dependencies. The products which were delivered as rents to the monastery were both raw and processed, with some properties delivering wheat, others bread, some wine, and others apples, beans, and chickens (Table 3). This system, which probably built on agreements established in previous

---

[139] 'vini hornas decem a tunc dare et atducere debeat de quod ibi seminaverit quantum ibi seminaturia de triticum introierit, preter de linum, item de sexta parte unam et item de mileum et de fasioli, de folia et de cepullas et de senas et de stivalium et de cucurbitas de quinta partem unam, et vinum ipse et abbas divident inter se per sex uncias', *RN* 233 (982), pp. 144–5.

[140] *RN* 379 (1019), pp. 236–7, *RN* 399 (1023), p. 249; Skinner, *Health and medicine*, p. 9.

[141] *RN* 275 (992), p. 170, *RN* 277 (992), pp. 171–2, *RN* 391 (1021), pp. 244–5.

[142] *RN* 268 (990), p. 166. Later documents describe a mill at Fullotani, which gave the monastery 10 or 12 *modii* of grain per week.

[143] *RN* 367 (1016), pp. 227–8. Other Neapolitan monastery payments in produce went to S. Marcellinus, wheat, wine, half the fruit, chestnuts, and acorns (*RN* 396 (1022)); to SS. Festi et Desiderii, 5 *modii* of wheat and 5 *modii* of beans from properties in the territory of Naples (*RN* 3 (915), p. 19); to SS. Severinus et Sossius, 2 *modii* of wheat and one of *favino* beans each August from property at Calvizzano (*RN* 281 (993), p. 174).

[144] David, *English bread and yeast cookery*, pp. 50–88, 246. I am grateful to Debby Banham for sharing her expertise about medieval bread.

Table 3 *SS. Sergius and Bacchus, Naples, stocks its larder*

	Spring	Summer	Autumn	Winter	Monthly	No time specified
RN 358 (1016)						½ the wine and oil from a property at Pomigliano d'Arco, to be taken to storage there
RN 362 (1016)						½ the wine, ½ the chestnuts from a property on M. Vesuvius to be taken to S. Basilii de Nonnaria (in a village between Portici and S. Sebastiano al Vesuvio)
RN 367 (1016)	1 *modius* of bread at Easter	27 *modii* of wheat in mid-Aug.		2 *modii* of bread in Dec.	5 *modii* of bread each month	
RN 368 (1016)	10 *modii* of wheat, and at Easter ½ a quart of *agnos*	5 *modii* of wheat in mid-Aug.		½ the millet and 1 gold taro in Dec.		10 *modii* of wheat, 2 *tari*, 1 *modius* of millet and a quart of *agnos* (a tree).
RN 370 (1016)		20 *modii* of wheat and a pair of breeding chickens in mid-Aug.				a meal for 5 people at the property
RN 373 (1017)						½ the wine and nuts to be taken to S. Basilii de Nonnaria
RN 378 (1018)						1 *modius* of wheat, 1 pitcher of wine, a *modius* of salt, and a quart *de ture* (?)
RN 379 (1019)		2 *modii* of wheat, 2 *modii* of millet in mid-Aug.				½ the wine and *saccapanna*, 3/5 of the apples, ½ the nuts and other fruits
RN 385 (1020)			every year at the *vendemmia*, 1 pitcher of wine from each *salma*	50 eggs in Dec.		2 parts of the hay and ½ the wine and sweet wine

Table 3 (cont.)

	Spring	Summer	Autumn	Winter	Monthly	No time specified
RN 391 (1021)			2 *modii* (11 quarts each) of red beans and a chicken in Sept.			
RN 399 (1023)						½ the wheat, wine and chestnuts to be taken to S. Basilii de Nonnaria
RN 398 (1023)						½ the produce from a wood on M. Vesuvius, converted to planting, to be taken to S. Basilii de Nonnaria

generations, provided a substantial amount of fresh food, processed wheat and wine, and eggs and hens.

The rents were staggered across the year, with significant arrivals at harvest time and midwinter, and these were mixed with cash payments, which may best be understood as cash-equivalents. If we consider only the wheat payments stipulated in this small group of contracts, the monastery took in 75 *modii* of wheat (405 kg of wheat makes in the order of 1,350 loaves at 500 g each) per annum, staggered through the year, and 15 *modii* of bread (81 kg is about 270 loaves per annum) for the monastery. We do not know the size of the monastery, but it is clear that the payments in kind were not sufficiently large for selling on. Indeed, we should hope that the monks had many other rental agreements beyond just these to keep them fed.

One of the payments was an obligation, a meal for five to the higumen in Naples. This should be understood as a payment in kind, produce converted into food, as well as a symbolic gesture. The offering of a meal – the giving and receiving – corroborated the relationship between landowner and renter. From the eleventh century, references to gifts of small amounts of food which were part of the annual obligations of tenants to landlords become more common. In southern documents, these are joints of meat, cakes, or eggs and are known as the *salute*; in the North they are the *amiscere*.[145]

In the absence of urban markets between late antiquity and the tenth and eleventh centuries, there were three main ways to get fresh foods: collect them as rents or payments from lots of land owned outside the city, plant and grow fruits and vegetables in the city, or seek charitable assistance from an urban church. Acknowledging that our documents describing properties tend to reflect higher orders of society, they nonetheless preserve a real range of people who had cultivated lands within Italian cities. Some plots of land were worked collectively, with shared ownership. At Naples, an urban plot was held by 'the men of Calbectianum', whose land neighboured a garden plot described in a document from Naples in 934.[146] Another group of men at Naples clubbed together to buy agricultural land, the 'men of Sol et Luna street' whose 'terra' bordered an orchard sold to a deacon in 1030.[147] These gardens from Naples suggest a sort of collective effort to acquire property and enter the property market. The documents might also speak to collective food-growing strategies, along the lines of community gardens of more modern periods.

Community Benefits

Beyond simply providing fresh food, there are considerable benefits to communities in developing urban cultivation, ranging from fostering social cohesion to securing land tenure. Research and policy on modern urban community gardens has made clear that shared growing spaces can positively build communities across socio-economic divides.[148] Urban cultivation provides therapeutic benefits to gardeners, and psychological benefits to the people who live and work among them.[149] Urban residents who participated in the planting of trees in communal spaces report greater opinions not only of the tree they planted, but of the improvements the tree brought to the neighbourhood and to the overall friendliness of the neighbourhood.[150]

---

[145] Andreolli, 'I prodotti alimentari'; Andreolli and Montanari, *L'azienda curtense*; for a wide-ranging discussion, see Kuchenbuch, 'Porcus donativus'.
[146] 'terra de hominibus de Calbectianum', *RN* 26 (934), pp. 33–4.
[147] *RN* 423 (1030), p. 266. Unusually the document does not specify whether the *terra* is within the walls or not; discussion in Skinner, 'Urban communities', p. 296.
[148] For better dietary habits on garden sites, see Blair et al., 'A dietary, social and economic evaluation'. For community development, see Morton et al., 'Accessing food resources'; Schukoske, 'Community development'.
[149] Ulrich, 'Natural versus urban'; Kaplan, 'Some psychological benefits'.
[150] Sommer et al., 'Social benefits of resident involvement'.

Community Benefits

In modern cities in the developed world, urban food gardens and allotment gardens increased in the post–World War II period, but not only due to the need to aid in household food strategies. In 1964 Harry Thorpe undertook an extensive survey of allotments in England and Wales (729,000 plots occupying about 78,000 acres) and determined that the primary aim for many allotment owners (51.5 per cent of those interviewed) was leisure.[151] During the economic recession of the 1970s, community gardeners and activists took over thousands of vacant lots left unbuilt and fallow as industrial and residential capital abandoned American cities.[152] The peak of urban vegetable gardens in the Barcelona metropolitan area occurred in the late 1970s and early 1980s, after a period of rapid informal urban growth and during economic crisis. Because early urbanisation around Barcelona had been informal, discontinuous, and often self-built, small-scale agriculture fit into gaps in peri-urban spaces, near roads, and between residential and industrial zones.[153] These expansions were principally aimed at creating access to fresh food, but there was also a desire to provide activities for some members of households, to craft an alternative urban environment, often occupying abandoned spaces. The intensity of urban cultivation is greater in the developing world, where city growth is rapidly expanding. In 1996, a United Nations report estimated 65 per cent of families in Moscow were engaged in urban agriculture.[154] Governmental policies encouraged urban cultivation to augment food resources as well as to improve community relations.[155] For example, the New Deal Federal Emergency Relief Administration (USA) allocated $5.5 million to food gardens in forty-three states in 1934.[156] In the 'Dig for Victory' campaign in Britain during the second World War, government policies encouraged male heads of households to garden plot, for personal health, family benefit, and national good:

> [The gardener] is generally better in spirit because cultivating his plot took his mind off the burdens of office or workshop; he has benefited his family by providing fresh vegetables that kept them fit and incidentally helped his wife in trying to make ends meet and avoid queues; he and his fellow 'Victory Diggers' benefited their country by contributing in every year a substantial and

---

[151] Thorpe, 'The homely allotment', p. 175. For a rich sociological analysis of British allotments in the late 1980s, see Crouch and Ward, *The allotment*.
[152] Schmelzkopf, 'Urban community gardens'; Brown and Jameton, 'Public health implications'; Lawson, *City bountiful*.
[153] Domene and Saurí, 'Urbanization and water consumption', p. 291.
[154] Cheema et al., *Urban agriculture*, p. 45.
[155] Brown and Jameton, 'Public health implications'; Lawson, *City bountiful*; McClintock, 'Cultivation, capital, and contamination', p. 28.
[156] Lawson, *City bountiful*, p. 326, note 2.

indispensable quantity of food to the national larder, without which the nation might well have had to go short.[157]

In the modern-day USA, urban community food-producing gardens in low-income areas led to solutions for other neighbourhood issues in Upstate New York counties, reportedly through the community organization facilitated through gardens which created informal networks and social support.[158] Neighbouring garden spaces, of the kind we see in many of our documents which attest to cultivated plots next to other cultivated plots, have been shown to contribute to the sharing of skills across property boundaries. The family members and neighbours may have used the neighbouring gardens as a place for sharing and communicating over generations, while working the plots that fed their households. The garden plots may very well have provided space for the development and strengthening of relationships, family obligations, and support.

Conclusions

The early medieval Italian peninsula was rich in fertile land with diverse growing conditions. Patterns of agriculture and structures of landholding were formed by the legacies of Roman farming and reshaped by the new conditions of early medieval society: minimal 'state-driven' production, absence of mega-elite owners, and the presence, instead, of smallholdings, a market in land, and new ideas about inheritance and land ownership by churches, ecclesiastical institutions, and women. As was similarly the case in fifteenth-century Languedoc in Emmanuel La Roy Ladurie's analysis, 'what capitalistic agriculture lacked at the end of the Middle Ages was not land and buildings, but money and labour'.[159] Practically, this meant that the countryside was filled with small-scale plots, most growing a range of crops to meet local or at best regional needs.

A reliable market of agricultural products, which had existed in late antiquity, was not present in early medieval Italy. This means that exchanges of goods were strongly local and small in scale. There were no major efforts in place to organise labour and extract surpluses – with the exception of some major monastic houses operating at very

---

[157] Ministry of Agriculture and Fisheries, Agricultural Statistics, 1939–1944: England and Wales, London, 1948, 2, quoted in Ginn, 'Dig for Victory!'.
[158] Armstrong, 'A survey of community gardens', pp. 324, 325.
[159] Le Roy Ladurie, *The peasants of Languedoc*, p. 39; cf. Lin Foxhall's comments drawing parallels to ancient Greece, Foxhall, 'Cultures, landscapes, and identities', p. 89.

large scale, and with the assistance of royal or imperial support – nor were there structures in place to buy fresh food from vendors, as it had been in antiquity and was again possible in the later Middle Ages. The wealthiest landowners lived in cities, as did many other people. The bulk crops of cereals, wine, and olive oil produced in the countryside came into the city through networks of rent or obligation. Urban agriculture played a role in the social lives of Italian cities and their economic lives as well. It is unlikely that early medieval cities were self-sufficient in terms of food production. Urban agriculture was never the sole mode of farming in Italy by any means, but cultivated lots were omnipresent in the cities for which we have documentary records, indicating that gardens played a key role in feeding cities.

In this chapter, I have suggested that economies of exchange were driven by household needs for the most part. Luxury goods appear to have passed through some cities in Italy, but large-scale, long-distance commerce to and through Italy was still a few centuries away. The significance of social ties and household structures in the movement of goods is apparent in the few wills, testaments, and dowries from the period, and these were the principal motors of exchange. Households fed themselves. These households may have been conceived as stretching beyond a single dwelling to include extended families which may have shared resources, or to houses of dedicated religious who shared resources collectively.

5 Values and Ideals

As the previous chapters have shown, the presence of food cultivation in the cities of early medieval Italy was not simply a by-product of a breakdown in urban density and fluctuations of markets for everyday foods. Intellectual and cultural attitudes to gardening also gave rise to new forms of gardens, lending the emerging systems of food provisioning and urban living a conceptual justification. Two elements shaped early medieval ideas and values around productive gardening: Roman esteem for land economy and Christian concepts of social welfare. The legacy of late antique estate-management underpinned household-level horticulture with a sense of noble tradition, and the transmission of classical texts and late antique redactions of them provided tools for the dissemination of thinking about this tradition. Admiration for the effective management of an estate and the welfare of a family group in the late Roman world endured into the post-classical period, even though structures of estates and the economic network around them changed. This regard for well-run estates provided a framework for emerging ideas about Christian households and dedicated religious communities. Written into the foundations and rules which shaped late antique religious communities in Italy were expectations about food cultivation, estate-management, self-sufficiency, and charitable support. The produce of gardens in the countryside as well as in cities went to feed households and communities, including houses of dedicated religious men and women, and the poor which were sustained by ecclesiastical institutions. In addition to feeding dependants, some of the produce of urban gardens also appears to have been used for medical products. The lines between what constituted quotidian nutrition and medical treatment are very blurred in our period, but we can look to the transmission of antique texts of medical knowledge and the compilations of recipes to gain some perspective on the value of garden products for medicinal purposes.

Values and Ideals

In Roman society, significant cultural esteem was accorded to growing things well. Despite or perhaps because of the fact that most wealthy Romans never touched a garden tool, there was a full array of positive values attached to agrarian pursuits and, in particular, as now, the efficient and profitable farming of the land. For Nicholas Purcell, 'deep in what the Romans thought about themselves ... we find intensive horticulture and the lots on which it took place; and the domestic nature is central'.[1] Being able to produce useful crops as well as ornamental plants was a source of pleasure, wealth, and ethical virtue. From poetry to prosaic agronomic texts with instructions and guidelines, Roman authors fostered an appreciation for working the land and producing food to eat, sell, and store for future use; there was also beauty in the cultivation of plants and trees. Thinking and writing about gardening fed into the 'myth of the peasant patriarch', an ideal of Rome's traditional leaders as men who worked their land, and texts about agriculture celebrated the religious duties and ethics in horticulture.[2] The main texts concerned with agronomy and botany in antiquity were the Geoponics, written in Greek and Latin, in prose and verse.[3] Cato, writing in the second century BCE, wrote an essay in Latin on Agriculture and estate management, *De Agri Cultura*, and Varro in the first century BCE wrote a synthesis of previous writing on agriculture. Cicero had accorded agriculture pride of place as the principal Roman value, the best of all human activities:

But of all the profit-making activities, none is better, more fruitful, more enjoyable, more worthy of a free man than agriculture. However, I have discussed this quite fully in my *Cato Maior*, so you can find there observations relevant to this topic.[4]

These values were celebrated in literature, too. Vergil's account in *Georgics* IV.125–48 of the old man of Taranto who 'lived under the arches and towers of the fort, on a little patch of land that nobody wanted, too poor for oxen to plow, unfit for pasture, not right for planting vines' is emblematic. The unnamed man planted flowers, herbs, vegetables, and fruit trees, and through his work, 'he made for

---

[1] Purcell, 'The Roman garden as a domestic building', p. 122. See also Marzano, 'Roman gardens', pp. 199–203.
[2] Myers, 'Representations of gardens in Roman literature', pp. 260–2. On the peasant and the myth of the peasant patriarch, see Garnsey, 'Non-Slave labour', p. 36, and Draycott, 'Roman domestic medical practice', pp. 62–4.
[3] Henderson, *Hortus. The Roman book of gardening*; Goodman, 'Agrarian writers, agronomists'; Gaulin, 'Tradition et pratiques de la litterature'.
[4] Cicero, *De officiis*, I, 42, trans. Walsh, p. 51.

himself a happiness that was equal to the happiness of kings, And when he came home at night his feast was free'.[5] The poem lauds the simple pleasure of working the land and realising a harvest, and, as Sara Myers makes clear, uses the well-tended garden to convey multiple positive associations: a philosophical virtue of self-sufficiency, a *colonus* as a farmer-hero, as well as gardening as a metaphor for poetical composition.[6]

Discussion of horticulture could also promote the virtues of Roman military expansion. The book on gardens in Columella's treatise on agriculture, *Cepuricus de cultu hortorum* (written *c.* 60–5 CE), is on the one hand practical. On the other hand it uses the planned gardens of Italian villas, the food-producing ones in particular, as a device to describe the geographic variety of the Italian peninsula and as a means to celebrate the imported plants, brought to Italy as trophies from conquered lands or as newly available products from the expanding territories of the Roman empire.[7]

Many of these classical agronomic texts survive but were not widely copied or circulated until the later Middle Ages.[8] In the third, fourth, and fifth centuries, writers produced new texts by compiling and extracting earlier ones, and these enjoyed wider circulation than their earlier counterparts. Rutilius Palladius's *De re rustica* was composed almost entirely out of reworked extracts from Columella, Gargilius Martialis, and an epitome of Vitruvius by Faventius.[9] It is broadly held

---

[5]   namque sub Oebaliae memini me turribus arcis,
       qua niger umectat flaventia culta Galaesus,
       Corycium vidisse senem, cui pauca relicti
       iugera ruris erant, nec fertilis illa iuvencis
       nec pecori opportuna seges nec commoda Baccho:
       hic rarum tamen in dumis olus albaque circum
       lilia verbenasque premens vescumque papaver
       regum aequabat opes animis, seraque revertens
       nocte domum dapibus mensas onerabat inemptis'

   Vergil, *Georgics*, Book IV, lines 125–33, trans. Ferry, p. 151.

[6] Myers, 'Representation of gardens in Roman literature', p. 268, with further bibliographic reference to several different readings of the poem.

[7] Columella, *De re rustica*, Book 10, esp. pp. 6–34; Marzano, 'Roman gardens', pp. 230–1; see Spencer, *Roman landscape*, pp. 95–6, and Pagán, *Rome and the Literature of Gardens*, pp. 27–30.

[8] Brunner, 'Continuity and discontinuity of Roman agricultural knowledge', esp. p. 32.

[9] Palladius, *De re rustica*, ed. Martin; Rodgers, 'The Moore Palladius', p. 203; Browning, 'Minor figures', p. 771. On the process of compilation as a preservation and transmission of knowledge in late antiquity, see Kaster, *Guardians of language*, esp. pp. 15–30, and Leyser, 'Shoring fragments against ruin?', pp. 66–8.

that the end of classical Geoponics or Agronomic texts came around the same time as Palladius at the end of the fourth or probably early fifth century.[10]

Ancient texts were, of course, transmitted to the early Middle Ages and later, sometimes in redactions and excerpts, parcelled in schoolbooks or compilations around a theme.[11] Not all ancient texts were of interest to early medieval readers, either as historical compositions worthy of study or as practical texts with contemporary applicability.[12] Leaving aside Vergil's *Georgics*, there are sixteen preserved manuscripts of Latin agronomists copied before the twelfth century, predominantly Columella, Gargilius Martialis, and Palladius.[13] (One manuscript from Florence, now lost but transcribed in the fifteenth century for Poliziano (Agnolo Ambrogini), was a ninth- or tenth-century compilation of all three.[14]) Gargilius Martialis, a third-century horticulturist, wrote a text based in part on Pliny, transmitted to the early middle ages most often as an appendix to the *Medicina pliniana*, a complication of remedies based on Pliny's *Natural History*.[15] One palimpsest from Bobbio, now in Naples, has several folios of his text in a sixth-century manuscript which was then written over in the late seventh century with text of the *Liber Pontificalis*.[16] Like Gargilius Martialis, Palladius was cited by Cassiodorus as an author whose work was desirable for a monastic library; Palladius was more common in some circles.[17] All extant medieval manuscripts of Palladius's *De re rustica* can be traced back to one original in France in the ninth century. Seven copies were made in Francia in the ninth, so this was certainly of interest to Frankish readers, but perhaps less so to readers in the Italian peninsula.[18] The value of

---

[10] Goodman, 'Agrarian writers, agronomists'.
[11] Contreni, 'Carolingian renaissance'; McKitterick, 'The written word and oral communication'; Reynolds, *Texts and transmissions*.
[12] Meyvaert made this point, but perhaps too forcefully, when claiming that classical texts were 'in all probability ... very seldom consulted by the monastic gardener. What these books contained was a literary tradition having little or nothing to do with the practical side of horticulture', 'The medieval monastic garden', p. 31. For the eastern, Greek-language traditions, see Rogers, 'Κηποποϊα: Garden Making and Garden Culture in the *Geoponika*'.
[13] Gaulin, 'Tradition et pratiques de la litterature', p. 109.
[14] The Marcianus from S. Marco in Florence, now lost.
[15] Gargilius Martialis, *De hortis*, ed. Mazzini; Reynolds, *Texts and transmission*, p. 40, note 2; discussion in Condorelli, *Gargilii Martialis quae exstant vol. 1*, pp. xi–xiv, 3–5.
[16] Naples, Biblioteca Nazionale, IV.A.88, ff. 40–7, s. vi, uncial, written over in s. vii; *Codices latini antiquiores*, vol. II, 403.
[17] On Cassiodorus's recommendations, see p. 167.
[18] Palladius, *De re rustica*, ed. Martin. All early medieval manuscripts trace back to a lost archetype, copied perhaps in the end of the eighth century, in north-east France. Examples include Cambridge UL Kk 5.13, s. ix$^{2/4}$ written at St-Denis; Paris, Bibliothèque Nationale, lat 6842B, s. ix^1, probably coming from Loire valley;

Palladius's text lay not only in its erudition, but also in its convenient format with a mind to practical instruction and application. The passages were organised sequentially around the seasons of the year with a further book on animal husbandry and a poem on the grafting of trees.[19] We can be clear that this was not transmitted simply because of its antiquity but perhaps also for its utility, though it is not obvious that these texts were copied directly in Italy nor read beyond ecclesiastical circles.[20] Agronomists nonetheless were influential, and distinctly so among churchmen. The great encyclopaedist Isidore of Seville, whose *Libri Etymologiarum* were widely circulated in Italy, named several ancient authors as his sources, but for agricultural matters he predominantly used Columella and Palladius, whom he called Aemilianus.[21]

Just as the dense urbanism of Roman Italy created a substructure which gave early medieval Italy its particularly urban character and provided a cultural frame for understanding cities and city living in certain ways, so too Roman ideas about agriculture and horticulture in particular shaped how people understood their cabbage patches. This knowledge was transmitted indirectly, however, not through the individual texts of specific ancient agronomists but more through codices of collected passages, encyclopaedias, and others.

In late antiquity cultural attitudes to agriculture changed in two key ways. First, classical interest in the symbolism of flowers and the uses of blossoms for ceremonies took radical new directions in Christian contexts. And second, traditional values of self-sufficiency and efficient management of estates were newly meaningful as religious houses took on responsibilities for charitable feeding in addition to the support of dedicated religious men and women.

Reynolds, *Texts and transmission*, pp. 287–8. Another transmission is Italian, but the first manuscript preserved is late for our period: Milan, Ambrosiana C.212 inf. s. xiii/xiv, northern Italy, perhaps Bologna. It is worth noting the restricted geographical and chronological patterns of this text and its transmission because it has been claimed that 'almost every monastic library owned a copy of [Palladius' work]', Opsomer-Halleux, 'The medieval garden and its role in medicine', p. 102.

[19] Palladius, *De re rustica*, ed. Martin; Martin, 'Introduction'.

[20] Epstein, *The medieval discovery of nature*, pp. 28–9, contra Meyvaert, who argued the books in monastic libraries 'contained a literary tradition having little or nothing to do with the practical side of horticulture', 'The medieval monastic garden', p. 31.

[21] On the sources for Isidore, and the sources that Isidore declared himself to be using, see Isidore, *Libri XX Etymologiarum*, Book XVII, i, ed. André ; *De agricultura*, Liber XVII, pp. 7–11, trans. Barney et al., p. 337; Barney et al., 'Introduction', p. 14.

Consider the Lilies of the Field (Mt 6:28)

At the end of antiquity, the flowers lost their appeal; esteem for cultivation shifted firmly towards food production and away from decorative and ornamental gardening. In the first century BCE, Vergil's *Georgics* would praise cultivation of both foodstuffs and flowers:

> It might be that I'd sing to celebrate
> The care it takes to cultivate the flowers
> That make our gardens beautiful. I'd sing
> Of Paestum and its roses and how they bloom
> Twice every year, and how the endive drinks
> With gladness from the brooks, and how the green
> Wild-celery plants adorn the riverbanks,
> And the gourd tendril winds and turns and coils
> Its way through the grass, and swells and becomes its fruit.[22]

The ancient city of Paestum was famous in antiquity for the roses farmed there in great quantities for garlands and perfume.[23] Pliny identified two plants in particular to be grown for garlands: roses and violets.[24] These were commercial crops, and Varro recommended growing these flowers, for which there was high urban demand, in farms near cities, where delivery was easy and costs were low.[25] Columella advised growing roses in rows, violets either in trenches in fertilized beds or like other annual herbs in beds.[26] Roses and violets were made into garlands and crowns for use in temples and in honour of the dead.[27] Some suburban tomb plots were planted with them, specifying that the blossoms should be offered to the deceased.[28] *Rosalia*, summer fests and banquets which

---

[22]   forsitan et, pinguis hortos quae cura colendi
       ornaret, canerem, biferique rosaria Paesti
       quoque modo potis gauderent intiba rivis
       et virides apio ripae, tortusque per herbam
       cresceret in ventrem cucumis

   Vergil, *Georgics*, Book IV, lines 118–22, trans. Ferry, p. 149 (though I translate *cucumis* as gourd). Poem discussed in Myers, 'Representations of gardens in Roman literature'; on cucurbits, see Paris, et al., 'Occidental diffusion of cucumber'.
[23] On the roses of Paestum, see Brun, 'The production of perfumes in antiquity', pp. 297–9. For a list of ancient authors who celebrated Paestum's *rosaria*, including Ovid and Martial, see ibid., p. 297.
[24] Pliny, *Historia naturalis*, Book XXI, 10, ed. and trans. Mayhoff.
[25] Varro, *De re rustica*, Book I.16, 3, ed. and trans. Hooper, pp. 220–1.
[26] Columella, *De arboribus*, Book XXX, ed. and trans. Forster and Heffner, pp. 408–11.
[27] Toynbee, *Death and burial in the Roman world*, pp. 62–3; Cumont, *Lux perpetua*, pp. 76–9. On garland flowers see Draycott, *Roman domestic medical practice*, pp. 73–4.
[28] Toynbee, *Death and burial in the Roman world*, p. 97, cites several examples from Italy of roses and also of grape vine, for wine to be offered to the deceased. See now Bodell, 'Roman tomb gardens', esp. pp. 222–31.

celebrated with fresh roses, continued to the later fourth century.[29] Augustine (d. 430) reports his misspent youth competing for 'popular renown ... garlands that would wither'.[30] For the imperial and late antique periods, images of flower garlands appeared in the decorative mosaics and paintings of villas, synagogues, tombs, and even churches.[31]

These traditional significations and uses of flowers transformed with the rise of Christianity. Where the rose had connoted beauty and honour for the person who was given the blossoms, in the writings of the early church fathers, it came to be viewed as a luxury to be eschewed. Clement of Alexandria (d. *c.* 215) in condemnation of floral garlands, wrote that 'roses and violets, being mildly cool, relieve and prevent headaches ... but we do not need the crocus or the flower of the cypress to lead us to an easy sleep'.[32] The first *Apologia* of Justin (d. 163/67), written in Rome to the emperor Antoninus Pius, proclaimed an ascetic approach to flowers among the emerging Christian community: 'Neither with frequent sacrifice nor with flower crowns do we venerate those whom they call gods, but whom men have formed and placed in churches. ... We do not bring libations, fragrances, branches or crowns for the dead'.[33]

Church fathers used the images of red roses and white lilies often, as expressions of beauty, pleasure, and fertility, but within a distinctly Christian lens. The pairing of roses and lilies in Latin poetry had started with Vergil's *Aeneid* and had appeared often among Classical authors, such as Ovid, and early Christian poets.[34] In imitation of

---

[29] Phillips, s.v. Rosalia, *Brill's New Pauly*, vol. 12, pp. 734–5. For the popularity of the festival in fourth-century Italy, see Salzman, *On Roman time*, pp. 97–9.

[30] 'hac popularis gloriae sectantes inanitatem, usque ad theatricos plausus et contentiosa carmina et agonem coronarum faenearum et spectaculorum nugas et intemperantiam libidinum', Augustine, *Confessiones*, Book IV, 1, ed. O'Donnell, vol. I, p. 33, commentary at vol. II, p. 23.

[31] Géczi, *The rose and its symbols*, pp. 357–86. I thank Paolo Squatriti for this reference.

[32] Clement of Alexandria, *Paedagogus*, Book II, viii, eds. Marcovich and van Winden, p. 112, trans. Wilson, p. 236.

[33] 'Ἀλλ' οὐδὲ θυσίαις πολλαῖς καὶ πλοκαῖς ἀνθῶν τιμῶμεν οὓς ἄνθρωποι μορφώσαντες καὶ ἐν ναοῖς ἱδρύσαντες θεοὺς προσωνόμασαν, ἐπεὶ ἄψυχα καὶ νεκρὰ ταῦτα γινώσκομεν καὶ θεοῦ μορφὴν μὴ ἔχοντα ... ὅπερ μόνον ἐγκαλεῖν ἡμῖν ἔχετε, ὅτι μὴ τοὺς αὐτοὺς ὑμῖν σεβόμενοι θεούς, μηδὲ τοῖς ἀποθανοῦσι χοὰς καὶ κνίσας καὶ δένδρα καὶ στεφάνους καὶ θυσίας φέρομεν', Justin Martyr, *First apologia* IX, 1; XXIV, 2, ed. Girgenti, pp. 40, 80–2. I thank Nick Evans for his help with this passage.

[34] Coffee, 'Intertextuality as viral phrases: Roses and lilies'. Compare the use of symbolism of violets and roses (on the head and pudenda of a statue of Venus) by the late Latin poet Luxorius, *Liber epigrammaton* no. 70, 'On a statue of Venus on whose head violets had grown', ed. Rosenblum, p. 153, and the *Passio Sanctarum Perpetuae et Felicitatis*, XI.5, ed. Heffernan, p. 114.

Vergil, Prudentius (d. c. 413) chose these flowers as an image of the profits of Christian wisdom: '[Wisdom] draws no nurture from moist earthly soil, yet puts forth perfect foliage and with blooms of blood-red roses intermingles white lilies that never droop on withering stem.'[35] Jerome (d. 420) paired roses, lilies, and violets in his commentaries on the Bible, elaborating on the lilies of the field of the Old and New Testaments by describing these different flowers as beautiful, laudable creations:

> We enter a meadow filled with flowers; here the rose blushes; there the lilies glisten white; everywhere flowers abound in all varieties. Our soul is drawn hither and thither to pluck the most beautiful. If we gather the rose, we leave the lily behind; if we pluck the lily, the violets remain.[36]

John Chrysostom (d. 407), writing in Greek, used the same grouping of three flowers when he likened reading Scripture to roses, violets, and lilies.[37] Floral scents were sometimes miraculously experienced at tombs of martyrs, though they were not tied to specific flowers.[38] Flowers, roses and lilies in particular, remained figures of beauty, but they were to be understood as the Christian God's creation.

Tertullian (d. c. 220), writing in Carthage in the early third century, juxtaposed crowns of garden flowers and Christ's crown of thorns, an opposition which endured among subsequent Christian writers throughout the Middle Ages:

> You may now be crowned with laurel, and myrtle and olive, and any famous branch and which is of greater worth, with hundred-leaved roses too, culled from the garden of Midas, and with both kinds of lily, and with violets of all sorts, perhaps also with gems and gold, so as even to rival that crown of Christ which He afterwards obtained. . . . If for these things, you owe your own head to Him, repay

---

[35] 'Quamuis nullus alat terreni caespitis umor, fronde tamen viret incolumi, tum sanguine tinctis intertexta rosis candentia lilia miscet nescia marcenti florem submittere collo', Prudentius, *Psychomachia*, lines 879–90, ed. Thompson, p. 340; cf. Prudentius, *Liber cathemerinon*, Hymn 5.113–24 (Christians gathering in a flower-filled garden; Hymn 3.21–80, a rustic garden).

[36] 'Venimus in pratum, habet flores plurimos: hinc rosa rubet, inde candent lilia, diuersi flores sunt. Anima nostra huc illucque trahitur, unde flores pulchriores capiat. Si rosam colligimus, lilium relinquimus; si lilium tulerimus, uiolae nobis supersunt', Jerome, *Tractatus de Psalmo LXXVII*, in *Tractatus sive Homiliae in Psalmos*, ed. Morin, p. 64, trans. Ewald, p. 79; *Commentary on Matthew* 6.28; cf. Jerome, *Vita Pauli*, 3, where lilies and roses grow in a paradisiacal garden of sensual delights.

[37] John Chrysostom, *Ad populum Antiochenum*, in *PG* 49, coll. 15–222, col. 17, trans. Schaff, p. 331.

[38] For example, Gregory of Tours, *Liber in gloria confessorum*, ch. 40, ed. Krusch, pp. 322–3. For discussion and relevant bibliography, see Roch, 'Inenarrabiles odores. Récits et contextes'.

164   Values and Ideals

it if you can, such as He presented His for yours; or be not crowned with flowers at all, if you cannot be with thorns, because you may not be with flowers.[39]

For Ambrose (d. 397), the fall of man caused the rose to have thorns, and the rose with its thorns should call to mind man's sin, ever near.[40]

With the winding down of traditional festivals, temple celebrations, and traditional funerals, flower garlands stopped being made, and the specialist farms where they were grown ended, too. Floral symbolism endured, though in changed form, increasingly disconnected from the farms and gardens where flowers were grown. Early Christian authors tended to construct figurative expressions around flowers of the field, growing wild, in part, to refer back to Christ's Sermon on the Mount and other Biblical passages. They may also have drawn upon these references because of the changing horticultural landscapes around them, where from the fourth century fewer flowers were cultivated, and what gardens there were, were increasingly used for food production.[41]

Gardening as a Monastic Principle

Esteem for agriculture and household gardening ran deep through the writings of the men and women experimenting with different forms of religious life. The connection between gardens and the dedicated religious was part of some of the earliest and most influential thinking about Christian life because the paradisiacal garden of Eden, where both flowers and fruits grew, was the site of man's fall. Augustine wrote in his *Confessions* (397–400) of his own conversion to the dedicated religious ascetic life under a fig tree, in an urban garden in Milan, where he heard

---

[39] 'Quae tunc Domini tempora et foedauerunt et lancinaueruntuti tu nunc laurea et myrto et olea et inlustriore quaque fronde et, quod magis usui est, centenariis quoque rosis de horto Midae lectis et utrisque liliis et omnibus uiolis coroneris, etiam gemmis forsitan et auro ? ut et illam Christi coronam aemuleris, quae postea ei obuenit ? Atquin et fauos post fella gustauit, nec ante rex gloriae a caelestibus salutatus est quam rex Iudaeorum proscriptus in cruce, minoratus primo a patre modico quid citra angelos, et ita gloria et honore coronatus. Si ob haec caput ei tuum debes, tale, si forte, ei repende, quale suum pro tuo obtulit, aut nec floribus coroneris si spinis non potes, quia floribus non potes.' Tertullian, *De corona*, XIV, 4, ed. Fontaine, pp. 173–6, trans. Cleveland-Coxes, p. 102.

[40] Ambrose, Exameron, III, 11 ed. Schenkl, p. 91 trans. Savage, pp. 102–3.

[41] On the use of cisterns for irrigating farms in the immediate outskirts of Rome for flowers, see Wilson, 'Villas, horticulture and irrigation infrastructure'. On taxa of ornamental gardens and the changes of late antiquity, see Goodson, 'Admirable and delectable gardens'.

a voice from a neighbouring garden.⁴² The garden could be a place of old-fashioned luxury, even a place of sin, but it could also provide a route to redemption. The Greek *Life* of the fourth-century Egyptian ascetic Pachomius describes Theodore, Pachomius' disciple, who started monastic life in his own garden.⁴³ His *Life* was influential among late Roman thinkers setting out new ways of living as ways in which men and women might reconcile the fall of man in Eden by setting themselves apart from the world in ascetic abstinence. The provision for growing food was an essential part of this withdrawal from society and asceticism.

If in ancient literature gardens and cultivated spaces had been places of leisure (*otium*), they were not in late antique religious communities. Church fathers were generally averse to traditional forms of leisure in this world, especially among communities of dedicated religious: 'Leisure (or idleness) is an enemy of the soul'.⁴⁴ Among the guidance for early religious communities, very often there was instruction to create gardens in communities of men or women living together for purposes of devotion to God, and they are clearly food-producing kitchen gardens.⁴⁵ *The Rule of the Master*, an anonymous rule composed in Italy in the early sixth century, specified that all that was necessary must be contained within a monastery's walls, including an oven for bread and a garden.⁴⁶

---

⁴² Augustine, *Confessiones*, Book VIII, 12.29, ed. O'Donnell, vol. I, pp. 101–2, see commentary at vol. III, pp. 55–71; Pagán, *Rome and the literature of gardens*, pp. 93–108. Cf. his mention of a *hortus* in the house in which he stayed at Ostia with his mother in 387, where the two of them could retire in intimate seclusion, Augustine, *Confessiones*, Book IX, 10.23, ed. O'Donnell, vol. I, p. 113, see commentary at vol. III, pp. 122–3; Shepherd et al., 'Giardini ostiensi', p. 70.

⁴³ *Sancti Pachomii vita tertia*, 45, ed. Halkin, p. 280; cf. *Historia monachorum in Aegypto*, ch. 17, in *PL* vol. 21, col. 439C; Meyvaert, 'The medieval monastic garden', pp. 25–7.

⁴⁴ 'Otiositas inimica est animae', Benedict of Nursia, *Regula*, ch. 48. See Leclercq, *Otia monastica*, pp. 27–41. Cf. Augustine, *De civitas dei*, Book 22, 19; *In Ps.* 110, I, cc 40; Dionysius Exiguus, 'Collectio decretorum pontificum romanorum', in *PL*, vol. 67, col. 232 against '*desidioso otio*'. However, see Fontaine, 'Valeurs antiques et valeurs chrétiennes', on a certain kind of Christian *otium* among Ausonius, Paulinus, Prudentius, and others.

⁴⁵ Troncarelli, 'Una pietà più profonda', has a sensible account of the different manuscript traditions and texts circulating in monastic contexts in Italy. On early rules, see Clément, *Lexique des anciennes règles*; de Vogüé, *Les regles monastiques anciennes*; Dey and Fentress eds., *Western monasticism ante litteram*.

⁴⁶ 'Omnia uero necessaria intus intra regias esse oportet, id est furnus, macinae, refrigerium, hortus uel omnia necessaria, ut non sit frequens occasio, propter quam fratres multotiens foras egressi, saecularibus mixti' (Everything necessary should be found within the gates, that is an oven, mill, cellar, garden and all that is needed, such that there should not often be reason to go out, to mix with laity), *Regula magistri*, ch. 95, 17 (ed. de Vogüé, p. 446).

Benedict's *Rule*, composed around 535, follows the earlier *Rule of the Master* closely in specifying that 'the monastery should, if possible, be so constructed that within it all necessities, such as water, mill, and garden are contained within, and the various crafts are practiced, so that there should be no need for the monks to roam outside, because this is not at all good for their souls'.[47] Compositions such as these Italian rules tended to imply a rural setting for religious communities. (Conrad Leyser makes the point that when Lombards attacked Montecassino in 577 and the monks came from a hilltop in Campania to Rome, the urban context may have been a shock.[48]) However, Gregory's letters from a few decades later attest to townhouses in which religious communities lived; they may not have had fields and mills, but as we have seen, they could have had ample cultivated spaces. Rules or letters of instruction for female religious communities in late antiquity tended to provide less detailed guidance about the structures which housed religious women than men's did, but dedicated religious women were without gardens for their own food provision.[49] There is little evidence from Italy about the shapes of early women's communities, but hagiographic material from elsewhere in sixth- and seventh-century Europe attests to religious women growing vegetables within their houses.[50]

In the mid sixth century, the retired statesman Cassiodorus composed guidance for a community of men who were living in a monastery created on his lands at Vivarium in what is now Calabria. Cassiodorus was a learned man himself, and men of his social status still lived in a world of books.[51] His instructions included suggested readings chosen for their ancient erudition, as his reading list was intended to facilitate the education of his monks.[52] But he also included practical texts, because he wanted the men to be able to grow food. A chapter of Cassiodorus's *Institutiones* recounts that his monastery was built on a site that had 'irrigated gardens and the fish-filled stream of Pellena' as well as the fishponds which give his monastery its name, and these

---

[47] 'Monasterium autem, si possit fieri, ita debet constitui ut omnia necessaria, id est aqua, molendinum, hortum, vel artes diversas intra monasterium exerceantur, ut non sit necessitas monachis vagandi foris, quia omnino non expedit animabus eorum', Benedict of Nursia, *Regula*, ch. 66, 6. On the *Rule* and its relation to the *Rule of the Master* and to Benedict, see Leyser, *Authority and asceticism*, pp. 101–7.

[48] Leyser, *Authority and asceticism*, p. 131.   [49] Smith, *Ordering women's lives*.

[50] See, for example, Willesuinda, in *Vita S. Columbani abbatis*, Book II, c. 17, ed. Krusch, p. 268.

[51] I borrow the phrase from Cooper, *The fall of the Roman household*, p. 57.

[52] These suggested readings come in Book 28, 'What Those Who Cannot Manage Texts of Logic Should Read'. On the *Institutiones*, see Vessey, 'Introduction'; Leclercq, *The love of learning*, pp. 24–30.

amenities should be used 'to prepare many things for pilgrims and the needy' as well as for the monks themselves.[53] Of Gargilius Martialis, Cassiodorus wrote that he 'has written most excellently on gardens and has carefully explained the raising of vegetables and the virtues of them, so that upon reading his treatise, under the guidance of God, everyone may be sated and restored to health'.[54] These combined benefits of gardens for food production and medicinal supplies continued to influence monasteries for centuries to come.

The craft of cultivation and knowledge of its methods were intellectual values, and they provided a practical exercise in property management. The anonymous seventh-century (?) *Regula monasterii tarnatensis*, composed probably in southern Gaul, describes the role of the gardener who should work with the cellerar and the *praepositus* to weigh and distribute evenly the vegetables or herbs.[55] Even women's rules in the seventh century include mentions of gardens among the monastic spaces; so Donatus's *Regula ad virgines*, also written in Gaul, advocates humility 'in the heart and body, at work, in the oratory, in the monastery, in the garden, on the road, wherever she is sitting, walking, standing, the head should be bowed'.[56] These 'rules' are part utopian aspirations, part practical instructions; they cannot be taken as straightforward accounts of how individual monastic communities worked, but their composition and compilation speak to the expectations and extent of the aspirations of these communities to live communally and separate from the wider world; food cultivation was a central part.[57]

In addition to rules and often differently from them, colourful stories also attest to the regular presence of productive gardens in religious communities. Gregory's stories in the *Dialogues* make clear that a garden was, for his audience, a common part of a monastery, and it

---

[53] 'ad multa peregrinis et egentibus praeparanda' 'habetis hortos irriguos et piscosi amnis Pellenae fluenta vicina', Cassiodorus, *Institutiones*, Book 29.1 (ed. Mynors, p. 73).
[54] 'de hortis scripsit pulcherrime Gargilius Martialis, qui et nutrimenta holerum et virtutes eorum diligenter exposuit, ut ex illius commentarii lectione praestante Domino unusquisque et saturari valeat et sanari', *Institutiones*, Book 28.6 (ed. Mynors, pp. 71–2).
[55] 'Hortulanus ita debet constitui, ut et praepositi et cellarii solatio sublevetur. Et quia olerum beneficiis cellariae juvantur expensae, oportet ut secundum dispensationem cellarii expendantur pariter et colantur', *Regula monasterii tarnatensis*, ch. 12 in *PL* vol. 66, coll. 977–86.
[56] 'Duodecimus humilitatis gradus est, si non solum corpore, sed etiam corde monacha humilitatem videntibus se semper indicet, id est in opere, in oratorio, in monasterio, in horto, in via vel ubicumque sedens, ambulans vel stans, inclinato sit semper capite', Donatus (d. 660), *Regula*, ch. 48 (ed. Zimmerl-Panagl, p. 169).
[57] Diem, 'Inventing the holy rule'.

was sometimes worked by the monks themselves.[58] The kitchen garden of one monastery, tended by a monk, was miraculously protected from a vegetable thief, who was then offered the vegetables as charity.[59] Saint Boniface, bishop of Ferentino, made sufficient wine from a too-small grape harvest at his monastery's vineyard and then commanded the caterpillars to stop eating the vegetables in his monastery's garden; they complied.[60] These miracles of the day-to-day give a sense of the ubiquity of monastic gardens and pesky garden bugs (anyone who grows cabbages seeks divine protection against caterpillars from time to time). The food supply of the community was a pressing concern for religious houses. Another monastic garden was tilled by men who had entered the garden as vegetable thieves, but they were miraculously convinced to change their minds and help out the monastery; they were charitably given vegetables.[61] There is a loose and widely held expectation in the early medieval West that dedicated religious houses might have food-producing gardens as part of the complex, and that one of the roles in the community might be a gardener. These are part of the landscape of late antique imagination of dedicated religious houses, largely rural but not only, and undertaking productive horticulture.

Ancient esteem for agriculture and estate-management persisted as a literary device, attesting to its continued currency. In late antique and early medieval literature, garden work was an appropriate and relevant skill for leading men. The *Dialogues* tell the story of Paulinus, the famous bishop of Nola, who offered himself as ransom for the return of a widow's son, held captive by Vandals. Paulinus describes himself as having few skills other than tending a garden, which he had done for his Vandal lord, until he converted his master and revealed himself to be the

---

[58] *Dial.* 1.7 (ed. de Vogüé, p. 65). On the *Dialogues* as '"ascetic pastorale" for city folk', see Leyser, *Asceticism and authority*, p. 153; Jenal, *Italia ascetica atque monastica*, vol. I, pp. 266–303.

[59] *Dial.* 1.3 (ed. de Vogüé, vol. II, p. 36).

[60] Wine: *Dial.* 1.9.3–4 (ed. de Vogüé, vol. II, p. 78); caterpillars: 1.9.15 (ed. de Vogüé, vol. II, p. 88).

[61] *Dial.* 3.14.6–7 (ed. de Vogüé, vol. II, pp. 306–8). See also 4.23.1 (ed. de Vogüé, vol. III, pp. 78–80), and 2.8.4 (ed. de Vogüé, vol. II, p. 162). In the latter, the Edenic associations of gardens remain clear: a presbyter, Florentius, envious of Benedict's fame, sends girls to dance naked in the garden of the monastery at Subiaco to tempt the monks. For vegetable thieves receiving garden produce from other monasteries, see Gregory of Tours, *Liber vitae patrum*, ch. 14.2, pp. 268–9, where Saint Martius, abbot of a monastery in Clermont, found a thief in the garden, gave him what the thief had picked to steal, and showed him out. For a tenth-century urban monastery at Rome with garden, olive groves, and orchards surrounding it, see *Papsturkunden* vol. I, 85 (938).

learned bishop.[62] Gregory's story turns on the humility of the bishop, acting as a servant in a garden and providing greens for his master's table, and through performing his humble yet worthy task nobly, he gained the trust of the master and was rewarded with his freedom as well as the freedom of all Campanian captives. For Gregory and his readers, working a kitchen garden was worthy labour for a great and pious man in lowly guise, an early medieval farmer-hero as bishop. In a similar way, Leontius's Greek *Life of Gregory of Agrigento* describes a vegetable garden in a monastery at Rome, which conveys the humility and moral nobility of a different Gregory, who was later bishop of Agrigento.[63] Into a garden of vegetables, perhaps at S. Saba, Gregory ran and hid to avoid being spotted by the bishops who had come to find him: 'Gregory recognized the bishops, and ran away and hid in the garden in the middle of the bushes ... And the abbot went down into the garden and found Gregory hidden in the middle of the vegetables (λαχάνων)'.[64] He was recognised by the pope, who had seen him in a dream vision, and was appointed bishop of Agrigento. The garden works here as a modest but nonetheless respectable place for the miracle-working monk to be found.

In late antique Italy, certain thinkers about the shape of monastic life, its values, and rewards were more influential than others. The tensions inherent among communities of devoted religious men and women, their desires to remove themselves from society, and the recurring need for sustenance for their bodies percolated from the earliest experiments with monasticism in deserts through to the end of the Middle Ages.[65] For Augustine, ascetic withdrawal from society could recreate the early community around Christ, and the world of the monastery served as a precursor of the world to come.[66] Augustine's influence was enormous throughout the Middle Ages, but for churchmen in the sixth century, alternative visions of the aims of separate community emerged, where the splendours of the world to come were occasioned by the

---

[62] *Dial.* 3.1 (ed. de Vogüé, vol. II, pp. 216–66).

[63] Leontius, *Life of Gregory*, ed. Berger. Berger dates the Greek *Life* to the end of the ninth century, pp. 23, 47–8; Martyn disagrees, suggesting a date closer to the lifetime of Gregory, 'Introduction', *A translation of Abbot Leontios*, pp. 20, 106.

[64] 'Καὶ ἰδὼν αἴτους ἀπὸ μακρόθεν ἐπέγνω τοὺς ἐπισκόπους, καὶ εἰσδραμὼν ἐκρύβη ἐν τῷ κήπῳ μέσον τῶν φυτῶν... Κατελθὼν δὲ ὁ ἡγούμενος ἐν τῷ κήπῳ εὗρεν αὐτὸν κεκρυμμένον μέσον τῶν λαχάνων.' Leontius, *Life of Gregory*, ed. Berger, ch. 41, trans. Martyn, p. 171. I thank Nick Evans for his help with this passage.

[65] Davies, 'Monastic landscapes and society'.

[66] Leyser, *Asceticism and authority*, pp. 3–32; MacCormack, 'Sin, citizenship, and the salvation of souls'. For a broad overview of attitudes towards property in the early medieval West, see Ganz, 'The ideology of sharing'.

humility of life in this world.[67] In both of these strands of thinking, absence of private resources was central, following the model of the apostolic community, among whom 'distribution was made to everyone, according as he had need'.[68] Ascetic withdrawal, eschewal of personal property and status, and study of scripture became, in Italy, foundational elements of monastic life and provided a new language of authority under Pope Gregory.[69] Underpinning the thinking about new forms of religious life in the fifth and sixth centuries was the long-lived Roman appreciation for agriculture and its benefits.[70]

Aristocratic Ideals and Men of the Church

In the period up to the sixth century, models of asceticism and communal living among the dedicated religious evolved. New theologies and practices were needed to resolve changing ideas and emerging circumstances. Teachings of agronomy informed the decisions not only about monasteries but also about households of churchmen. Benedict, Cassiodorus, Augustine, Gregory, and several others who composed 'rules' and instructions for religious life and who took on the leadership of the early churches of the West lived their lives as aristocratic men of high social standing.[71] Their backgrounds and social status provided them with a paideia which included the books, poems, and images which revered agriculture and estate-management, as we analysed above.[72] The discourse on how to manage an estate and a household also proved to be directly influential, not only to monastic thinkers but also to bishops of late antiquity who developed strategies to run their households and who, in turn, provided models for subordinate priestly households. *Oikonomia* was a 'specialized branch of practical knowledge and personal ethics' in antiquity.[73] The architectural theoretician of the first century, Vitruvius, provided six principles desirable in architectural design, the last of which was 'oikonomia' (allocation): 'the efficient management of resources and site, and the frugal, principled supervision of working expenses'.[74] In

---

[67] On Augustine's influence, see Marrou, *Saint Augustin*. On the *Rule of the Master*, Eugippius, and their dependence upon the language of the *passiones*, see Leyser, *Asceticism and authority*, pp. 124–5.
[68] Acts 4.35. [69] Leyser, *Asceticism and authority*, pp. 150, 180–1.
[70] Fontaine, 'Valeurs antiques et valeurs chrétiennes'.
[71] Sotinel, 'Le recrutment des évêques'.
[72] Leclercq, *Love of learning*, pp. 14–15. For analysis of paideia in Greek-language monastic traditions, see now Larsen and Rubenson, *Monastic education in late antiquity*, and on transmitted views of manual labour, see Cracco Ruggini, 'Graduatorie fra "utillimae artes"'.
[73] Sessa, *The formation of papal authority*, p. 5.
[74] Vitruvius, *Libri X*, I.2, 2, trans. Rowland, p. 25. On Vitruvius' significance in late antiquity and the Middle Ages, see Reynolds, *Texts and transmission*, pp. 440–5.

late antiquity, *oikonomia* fed into emerging ideas about the practice of power and stewardship within the ecclesiastical households, including monasteries and bishops' and priests' households in the fourth and fifth centuries.[75]

Kristina Sessa has made the case that the paradigm of good estate-management and provision for the welfare of dependents was critical to the shaping of the role of the bishop of Rome[76] between the fourth and sixth centuries (in particular from the late fifth century). As Sessa argued, 'To lead the church, [bishops] had to be seen as expert estate managers, men who could be trusted with the orderly and ethical oversight of people and property'.[77] Her argument locates one branch of the authority of churchmen in Italy in a role which drew upon the roles of *paterfamilas*, head of household.[78] In the changing social orders of late antiquity, the responsibilities of leadership incumbent upon the *paterfamilias* endured as a role for high-status men. Among the *Novels* of Justinian is a law of 539 by which any man elected to the episcopate became a *paterfamilias*, as they must be independent of any of their living male relatives.[79] The other branch of authority invoked both in rhetorical discourse and in practice among church men was that of the steward. This role went by many names in late antique Italy; fundamentally stewards acted as agents of the *dominus* of an estate to oversee finances, personnel, and other management duties related to agriculture land and household, without being the owner of the estate. In late antiquity, activities of stewardship, the practice of *oikonomia*, developed as a political philosophy, accruing specific relevance in analogy to the ordering of divine and human life.[80]

Appropriate allocation was an essential duty of bishops, abbots, and also priests who ran households for other churchmen in an evolving value of support and charity. Ambrose, bishop of Milan (d. 397), in his comments on II Corinthians accords God the highest responsibility

---

[75] On the rising power and influence of bishops, see Brown, *Power and persuasion in late antiquity*, pp. 89–117.

[76] Sessa, *The formation of papal authority*. For a critique of Sessa's argument, see McLynn, *Bryn Mawr Classical Review* 2013.02.18; for a view of Sessa's argument in relation to papal decretals, see D'Avray, 'Half a century of research'.

[77] Sessa, *The formation of papal authority*, p. 87.

[78] Sessa, *The formation of papal authority*, pp. 45–62; Cooper, *The fall of the Roman household* and especially for women and changing expectations upon them in relation to the household, pp. 107–22; Cooper, 'The household and the desert'.

[79] Justinian, *Novellae* 81.3, trans. Miller and Sarris, p. 562.

[80] Sessa, *The formation of papal authority*, quote from p. 5. For the spiritual dimensions of *oikonomia*, see Agamben, *The kingdom and the glory*; Demacopoulos, *Five models of spiritual direction*.

for the ordering of life in an agricultural metaphor: 'Everything belongs to God, both the seeds and the seedlings that grow at his nod, and are multiplied for the use of mankind. It is God, therefore, who gives these things and he himself who orders them to be shared with those who need them.'[81] Ambrosiaster, writing in Rome in the time of Pope Damasus (366–84), commented on a passage in I Timothy to make clear the bishop's relationship as steward: 'Although the entire world belongs to God, the church may nevertheless be called his house, whose rector is presently Damasus'.[82] In a broad sense, but resting upon very old and deep values, Damasus and other bishops understood their duties as the management of God's estate and its appropriate allocation.[83] The *Rule of the Master*, composed in the early sixth century in Italy, specified that at meals, the community came to the table of the abbot, over which baskets of bread and the rest of dinner hung. At the abbot's command, the food was 'to descend by the rope of the pulley, so that it might appear that the provisions for God's workmen are coming down from heaven'.[84] The abbot then distributes to the deans (mid-ranking officials within the community envisaged by the *Rule*), and the deans distribute to the brothers. As the institutions and frameworks of early Christian communities developed in the fifth and sixth centuries, very old ideas about agriculture, growing food, and sharing the produce of the land provided a rich structure supporting early medieval urban cultivation.

Emerging Ideas about Charity

Many late antique and early medieval bishops gave their homes over for a range of ecclesiastical charities. They became monasteries, households for priests, hostels for the poor, or hospitals, and these sometimes had gardens in them which were then used to produce food for the communities.[85] It may be that a bishop moved into an *episcopium* and liberated his personal or family home for a new purpose, or he may have

---

[81] 'Omnia Dei sunt, et semina et nascentia Dei nutu crescunt, et multiplicantur ad usus hominum: Deus ergo quae dat, ipse et iubet de his communicari eis, qui indigent', Ambrose, Commentary on II Cor. 9.10–11, in *PL* vol. XVII, col. 314, trans. Sessa, *The formation of papal authority*, pp. 67–8.

[82] 'ut cum tutus mundus dei sit, ecclesia tamen domus eius dicatur, cuius hodie rector est Damasus', Ambrosiaster, '*Commentarius in Epistulam ad Timotheum primam*', 3.15.1 (p. 270), trans. Sessa, *The formation of papal authority*, pp. 90–1.

[83] Sessa, *The formation of papal authority*, pp. 90–2.

[84] 'et omnibus adhuc ad suas mensas stantibus, canister supra mensam abbatis pendens trocleae fune descendat ut a caelo uideatur operariis Dei annona descendere', *Regula Magistri*, ch. 23, 2, ed. De Vogüé, vol. II, p. 110; cf ch. 21, 13.

[85] Horden, 'The earliest hospitals in Byzantium', esp. p. 377.

used his episcopal residence for distribution to the poor.[86] Bishops of Rome and other Italian cities left their personal houses to monasteries in the early Middle Ages.[87] From the eighth century to the tenth, in addition to the creation of monasteries, some bishops and priests created new institutions for the training of priests, *scolae*, and *xenodochia*, which were ecclesiastical institutions which provided care for foreigners, travellers, pilgrims, sick, and poor.[88] These two structures were different kinds of post-classical charitable institutions which went by various names; they were generally separate from monasteries or churches, though they might be administered by personnel from them, and often had their own property endowments. *Xenodochia* were founded in late antiquity by aristocrats and churchmen alike.[89] Increasingly from the eighth century they were formed around a donation from a cleric or bishop of his own house or properties for charitable purposes or for the education of clergy. In Lucca in the mid eighth century, a priest and two men created a church and *xenodochium* next to the walls, called SS. Gemignano, Paolo e Andrea, and they endowed it with their neighbouring two-story townhouse with its curtilage (adjacent land), courtyard, garden, granary, and trees, as well as a substantial portfolio of rural properties, such that pilgrims 'might take daily support'.[90] The properties are enumerated and include houses, servants, fields, woods, barnyard animals, and the

---

[86] Sessa, *The formation of papal authority*, p. 101. See Leontius, *Life of Gregory, Bishop of Agrigento*, ch. 92, for his creation of a hostel.

[87] Rome: Houses of Bishops Gregory (and that of his mother, Silvia), Honorius, Gregory II, and Paul I were all converted to monastic residences; see references in Coates-Stephens, 'Housing in early medieval Rome'. Milan: Will of Andreas, archbishop of Milan (903), in Natale, 'Chartae saeculi X (901–928)', 3 (903) (pp. 414–8), on which see below.

[88] On *xenodochia*, see Stasolla, 'A proposito delle strutture', p. 9; Dey, 'Diaconiae, xenodochia, hospitalia and monasteries'; for the East, Nutton, *Ancient medicine*, pp. 314–5; on charity of food in Southern Italy, see Skinner, *Health and medicine*, pp. 19–20.

[89] For Jerome's praise of Pammachius for founding a charitable *xenodochium* in Portus, see Epistola lxvi, 11, ed. Hilberg, p. 661. For the donation of two vineyards in Rome along with several other estates from Eustathius, dux and dispensator to the *diaconia* of S. Maria in Cosmedin in the mid eighth century, see Table 1.

[90] 'Sicherad uir uenerabilis presbitero, Filerad et Alapert ... in propriis territurio nostro ecclesia in honore sancti Geminiani, sancti Pauli et sancti Andree fabrire uisi sumus, hic prope muro ciuitati ista Lucense, ... iniui senedocium inistituere uidemur; et uolomus iuidem, quamuis in paruis, de res nostra unusquisque offerere, ut peregrinos adque eginos cotidie consulationem adcipiant. Unde in primis omnium nus qui supra Sicherad, Filerad et Alapert offerere uidemur Deo et tibi iam dicta eclesia, qui ad nus fabrita uideris esse, casa illa qui est solario, qui nouis hic prope iam dicta ecclesia ad Paulecione abuinet, cum fundaminto ubi ipsa posita est, cum curte, orto, granario, uel omnis fabricis, cum suis edificiis, cum petras et ... is uel arboribus uel omnia quas nouis hic in iam dicto loco ad ipso Paulecio abuinet, in integrum', *CDL* vol. II, 127 (757) pp. 7–11.

provision of firewood, wine, and quantities of oil annually to the *xenodochium*. The document does not make explicit the means by which this charity would be distributed to the poor but sets out the motivation as the love of God.[91]

Three early tenth-century examples make clear the nature of these new institutions and the convergence of clerical training and charity for the indigent in some Italian cities; in each of these cases and in many more, townhouses with gardens form the nucleus of the new institution. Andreas, archbishop of Milan, created an urban *xenodochium* in his will, dated 903:

> For the love of God and our Lord Jesus Christ and for the salvation of my soul and those of my aforementioned father and mother, deceased, and other family ... after my death there should be a *xenodochium* for the care of the poor in my own house, which I have in the city of Milan, not far from the church called 'Summer', and near the monastery which is called 'Wigilinda' [S. Maria], and that *xenodochium* should possess the rooms and buildings which comprise it, and that chapel erected in it, built in honour of the blessed archangel of Christ, Raphael, and the bath with the land on which they stand, also similarly holding the yard (*area*) and garden, and all that has been built or will be built there for me.[92]

He endowed it with a number of further properties, including two nearby townhouses with yards, of which his nephew reserved the use during his own lifetime, and several suburban fields and rural farms, some of which were to be used by his niece for her lifetime, and his olive orchard at Lake Como, should all eventually go to support the *xenodochium* and its operations. Each year upon the anniversary of Andreas's death, 100 poor should be fed half a loaf of bread and relish (*cumpanaticum*), 1/4 pound of lard or cheese, and a *starium* of wine.

Iohannes, bishop of Pavia, was given a small piece of land (*terrula*) and parts of the substructures of the theatre of Verona in the late ninth century

---

[91] For another *xenodochium* in the city of Lucca for feeding the poor, see *CDL* vol. II, 175 (764) pp. 137–41.

[92] 'Ego qui supra Andreas, humilis archiepiscopus ... pro amore Dei et Domini nostri Iesu Christi atque pro remedium anime mee vel suprascripto quondam genitori et genitrice mee ceterisque parentibus meis, ... post meum obitum sit senedochium in elemoniis pauperum infra casa meam propriam, quam habeo infra hac Mediolanensis civitate non multum longe ab ecclesia, qui dicitur estiva, et prope monesterio que vocitatur Vuigelinde, et in eundem senedochium deveniant potestatem salas et casas earum inibi constitutes, et capellam illam inibi edificatam constructe in onore beati Christi archangeli Rafaelis, atque balneum, cum areas in qua extant, curte et orto omnia simul tenente, et omnes edificias vel fabricatura inibi constructas', Natale, 'Chartae saeculi X (901–928)', 3 (903) (pp. 414–8) (= *CDLangobardiae* 402, though I provide the text as edited by Natale). On this document, see Balzaretti, 'Women property, and urban space', pp. 547–51.

(this gift will be discussed in Chapter 6). His written testament leaves this land and other properties to a *xenodochium* he created at the oratory of S. Siro, which he founded in Verona:

> that the two-storey house in which I live, in the castrum of Verona not far from the fountain, just as the oratory of S. Siro, confessor of Christ, which I, unworthy and a great sinner, founded with God's aid, ... should presently be a holy and venerable *xenodochium* in the aid and sustenance of the poor and the dependents of God ... The place therefore I offer as the oratory is between seven arches and vaults and the garden located in the castrum, which I did buy from a certain Idelbertus ... also one tenth of the grain which is given to the dominus, and in my house it will go in through my small courtyard, in Mareliano. To that *xenodochium* of mine I offer my kitchen, two-storey house, and stable, and the small piece of land next to it located in nine arches and vaults which my lord Berengar, emperor, gave to me by earlier documents, as declared in the same precepts and my gardens which are next to the mansio and the oratory.[93]

At Verona, the will of deacon Dagibert, dated 931, left an oratory he had built along with its adjoining house, hearth, kitchen, wine cellar, latrine, courtyard, and kitchen garden, as well as two other townhouses and many rural farms, to create a *xenodochium* 'for housing and sustaining priests and paupers and pilgrim guests'.[94] In his endowment, we can see the blending of structures for the training of priests and charity for pilgrims and the poor; all of these were to be looked after in a new *xenodochium* next to Porta S. Firmo, created out of existing structures. He stresses that the purpose of the endowment is the redemption of his soul and that of his parents.

---

[93] 'ut casa habitationis mee solariata infra castrum veronense non longe a fontana posita, simul cum oratorio beati Syri confessionis [oris?] Christi, quod ego indignus et maximus peccator Deo adiuvante in proprio me fundavi ... sit presentialiter sanctum et venerabile Xenodochium in elemosina et sustentatione pauperum Deoque famulantium ... Loco igitur dotis offero eidem oratorio inter arcovolutos et arcovalos numero septem nec non et hortum in eodem castro positum, quod dudum a quodam Ildeberto libero homine comparavi ... seu omnem decimam illam frugum quas Dominus annue dederit, et in mea mansio intraverit de curticella mea ... in ... Mareliano ... Cui etiam xenodochio meio offero cocquinam meam solariatam et stabulum meum nec non et terrulam iuxta se positam et inter arcovalos et arcovolutos numero novem quos mihi meus senior dominus Berengarius imperator per praeceptorum paginas contulit sicut in eisdem preceptis declarator seu et hortos meos qui iuxta mansionem et prefatum oraculum constat', *CDV* vol. II, 186 (922).

[94] 'xenedochium ad refugium et sustentationem sacerdotum et pauperum et ospicium peregrinancium, ... do et cedo presentialiter terram cum casis super se habente que sunt terranee cum caminatis, quoquina caneva secesso curtis orto totum in simul tenentem', *CDV* vol. II, 214 (931). On the *xenodochia* at Verona, see Miller, *The formation of a medieval church*, pp. 87–8, 101, but – critically – note the identification of several of the relevant documents (e.g. *CDV* vol. I, 101 (813) and *CDV* vol. I, 176 (844)) as later forgeries by La Rocca, *Pacifico di Verona*, pp. 54–81, 105–20.

Not all properties which went to form *xenodochia* were urban townhouses with gardens but many were. The regular presence of kitchen gardens among the houses donated for these charitable institutions suggests that these urban amenities were particularly suited to be donations for charitable purposes. In our examples, any produce of the urban plot was increased by the produce of rural properties which formed the endowment – these institutions did not survive on fresh food from the urban garden alone. Nonetheless the frequency with which houses with gardens were put to use for religious communities and charity suggests that the small degree of sufficiency that a townhouse garden afforded was desirable for this purpose. It is intriguing, in this context, to note Wendy Davies's observation that in the tenth century, Iberian monasteries were actively acquiring gardens.[95]

Ancient ideas about the cultural value of agriculture and estate-management endured into late antiquity and the early Middle Ages through separate strands of thought, some of which intertwined in the emerging culture of Christian institutions. Working the land for food continued to be viewed as a noble, esteemed activity; it appears in poetry and hagiography as a pursuit for especially pious men. Decorative gardens and flowers, while cherished among high-status homeowners and used for religious and commemorative ceremonies in antiquity, appear to have declined in value in Christian culture in Italy. Early Christian fathers such as Clement, Justin, and Tertullian distinguished their communities from earlier ones by the fact that Christians did not use flowers, and subsequent churchmen understood flowers and decorative gardens allegorically through biblical frames. Old values of estate-management nonetheless shaped the thinking of men who defined the shape of monastic communities and also the practice of urban church leaders such as bishops. The end result of efficient economic management of lands, the production of useful crops, shaped new ideas about charity and suitable distribution of resources. Urban townhouses with gardens formed the core of charitable ecclesiastical centres and households for the training of priests.

Medicine

Alongside the allocation of food resources, some early medieval religious communities provided medical care, knowledge about health, and medicine. To what degree were gardens of clerics or monks, or indeed any urban gardens owned by anyone, useful for the cultivation

---

[95] Davies, 'Gardens and gardening in early medieval Spain', pp. 347–8.

of plants for medicinal purposes? It is often assumed that gardens in medieval religious houses provided materials for healing medicines made by monks, as among the emerging roles of houses of dedicated religious men and women was also care of the sick.[96] Cassiodorus listed medical books for study at his monastery at Vivarium in a chapter for the brothers who 'vigilantly attend to the health of the human body'.[97] Cassiodorus's own advice about the practice of medicine among the monks was cited by later writers in support of monastic medicine.[98] The early ninth-century playful poem on gardens by Walahfrid Strabo, *Hortulus*, describes the medicinal values of two dozen plants, including melons and gourds, sage, rue, lilies, poppies, and many others growing in his monastic garden at Reichenau in southern Germany.[99] Many of the plants in the poem are also listed in the *Capitulare de Villis*, an idealised description of royal estates in Francia, probably composed in Aquitania in about 794.[100] What was described by a clever monk imitating Vergil in the centre of Lake Constance, or what may have been envisioned for an idealised drawing of a Carolingian monastic complex, such as the Plan of St-Gall which includes an 'herbarium' next to the physicians' house and infirmary, or an idealised vision of a royal estate such as the *Capitulare de Villis*, may not serve to accurately report any actual cultivation in Francia. These sources do, however, imply that monastic and estate gardens north of

---

[96] On care of the sick in early medieval Christian thinking, see these introductions to the topic: Horden, 'Sickness and healing'. For an example of a claim that monks used their gardens for healing remedies, see Vitolo, 'Prodotti della terra', p. 185. For evidence of domestic gardening for medical purposes in al-Andalus, see García Sánchez, 'Utility and aesthetics in the gardens', pp. 223–6.

[97] Cassiodorus, *Institutiones*, Book I.31, pp. 78–9. His list includes the Herbal of Dioscorides [*De materia medica* or Ps. Dioscorides, *Ex herbis feminis*], Hippocrates and Galen translated into Latin, a miscellany, which Everett suggests might be the *Alphabet of Galen*, Caelius Aurelius, *Medicine* [either *On acute diseases* and *On chronic diseases*], Hippocrates' *Herbs and cures*, and various others which have been left in the library. Cassiodorus, *Institutiones*, I.31, ed. Mynors, pp. 78–9; trans. Halporn, pp. 166; discussion in *Alfabetum Galieni*, ed. Nicholas Everett, p. 24; Nutton, *Ancient medicine*, pp. 307–8; Collins, *Medieval herbals*, pp. 164–5.

[98] Cassiodorus, *Institutiones*, I.31 is cited in the 'Defensio artis medicinae' of the ninth-century Lorscher Arzneibuch (Bamberg MS *Msc.Med.1, olim* L III 8, fol. 5r), transcription in Sudhoff, 'Eine Verteidigung der Heilkunde', pp. 224–33. See also MacKinney, 'Medical ethics and etiquette', pp. 5–6 and Meyvaert, 'The medieval monastic garden', p. 40.

[99] The plants he lists were common among classical agronomists, such as Columella, Palladius, and Dioscorides. For the text, *MGH, Poetae latinae*, II, pp. 259–473 and new edition of Berschin, *Walahfrid Strabo: De cultura hortorum (Hortulus)*. See also Butzer, 'The classical tradition of agronomic science', esp. pp. 573–6.

[100] *Capitulare de Villis*, ch. 70, in *MGH Capit.*, vol. I, ed. Boretius, no. 32, p. 102. On this text, see now Campbell, 'The *Capitulare de Villis*'. Cf. the *Brevium Exempla*, *MGH Capit.*, vol. I, ed. Boretius, chs. 29, 37, pp. 255–6.

the Alps grew a range of plants, most of which were familiar from Roman horticulture, and that these were useful for nutrition and health.[101]

Were urban gardens used to grow medical products? What medical ingredients were grown, by whom, and who used medical plants? As we have seen, in early medieval Italy, households of religious men and women often had gardens and charitable institutions sometimes also had large endowments including agricultural estates; the produce of these was used by dependants or sold on (or exchanged) for other goods. Did these include produce with medical properties? The example of Pertuald's donation to S. Michele, Lucca described the church and monastery as having a garden and medicinal garden (*ortum uel pigmentarium*); it had some land dedicated to products specifically for *pigmenta* (unguents or remedies), though such a designation is unusual among our documents. It is critical to examine what constituted medieval knowledge in early medieval Italy. The cities of the Italian peninsula were centres of the transmission of some kinds of medical knowledge and – it has been argued – the movement of some exotic products into continental Europe.[102] The study of Italy thus provides a significant case study for medical practices in the early medieval world. Such a study would take us far away from the present research, but a small detour in the direction of early medieval medical practice might help us to resolve a question about the degree to which medicine might have driven urban cultivation in religious houses or beyond them. We will briefly consider what constituted medical knowledge and medieval practice in our period and how ingredients for it might have been sourced.

In the early Middle Ages, there was a substantial body of information about medical theory about how the body and health worked and how remedial corrections to health might be made. This knowledge was both inherited from antiquity and evolving in new contexts. Medical knowledge was communicated in many ways, among which theoretical texts are the most visible to us now. Ancient texts were recopied and all kinds of literature were redacted, abbreviated, reorganised, and recompiled. Peregrine Horden referred to this as the 'triumph of the miscellany', and like other forms of the miscellany, the compilation of texts from disparate sources speaks to shifting taxonomies of knowledge.[103]

---

[101] On St-Gall, see Stiftsbibliothek St-Gallen, 1092. Horn and Born, *Plan of St Gall*, vol. II, pp. 203–8, discussion of the nature of the drawing in McClendon, *Origins of medieval architecture*, pp. 163–72. On the evidence it provides for healthcare, see Everett, 'The manuscript evidence for pharmacy'.
[102] On the movement of medical products, see Chapter 4, p. 130.
[103] Horden, 'What is wrong with early medieval medicine?' p. 16. See Touwaide, 'The legacy of classical antiquity' and on miscellanies, Dorofeeva, 'Miscellanies, Christian reform and early medieval encyclopaedism'.

Treatises clumped along linguistic lines, so Greek and Syriac texts moved in Greek-speaking lands, Latin in Latin-speaking lands, and after the seventh century, Arabic in Arabic-speaking lands. There were, of course, bilingual contexts in which both or several languages might be used, and there were locations for translation from one language to another, such as Constantinople, Baghdad, and Ravenna.[104] Within Italy, Ravenna in the fifth to seventh centuries, Salerno in the tenth to twelfth centuries, and Sicily in the eleventh and twelfth centuries have often been considered places for transmission and translation from Greek to Latin and, later, from Arabic to Greek or to Latin.[105] Medical treatises and recipes claimed authority through different means, from the antiquity of a text and its presumed author, to the theoretical principles which underpinned its composition, to the demonstrability of its effectiveness – some of these ways of knowing overlapped in some of our texts, others did not. For the period from the fifth century to the late eleventh century, we have a wide range of evidence for people in the Italian peninsula writing about or talking about improving or correcting health through diet and remedies of plant, animal, and mineral components. That evidence comes in part through a corpus of manuscripts in Greek and Latin written with varying degrees of polish, with compilations of calendars, excerpts of the writings of classical physicians, ancient letters on how to preserve health, and, of course, recipes for remedies, whether simples, that is, single ingredients, or more complex products to be externally applied, internally consumed, or taken in.[106] Some of these texts were intended for the use of specialists: 'physicians', court officials, or even monks or churchmen, whether practicing medicine or advising others on how to do so; others were produced for laymen and women to practice medicine on their own.[107] Of the few hundred early medieval manuscripts

---

[104] McCabe, 'Imported Materia medica'; Butzer, 'The Islamic traditions of agroecology' and references in the next note.

[105] Ravenna: Mazzini and Palmieri, 'L'ecole medicale de Ravenne: Programmes et methods d'enseignement, langue, hommes'; see also the skepticism of Vázquez Buján, 'Remarques sur la technique de traduction; Vázquez Buján, 'Problemas generales de las antiguas traducciones médicas latinas. Salerno: Jacquart and Paravicini Bagliani, *La scuola medica salernitana*; Skinner, *Health and medicine*, pp. 127–36; Sicily: Ieraci Bio, 'La trasmissione della letteratura medica Greca'; Ieraci Bio, 'Centri di trasmissione della letteratura medicale'.

[106] Other evidence comes from charters and legal codes, admirably analysed by Pilsworth, 'Beyond the medical text'; Pilsworth, 'Could you just sign this for me John?'; Pilsworth, *Healthcare in early medieval northern Italy*.

[107] For a broad overview, see Nutton, 'Early-medieval medicine and natural science'; Pilsworth, 'Could you just sign this for me John?' On self-care and the texts used for it, such as Marcellus of Bordeaux's early fifth-century collection of classical recipes from Scribonius Largus, charms, chants, and other remedies, see *Alfabetum Galieni*, ed.

collecting medical theory, instruction, or recipes from Greek- and Latin-speaking Eurasia, not one is identical to another.[108]

A fair reading of the preserved literature for early medieval medicine – one that does not simply focus exclusively on certain kinds of texts, either theoretical or practical – makes clear that much of what was written about health and illness advocated the moderation of everyday diet to rectify and improve health and, sometimes, the use of remedies; these take the form of tonics of single ingredients or compounds of several.[109] The ingredients for these remedies were often locally sourced. A large portion of classical-period medical theory concentrated on modifying the diet to improve health, and this legacy shaped profoundly the practice of the early Middle Ages. The instructions of Anthimus (c. 475–525) are a clear example of this principle. Anthimus may have been a native Greek speaker, and may have been a physician or diplomat exiled from Constantinople to Ravenna; he served on an embassy to Francia from the court of Theodoric in Ravenna. Anthimus composed a letter to Theuderic, king of the Franks, 'On the Observance of Foods' (*De observatione ciborum*)[110] which provides insight into the principles about diet, health, and remedies current at Ravenna. Anthimus's letter advocates eating a variety of foods and drink, preferably cooked (except for cheese, which he thought should not be cooked) and 'well prepared'; he provides considerable instruction about the preparation of meats, grains, vegetables, and fruits.[111] His understanding of illness and health, and the means to rectify one to improve the other, was based upon Galenic principles even if he cited no authority explicitly.[112] Ravenna seems to have been a centre of medical knowledge.[113] Some lectures on Galenic theory were transcribed 'in Ravenna' in the mid sixth to mid seventh century; Cassiodorus, who served Theodoric at Ravenna from about 500 to 540, might provide an index of medical training at Ravenna.[114]

Everett, p. 27; Stannard, 'Marcellus of Bordeaux and the beginnings of medieval *materia medica*'.

[108] The fundamental catalogues are Beccaria, *I codici di medicina del periodo presalernitano* and Wickersheimer, *Les manuscrits latins de médecine*.

[109] Wallis, 'The experience of the book'.

[110] Anthimus, *De obseruatione ciborum*. The earliest manuscript is Stiftsbibliothek St-Gallen, lat 762, s. ix; the text seems to have circulated in Francia, but not in Italy, see Grant, 'Introduction', esp. pp. 43–4.

[111] He includes rice (ch. 70), millet, and panic (ch. 71), which were not commonly eaten for food, but had been used for medical purposes and animal fodder, ed. Grant, p. 75.

[112] On his sources, see Grant, 'Introduction', pp. 38–42.   [113] See note 105 and p. 179.

[114] A ninth-century manuscript (Milan, Biblioteca Ambrosiana, G.108.inf) records notes on Hippocratic works, and a copy of lectures on works of Galen given by someone

Many of the ingredients for promoting health and correcting illness were simply foodstuffs, and these were relatively accessible and consistent in the post-classical west. There was a broad range of meats, grains, legumes, vegetables, and fruits which were common to the lands of the late Roman and post-Roman world, so foodstuffs mentioned in the ancient texts may well have continued to be grown.[115] Thus, rice, apples, and coriander had been spread in Europe and propagated by the Roman army; it is not a struggle to imagine these at a sixth-century Frankish court – we know they were in Ravenna (rice is attested archaeologically at Classe, imported to the port).[116] At the court of Theuderic near Metz, to where Anthimus seems to have directed his advice, he notes that bustards (a wild fowl) and gourds or melons are not available, though he commends eating them.[117] Issues of the difference between what would grow in the Mediterranean and what would grow north of the Alps persisted in the early Middle Ages. Thus, in the *Formula Augiensis* of the ninth century, there is the model of a letter to an abbot asking for seeds of leeks (*porra*) which apparently could not be acquired in Francia.[118] Leeks are members of the *allium* genus, and while their seeds were apparently difficult for at least one monastic household to acquire in Francia, they were common cultivated plants in the Roman and post-Roman world, grown from seed; Pliny reports they were eaten to improve the voice, and they appear among the garden plants of the *Capitulare de Villis*.[119]

Those with a maximalist view of long-distance trade in the early Middle Ages have made the argument that not only ingredients but also manuscripts with medical texts arrived north of the Alps through Italy. John Riddle suggested that medical goods moved from east to west through what he called 'folk-communication', a mysterious process invisible to us in the written record but akin to the means by which tin

---

named 'Agnellus, yatrosophista' and also termed 'archiatrus', recorded by someone named Simplicius 'medicus' 'in Ravenna' along with other works, *Alfabetum Galieni*, ed. Everett, p. 22. For Cassiodorus's recommendations, see note 97.

[115] See the list of foodstuffs in Opsomer-Halleux, 'The medieval garden and its role in medicine', pp. 106–12.

[116] Augenti et al., 'Indagine archeologiche a Classe (Scavi 2004)'.

[117] Anthimus, *De obseruatione ciborum*, ch. 33, 57, ed. Grant, pp. 63, 71.

[118] 'Ceterum obnixe deposcimus, ut, si ulla facultas assit, pro semine porri nos adiuvetis, quia in tota Francia nec ad conparandum aliquid huiusmodi adinvenimus', Formulae Augienses C, Formula 8, *MGH Form.*, p. 368.

[119] Pliny, *Historia naturalis*, Book XIX. 33. See John of Cassian, *De coenobiorum institutis*, Book IV.22 (ed. Petschenig, p. 63) on monastic diet including leek tops, and on leeks in other Frankish monasteries, see Meyvaert, 'The medieval monastic garden', pp. 34–5; *Capitulare de Villis*, c. 70, in *MGH Capit.*, vol. I, ed. Boretius, no. 32, p. 102.

and amber arrived in Europe in prehistory.[120] Michael McCormick argued rather that medical ingredients, like silks and other luxury goods, moved through ecclesiastical networks through Italy into northern Europe. McCormick argues that there was a real difference in the availability of exotic products between early medieval Italy and Francia: 'on the Italian side of the Alps ... pepper was reckoned in pounds or sacks (presumably a multiple of pounds). Cumin also was counted in pounds; cinnamon and costus were measured in ounces'.[121] Peregrine Horden, in his recent survey of the state of early medieval medicine, followed McCormick in arguing that the medical codices brought to St-Gall from Italy attest 'the vigour of trade [between Italy and] the eastern Mediterranean in the Carolingian period', and the arrival in Western Europe of exotic culinary/medicinal ingredients such as pepper because recipe books from Italy included ingredients which came from beyond western Christendom and because some spices and exotic ingredients appear to have been acquired through Italian networks.[122]

There are two reasons for which I am sceptical of such a view. First is the conservatism of medical literature in the early Middle Ages.[123] For example, the so-called *Alphabet of Galen*, a text produced in the seventh or eighth century in Italy, includes many items which are grown locally as well as many more which are described specifically as imports to the Mediterranean world. Among its list of substances – just from the Cs:Cardomom, from Arabia and other places, which heats and loosens, so it 'relieves cramps and gas in the bowels, causes urination and menstruation, and expels the foetus'. [*AG* 71];

Cumin, from Ethiopia and Arabia which softens and warms, 'hence it is good for flatulence and stomach cramps, is a powerful pain-reliever, and when drunk it turns the skin pale' [*AG* 69]; the mineral Chrysocolla, from Armenia, Macedonia or Cyprus, which is styptic, meaning it stops

---

[120] Riddle, 'The introduction and use of eastern drugs in the early Middle Ages', p. 197. Further on models of the early medieval economy of Italy, see Chapter 4.
[121] McCormick, *Origins of the European economy*, p. 708, cf. pp. 712, 727. On incense, recipes for it and the ingredients they use, see now Burridge, 'Incense in medicine'.
[122] McCormick's and Horden's comments consolidate decades of consideration of the questions; see Voigts, 'Anglo-Saxon plant remedies'; Riddle, 'The introduction and use of eastern drugs in the early Middle Ages', and now Burridge, 'An interdisciplinary investigation into Carolingian medical knowledge and practice'.
[123] For new interventions in the long debate about the degree to which early medieval European medical texts were derivative or inventive, see now Burridge, 'An interdisciplinary investigation into Carolingian medical knowledge and practice' with citation and discussion of the relevant literature.

bleeding and 'is mixed with eye salves for healing watery eyes' ... and 'strips away overgrown flesh'. [*AG* 66].[124]

The entries on these substances derive nearly *verbatim* from the Latin translation of Περὶ ὕλης ἰατρικῆς by Dioscurides (*c.* 40–90 CE), his collection of simples.[125] Dioscurides' text continued to be highly influential in early medieval Italy; the list of plants and minerals cannot be taken as evidence for cultivation patterns or trading networks of seventh- or eighth-century Italy, but rather of the continuing use of Dioscurides. Remedies written in early medieval Italy vary considerably in the obscurity of their ingredients, however. The second reason for which we should avoid drawing conclusions about trade in exotic substances through Italy based on medical literature is that there was enormous variation in the texts themselves. Two recipes from a single codex written in Italy make this point clear: BAV pal lat 187 is a small codex (109 mm × 177 mm, 66 folios), almost a pocketbook, which includes fragments of a psalter and the earliest manuscript copy of the *Alphabet of Galen* (ff 8-66 v), written probably in Northern Italy, in the seventh or eighth century.[126] On folio 7, the final page of the quire onto which part of a psalter had been copied, there are two recipes written out somewhat informally in a cursive script of Northern Italy, perhaps a notarial hand, of the mid to later eighth century (Table 4, Fig. 25).[127] One recipe is for an unguent to loosen the belly, and it includes as ingredients aloe, myrrh, basil, costus root, cardamom, galbanum, and saffron. Some of these ingredients would have been relatively easy to get in Northern Italy, such as rose, basil, and juniper berry, but galbanum is, according to the *Alphabet of Galen*, a 'sap from a shrub grown in Syria';[128] cardamom, as we have just seen, was known as an Arabian spice; and several others were known through texts like the *Alphabet of Galen* as products of distant lands. Claire Pilsworth suggests that given the ingredient list, this was a recipe which might have been originally translated from Greek, the recipe itself being

---

[124] *AG* s.v. Cardomom no. 71; s.v. cumin no. 69, and *AG* s.v. Chrysocolla no. 66.
[125] Pedanius Dioscorides, Book I.6 (ed. Wellmann, vol. I, pp. 10–11), Book III.59 (ed. Wellmann, vol. II, pp. 71–2), Book V.89 (ed. Wellmann, vol. II, pp. 62–3).
[126] Vatican City, BAV, pal. lat. 187 (s. viii$^{2/2}$) measures 109 × 177 mm; digitised here: https://digi.vatlib.it/view/bav_pal_lat_187 [accessed: September 2019]. On the codex and its script, see *Codices Latini Antiquiores*, vol. I, nos. 80, 80a, and 81 (p. 24); *Alfabetum Galieni*, ed. Everett, pp. 122–4. On the condition of the codex and the implications of its signs of wear for questions of practical use, see McCormick's colourful description of the 'filthy little book', 'one of the dirty and well-worn medical manuscripts of convenient pocket size', McCormick, *Origins of the European economy*, p. 713 and note 77.
[127] Pomaro, 'Prolegomeni alla "classe carolina"' has a guide to the letter forms on Tav. IV, no. 15; see also Petrucci, 'Alfabetismo ed educazione grafica', p. 118; Angrisani, 'Materiali per uno studio', p. 129, gives it as s. viii, 'probably northern Italian'.
[128] *AG* s.v. Galbanum no. 119.

Table 4 *Recipes of BAV, pal. lat. 187, f. 7r, transcription C. Burridge* [i]

1 **Unguentum ad uentrem soluendum**	**An unguent to loosen the belly**
2 recipet haec . Aloe rosas agrestes . libanu /	This is the recipe. Aloe,[ii] wild rose,[iii] frankincense,[iv]
3 mastice . opopanace galbanu crocu cinicum /	Mastic,[v] opopanax,[vi] galbanum,[vii] saffron,[viii] safflower,[ix]
4 titimalum . storace locia . sucus absenti /	spurge,[x] storax,[xi] *locia*, juice of absinth,[xii]
5 basilico costu foliu cyperum cardamomum /	basil,[xiii] costus,[xiv] *folium* (leaf of malabar?),[xv] galingale,[xvi] cardamom,[xvii]
6 murra larice maratri . semen archiotides /	myrrh, larch, fennel,[xviii] seed of juniper berry,
7 coloquintidis diagridiu. oleum commun\<em\> /	colocynth or wild gourd,[xix] compound of scammony,[xx] common oil,
8 \<cera\> quod sufficit **Potio ad psysicos** /	wax to suffice. **Potion for health**
9 pullum crassum adipes recentes omnes quales /	Fresh fats of a heavy hen, all that comes.
10 inuenire potueris lardu medulla et suina sebu /	You mix pork lard, marrow, and suet,[xxi]
11 et suinum et taurinum hircinum uel uerbicinum /	And pork, beef, goat or sheep
12 axuntia buturum mel oleum nuoleus \<pinto\> /	fat, butter,[xxii] honey,[xxiii] oil,[xxiv] [???]
13 a modalas nuces abellanas tritas radices /	In amount that corresponds to a hazelnut,[xxv] roots
14 enule radices anagallici euisci apii petrosilini /	of elecampane,[xxvi] roots of pimpernel,[xxvii] mallow,[xxviii] celery,[xxix] parsley[xxx]
15 feniculi radices porri capitta libistici radices satu /	Fennel roots,[xxxi] head of a leek,[xxxii] lovage roots,[xxxiii] savory,[xxxiv]
16 regia ysopum origanum . sarpullum trita omnia /	hyssop,[xxxv] oregano,[xxxvi] wild thyme,[xxxvii] all ground.
17 bulliat in uino albo usqe dum solum modo ossa /	It should be boiled in white wine until only the bones
18 ex eodem pullo remaneat colabis per lenteolum /	of that chicken remain, you will filter through linen
19 et \<rep\>onis in baso et dum opus f\<uerit\> facis condi\<o\> /	and you will replace it in the vessel and while this is done, you make *conditum* (seasoned wine).
20 et calefacis et cum loro condito bibat in balneo /	And you heat it up and let him drink it with *conditum* (seasoned with laurel) in a bath
21 aere ieiunus ue\<l\> foris t\<ant\>um modo ieiunus /	of copper, on an empty stomach, or out in the same way, on an empty stomach,
22 nam et sagappinum cum \<lacte datum\> in balneo /	And also sagapenum[xxxviii] with milk, in a bath,
23 in ore iubat /	By mouth. It helps.

[i] Digitised image here:

https://digi.vatlib.it/view/bav_pal_lat_187
Transcription by Claire Burridge, whom I thank for sharing her thoughts on this manuscript, these recipes, and their translation.
[ii] *AG* s.v. Aloe, no. 5.
[iii] *AG* s.v. Rosa, no. 232.
[iv] Du Cange et al., *Glossarium*, s.v. Olibanum.
[v] *AG* s.v. Mastiche, no. 186.
[vi] *AG* s.v. Opoponax, no. 201.
[vii] *AG* s.v. Galbanum, no. 119.
[viii] *AG* s.v. Crocus, no. 44.
[ix] AG s.v. Cnicum, no. 82.
[x] *AG* s.v. Tithymallum, no. 280.
[xi] *AG* s.v. Styrax, no. 254.
[xii] *AG* s.v. Absinthium, no. 17.
[xiii] *AG* s.v. Ocimum, no. 205.
[xiv] *AG* s.v. Costum, no. 64.
[xv] *AG* s.v. Folium, no. 111.
[xvi] *AG* s.v. Cyperus, no. 61.
[xvii] *AG* s.v. Cardamomum, no. 71.
[xviii] Du Cange et al., *Glossarium*, s.v. Maratrum.
[xix] *AG* s.v. Quolocynthis, no. 226.
[xx] *DMLBS* s.v. dia.
[xxi] *AG* s.v. Sepum, no. 244.
[xxii] *AG* s.v. Butyrum, no. 41.
[xxiii] *AG* s.v. Mel, no. 179.
[xxiv] *AG* s.v. Oleum, no. 203.
[xxv] Du Cange et al., *Glossarium*, s.v. avellane.
[xxvi] *AG* s.v. (H)Elenion, no. 99.
[xxvii] *AG* s.v. Anagallis, no. 25.
[xxviii] *DMLBS* s.v. Ebiscus; AG s.v. Ibiscus, no. 138.
[xxix] *AG* s.v. Apium, no. 14.
[xxx] *DMLBS* s.v. petroselinum.
[xxxi] *AG* s.v. Foeniculum, no. 110.
[xxxii] Du Cange et al., *Glossarium*, s.v. porrus.
[xxxiii] AG s.v. Libysticum, no. 148.
[xxxiv] *AG* s.v. Satureia, no. 268.
[xxxv] *AG* s.v. (H)Yssopum, no. 297.
[xxxvi] *AG* s.v. Origanum, no. 206.
[xxxvii] *DMLBS* s.v. Serpullum.
[xxxviii] *AG* s.v. Sagapenum, no. 243.

an eastern product which required imported ingredients.[129] On the same page, written with the same hand, is another remedy, made of ingredients

[129] Pilsworth, *Healthcare in early medieval northern Italy*, pp. 94–5. On Byzantine recipes, see Baader, 'Early medieval Latin adaptations of Byzantine medicine in Western Europe'.

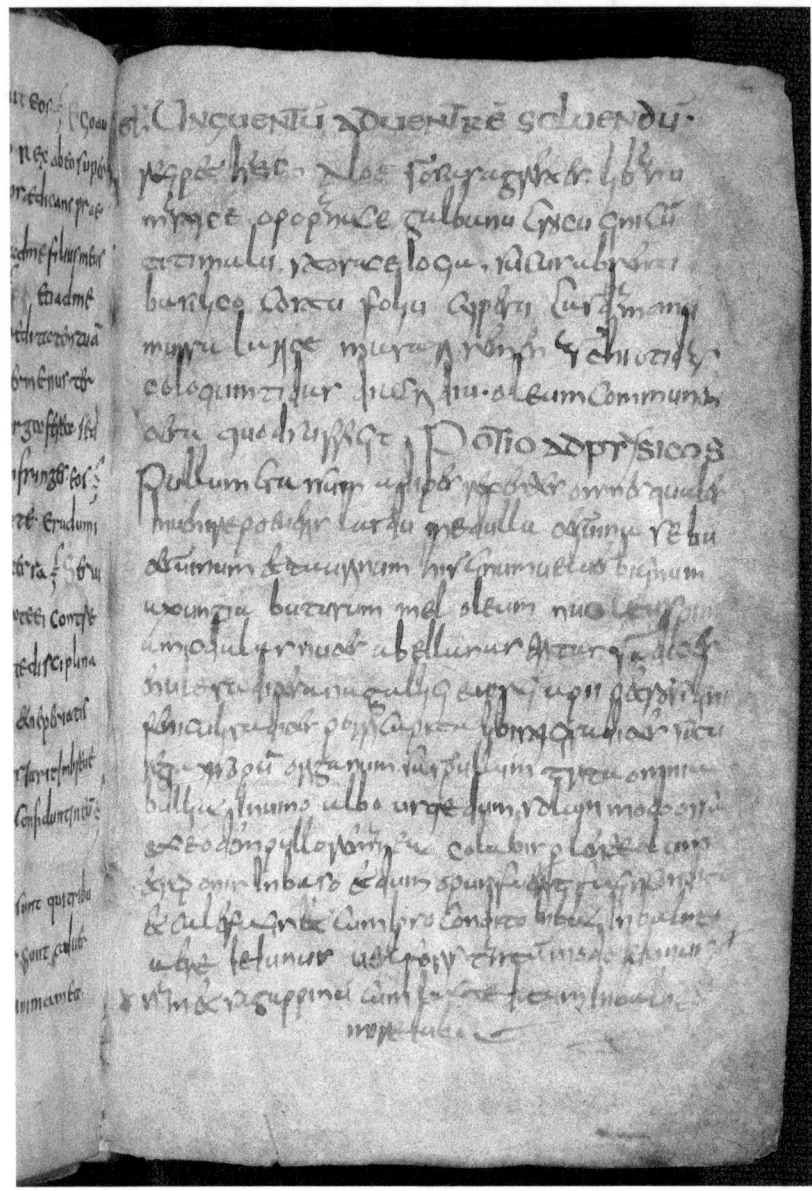

Figure 25 BAV pal. lat. 187, f. 7r. Photo © Biblioteca Apostolica Vaticana, reproduced by permission of Biblioteca Apostolica Vaticana, with all rights reserved.

including animal products, roots of several garden plants, oils, and honey. These ingredients, Pilsworth suggests, might be found in the larder of a well-furnished house in Northern Italy, and the presence of lard suggests, further, that the source of the recipe is probably not Mediterranean in origin.[130] I agree with Pilsworth's broad characterisations of the differences in the ingredients of the two recipes but draw different conclusions. First, many of the exotic ingredients in the first recipe are to be found in treatises circulating in Italy. They were familiar names, even if the products were not easily to hand. The presence of these ingredients in this recipe, however, does not mean that these products were easily accessible in Italy. The fact that the two recipes appear in the same hand, on the same folio of a manuscript with other kinds of medical texts, suggests that there was a very broad range of practices, ingredients (or desired ingredients) for recipes, and forms of knowledge in circulation in early medieval Italy. There were substitutions for different ingredients, as are attested in later recipe collections, and it may be that without ingredients for one recipe, another with available products was used.[131]

A manuscript-based approach to the evidence for medical literature and remedies, one which takes regional differences into account, reveals a profile of medical practice which was diverse and varied even within Italy. Some cities in Italy, such as Ravenna and later Salerno, fostered the transmission and translation of texts, the teaching of traditions and principles; in others, such as Rome or Genoa, exotic ingredients might have been exchanged. But this sheds very little light on what plants might have been grown for medical purposes or where. A further complication regarding the cultivation of medical plants is the principle commonly expressed in classical treatises that wild ingredients are more efficacious than domestic ones.[132] For example, Dioscurides claimed about the opium poppy (*papaver somniferum*) that there are garden-variety poppies with no narcotic effects and wild ones which were preferable for medicine; these differences were repeated in Latin translations and in other texts based on Dioscurides, such as the *Alphabet of Galen*, and also by modern scholars.[133] Those authors made distinctions also between wild and cultivated asparagus, poppy, and many other plants. Early medieval recipe collections sometimes specify wild ingredients, such as asparagus *agrestis* or *silvaticus* or *papaver silvaticum*. Given that many of the ingredients for remedies were commonplace plants in post-Roman Europe and some grew 'wild' without cultivation, it is impossible to identify

[130] Pilsworth, *Healthcare in early medieval northern Italy*, p. 95.
[131] On replacements, see Touwaide, 'Quid pro quo: Revisiting the practice of substitution'.
[132] Opsomer Halleux, 'The medieval garden and its role in medicine', p. 103.
[133] Dioscurides, Book IV, 64 (ed. Wellmann, vol. I, pp. 218–21), *AG* s.v. Opium, no. 199.

a specifically medical garden, and we struggle to know what Pertuald's *pigmentarium* (p. 81) might have been.

Given the overlap between the ingredients for everyday meals and health remedies in the early Middle Ages, and the wide range of practices aimed at health and medicine that the textual evidence attests in our period, some of it evidently illusory, to what degree did medical aims motivate urban cultivation? Archaeobotanical evidence does not provide any clear answers to the question, because some plants identifiable in the record were potentially used for everyday foodstuffs as well as for medicine. Some plants like violets (*Viola sp*) or chamomile (*Matricaria chamomilla*) grew spontaneously as weeds but also had medical applications. For instance, excavations of an urban garden at Ferrara, discussed in Chapter 3, revealed a wide range of archaeobotanical remains of foodstuffs, a few plants that might have been used for textiles or food, and a few plants which may have been medical.[134] The excavators stressed the preponderance of cultivated poppy (*papaver somniferum*) among the plants identified; this might have been used as seed in foods, as the excavators suggest, or perhaps for medical purposes.[135] Through food came health, and urban gardens were a source of food for early medieval city-dwellers, but it does not appear that providing resources specifically for medicine was an aim for urban cultivation.

Conclusions

Roman views on horticulture ran deep and remained influential in the early Middle Ages. Among Romans of the imperial period, there was widely felt esteem for working the land to produce useful products efficiently, an esteem strongly rooted in legends about the foundation of Rome and early leaders and gardens' noble modesty and productivity. Efforts to improve upon agricultural techniques prompted scholars to compose new treatises and collect knowledge of the natural world, as well as to celebrate plants and farming in verse. In the transformations of late antiquity, some of these views and values endured: the role of cultivated space in noble estates, and the sense of pride in effective management of an agricultural estate. Some Roman authors on horticulture were reproduced and transmitted into late antiquity, often in redacted and reordered compilations. Other Roman traditions of horticulture were suppressed, in particular the practice of growing flowers for garlands and using garlands to celebrate, commemorate, and worship. A much narrower canon of

---

[134] See Table 2, Chapter 3; Bosi et al., 'Applicazioni morfobiometriche'.
[135] Fritsch, 'Zur Samenmorphologie des Kulturmohns'; Scarborough, 'The opium poppy'.

Conclusions

flowers and flower uses were invoked by early Christian writers and churchmen. Violets and roses, the traditional flowers of garlands, were still grown, sometimes wild and used for medicinal purposes. Food horticulture continued to be praised in Christian literature and poetry. Roman traditional views on horticulture informed the shape of new Christian institutions through the models of household leadership. Urban gardens formed the core of many urban ecclesiastical residences, both high-status episcopal residences, monasteries, and also new charitable institutions founded by churchmen. In these contexts, the self-sufficiency – even limited self-sufficiency – provided by a garden appears to have been key to the running of an urban *xenodochium* or *scola* for priests. Medical plants may have motivated urban cultivation in the early Middle Ages, but the wide variety of practices which can be grouped under the heading of medicine and the enormous difficulty we have in identifying strictly medical plants make it impossible for us to assess the degree to which urban gardens were considered medicinal.

Through the transformations of late antiquity and the early middle ages, urban living took on new forms, and urban horticulture played a key role in social interactions, both those around new religious communities, as we have seen, and across the vertical hierarchy of early medieval Italian societies. Reconsidering the ways in which power was manifest in cities helps to show further the ways in which ideas about cultivation transformed and came to underpin urban socio-politics, as we shall see now.

6   Conspicuous Cultivation

How was power communicated in early medieval Italy? What forms did power take and how was it enacted or embodied? What role did urban patronage play in this? Many of our ideas about the performance of power in the early Middle Ages can be traced to ideas about how power worked in imperial Rome: munificence and euergetism, especially of churches. In reviewing the strategies of performing power in antiquity and the conventional understandings of power in urban contexts of the early Middle Ages, we can re-evaluate the ways in which cultivated lands within a city might have participated in social mobility and the achieving of status in the early Middle Ages.

Being and remaining powerful in the later Roman Empire involved spending money on public goods. Emperors laid out new public sectors of cities and individual monuments, especially in the capitals but also in other cities of the empire. Imperial public buildings were vehicles for imperial beneficence, munificence for the benefit of all, and for the pleasure and sustenance of the populace. During the late Republic and principate, wealthy Romans lavished gifts of buildings or games upon their cities. Some of these gifts were from urban patrons to their city in a quasi-official exchange: financing of projects to be reciprocated by political support and honours. In other cases, local elites paid for honorific statues, shrines, and monuments (usually accompanied by inscriptions) in honour of a higher-status patron with the expectation of protection and munificence. These were part of a loosely structured, ubiquitous reciprocal relationship between elite clients and their imperial patrons, whereby paying for projects or gifts was reciprocated with honours, loans, or other *beneficia*.[1] Imperial officials and local administrators in the imperial government often paid for buildings or restorations of public buildings and infrastructural works in Italian cities. Private citizens

---

[1] The classic statement is Saller, *Personal patronage under the early Empire*, and the essays in Wallace-Hadrill (ed.), *Patronage in ancient society*.

also gave public gifts for love of their city and its citizens or as part of the specified duties of their position as a magistrate. From the inscriptions that commemorate the donations of buildings, statues, restoration projects, or games, we read of men and occasionally women who paid for gifts on behalf of their cities.[2]

The first part of this chapter will focus on the means by which power was performed and experienced in the urban landscapes of Italian cities of late antiquity, considering the paired legacies of providing public food provision and architectural and infrastructural patronage as markers of high social status. I will then consider the means by which we currently understand patronage within early medieval environments, based in part upon late antique patterns, and how pervasive remained the understanding that architectural commissions – building or renovating or restoring – were key to achieving social prestige or spiritual benefits. I finally will consider some of the other means by which power was conveyed in early medieval Italy, namely through the exchange of agricultural property, as a means to suggest how these tools were employed in urban contexts as well, which will bring us back to gardens.

The patterns of the movement of cultivated land within elite networks attest to the high value that contemporaries placed on it and suggest that urban cultivated spaces had a particular social capital. The ideals associated with this kind of property, as we have seen in Chapter 5, preserved some commonalities with antiquity and also revealed new ideas about cultivation within the context of new views of households and ecclesiastical communities. Other factors, also related to both ancient precedents and emerging social structures, shaped the significance of household gardens among urban elites. I argue that the ownership of cultivated spaces and their transfer through gift or sale were influential for social status, just as the building of monumental churches was. Though early medieval urban churches and their decorations are more likely to have survived to the present day than an orchard is, agricultural properties and the gardens, orchards, and vegetable patches in early medieval Italian cities were similarly integral tools of elite expression and social mobility.

Patterns of patronage and euergetism were visible in the late antique urban landscape. Strolling through the Roman Forum, for instance, a visitor to late antique Rome would have seen the paved central area between the old and new *rostrae*, in front of the Curia Senatus, marked by inscriptions commemorating restorations. Some of the major buildings in the lower Forum had been recently restored, by individuals or by the

---

[2] See the fundamental study by Veyne, *Le pain et le cirque*, and for Roman Italy into late antiquity, see the essays in Lomas and Cornell, eds., '*Bread and circuses*'.

Senate, and some of the inscriptions celebrated the patrons' love of the city. The roads of the Forum and parts of the Imperial Fora nearby were lined with columns and statues, their bases inscribed with patrons' names and titles.[3] Lavish architectural programmes such as the Forum of Peace, built by Vespasian in 71 CE, stood as monuments to the patron's resources and his aesthetic sophistication. The Forum of Peace showcased ancient statuary and was planted with fountains surrounded by beds of short, bushy flowering roses, the red *Rosa gallica*; and perhaps also trees brought from conquered Judea are a statement of territorial domination.[4] This part of the urban landscape was filled with competing expressions of a certain kind of social and political virtue, which was corroborated by other kinds of building elsewhere. Up to the fourth century, the cities of Italy were the canvases upon which urban elites of Italy projected their social status and mobility, and the commemoration of this patronage was a strategy for competition among families and the building of legacies for the future.[5] The practices of private urban euergetism, well established in the principate, changed over the course of the fourth and fifth centuries in relation to two major factors: the increasingly limited opportunities for social mobility among the high ranks of late Roman society, and the rise of Christianity.[6]

In late antiquity, the erection of an honorific statue or a commemorative monument was controlled by the Senate (notionally) and the emperor (practically).[7] Wealth in late antique Italy was in the hands of a smaller number of families, bound up in the Imperial administration and, eventually, the church. At Rome itself, civic patronage by private people continued through the late fifth and early sixth centuries; elsewhere in Italy, private euergetism declined already in the fourth century.[8]

---

[3] See Weiswelier, 'Making masters, making subjects', on the changes in honorific statues at Rome from Republican to early Imperial, and early Imperial to late antique.

[4] Meneghini and Santangeli Valenzani, *I Fori imperiali*, pp. 61–70; Carroll, 'Contextualising art and nature', p. 546; on the plantings in the rectangular beds, see Rizzo, 'Indagini nei Fori Imperiali', pp. 238–9; and for suppositions about what trees were planted, see Pollard, 'Pliny's *Natural history*'.

[5] On the patronage of buildings in Roman Italy as a social tool, see Millar, 'Italy and the Roman Empire', p. 317, and for late antiquity and the Middle Ages, Ward-Perkins, *From classical antiquity* remains apposite; see now also Brown, *Through the eye of a needle*, pp. 53–92.

[6] Smith, 'Restored utility/Eternal city'; Kalas, 'Writing restoration in Rome'; Kalas, *The restoration of the Roman Forum*; Alföldy, 'Urban life, inscriptions'.

[7] Weiswelier, 'Making masters, making subjects'; Smith and Ward-Perkins, *The last statues of antiquity*; Machado, *Urban space and aristocratic power*, pp. 139–45, 266–7. For the complex tensions between senate and emperor in the erection of monuments, especially on the Forum of Rome, see Marlowe, 'The multivalence of memory'.

[8] Ward-Perkins, *From classical antiquity*, points to a marked decline in non-imperial patronage already in the early third century, pp. 14–37.

Changes in who spent money on buildings and where they spent it, concomitant with the changes in the urban fabric of the cities of Italy discussed in Chapter 2, fostered new and different strategies for social mobility and elite representation in the urban context. The rise of Christianity, as has long been known, provided new opportunities for social mobility and peer-polity interaction in the promotion of cults through church building, decoration, and furnishing, as well as through support – direct or indirect – for the poor.

In order to understand support for the poor in late antique cities of Italy, it is essential to recognise the distinction between models of euergetism at Rome and those elsewhere. At Rome, a key expectation of the emperor was that he would ensure the distribution of grain and pork, and later also bread and wine, to citizens of Rome.[9] This system, the *annona*, was not principally a measure of charity, but rather it was the right of certain citizens and meritorious individuals to receive food provisions from the state:[10] grammarians, orators, physicians, and lawyers,[11] as well as military men.[12] Enormous energies were expended to make this possible. Despite periods of shortage and changes in provisioning after the Vandal conquest of North Africa, emperors still provided food to members of the Roman populace, and there existed a significant administration to facilitate this.[13] From the fourth century and through the fifth century, emperors also began to consider provision for the needy, and typically through endowments and incomes to episcopal churches and their facilities which allowed them to feed, bathe, and look after the poor.[14] Bishops encouraged almsgiving, through the church, for the care of the poor, and as Michele Salzman has shown, through the fifth century both the tradition of civic euergetism to provide food for individuals in Rome and new ideas about Christian charity for the indigent moved in parallel to influence imperial funding, at least until the middle to late sixth century.[15] By the end of the century, the bishop of Rome was responsible for the feeding of the (by now somewhat less populated) city, and the managing of the grain supply for doing so. Elsewhere in Italy (and the Empire) bishops

---

[9] Lo Cascio, 'Canon frumentarius, suarius, vinarius'; and Rickman, *The corn supply of ancient Rome*.
[10] Virlouvet, *Tessera frumentaria*.
[11] Justinian, *Novellae*, Pragmatic Sanction, 22 (532), trans. Miller and Sarris, p. 1127.
[12] *Codex Theodosianus* 14.17.10 (392) and 14.17.11 (393).
[13] Sirks, *Food for Rome*; Durliat, *De la ville antique*.
[14] Salzman, 'From a classical to a Christian city'; Brown, *Poverty and leadership in the later Roman Empire*.
[15] Neil, 'Imperial benefactions to the fifth-century Roman church'.

negotiated the appropriation of certain public responsibilities, including the commissioning of certain public works.[16]

Outside of Rome, civic euergetism took slightly different forms, tending towards the provision of entertainment and the erection of statues and buildings.[17] In paying for buildings and entertainment, patrons showed themselves to be members of the elite and invited the support of the populace, hoping for help in elections or appointment as civic patrons. Thus at Benevento a certain number of inscriptions attest to renovations of buildings by private individuals from the later fourth and fifth centuries. An earthquake is attested in the area, in either 346 or 375; it may have provoked damage requiring restorations. In addition to restorations, twenty-two inscriptions from honorific statue bases dating to the fourth and fifth centuries make clear the extent of patronage in the city through late antiquity. Members of the plebs of Benevento, *viri clarissimi*, civic patrons, and then (after 333) governors erected statues in honour of the emperor, of patrons, and for the ornament of the city, proclaiming their names, rank, and sometimes ancestry in the inscribed bases. The urban fabric of Benevento was restructured on a smaller scale, with a reduced circuit of walls dating from the later fourth century and the construction of a major church, the episcopal basilica. Despite the smaller scale of late antiquity, there was nonetheless attention paid to the ornament of the city and civic euergetism. The major aristocrat Quintus Aurelius Symmachus (d. 402) wrote to his father in 375 from Benevento describing how, after the earthquake, citizens 'exhaust their private fortunes in competition over the adornment of the city'. He remarked upon the honours the city bestowed upon him, in expectation of his own patronage: 'I was feted with such great honours that I am now weighted down by obligations', making clear that the city certainly hoped for his assistance with private contributions to the decoration of the city.[18] As a consular capital, Benevento may have enjoyed more civic patronage than, say, Catania or Pavia, but the point nonetheless remains that among provincial centres in late antiquity the culture of private euergetism and display of civic patronage remained a meaningful expression of social status and tool of social mobility.[19] Bishops increasingly participated in this process, even in terms of the

---

[16] See the essays in Rebillard and Sotinel, *L'évêque dans la cité*, esp. the contribution of Sotinel.
[17] Cébeillac-Gervasoni, *Les élites municipales*; Lomas, 'Public building, urban renewal'.
[18] 'privatam pecuniam pro civitatis ornatu certatim fatigant ... Ibi summo cultu civium plausuque susceptus tanto honore celebrabar, ut iam gravarer officiis'; see Symmachus, *Ep*. I. 3.3–4, trans. Salzman and Roberts.
[19] Using the database of Smith and Ward-Perkins, *The Last Statues of Antiquity* (website: http://laststatues.classics.ox.ac.uk).

construction of churches, such as the basilica of Benevento, which may have been funded by a bishop – we know of no other patron for it.[20]

The urban fabric of major cities in Italy and the large number of inscriptions, statues, and shrines in them reflected the jostling of families for social status and support. Between the fourth and seventh centuries, as churches were built in cities, they too bore the names of their patrons, whether clerical or lay.[21] Thus, the mosaic pavements of the cathedrals of Florence (c. 400), Parma (late fourth or early fifth centuries), Brescia (late fourth or early fifth), and several other early churches were inscribed with the names of the men and women who financed the pavement, with the number of feet of mosaic that they endowed.[22] Other mosaics recorded votive donations from individuals, such as the monumental mosaic of S. Maria Maggiore, at Rome, reading 'Xystus Episcopus Plebi Dei', or the pavement of the cathedral of Bari, recording the patronage of clerics towards the decoration of the church.[23]

Epigraphy was essential in recording this kind of urban investment. There was a strong correlation between urbanism, literacy, and the epigraphic habit, continuing through late antiquity. Through the course of the fourth and fifth centuries and beyond, the display of writing in urban contexts declined and became increasingly attached to sacred functions and religious buildings. Lay use of epigraphy continued – for funerary markers of high status, for instance, and occasionally to celebrate a commission – but the numbers of preserved examples are considerably reduced with respect to previous centuries.[24] Other aspects of urban display became important.

Late Antiquity

In the cities of Italy, competitive patronage remained a useful strategy for social mobility beyond late antiquity, as we shall see. It began to take different forms, in particular through the vehicles provided by the church and its increasing range of activities. The foundation of oratories and private churches, monasteries and charitable centres, as well as their decoration and furnishing became increasingly visible among urban elites, both lay and ecclesiastic, in the sixth and seventh centuries, in all

---

[20] For North Africa, see Lepelley, 'Le patronat episcopal'.
[21] Caillet, L'évergétisme monumental chrétien.
[22] For example, Caillet, L'évergétisme monumental chrétien, pp. 25–9, 55–8, 59–66.
[23] On S. Maria Maggiore, see De Blaauw, Cultus et decor; on Bari, see Caillet, L'évergétisme monumental chrétien, pp. 12–17.
[24] The mid seventh century was the low point of inscriptions which are preserved to us in Italy: Durliat, 'Épigraphie chrétienne', p. 231; Mitchell, 'The display of script'.

the cities of Italy for which we have sufficient material or textual evidence.[25] The patronage of religious buildings as well as their services became a strategy of early medieval Italian elites to promote their families' interests, attract attention at court (episcopal and royal), as well as save their souls. Inscriptions recording patronage were again painted or carved on buildings, making clear that investing in a church or religious building was motivated, at least in part, by the desire for secular prestige within the urban context, just as classical urban euergetism had been.

New political forces, such as the Lombard kings and their courts, encouraged euergetism of building, and their patronage was attested sometimes in inscriptions and sometimes even inscribed on building materials, such as the roof tiles stamped with the names of King Agilulf (reg. 590–616) and his son Adaloald (reg. 616–25) recovered from the major urban church of S. Simpliciano, Milan.[26] These tiles certainly record the royal patronage and a financial outlay for a major building, though stamps on tiles were not as visible as the monumental epigraphy or statue bases which typify late antique patronage.

Funding the construction of buildings in the early medieval city worked to the benefit of those funding them in three ways: promotion of individual or group assets in view of contemporaries, consolidation of memory for successors, and conspicuous piety. Each of these functions was not only material but also social in nature. Fundamentally, funding a building was patronage in the sense it held in late antiquity, where a patron expected something in return, though in this case the expectation may have included a hoped-for reciprocal obligation from God, a bishop, or another ruler.

In the Lombard territories of Northern Italy, much elite patronage involved the construction of private churches or monasteries on rural private land.[27] This was encouraged by Lombard legislation from 713, when an edict issued in the first year of Liutprand's reign permitted Lombard men to pass on their wealth in donations *pro anima*. The laws related to inheritance provided new permission, and possibly even encouragement, to transmit wealth through a donation 'of what he

---

[25] Ward-Perkins, *From classical antiquity*, 51–84; Ghilardi and Goddard, *Les cités d'Italie*, and Chavarría, 'Local churches and lordship'. For Lucca, see Wickham, 'Economic and social institutions in Northern Tuscany', pp. 25–6.
[26] See examples in Milan – Castello Sforzesco, Civiche Raccolte D'Arte, and Museo D'Arte Antica – discussed in Monneret de Villard, *Catalogo delle iscrizioni*, cat no. 22. Cf. the bricks and tiles with Theodoric's name stamped in them, discussed by La Rocca, 'An arena of abuses'.
[27] Stoffella, 'Aristocracy and rural churches'; La Rocca, 'La reine et ses liens'; Brogiolo, 'Architetture, simboli e potere'.

wants to whom he wants' rather than through conventional transmission to heirs.[28]

Contemporary histories and chronicles praised Lombard kings of Italy for their restoration of cities and foundation of new cities. In the seventh and eighth centuries, the kings of Italy were credited with rebuilding walls, restoring churches which had been ruined by abandonment, and reoccupying late Roman palaces, such as the Palace of Theodoric at Pavia, or those at other cities which had recently served as defensive centres, such as the Byzantine castrum of Cividale (Friuli).[29] Modern historians have followed Paul the Deacon and others in celebrating certain rulers such as Liutprand (reg. 712–44) at Corteleona and Arechis (reg. 774–87) at Benevento for the flourishing of art under their patronage, the fostering of collective cults under the royal umbrellas of palace chapels and monasteries, and the promotion of royal culture in cities. In Southern Italy, and in some major cities of the North, the construction or refurbishment of urban churches constituted a major strategy for social display in urban contexts.[30] Between legacy and contemporary social networks, urbanism and the urban landscape were essential tools for early medieval rulers.

In addition to patronage of religious facilities, early medieval elites contributed to the infrastructure, water supply, and bathing facilities of Italian cities. From the cities of Italy we know of a range of baths, from those intended to wash the poor to those enjoyed by clerics and churchmen, and those used by royalty and even visiting emperors.[31] Bath buildings were built and repaired, aqueducts restored, and wells refurbished by the rulers and elites of early medieval cities. Legislation from Carolingian Italy makes clear the responsibility of the palace to maintain open areas and sewers in the cities of Italy, though there is no evidence that this law was actually acted upon.[32]

---

[28] See Edict of Liutprand (713), 6, in Gasparri and Azzara, *Le Leggi dei Longobardi*, pp. 140 and 236, note 8, and discussion in Wickham, 'Economic and social institutions', p. 20.

[29] Such as S. Ambrogio and S. Michele, at Pavia, restored by Grimoaldo (662–71). Cuniperto (688–700) built a monastery in honour of S. Giorgio in campo Coronate, and Ariperto II (701–12) a female monastery in honour of S. Agata. Bullough, 'Urban change in early medieval Italy'; Brühl, *Fodrum, gistum, servitium regis*; Rotili, 'Architettura e scultura', p. 295.

[30] On the differences between north and south, Latin and Greek, see Goodson, 'Urbanism in the politics of power'; Gelichi, 'Note sulle città bizantine', esp. p. 68.

[31] Squatriti, *Water and society*; Ward-Perkins, *From classical antiquity*, pp. 119–54, provides a useful summary but perhaps overemphasizes charity and washing the poor as motivation for paying for bathing facilities (140) and the absence of patronage concerned with domestic water supplies (149).

[32] See, for example, *MGH CRF*, I, p. 216, ch. 3; Azzara, 'La ricezione dei capitolari'.

A capitulary of Pippin I for Italy, dated 782 or 786, stipulates that 'All must contribute to the restoration of churches, building of bridges, and repair of roads, as was the old custom'.[33] Another from 850, under Louis II, specifies that:

In each [scil. Italian] region on a river, where ancient custom has made bridges, we wish these to be repaired at once; and if there is anywhere a need for a new bridge, we wish this to be built by the common labour of all those who live nearby.[34]

Popes' restorations of the aqueducts of Rome have been taken as evidence that the popes were de facto ruling the city in the eighth and ninth centuries.[35] Much attention also went to the funerary monuments of elites, including funerary oratories, or tombs within existing churches.[36]

The Role of Architecture

When seeking to document and analyse power and elite competition in the cities of early medieval Italy, we tend to look at buildings as our principal indicator. I plan to nuance this considerably in the next pages, but the basic point remains valid and central to the understanding of cultivation within cities. Gian Pietro Brogiolo claimed that 'by far the most meaningful expression of power is to be found in architecture'.[37] At its essence, commissioning in the built environment whether building something new or restoring something existing projected to contemporaries the scale of individual or group assets, and his or their command of resources in the form of property, building materials, and labour. Prestige building made use of prominent locations, valuable materials, and skilled techniques of craftsmanship. Ancient monuments were sometimes taken over to create new ones, both major public monuments and domestic private ones. From the seventh century onwards, new churches were often located within the urban fabric of cities, sometimes even within ancient buildings; these formed the poles of new agglutinative clusters of settlement and patronage.[38]

Interventions, such as a new monument inserted into an existing and ancient context, assured the visibility of the project and its patron;

---

[33] 'Ut de restauratione ecclesiarum uel pontes faciendum aut stratas restaurandum omnino generaliter faciant, sicut antiqua fuit consuetudo', *Capit.* vol. I, p. 192, ch. 4.
[34] *Capit.* vol. II, pp. 87–8, ch. 8; cf. p. 84, ch. 3 and p. 85, ch. 5. See discussion in Ward-Perkins, *From classical antiquity*, pp. 186–9.
[35] Coates Stephens, 'The walls and aqueducts of Rome'.
[36] Brogiolo, *Le chiese rurali tra VII e VIII secolo*; La Rocca, 'Le aristocrazie e le loro chiese'.
[37] Brogiolo, 'Architecture and power', p. 452.
[38] Vaes, 'Nova construere'; Brogiolo, 'Aspetti economici e sociali'; Gauthier, 'La topographie chrétienne'.

differentiating his commissions from the rest of the urban fabric. Thus, high-status houses were set out by their presentation of recherché materials, and churches, likewise. Previous scholarship on power in the early medieval city has stressed the ways in which building something was a key means to express power. Thus people living in early medieval cities had a 'monumental concept of their palaces and of their churches' but 'they allowed the paved streets to be covered by debris ... and simple houses and huts were erected'.[49] Gian Pietro Brogiolo here highlights a tension between monumental buildings on the one hand and the rest of the city, on the other, which he attributes to the 'sharp fragmentation of [Lombard] society and consequently also its material manifestations'.[50] He goes too far, however, in suggesting that ordinary houses were not tools by which families asserted status. Documents from Ravenna for the eighth and ninth centuries preserve a strong association between houses and their owners, with toponyms and anthroponyms.[51] Within such an urban landscape, in which houses and churches could relate so closely to the projection of social status, the creation or manipulation of unbuilt areas, namely cultivated spaces, hitherto has been underestimated. The recognition that the built environment not only reflected but also fuelled social advancement can make sense of architecture as well as gardens and orchards.

Power in the Unbuilt Environment

In what follows I will consider the urban agricultural properties of high-status individuals and how they relate to strategies of representation and the reproduction of social order in the cities of Italy. These can be understood along some of the lines described in 'The Role of Architecture', namely the strategies of making public patronage, allegiances, and wealth by commissioning monuments and building works in cities. Secondly, we can understand the value of urban gardens and cultivated lots, using ideas historians have employed to analyse the exchange of agricultural properties in general.

To have land in the early Middle Ages did not necessarily mean having wealth, but it did mean having an identity. Possessing land on the one hand provided an income, if the land was worked profitably or if it was rented out for a payment in kind or in cash. On the other hand, land held by gift or purchased or even rented attached owners to a place, its history, and the history of others who had owned the same land. The means by

---

[49] Brogiolo, 'Conclusions', p. 253. [50] Brogiolo, 'Capitali e residenze regie', p. 143.
[51] Cavalieri Manasse and Bruno, 'L'edilizia abitativa', p. 183.

which lands were transferred also connected owners to other people: the seller, the renter, the donor, or the witnesses to the transaction. The social networks achieved through land ownership and exchange were a fundamental practice of power in the early Middle Ages. The 'politics of land' has become a key tool for examining power relationships and social mobility in the early Middle Ages.[52] I have considered how ancient systems of patronage, control of foodways, and commissioning of architecture and infrastructure changed over time into new forms of patronage and display in cities. In what follows, I will examine the ways in which exchanges of land, and in particular urban properties which included areas for cultivation, contributed to the construction and maintenance of power in early medieval cities.

There are many ways in which land changed hands in early medieval Italy; among the preserved documentary record, we have original charters of donations, sales, leases or rental agreements, and also testaments of inheritance or endowments, cartularies, letters, or narrative sources which report exchanges, and records of disputes about them, ranging from very large rural estates to very small urban plots.[53] There are two related concepts related to property transactions which are fundamental to the argument I advance in this chapter. First, that cultivated land within cities was sometimes a highly privileged gift, and we can see this privilege in the agents, in the status of the transactions, and the locations of the cultivated lands. Second, the commercial exchange of urban cultivated properties was a means by which people and institutions negotiated power and economic potential. A brief discussion of these concepts is needed before moving on to examples of the practices.

Giving lands in gift to another person or to an institution was a means of asserting social status, both of the giver and the receiver, throughout early medieval Western Europe. Gothic soldiers received allotments in grant from the king, as payment for services rendered and in order to support their households.[54] Merovingian and Burgundian rulers rewarded their supporters with gifts of land.[55] Carolingian kings used gifts of benefices, lands from the fisc, or even church lands surplus to needs to draw together families of supporters and those in a special relationship with the king in

---

[52] Bloch, *Feudal society*, pp. 68–9; cf. Tabacco, 'La connessione fra potere e possesso', pp. 138–9. The Bucknell Group has determined the contours of this aspect of early medieval life over from the past twenty-five years: Davies and Fouracre, eds., *Property and power*, especially Chris Wickham and Tim Reuter, 'Introduction', pp. 6–7.

[53] For a helpful introduction, see www.charlemagneseurope.ac.uk/charter-basics/.

[54] Goffart, *Barbarians and Romans*, pp. 72–9, 80–8; Cassiodorus, *Variae* 8:26. See also Innes, 'Land, Freedom'.

[55] Wood, 'Teutsind, Witlaic', which complicates the position of Wallace-Hadrill, *The long-haired kings*, pp. 237, 247.

a vast network.[56] To receive gifts or honours from the king was to belong to a preferred social group.[57] The extension of these benefices may have been a reward for past support, or aimed at achieving support in the future. They may have carried the expectation of military support; they undoubtedly activated links of patronage to extend the social relationships achieved within the court beyond it.[58] The main model of this network of royal patronage in our period was the Carolingian court, and there were systems for petitioning and requesting grants through counts and other members of the aristocracy.[59] The practice was hardly unique, however, and the donation of land, whether as a temporary gift for a lifetime, or permanently, was a key practice of power throughout early medieval Europe, from Anglo-Saxon England to Italy and beyond.[60] The ubiquity of this practice notwithstanding, there was variation across different regions and within different societies. Thus, in Italy after 774, Carolingian rulers gave land within the former Lombard kingdom to Franks, though Italian kings generally did not give away major tracts of their land until the end of the ninth century, and dukes and rulers of southern territories gave gifts of properties only to special groups around their courts.[61]

In some cases rental arrangements acted almost as benefices in providing political more than economic benefit. A landlord such as a monastery may have let out properties to a family at favourable rates and received rent and often a symbolic gift in return; a community was created among the tenants of the same landlord, all of the donors to a given church, or the group of neighbours who all sold to the same acquisitive proprietor. We can see from a document of 883 that a group of *consortes* sold a house and its little courtyard, in vico Coraria, near the Sede Furcillense (Naples), to the rural monastery of S. Vincenzo al Volturno. Maria, the wife of Peter, a tribune of Naples, acting on his behalf and in the name of their son, Iohannes, 'a captive of malign Saracens', sell their two parts of the

---

[56] Ganshof, 'Note sure la concession', and Gladiß, 'Die Schenkungen'.
[57] For a broad summary, see Costambeys, Innes, and MacLean, *The Carolingian world*, pp. 315–9; Innes, *State and society*, pp. 87–93.
[58] For Italy, see Wickham, 'Aristocratic power', esp. pp. 164–70; Gasparri, 'Strutture militari'.
[59] See, for example, Innes, *State and society*, pp. 85–8; Rosenwein, *Negotiating space*.
[60] On royal gifts of land, see Davies and Fouracre, eds., *The languages of gift*, and in particular Davies, 'When gift is sale', p. 230, and Nelson, 'The role of the gift'; Wickham, *The mountains and the city*, ch. 7.
[61] Tabacco, 'La connessione fra potere e possesso'; Cutler, 'Significant gifts'; Tabacco, 'L'allodialità del potere'; Taviani-Carozzi, *La principauté*, pp. 709–25. On Carolingians in Northern Italy, see Hlawitschka, *Franken, Alemannen, Bayern*. For the tenth century, see Skinner, 'Noble families'. The characterisation of Italy in Innes, 'Land, freedom', p. 67, is helpful for the earlier period, if overly reductive.

property, to join with the other three parts of the property previously sold by their *consortes* to the monastery; the house and courtyard were contiguous on two sides with a garden owned by the monastery.⁶² Up to the mid eighth century S. Vincenzo had acquired parcels of land not only in its rural base in the Mainarde mountains, but also throughout the region, including in towns such as Benevento, Salerno, and Capua; in the 860s and 870s it consolidated holdings in all of these areas, and here it is consolidating its holdings within a neighbourhood at Naples.⁶³ For the seller, in addition to the 80 'Sicilian' *solidi* (dinars or quarter-dinars), Petrus joined his *consortes* in transacting with S. Vincenzo. Petrus also sold a garden in the same street along with a cellar in the same neighbourhood to the Neapolitan monastery of S. Maria, located in the via Furcillense, and in 886 these were sold to S. Vincenzo al Volturno.⁶⁴ Petrus may have intended that these properties should always end up with S. Vincenzo, but in their passage over twenty years, his family house, a garden, a cellar, and other utilitarian and residential properties joined together a horizontal network of neighbours and links of affiliation between urban church and rural monastery. Essentially, gifts of land created a vertical bond between giver and receiver; they nearly always required a reciprocal gift of some form, whether spiritual or physical, and they created horizontal bonds between groups who had all been the recipient of similar gifts.⁶⁵ This pattern held true not only for the highest social orders, but also at smaller scales, so land owners, even middling or

---

⁶² 'petrus tribunus una cum Maria coniuge mea, invice mea, et invice iohannis legitimo filio mio, qui a malignis sarracenis captus est ... dedimus ... idest omnes porciones nostre in integrum de domum nostram una cum porcionis nostre de curticella ante se cum adiacentibus suis, et introituum suum, omnibusque eius pertinenciis, positis vico quam coraria sego furcillense, et sunt ipse porciones nostre partes duas, et reconiungitur et indivisas reducentur cum alias tres partes porcionis consortibus nostris, quod vos iam epmtum [sic] habetis ... et coherentur sibi in simul de uno latere et de uno capite hortum vestrum santique monasterii, et de alio latere est suprascriptus vicus publicus quam coraria, et de alio capite corticella nostra', *MNDHP*, Appendix II, 4 (863), pp. 266–7; cf. Martin et al., *Regesti dei documenti dell'Italia meridionale*, 1059, p. 501.

⁶³ Wickham, 'Monastic lands and monastic patrons', pp. 144–5, fig. 11.2.

⁶⁴ 'Idest in priora cellareum in integro cum domo et omnibus possessionibus eius, cubiculum quoquo ipsum insimul concessi. tradidi vobis et hortum nostrum, qui est inter hortum domini aceprandi, et leonis magni viri. Ipsum verum supra scriptum cellareum et hortum positum intus hanc civitatem inter duo vicora, unum qui vocatur corarium, et alium vicum placidum, sego furcillensem', *MNDHP*, Appendix II, 5 (883), pp. 267–9; cf. Martin et al., *Regesti dei documenti dell'Italia meridionale*, 1077, p. 510. In 883, Abbot Maius, who acquired both of these parcels, may have had different motivations, as the monastery in the Mainarde had been destroyed in 881. The bishop of Naples signed this transaction and supervised the acquisition of others at Naples; Hodges, *Light in the Dark Ages*, pp. 153–4.

⁶⁵ For the most influential theories about gifts and counter-gifts in terms of medieval properties, see Rosenwein, *To be the neighbor of St Peter*, pp. 125–43, who focusses on gifts to the monastery of Cluny; Duby, *The early growth of European economy*, pp. 48–72.

small holders, might have associated themselves with local aristocrats or comparatively higher-status families by entering into relationships with a family church owned by local aristocrats, or donating to a large monastery.[66] Within that matrix there may have been competition for resources and thus strategies for achieving more or better gifts. There was certainly a circulation of wealth and resource within communities, and there was a shared participation among the elite in the land grants of others, whether through petitioning or through witnessing the documents recording transactions. These were, fundamentally, practices of social hierarchisation and reproduction.

The nature of land transactions in early medieval Europe, such as we presently understand it, was social. As I have just described, the gift of land, whether urban or rural, provided opportunities for social manoeuvre. The mechanics of achieving a transaction such as a royal gift were not entirely different from those of any private gift or sale as far as we can tell from the charter evidence. A charter was composed by a notary, using to greater or lesser degrees a formula, and the document was signed by all parties, plus several other witnesses.[67] The document may identify the parentage of the signatories and the source of the land, whether inheritance, gift, or previous purchase. It may have identified the boundaries of the property or properties by naming the neighbours, and the list of witnesses attests to those who were present for the agreement of the document.[68] The analysis of the relationships recorded by early medieval charters has been the stuff of very rich social history because each document provides a snapshot of a 'small world'.[69] Through this kind of research we can see the noble families of Naples, in the tenth century, serving as witnesses for each other's documents and concentrating their gifts of properties to certain ecclesiastical institutions, fathers witnessing sons' transactions or formally consenting to their children's property

---

For an overview, see Wickham, 'Rural economy and society', and now Bijsterveld, 'The medieval gift as agent of social bonding'.

[66] Wickham, 'Aristocratic power', pp. 166–7; for the example of Toto of Campione, see Balzaretti, *The lands of Saint Ambrose*, pp. 316–7, and above all, Gasparri et al., *Carte di famiglia*.

[67] See Chapter 1, Sources: Documents, p. 18.

[68] Guyotjeannin et al., *Diplomatique médiévale*. For a broad discussion and historiography, see Koziol, *The politics of memory and identity*, pp. 17–62, and the extensive literature laid out usefully in the footnotes there. On the public nature of conflict resolution and the involvement of witnesses and public pressure in the process, see Davies and Fouracre, eds., *The settlement of disputes*, pp. 234–5.

[69] The term comes from Davies, *Small worlds*. The social histories written through charter transactions are too many to name here: see Davies and Fouracre, eds., *Property and power*, and for Italy, Gasparri and La Rocca, *Carte di famiglia*; Costambeys, *Power and patronage in early medieval Italy*; Skinner, *Family power*.

transfers, and siblings serving as witnesses for documents: as Ross Balzaretti points out, 'family relations structured economic activities'.[70] So too did power relations structure economic transfers, as we will see with the examples below.

Because land transactions were essentially social, land ownership should likewise be understood as having been a social practice. Some documents about urban gardens reveal how land held the memory of those who owned it previously; by preserving toponyms of their environment, recording names of previous owners such as the will of Iohannes, bishop of Pavia, who identifies the previous owners of the garden in the castrum of Verona which he purchased, and especially the 'little land' at Verona given to him by King Berengar 'by earlier documents'.[71] Barbara Rosenwein reminds us that not all social ties were amicable, and so our documents could record enmities, conflict, and rivalries. Indeed, the choice of sale or donation, especially to an ecclesiastical institution, might have been an act of eliminating the possibility of another claimant or purchaser.[72]

Given just how much urban land was agricultural, transactions of cultivated properties in cities should be examined with the same view to examining social relationships as transactions of larger-scale rural land. There may have been a difference in the way that land for specialised production was bought or sold, as opposed to land for mixed use.[73] Should the urban context of these cultivated lands be considered differently from the context of rural lands which are more typically the subject of study? I argue that yes, urban properties, while exchanged in ways that were similar to rural properties, were indeed much more highly visible commodities, and, as such, they formed sharper tools in the exercise of power renegotiations. In Italy, a profoundly urban society, cities were fundamentally places of competition; they may have been dominated by a ruler, but they were also populated by many competing families.[74] The cities of Italy were intense political and social foci for upper classes, and their properties – what they owned and what they exchanged – were key aspects of this focus.

---

[70] Balzaretti, 'The politics of property in ninth-century Milan'; see also his unpublished paper 'Fathers, sons and property transfer'. For Neapolitan families, see Skinner, 'Urban communities in Naples'; Skinner, 'Noble families', p. 365.

[71] 'nec non et hortum in eodem castro positum, quod dudum a quodam Ildeberto libero homine comparavi'; 'nec non et terrulam iuxta se positam et inter arcovalos et arcovolutos numero novem quos mihi meus senior dominus Berengarius imperator per praeceptorum paginas contulit', *CDV* vol. II, 186 (922). Cf. the example of Maru and Barbaria at Naples later in this chapter. On the memory through place, see Nora et al., *Les lieux de mémoire* and now Fentress, 'Topographic memory'.

[72] Rosenwein, *To be the neighbor of St Peter*, pp. 130–2.

[73] So Laurent Feller has suggested. See Wickham, 'Conclusions', p. 632.

[74] Wickham, 'Aristocratic power', esp. p. 159.

Three examples will make clear the modalities of cultivated property within the cities of Italy and exchanges of it among the highest echelons of Italian society. The examples here range from the eighth to the early tenth century and from northern to southern Italy.

Fulrad

Fulrad of St-Denis was given a house with a garden in Rome by Pope Stephen II in 757. We know about the donation only from a single source, so it is impossible to know how big the garden was, what was grown, or in what way it might have sustained Fulrad's household while in Rome. The context of the documentation of the gift, however, makes clear that this was a donation of significant prestige, a statement to all in Rome of the allegiance of the papacy to the Frankish court.

Fulrad was a long-time close advisor to the Carolingian king Pippin. He became the abbot of St-Denis, the royal Frankish monastery near Paris, in 750, and the royal *cappellanus* in 751. Later sources report that he travelled to Rome with Burchard of Wurzburg to seek the opinion of Pope Zacharias (741–52) on the palace mayoralty, a trip which was used to authorise Pippin's usurpation of the Merovingian throne.[75] Fulrad was sent by King Pippin to meet the papal party arriving from Rome in 753, and he hosted Pope Stephen II (752–7) at the abbey of St-Denis, perhaps for several months, and eventually escorted the pope to the royal court at Ponthion in January 754.[76] At this point, a strong alliance was forged between the Frankish king and the pope, forcing a political reshuffling in each party's relationships with the Lombards. In these renegotiations, Fulrad was a key figure. He was sent to collect the keys of all the cities in Italy which were released by the Lombard king Aistulf and returned to papal control, including Ravenna, Rimini, Pesaro, and several others.[77] He was also sent in the papal party to Desiderius in 756.[78] Fulrad was rewarded for his loyalty to the Frankish king by awards of land and offices, starting with gifts of land and rights for income to St-Denis.[79] In 757

---

[75] *ARF*, s.a. 749 and 750, trans. Scholz, *Carolingian chronicles*, p. 39. On the sources, see Costambeys, Innes, and MacLean, *The Carolingian world*, pp. 61–3.
[76] Fleckenstein, 'Fulrad von St-Denis', pp. 19–20; Semmler, 'Verdient um das karolingische Königtum'. For the events and the sources which recount them, see McKitterick, *History and memory*; Costambeys, Innes, and MacLean, *The Carolingian world*, pp. 134–5; Jarnut and Becher, *Der Dynastiewechsel*.
[77] Noble, *The republic*, pp. 92–3; *LP*, Vita Stephani II, chs. 46–7 (vol. I, pp. 453–4, 460).
[78] *LP*, Vita Stephani II, chs. 49–51 (vol. I, p. 455); *Codex Carolinus*, 11 (757).
[79] Pippin gave an estate, Saint-Mihiel, to the abbey of St-Denis in 755, *DKar I*, no. 8 (755) = ChLA XV 599. *DKar I*, 1 (752), *DKar I*, 6 (753), and *DKar I*, 7 (754) are decisions in favour of St-Denis. See Stoclet, *Autour de Fulrad*, for analysis of the properties of Fulrad, based upon his will.

Fulrad also received gifts from the pope as a reward for his services.[80] In 757, Stephen II wrote a number of letters extending gifts and privileges to Fulrad, including one awarding him a house with a garden located near St Peter's at the Vatican.

These letters are not preserved in the original, but in a formulary book transcribed in the ninth century (Paris, BnF, MS lat. 2777, fols. 43r–61v). This manuscript is famous among scholars of Carolingian history because it includes some of the only transcriptions of texts which seem to have been fundamental in the development of a distinct new practice of kingship by the Carolingians, and the carving up of different kinds of ecclesiastical and secular authority.[81] Jo Story argues that the compilation lies somewhere between a formulary and a history book. Some names were removed from letters of the second half of the collection to facilitate their reuse as exemplars,[82] but the order of the elements within the manuscript, the themes which unite them, and the pressing political context of the last quarter of the eighth century, when the letters of the first section appear to have been gathered, suggest that there was 'a historical and archival motive for gathering copies of these letters together, a motive that outweighed the need to preserve them simply as models or patterns of letters' (Table 5).[83]

The gift of property from Stephen II to Fulrad, no. 7, reads as follows:

Bishop Stephen, servant of the servants of God, to Fulrad, lovable priest and also one other person. So it is fitting that we bestow approval that in future times nothing ecclesiastical of use should decrease in value. That now a suitable request has been made, let it be seen that it is carried out, when ecclesiastical property can be improved it should be without doubt effected. Thus, because you seek from us that hostel located near the basilica of St Peter, next to the tomb of St Leo I, the pope, which Ratchis the monk held, in the jurisdiction of the basilica of St Peter, and also the house located next to the monastery of S. Martino, with its upper and lower parts, with its entrance and garden, which was owned by Nazarius the monk, under the jurisdiction of the monastery of S. Stephan cata Galla Patricia, to you we must concede at this time; your prayers have been sent, for this abovementioned hostel and house with upper and lower parts, and all pertaining to it wholly, from the present days of the tenth indiction we conceded to you to have [it]. After your death, the hospital noted here and the house described above to the

---

[80] See Stephen's letter to Pippin, *Codex Carolinus*, 11 (757).
[81] Levison, 'Das Formularbuch'. For a detailed summary of the contents of the manuscript and references to the pertinent literature, see Story, 'Cathwulf', esp. pp. 12–17; see also McKitterick, *Charlemagne*, pp. 43–9.
[82] *Form.*, ed. Zeumar, pp. 500, 503. On formularies, and this one in particular, see Rio, *Legal practice*, pp. 141–4. On these letters and their resemblance to a papal formulary book, the *Liber diurnis*, see Rosenwein, *Negotiating space*, p. 109.
[83] Story, 'Cathwulf', p. 12, note 45; Rio, *Legal practice*, p. 143.

Table 5 *Letters to Fulrad in Paris, BnF, MS lat. 2777.**

4 (ff. 46 r-v)	Stephen II–Fulrad (757)	Ornaments for vestments conceded to Fulrad	=Jaffé 2330
5 (f 46 v)	Stephen II – Fulrad (757)	Fulrad can establish six deacons at St-Denis who can wear dalmatics	=Jaffé 2331
6 (ff. 46 v-47 r)	Hadrian to Fulrad and/or Maginarius (781)	Confirmation of lease of hostel at Rome to Fulrad and/or Maginarius for life	(=Jaffé 2435), ed. in Stoclet, 'Les établissements', pp. 245–6.
7 (ff. 47 r-v)	Stephen II – Fulrad (757)	Gift of hostel of Ratchis and house with garden at Vatican to Fulrad for life	(=Jaffé 2333), ed. in Stoclet, 'Les établissements', p. 244.
8 (ff. 47 v-48 r)	Hadrian – Fulrad (774–84)	Concessions for the Valtellina	(=Jaffé 2443), see Rosenwein, *Negotiating*, pp. 108–9, cf. Pippin's gifts and immunities in Valtellina, *ChLA* 15.95, no. 616).
12 (ff. 53 v-54 r)	Stephen II – Fulrad (757)	Series of privileges, right to found monasteries on his property, right of immunity from local interference, right to bring disputes before the papacy	(=Jaffé 2331), ed. in Stoclet, 'Fulrad de St. Denis', pp. 234–5.[84]

* The numbers are those used by Zeumar in the *MGH* edition of the manuscript, which have been followed by Levison, 'Das Formularbuch' and most other scholars of the manuscript.

ius of the above-named places and the property wholly and nothing the less, should be reverted. Farewell.[85]

---

[84] See discussion in Rosenwein, *Negotiating space*, p. 122. On authenticity of the claims, see Karl Hauck, 'Paderborn', p. 115, note 141.

[85] 'Stephanus episcopus servus servorum Dei Fulrado amabili presbitero et item alie uni persone. Petentium desideriis ita nos convenit inpertire assensum ut tamen sequentibus temporibus nulli ecclesiastica utilitatis valeat summitti dispendiis. Nam tunc petitorum postulatio congruum videtur suscipere effectum, quando ecclesiastica praedia oportune ordinata ad meliorem fuerit sine dubio statutum perducta. Igitur, quia petistis a nobis quatenus hospitalem positum infra basilicam beati Petri, iuxta sepulchrum beati Leonis pape, quem tenuit Ratchis monachus iuris ipsius basilice beati Petri; nec non et domum positam iuxta monasterium beati Martini, cum inferioribus et superioribus suis, cum metata dua et horticella [scil. metatu suo et horticello], quam tenuit Nazarius monachus, iuris venerabilis monasterii sancti Stephani cata Galla patricia, vobis ad tempus emissa preceptione concedere deberemus; inclinati precibus vestris, per hujus praecepti seriem suprascripto hospitale et domum cum inferioribus et superioribus suis vel omnibus in integro pertinentibus, a praesenti decima indictione diebus vite vestrae vobis concedimus detinendum. Post vero obitum vestrum utroque memoratum ospitale et domum ut superius leguntur ad ius suprascriptorum piorum locorum cuius et est proprietas in integro nihilominus revertantur. Bene Valete'. See the edition of the text in Stoclet, 'Les établissements', pp. 243–4.

The hostel or residence that Fulrad sought and received was located behind the basilica of St Peter, south-east of the apse of the ancient basilica near the tomb of Pope Leo I.[86] It was most probably outside the door located south of the apse.[87] The house and garden had been owned by Nazarius, about whom we know nothing more. The house was nearby, at the monastery of S. Martino similarly south-west of the apse, and administered by the monastery of S. Stefano, also known as S. Stefano *maioris*, which, like S. Martino, may have been sacked in 771; perhaps the house was damaged at that point, as it is not referred to again.[88] Stoclet suggests that it may have been incorporated into the construction of the palace of Charlemagne, built in that area.[89]

The Lombard king Ratchis, who had previously owned the hospice, had abdicated in 749; he and his wife and children went to Rome; in front of Pope Zacharias they took monastic vows.[90] Ratchis then retired to the great abbey of Montecassino, south of Rome; but in 756, at the death of his brother and heir, Aistulf, he seems to have returned to the capital, Pavia, and attempted to rule briefly. In 756, Rome was besieged by Lombards and defended, in part, by Franks.[91] In 757, when Stephen ceded the property at St Peter's to Fulrad, such a donation would have been a pointed expression of the papal alliance with the Franks, a new world order at Rome, in rejection of the Lombards and, indirectly, of the Byzantines.[92]

This area of the Vatican, where both of these properties were located, was transformed in the late 750s by the construction of the chapel of S. Petronilla by Pope Paul, Pope Stephen's brother and successor, in apparent fulfilment of a promise made by Pope Stephen.[93] Charlemagne

[86] On the location of the properties, see Stoclet, 'Les établissements', who thinks that the hostel was inside the basilica. This seems improbable. See the archaeology of the transept and the door to the exterior, which was original to the fabric of the building, Krautheimer et al., *Corpus basilicarum*, vol. V, pp. 193–4.

[87] The door is marked '13' on the Alfarano plan, the monastery of S. Martino is marked 'a' on the Alfarano plan, and the tomb of Pope Leo I is '14', just to the south of the door, on the western wall of the south transept.

[88] Hints at damage come from a chronicle of Creontius, reported in fragments in a sixteenth-century history: Aventinus, *Annales ducum*, vol. II.1, p. 410, though this must be taken with a grain of salt. Duchesne believes it: 'Notes', pp. 318–19.

[89] Andrea of Bergamo, 'Historia', ch. 5, p. 224.

[90] *LP*, Vita Zacharia, ch. 23 (vol. I, pp. 433–4). On Ratchis, see Andreolli, 'Una pagina'; Hallenbeck, 'Pavia and Rome'. The first law of his successor, Aistulf, rescinded all of his donations of properties (*Legem*, vol. V, p. 196, item 1). See Pohl, 'Frontiers in Lombard Italy'.

[91] Hallenbeck, 'Rome and Pavia', esp. pp. 81–4; Duchesne, 'Notes', p. 317.

[92] On papal politics in 757, see Goodson, 'To be the daughter of Saint Peter'; McKitterick, 'The illusion of royal power'.

[93] For the sources reporting the construction of these buildings and their analysis, see Goodson, 'To be the daughter of Saint Peter'.

began construction of a palace in 781 near this.[94] Fulrad's house and hospice enjoyed prestige not only from the previous royal owners, and the proximity to the apse of St Peter's, but also we might imagine that it formed part of a new locus of Frankish presence at the Vatican.

Between 751 and 757, Fulrad also sought and received saints' relics from Rome; the ninth-century *Translatio sancti Viti martyris* reports Fulrad's desire for Roman relics, his trip to Rome, and his acquisition of the relics of Saints Vitus, Alexander, and Hippolytus, though it does not even hint that Pope Stephen gave them.[95] Popes were very reluctant to translate corporeal relics of Roman saints in this period, though visitors did sometimes steal them away.[96] Given the infrequency of relic translations in this period, Fulrad's acquisition speaks to his social capital at Rome, where, by hook or by crook, he was able to secure these relics and move them to his monasteries in Francia.[97]

The letters from Pope Stephen extended to Fulrad a range of privileges: the use of special vestments for celebrants in St-Denis, the installation of new celebrants, and a series of privileges including the right to found, on any of his properties, monasteries which would be in the jurisdiction of the papacy; and Fulrad had the right to bring any conflicts before the papal court for resolution, rather than any local episcopal court. In some respects, the privileges of letter 12 were extraordinary in that they exempted the royal monastery of St-Denis, already exceptional for its wealth and royal patronage, from the hierarchy of local and regional ecclesiastical control; the bishop of Paris no longer had jurisdiction over it.[98] Other institutions already enjoyed such privileges; St-Denis was not the first.[99] Indeed, in the same manuscript an earlier letter from Pope Adeodatus (615–18) to the monastery of St-Martin of Tours offered similar exemptions.[100] The multiple letters of papal gifts and privileges recorded in this manuscript, nonetheless, speak to huge rewards heaped upon Fulrad in 757.

---

[94] Noble, *The republic*, p. 288. On the Frankish presence at the Vatican, especially in St Peter's, see Story, 'The Carolingians' and Angenendt, 'Mensa Pippini Regis'. See also Brühl, *Aus mittelalter und Diplomatik*, vol. II, 7, citing the *Libellus de imperatoria potestate*, 204, 1.

[95] *Translatio Sancti Viti martyris*, ch. 2, discussion in Stoclet, *Autour de Fulrad*, pp. 367–75.

[96] On relic translations in this period, see Smith, 'Old saints, new cults', pp. 322, 355; Goodson, 'Building for bodies', and Goodson, 'To be the daughter of Saint Peter'.

[97] Röckelein, *Reliquientranslationen*, pp. 177–9.

[98] St-Denis was given royal immunity in 768, *MGH DKar I*, no. 25; for the full list of immunities, see Rosenwein, *Negotiating space*, pp. 109–10.

[99] In 628, Pope Honorius granted exemption to Bobbio, *Codice diplomatico del monastero di S. Columbano di Bobbio*, vol. I, p. 100, no. 10.

[100] Paris, BnF, MS lat. 2777, ff. 44r-v; discussion in Ewig, 'Beobachtungen zu den Klosterprivilegien'.

Fulrad returned to Rome only once, after 757, during the pontificate of Hadrian; the value that he derived from owning this house surely did not lie in his living there. We should understand the papal donation of these properties to Fulrad for the use of his lifetime through the same lens as the gifts of lands and estates that Pippin gave to Fulrad in Francia. These were prestigious gifts offered to a trusted ally. From the eighth century we have very few documents or material remains from houses at Rome, but most of those that we know about include gardens or cultivated spaces, perhaps because those we know about tend to be high-status properties, such as papal properties recorded in inscriptions.[101] This house with a garden and the hospice at the Vatican were likewise high-status properties. Fulrad in these years and in the subsequent decades had controlled many estates and properties; some of these were given to him as gifts, and some of these he gave away as donations.[102] His transactions of property with bishops, abbesses, and other aristocrats in the Carolingian circle brokered a currency of prestige; they reified relationships between people and between people and institutions, signalling alliances and peer-polities. The documents in which they were recorded also permitted an expression of piety and restrained devotion. Fulrad wrote a testament in 776 or 777, bequeathing some of the properties he had amassed to the abbey of St-Denis, 'pro animae meae et animabus famulorum famularumque' (for my soul and those of my family and dependents).[103]

Berengar[104]

Berengar I, king of Italy (888–915), later emperor, gave urban properties with cultivated (or cultivatable) plots at Verona.[105] In 889, upon the petition of Count Vualtfredus, Berengar gave a garden (*ortum*) in Verona to his *fidelis* Atto.[106] It was next to an ancient warehouse (*cum horreo*) and surrounded by walls, next to the church of S. Pietro in Curte; this was most probably located on the left bank of the River

---

[101] See Chapter 3, Rome, p. 37.
[102] See the full list and discussion by Stoclet, *Autour de Fulrad*, and Rosenwein, *Negotiating space*, pp. 122–4.
[103] *ChLA* 16.24, no. 624, ln 14. On the will, see Stoclet, *Autour de Fulrad*.
[104] A preliminary version of this section was published in Goodson, 'Garden cities in early medieval Italy', pp. 346–9.
[105] On Berengar, see Rosenwein, 'Family politics'; Rosenwein, 'Friends and family'.
[106] 'Vualtfredum illustrem comitem ... Attoni fideli nostro ortum in ciuitate Verona situm cum horreo antiquo murisque precingentibus concederemus', *DBI* 6 (889), pp. 29–31.

Adige, opposite the main city but near the ancient theatre in the area that had been the royal palace since the Ostrogothic period.[107] Berengar also gave a small garden (*hortellum*) in the centre of Verona to a certain Ingelfredus upon the petition of his consort Bertilla (Fig. 26). According to the dimensions of the parcel provided in the document, this 'little garden' measured about 625 sq. m, so it was not an insignificant parcel of agricultural property within the city.[108] It was located near the 'Corte Alta', in what appears to have been a relatively densely built-up neighbourhood near the former Roman forum, with a number of houses and churches.[109] In 913, Berengar also gave a *terrula* in the 'arena' of Verona, the ancient theatre in the part of the city next to the palace and *castrum*, across the river; it was called the 'arena' in the early Middle Ages. Berengar, having been petitioned by a courtier, Grimaldus, gave the land to a cleric, Iohannes, his chamberlain.[110] The document, preserved in the original, gives dimensions in *perticae* of a polygon, of 10 × 7 × 2 × 6 *pedes*. It is tempting to think that they correspond to a segment of the *cavea*, the vaulted substructures of the theatre's seating, and that the 'eminentior murus theatri in meridiana et in orientali parte' are the southern limits of the *cavea* at the *aditus maximus* of the theatre, or the double wall of arcades of the *scenae frons*, which ran along the south side near the river.[111] Whatever the correct dimensions were, the *terrula* given to Iohannes was most probably cultivated, 'terra' being a term usually used for fields for grain. Other plots in the 'arena' included

---

[107] La Rocca [Hudson], '"Dark Ages" a Verona', p. 40 and pp. 66–8.

[108] 'ortellum unum in proprietatem, pertinentem de Veronese comitatu situm infra civitatem Veronam non longe a Corte Alta ... extendentem de uno latere per longum perticas legitimas quinque additis sex pedibus, de altero uero latere per longum perticas quattuor additis pedibus .x., ex uno capite extendentem in latitudinem perticas iiii additis quattuor pedibus de altero uero capite perticas quattuor additis octo pedibus, concedimus', *DBI* 14 (896), pp. 48–9. One early medieval Veronese *pertica* measured either 5.25 m (12 piedi) (Cracco Ruggini, *Economia e società*, p. 505) or 2.057 m (6 piedi) (Zupko, *Italian weights and measures*, p. 189). This diploma, preserved in the original, gives as a length of the parcel 'perticas quattuor additis pedibus .X'), which means that the *pertica* used here had more than 10 *piedi*. For this document, Cracco Ruggini's figures are more likely correct, and this parcel of land would measure about 625 sq. m.

[109] La Rocca, '"Dark Ages" a Verona', pp. 31–78.

[110] 'Berengarius divina favente clementia rex ... Grimaldus glorio[su]s comes ... Iohanni clerico et fidelissimo cancellario nostro iure proprietario concedere dignaremur ... terrulam iuris regni nostri infra Arenam castri Veronensis ... in longitudine ab uno latere spatio perticarum decem, ab alii latere in longitudine consistunt pertice septem, ab uno capite adiacent perticae due, ab alio capite sunt pedes legitimi sex', *DBI* 89 (913), pp. 240–2. La Rocca, '"Dark Ages" a Verona', p. 67, suggested that the gardens might be located in the orchestra of the theatre.

[111] Geometry, however, does not permit those dimensions to describe a polygonal plot, so perhaps Berengar's notary made an error in the dimensions.

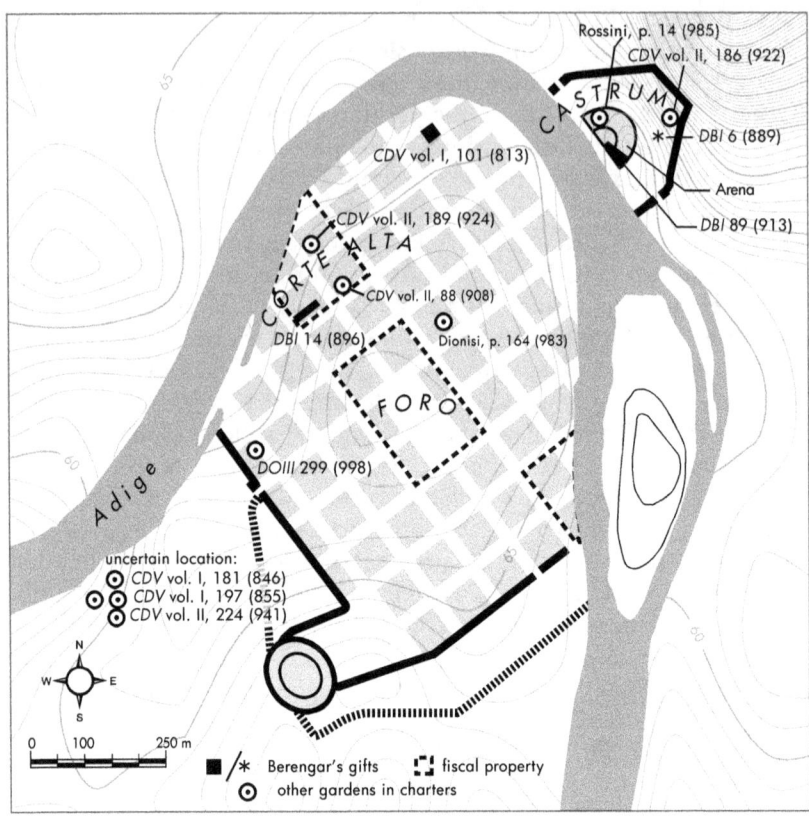

Figure 26 The gardens of early medieval Verona.

houses which were built into the *cavea* of the ancient theatre seating (*covalos/artovalis*), with *terrae* in front of them, as specified in the documents.[112]

The charter is preserved in the original, a large single sheet of parchment, elegantly laid out (Fig. 27).[113] The protocol and signature are written in uncial script, the text in a wispy minuscule, and the king's name appears as a box monogram. The format of the document and the wax seal with the king's portrait follow very closely earlier Carolingian

---

[112] Cf. *CDV* vol. II, 186 (922), discussed in Chapter 5, note 93; *DBI* 57 (905) pp. 160–2; La Rocca, '"Dark Ages" a Verona', p. 67. On the terminology, see Cappiotti and Varanini, 'Il pons marmoreus', p. 118.

[113] London, BL, Additional Charters 29242. s. ix. H: 500 w: 660 mm.

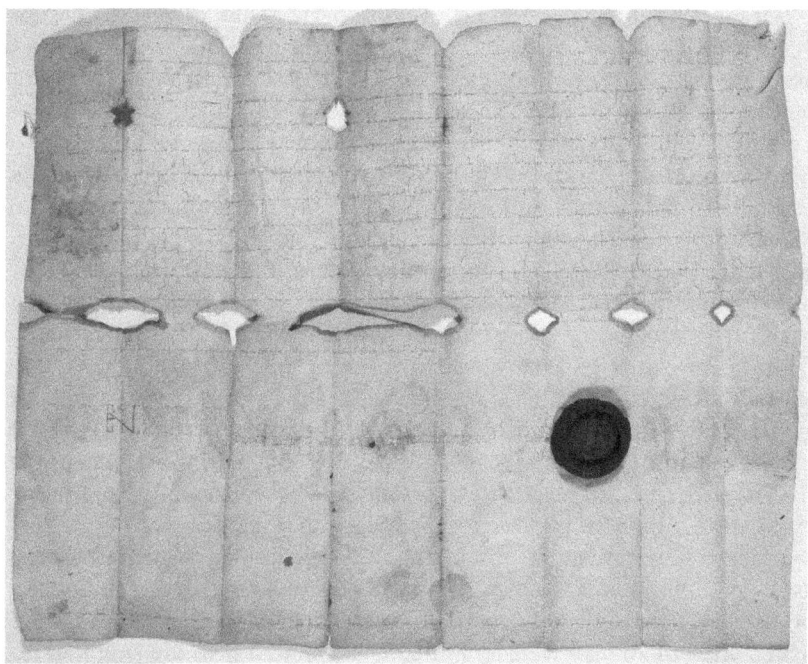

Figure 27 Diploma of Berengar I concerning a garden in Verona, 913 (=*DBI* 89). Photo © The British Library Board, Add Ch. 37631.

royal models, such as a diploma of Charles the Fat from Milan.[114] This was not a minor transaction of an insignificant vegetable patch but a donation of prestige.

Iohannes had received royal gifts before, of mills on the Adige, for example, and appears to have been within the close circle of Berengar, a key ally to a contested and difficult rule. He had been an advocate for earlier transactions and witnessed others over the years.[115] These urban lands at Verona were only part of the gifts of land that Berengar gave away to his followers, and they were tiny when compared with the fortified *castra*, estates, and mills he gave in Northern Italy, but they were valuable and significant within the context of the capital.

---

[114] *Museo* vol. I.2, 141 (880) is laid out very similarly, with uncial script at the top and for the signature, the same elaborate and wispy lettering, and a big wax seal. The parchment sheet has similar dimensions: h: 425 × w: 628 mm. On the chancellery of Berengar, see Bougard, 'La cour et le gouvernement', esp. pp. 266–7 and Keller, 'Zur Struktur', pp. 159–60.

[115] Rosenwein, 'Family politics', p. 261, note 62.

Berengar's diplomas handing over properties and privileges to supporters have received extensive scholarly attention. Berengar's rule over northern Italy was tumultuous and contested for decades, and it is evident that he used gifts to secure support.[116] Giovanni Tabacco labelled him a profligate ruler for giving away so much royal property and so many rights into private hands.[117] Barbara Rosenwein re-evaluated Berengar's handling of fiscal lands and institutional rights by examining the social relationships he formed by them. She determined that the recipients of his gifts fell into three distinct groups: related to his first consort, Bertilla, or his daughter by her, members of his court at Verona, or adherents of the Marquis Adalbertus.[118] The gifts of these three urban gardens certainly fall into the pattern she observed, two given to 'faithful' followers and another given to one of his own officials, a cleric who received extensive gifts from the king, both inside and outside the city of Verona. His gifts of parcels of lands around the royal palace at Verona, on the left bank of the river, were part of that process of surrounding his court with loyal followers by dismantling his royal centre and placing properties, such as parts of the theatre, into private hands.[119] The block of the city which had been associated with kings for centuries gave way to small parcels of houses, proprietary churches and oratories, and, not least, gardens. The people who owned them now were still directly associated with the king and his court, indeed the transfer of property and the honorific terms of the diplomas had ensured that association, and the people who received these parcels in gift derived social prestige from highly explicit and possibly quite visible connection to the king.[120]

Berengar gave gifts of urban gardens in other cities to powerful ecclesiastical institutions. In 889, on the intercession of Adelardus, Berengar left to S. Salvatore in Brescia a small estate with a small garden at the royal court of Brescia, Muciana. These were part of the royal properties within the city, transferred to the royal monastery.[121] In 909, upon the intercession of Adelardus, he endowed the urban church of S. Giovanni Domnarum of Pavia with a chapel, houses, a *uiridarium*, two gardens, and a *braidam*.[122] These were properties located next to the palace at Pavia. So, in both cases, these were prominent urban properties located in

---

[116] On Berengar's uses of gifts, see now also Feller, 'L'exercice du pouvoir'.
[117] Tabacco, *The struggle for power*, p. 154, and for a summary of the historiography, see Rosenwein, 'Family politics', pp. 248–9.
[118] Rosenwein, 'Family politics', p. 276.
[119] La Rocca, '"Dark Ages" a Verona', p. 39 note 35, 41, 48.
[120] Feller, 'L'exercice du pouvoir', pp. 143–5.
[121] 'quandam masiunculam cum orticello pertinentem de curte rei publicae nostrae Muciana civitate Brixia concedimus', *DBI* 5 (889), pp. 28–9.
[122] *DBI* 69 (909), pp. 185–8.

proximity to the court, which were transferred to the major urban churches. The prestigious properties and their gardens became ecclesiastical property.

His properties – those he gave away – were not the only properties with urban gardens in Verona. Many houses that appear in our documents included gardens, and some properties which were bought, sold, or donated were simply plots for cultivating. La Rocca has gathered together a list of townhouses known from the documentary record, and of nineteen houses which changed hands between the mid eighth and mid tenth centuries, nine included annexes of yards, gardens, or fields.[123] It was common but not universal that townhouses had some kind of growing space.

Within the context of urban Verona, to be given productive lands by the king would have worked to the benefit both of Berengar in his precarious rule and the men who received his gifts by showing the solidarity and mutual support of those with ample resources. They supported Berengar, and their new lands made clear that all of Verona knew of their support; Berengar ensured sources of income for them from these lands, with supplementary income and the possibility of stocking the pantries for their households. Within the medieval city, properties served as representations of wealth and control of resources, as signs of status and access to money or to power which dispensed the property.

These three parcels, however, did not remain in private hands for long. One went to the Veronese monastery of S. Zeno and another to a *xenodochium*, founded by Iohannes the cleric. Ingelfredus gave his garden to the Veronese monastery of S. Zeno, in a donation which was confirmed by Berengar himself in 901; perhaps it had always been destined for the monastery.[124] The garden within the vaults of the theatre appears in the will of Iohannes, bishop of Pavia, probably the same person who received it from Berengar.[125] A will of 922 lists his numerous properties, including his house and the oratory he founded in the *arena* (theatre), as well as the *terrulam* we have already discussed, and several other gardens, plots, and parts of the substructures and elevations of the ancient theatre, acquired in different ways.[126] Having accumulated gardens, Iohannes left these to a *xenodochium*, a hospice for the poor, which he founded in the area of the theatre, while reserving the use of some of these parcels for his nephews and for two female neighbours for their lifetimes. This donation of the

---

[123] La Rocca, '"Dark Ages" a Verona', p. 61, tav. 6.
[124] *DBI* 14 (896), pp. 48–9; 34 (901), pp. 100–2.
[125] On the problems of identification, see Rosenwein, 'Family politics', Appendix I; Scaravelli, s.v. Giovanni. On the will, see Cipolla, 'Attorno a Giovanni'.
[126] La Rocca, '"Dark Ages" a Verona', pp. 67–8; Cappiotti and Varanini, 'Il pons marmoreus', pp. 123–4.

garden to a *xenodochium* founded by a layman or priest replicates a pattern attested across Italy in the early Middle Ages: putting urban gardens into clerical hands. While many properties owned by laymen eventually made their way into ecclesiastical ownership, at least those that are known to us through documents (which are generally preserved in ecclesiastical archives), looking broadly at the movement of urban properties, there is a tendency for urban properties with cultivated spaces to be donated to ecclesiastical institutions in particular.

Maru and Barbaria, Naples[127]

A document from Naples provides a clear example of an urban kitchen garden in a neighbourhood with many similar gardens and the strategies by which a single high-status family retained control of it. In 920, the widow Maru and her daughter Barbaria, a nun, of a noble family at Naples, the Isauri or Isabri, gave a garden adjoining the urban church of S. Eufemia in Duos Amantes to the same church.[128]

Maru and Barbaria the nun, mother and daughter, sinner, widow and daughter of Iohannis, for the redemption of their souls, give to their own church of S. Eufemia, martyr of Christ, which is located in the region Duos Amantes, near the public wall, an entire garden located in front of the church, with trees, a pool, and all that pertains to it, which is adjacent on the eastern side to the garden of dominus Anastasius the prefect, to the garden of Maria, sister and aunt of them, and on the other side to the west, a road which runs from the public wall up to the entrance to the church and to this garden, and the entrance to the garden of Iohannis Isauri, and on the southern end, adjacent to the garden of Iohannis and Gregorius Isauri, and also the garden of Iohannes son of Stefanus the tribune, and on the other end, to the north, the church and the garden of Iohannes son of Elias. Likewise, we offer another garden, which is next to the communal pool, with its entrance and all that pertains to it. It is held that in all the days of their lives, this mother and daughter have the usufruct of these things, and both or whichever of them survives the other likewise from that point should do or decide in her power. Notwithstanding, provided that they appoint a guardian to the church, no one, whether priest or monk, should presume to change him or argue the price; and if after their deaths, this church should fall into disorder, then it is ordered that the higumen, who will be of the community of SS. Sergio e Bacco, which now is located in 'Viridario', without any price, from then all should be in the power of the priest, who will be the guardian. If anyone should presume to counter this offer, let him have the bonds of anathema on the part of the fathers, with Jude, traitor of Jesus Christ, and with all heretics and your contemptive judgement, S. Eufemia, before the tribunal of Christ, and additionally reconcile to

---

[127] A preliminary version of this section was published in Goodson, 'Garden cities', pp. 350–3.
[128] *RN* 6 (920), pp. 21–2. On the nobility of this family, see Skinner, 'Urban communities', pp. 291–2; Skinner, *Family power*, pp. 134–5.

the guardian and higumen 2 Byzantine gold pounds. Written and enacted by Leo the curate. Sign of the hand of Maru and Barbaria, and Marie and Iohannes Isauri.[129]

As the description of the boundaries makes clear, the donated gardens were hardly isolated. They were surrounded by six other gardens and a road leading to the city wall; this was an area called Ficariola, with many kitchen gardens owned by Neapolitans.[130] The document indicates that the widow Maru's brothers, John and Gregory, owned properties bordering one of her gardens, and it may be that this part of the city was under their control. Through this document, the donors established that the abbot of the powerful church of SS. Sergio e Bacco should protect their small church and their donation of lands to it. In 970, other members of the Isauri family gave donations both to the large monastery of SS. Sergio e Bacco and the small church of S. Eufemia.[131] The document of the donation from 920 crafted a network of social bonds, between the men of the major monastery of SS. Sergio e Bacco, the priests of the small proprietary church, the saint Eufemia who is invoked in the sanction clause, and the family.[132]

---

[129] 'Die 20 m. aprilis ind. VIII. Neapoli. Imperante d. n. Constantino m. i. an 12. Maru et Barbaria monaca, mater et filia, peccatrix, relicta et filia q. Iohannis pro redemptione anime offerunt in ecclesia propria earum, o b. Eufimia martira Christi, que sita est in regione duos amantes iuxta murum publicum, integrum hortum positum ante dictam ecclesiam, una cum arboribus, piscina et omnibus sibi pertinentibus, qui coheret de uno latere parte orientis cum hortu q. d. Anastasi prefecti, et cum hortu q. Marie germane et thie earum et de alio latere a parte occidentis cum via, que pergit at murum publicum, unde introitum habet in memorata ecclesia et in memorato horto, et introitum de hortum q. d. Iohannis Isauri, et de uno capite parte meridiana coheret cum hortu d. Iohannis et Gregori Isauri, nec non cum hortu d. Iohannis filii d. Stefani tribuni, et de alio capite a parte septentrionis cum memorata ecclesia et cum hortu d. Iohannis filii q. d. Elie. Iterum offerunt alium horticellum earum, qui est iuxta piscinam communalem una cum omnibus sibi pertinentibus. In eo vero tenore, ut in omnibus diebus vite earum ipsa matrix et filia usumfructum dictarum rerum habeant, et ambe vel que ex eis supervixerit qualiter exinde facere iudicareque voluerit in sua sit potestate. Verumtamen si in memorata ecclesia custodem ordinaverint, sive sacerdotem sive monacum, nemo presumat illum commovere vel quodvis premium querere; et, si post obitum earum ipsa ecclesia inordinata remanserit, tunc ordinetur ab igumeno, qui fuerit in congregatione Ss. Sergii et Bachi, qui nunc congregata esse videtur in viridiario absque omni premio, et a tunc omnia sint in potestate sacerdotis, qui ibidem custos fuerit. Si quis vero contra hanc offertionem venire presumpserit sub anathematis vinculis a patrum parte possideat cum Iuda traditore d. n. Ihesu Christi, et cum omnibus hereticis et iudicium contemnat tecum, b. Eufimia, ante tribunal Christi, et insuper componat custodi et igumeno auri libras 2 byth. Scriptum et actum per Leonem curialem. Signum manus Maru et Barbarie, nec non Marie et Iohannis Isauri. Gregorius subscribit. Testes: Leo filius d. Sergii, ΙΟΑΝΝΕC ϕΙΛΙΟΥC ΔΝ ΘΕΟΔΟΡΙ ΜΑΡΙΝΟΥC ϕΙΑΙΟΥC ΔΝ ΠΕΤΡΙ ΤΡΒ', RN 6 (920) pp. 21–2.

[130] Capasso, 'Pianta della citta', esp. pp. 436–7.   [131] RN 185 (970), p. 119.

[132] For analysis of the social and spiritual benefits of a similar – though not identical – donation, the testament of Ercanfrida to Lorsch (851), see Innes, State and society, pp. 40–2, and Nelson, 'The wary widow'.

The garden, orchard, and small garden of this document were owned by an apparently aristocratic family; some members of the family preserved their kitchen gardens, and these two women gave theirs to the church, retaining access to one part, presumably for their personal use, during their lifetimes. The gift of the garden to the church, then, strengthened the ties between the family and the church while maintaining the family's strong presence in the neighbourhood. This example provides some sense of the strategies that families used to preserve their blocks of property – they are not different from the strategies employed with rural lands. The donation of rural properties to ecclesiastical institutions, and the preservation of the use of that land for the duration of the life of the donor, was an extremely common means by which families created a social bond with the dedicated religious of a monastery or church, and ensured that the land would not be seized by another claimant. In tenth-century Naples, just as everywhere else, there was a hierarchy of social status, from the dukes and bishops down to the urban poor. The preserved documents from Naples attest to a range in housing types, and houses of widely different value are sold, donated, or exchanged. The analysis of these documents reveals several different important families in the city in the tenth century; their residential arrangements will have been an important part of social display and the performance of their social position. Thus the document attests to a number of widely practiced elite behaviours, with particular relevance to the urban context of early medieval Naples: the preservation of a family's hold on a number of gardens in their neighbourhood, the endowment of a proprietary church with a garden, and the forging of links in the family lasting beyond generations and indeed with the saint herself.

The examples, of a papal gift to a Frankish courtier, a king's gift to a local vassal, a family's preservation of two gardens in their neighbourhood, and a widow's sale of a garden to a prince, all concern gardens as high-status properties. The status is revealed in different ways, whether through the manuscript evidence of the document recording the transmission, the agents involved in the transactions, or the relative monetary value of the parcel, compared to rural agricultural property.

Several commonalities run through our examples, notwithstanding the differences in agents, locations, and chronology. In two examples, the location of the garden is suggestive of the high value accorded the property. Fulrad's house with a garden was located at the Vatican in close proximity to St Peter's; Iohannes' garden in Verona was located within the ancient arena in an area of town that had been recognised as the royal palace since the Ostrogothic period. In the case of Maru and Barbaria's gardens, they were located in a neighbourhood of elite-owned gardens, many owned by their family. The value of the properties exchanged lay not exclusively in their productivity and the amenity of food cultivation but also in their proximity to a major shrine, to other residential buildings of antiquity and celebrated history, or to other residences of other living people of note. The history and the antiquity of a place were key to the legitimacy of the rulers and aristocracy.[133] In some instances, ancient buildings and building materials were reused in such ways, as they preserved and even put on display the original elements, unmistakably ancient in their appearance. These were, most scholars agree, deliberate efforts to emulate and to project to their contemporaries the architectural craftsmanship of a bygone past, and thus to mimic the command of resources of previous patrons, motivated by ideology or pragmatism or a combination of both concerns.

In this chapter, I set out to link the late antique practices of civic euergetism and urban patronage with early medieval commissioning of building projects and assuming responsibility for infrastructure and some charitable works. In understanding the convergence of social values around the provision of food, entertainment, and urban amenities in the late Roman world, it is possible to reconstruct various strategies for attaining social capital in early medieval urban contexts.

---

[133] For example, Di Santo, *Monumenti antichi*.

7   Conclusions

This book has grown out of the observation and analysis of the spaces for urban cultivation which have long been seen but not examined. Most historians and archaeologists, and even many non-specialists will agree wholeheartedly that there were vegetable gardens, orchards, and vineyards in early medieval cities, including those of Italy. Scholars have long known, or assumed, that in the Middle Ages there were cultivated spaces within the city walls of Rome. Few previous scholars have looked at urban horticulture for what it might tell us about the nature of the city and its people.[1] The exploration of when and where productive gardens appeared, who owned them, and what these cultivated properties did reveals changes in how people interacted with each other and their environments, at the levels of their households, their neighbourhoods, and their countryside. Urban gardens existed in some forms in antiquity, in some Roman cities, and they existed in the cities of medieval Italy after the eleventh century. Yet for the period of this study they took on a critical role in urban life, making possible new forms of interaction between city dwellers. By concentrating on a period of considerable social, economic, and political change in the Italian peninsula, from about 500 to 1050, the focus on one element of city life permits us to gauge how people coped with changes, adapted their ways of life, to consider what remained consistent with the past and what did not, and to hypothesise about why. It also suggests that some of the salient aspects of central medieval society, such as charitable bequests in wills, and the structures of caring for the poor through ecclesiastical institutions arose from the reconfiguration of the household in late antique and early medieval Italy; household-scale cultivation played a role in this change.

The fresh food produced from urban gardens and the habits of cultivation alongside houses within cities emerged out of specific contexts and

---

[1] For a rare exception, see Meneghini and Santangeli-Valenzani, *Roma nell'altomedioevo*, pp. 127–32.

because of specific changes in ideas and values. In early medieval Italy, the production of food served to meet a quotidian biological need. As well, it was constrained by environmental and economic factors; growing food was prompted both by basic needs for calories as well as ideas, habits, traditions, and social distinctions.[2] In his analysis of water in early medieval Italy, Paolo Squatriti eloquently pointed out that 'water was indissolubly both matter and custom, both nature and culture in the diverse landscapes of Italy during the early Middle Ages. This duality shaped the modes of water procurement, distribution and usage'.[3] I seek to make analogous claims for urban cultivation. My research for this book places urban gardens at the intersection of practical concerns and symbolic significance in order to reveal the relationships between realities and ideas in how people expended their energies and considered care for their community. By paying attention to urban gardens we can chart a fundamental element of life in early medieval Italy and suggest new frames through which we can explore the early medieval past through consideration of material realities – including plants and food cultivation as key constituents of those realities. One of these frames is economic, another frame is the intersection between ideas and cultural value, and a third is about power and prestige. Through each of these frames, the material evidence and the texts which described and recorded medieval material realities come into sharp focus and we can see how the attention paid to growing fresh food took a new and prominent role in the shape of cities. We cannot ascribe the rise of urban gardening simply to a decrease in population density in cities, nor to a cultural shift towards self-sufficiency, nor to a downturn in marketing. Each of these factors correlated one with the others, and each prompted different responses in different contexts.

The documentary evidence for urban life in early medieval Italy is rich and thick; we have chronicles of bishops and other civic leaders and documents recording sales, donations, exchanges of properties, disputes and their resolutions, and testaments, many of which were preserved in archives and libraries at Rome, Milan, Lucca, Verona, Naples, Montecassino, and elsewhere. Charters recording property transactions are themselves a fertile seam for historians; they are filled with details of names and places, people's social status and title, and measurements of lands and their values in cash and kind. Sometimes we are able to view patterns in a collection of documents, such as the twenty-two charters dating from 721 to 877 in the dossier of the family group of Toto of Campione near Milan, which reveal long-term strategies of the men and

---

[2] Montanari, *Food is culture*.   [3] Squatriti, *Water and society*, p. 4.

women of the family to further its social advantage through acquisition, marriage, and association with a private church and subsequently a major royal monastery, S. Ambrogio.[4] Documents from Italy make clear the relevance of a distinction between urban and rural; the texts of medieval documents very often specify whether a given place was inside the city walls, or out; a wealthy owner might hold several different parcels of land in different places in the landscape, but the urban ones will nearly always be set apart by a locating phrase such as *infra civitate*. The formulae that notaries used when compiling some documents recording property transactions reveal a general expectation that properties in the city might include cultivated areas, and that these cultivated areas are qualitatively different from rural agricultural lands. Formulae for the latter often include a long phrase encompassing a range of landscapes (e.g. 'Half of all my possessions, including house with structure, houses, foundations, courtyard, garden vineyard, lands whether cultivated or not, trees whether fruiting or not, movable or immobile, or semi-mobile'[5]). Documents for the city, however, seem to have been less reliant on formulae and more individual in their composition, such as another example of houses at Milan and Pavia: 'and a house of my *ius* which I have inside this city next to the public Forum not far from the Mint, with surrounding lots, courtyard, land and its entrances, wholly, similarly he should have houses of my use which I have in the city of Pavia, near the houses which are called "cells of Nonantola" with curtilages, courtyard, garden and well'.[6] Thus many urban properties describe what is called variously (*h*)*ortus*, *orticellus*, *iardinellus*, or *terra*; for other terms such as *curtis* or *curticella* it not always clear from the document whether they were cultivated, and these require scrutiny against other contemporary documents in which it is often possible to identify local habits of usage.

Archaeological research has also provided ample evidence for the analysis of cities and cultivated areas within them. The nature of the archaeological record is fundamentally different from that of the documents, lacking names and dates but rich in topographic specificity and sometimes organic matter. The material record of the transformation of late Roman cities without household-level planting spaces to early medieval cities with areas of cultivation suggests a chronology a bit earlier than the

---

[4] Gasparri et al., *Carte di famiglia*; Balzaretti, *The lands of Saint Ambrose*, pp. 299–344.
[5] 'omnes res mea medietatem, tam casa cum structura case, fundamento, curte, orto, uineas, terris, cultum uel incultum, arboribus fructiferas uel infructiferas, mobile uel inmouile seo seomouentibis', *CDL* vol. II, 133 (759) pp. 21–3.
[6] 'et casellam illam iuris mei, quam abeo intra hanc civitatem iuxta Foro puplico non longe a Moneta, cum areas curte terra [e]t a[cc]essis suas in integrum similiter abeat casas illas iuris mei, quas abeo intra civitati Papie prope casas, qui dicitur cella de Nonantolas cum areas, curte, orto, puteum', *Museo* vol. I.2, 138 (879).

documents attest: about 500, while the first documents which mention gardens appear about 100 years later. The archaeology suggests that the few very early documents attesting to cultivated spaces attached to houses are not anomalous, but rather indicative of wider patterns. The material evidence for houses with cultivated areas gives a clear picture of Italian cities transformed as new structures of life emerged: large townhouses were subdivided or partially destroyed in order to provide compact living areas with gardens and backfilled areas between houses. Cultivated areas were created in places which in the late Roman period were open spaces, along main roads and over abandoned buildings. Urban gardens were not opportunistically eked out of abandoned spaces but rather were built with imported soil, manure, and retaining walls. The kinds of plants which were cultivated – when we can see their traces in the archaeological record as pollens or as carpological remains – were rather fewer in number than in antiquity. Indeed, the scale of urban life in antiquity was reduced: fewer people, smaller houses, less luxurious decorations in houses and buildings (though churches were gloriously adorned), and fewer imported goods in circulation. As Peter Brown has so clearly shown, new ways of living emerged as the largesse of late antiquity was replaced by charitable bequests and endowments of the church; urban gardens played a part in that transformation, too, and they attest to its extent and its effects in ways which have previously been misunderstood.[7]

In the period between about 500 and 1050, the Italian peninsula was a patchwork of kingdoms, duchies, semi-autonomous city-states, or provinces of other polities. The languages, customs, legal systems, and trade networks varied somewhat throughout the peninsula, and many scholars would avoid considering Italy as a single entity in the early Middle Ages. In this book, I have approached Italy not as a single unified entity, but as a peninsula with a great degree of shared history.[8] There were smaller administrative structures within these, but many of the same patterns of urban investment, taxation, and rural land use applied equally to these broad areas. Geography varied enormously across the peninsula, with some areas more densely urbanised than others, or more closely connected to riverine or maritime trade networks. Under Ostrogothic rule, Italy included parts of Gaul and Dalmatia; these and other parts of eastern and southern Italy, including Sicily, then joined the Eastern Roman (Byzantine) empire in the mid sixth century. Despite these political shifts, the differences between Milan, Pavia, Verona, Ravenna, Rome, and Naples in late antiquity had more to do with scale than any other

---

[7] Brown, *Through the eye of the needle*.
[8] Giardina, 'Le due Italie'; Millar, 'Italy and the Roman Empire'.

structural difference. In the second half of the first millennium, the different regions of Italy underwent very different trajectories into the Middle Ages, with some becoming vibrant capitals, others becoming footholds for foreign governments, others being dominated by their bishops. Throughout the period examined by this book, nonetheless, the differences between city and country remained far greater than the differences between cities in the North or the South, or cities in the Byzantine or Lombard areas. For these reasons, I have been able to consider in one study the urban transformations of Brescia, Bari, and Palermo; each of these had cultivated lands within the walls, and these areas of cultivation arose for broadly the same reasons and were used in broadly the same ways. While it was by no means a single political entity in this period, Italy remains a useful flexible geographic and historical entity in which we might observe the phenomenon of urban food cultivation and the reformation of early medieval households.

This book is an urban history of early medieval Italy, exploring the experience of early medieval cities, who lived there, how they put food on their tables, and how they read the urban landscapes around them. The relative density of living in cities pressurised life, and so we can see social interactions in sharper relief than in a rural landscape. For people living in a city, changes in property use, new buildings, or buildings left in dereliction are all more visible than if in dispersed rural settlements. In early medieval Italy, urban life was central, and urbanism was a fundamental aspect of governance and the exercise of power. Rulers and aristocrats lived in cities; urban churches and monasteries owned rural land, but they were predominantly controlled through urban networks. Throughout early medieval Italy, people used urban officials to authorise and record their property transactions, and often (though not always) convened in cities to resolve disputes. Because of the nature of urban existence and because of the key roles played by urban life in early medieval Italy, this study of urban gardening provides a keyhole view into early medieval society in the Italian peninsula that is, on the one hand, representative of wider patterns of land use, and social relations as they were formed and reformed around agricultural properties and, on the other hand, peculiar to urban contexts and the exigencies of life in a city. The archaeological evidence of Dark Earth from cities also speaks to the ways in which cities concentrated a range of activities common to rural areas into single sites: cultivation, manuring, and rubbish dumping took place outside cities as well, but when they were concentrated in given areas and other natural processes such as weathering and animal activity took place, the combination of materials and processes created the particular material we call Dark Earth. The examination of how people lived in cities and how they modified city spaces for new or different activities provides specific insights into the experience of economic and political transformations.

Across the cities of Italy, gardens came to be typical elements within the urban landscape and significant contributors to putting food on the table in urban households. While crops of cabbage and celery can be planted and harvested within months, the urban transformations by which urban townhouses sometimes included gardens were long-term evolutions. Some towns in the Roman period had landscaped parks and planters, some houses in Roman-period cities had courtyards which may have been planted – even with fruiting trees such as pear, apple, or cherry, or aromatic plants such as bay – but these did not constitute major food-producing areas for urban households.[9] Villas and rural residences made very deliberate use of their landscaped areas to grow fresh food which could be eaten at the villa or transported to the owners' townhouses for consumption, but the major cities of Roman Italy generally preserved a distinction between densely built-up urban areas and less-dense rural areas where space was made for cultivation. Suburbs of cities, including tombs and suburban villas, incorporated buildings and gardens, including sometimes gardens for fresh food. Contraction in the Roman economy of the late antique period blurred the distinctions between urban and rural as productive agriculture around cities shrank, and urban populations shifted out of cities, or out of Italy. By the sixth century houses had gardens attached to them, or between them; there were also separate plots of cultivation.

No city was ever fully self-sufficient: rural cultivation was always the major source of food production. Grain and cereals, eaten as bread, flat cakes, porridge, or stew, were the basic foodstuff of ancient and medieval Italy. Cerealiculture requires space, but not necessarily watering, fertilising, or pruning; it would be rare indeed to find evidence for people growing any significant amounts of wheat, barley, or rye in cities. These were grown in fields outside cities, worked by people living in villages or living in cities and walking out to work the fields when necessary. Surveying the overall panoramas of preserved property documents from various collections provides a sense of the profiles of property ownership: the majority of documents, whether from Rome, Lucca, or Naples, record rural landholding: grain fields, olive or chestnut groves, vineyards, and

---

[9] Palaeobotanical evidence from the new excavations from the Metropolitana C line have identified the plantings in gardens on the far side of the Caelian hill from the first century: a portico opened onto plantings of *Prunus* (peach tree or plum tree), *Juglans regia* (walnut tree), *Buxus sempervirens* (box), and *Rubus* (blackberry or raspberry bush); Rea, 'Archeologia nel suburbio di Roma', pp. 438–9; Rea and Saviane, 'At the foot of the Lateran Hill' [forthcoming].

sometimes gardens in villages; a significant minority are gardens, orchards, olive groves, or vineyards in cities.[10] While recognising that feeding a family always required some rural products, many if not most urban households grew some of their own fresh food and took care to refer to their gardens or orchards in documents recording transfers of properties. Sometimes it is possible to see clusters of gardens in neighbourhoods, when adjacent gardens are mentioned in the boundary clauses of a property being sold, exchanged, or donated. They were an increasingly visible part of the urban landscape in our period, comprising significant elements in the cityscape and the wider system of urban food provision.

It is nearly impossible to determine whether there was more urban cultivation in the earlier part of our period than the later, or vice versa. The nature of the early medieval documentary record is that there were ever more written documents produced over the period between 700 and 1200 (and later) and that there was a virtuous cycle which made more documents increasingly relevant in reporting transactions and thus further increasing the number of documents produced.[11] It is therefore inevitable that there is more evidence for urban cultivation in the later part of our period, but it may not reflect an actual increase in the amount of urban gardening taking place. This conundrum is difficult to resolve. Archaeology offers rather little in the way of a control against written records, as, while there are many kinds of material-culture chronological indicators in the late antique period from coins to distinctly dated pottery forms, there were far fewer coins in use in early medieval Italy and therefore fewer in the archaeological record than in phases of late antique occupation.

Like the documents of property exchange, the documentary evidence for marketing also increases and is subject to the same overall expansion in documents. For our period, the evidence for markets, their creation, and control clearly suggests changes in marketing activity, notably a movement from rural or coastal locations to urban ones, and, for the period around 1000, from periodic events to fixed markets with permanent structures within cities. Property transactions reflecting agricultural specialisation emerge in the early eleventh century, confirming a change in the systems of production and distribution with respect to the earlier period. It is not possible to say whether urban gardening expanded, declined, or remained constant over the period examined here, but it is possible to situate the phenomenon of urban gardening against

---

[10] For figures, see Chapter 1, pp. 5–6.
[11] Cammarosano, *Italia medievale*; Maire-Vigueur, 'Révolution documentaire'; Brown et al., *Lay documentary culture and the laity in the early Middle Ages*.

Conclusions 229

a changing economy, a system of commercial exchange which is more complex and more urban at the end of the period under examination.

Did urban cultivation end in the mid eleventh century when urban markets again made it possible to purchase fresh food in cities, and when there was increasing need for urban houses, as city populations rose? In short, it did not end completely. New residential plots at Rome appeared in the eleventh century, some of which expanded in areas that had previously had many gardens.[12] In 1019, SS. Ciriaco and Nicola in via Lata gave over three parcels of orchards to build new houses in Regio 9, near S. Maria in Trivio on the Campus Martius.[13] The fruit trees of the orchard remained in place between the houses because rental payments were partly in kind.[14] But the pressure for new housing and the opportunities for rental income prompted the creation of new houses.

Documents from the late eleventh century and beyond do describe gardens among urban houses and properties; there are examples from throughout Italy. One from the late eleventh century refers to a donation from Iohannes, gastald and *iudex*, who gave houses and a garden in Benevento to the church of S. Bartolomeo and S. Gennaro; it is surrounded by gardens of S. Modesto.[15] In many ways these are entirely consistent with the documents considered in the previous chapters. Of the documents recording cultivated properties at and around Benevento, the majority pertain to suburban or rural lands in the environs, and while there were cultivated spaces in the city after the mid eleventh century, they constituted a considerably less significant part of the wider economic pattern of food production than they had before. We are able to recognise the change in the role played by urban gardening by looking holistically at economic patterns for the period. At Naples, cultivated spaces were often outside of the city, and increasingly so from the eleventh century.[16] Efforts to quantify the rate and scale of this kind of change are difficult;

---

[12] Hubert pinpointed the beginning of rise in the property market at Rome, noting the increase in plots *ad domum faciendam* and similar phrases from the year 1000, *Espace urbain*, pp. 334–7; Wickham, *Medieval Rome*, p. 229.

[13] 'Idest terra bacante ad domum faciendum sedium unum in integrum cum arboribus pomarum infra se habentem, quod est in longitude pedes numero quadraginta hocto et per latum triginta sex, omnia pede semmissali iusta mensura ... atque omni anno de poma quem ibidem dominus donaverit medietatem,' *SMVL* 41 (1019) pp. 51–2.

[14] See also from Rome, a plot of land where there was once a vineyard, in a document of 1042: 'terra vacante ubi holim fuit vinea ... Posita Rome regione quarta in Aura infra locum qui dicitur Domus Nova [scil. Basilica Nova]', in *TSMN* 13 (1042), pp. 206–9.

[15] 'casas fabritas et casas ligneas et casalinas et terram que est ortum pertinentem habere intus hac nova Beneventanam civitatem', *Benevento* 51 (1092).

[16] A similar observation has been made by Paul Arthur, 'Naples. A case of urban survival', p. 770, pointing out that monasteries and urban elite were the only ones who commanded open areas.

230   Conclusions

we will never know the GDP of the Lombard duchy of Benevento, nor of any political entity of Italy in the early Middle Ages. These difficulties notwithstanding, considering the overall shape of the picture which emerges both from evidence for production and evidence for market distribution over the centuries of the early Middle Ages, we can see that household-level production plays a major role in the economy of early medieval cities for a period between about 500 and 1050. The dominant paradigms for urban economies, even early medieval ones, have previously not considered sufficiently the contributions of urban cultivation in economic systems, nor in political economies, to which we will turn shortly. Before considering political economies, it is worth reflecting on how analysis of urban food production has suffered under antiquated models and our limited understandings of urban provisioning.

In antiquity, the demands of a city, whether Rome or another city of the Italian peninsula, commanded the resources of its hinterlands and sometimes lands even further away. Von Thünen's model of urban consumption of suburban and rural products has periodically formed the basis of discussions of Roman cities, Rome in particular, and their provisioning. Two concepts of the model, crop location and intensification based on proximity to urban market and transport routes, have been invoked by many scholars of ancient economies to explain the ways in which food and firewood came to Rome and other cities in antiquity.[17] Because early medieval cities were productive, however, the model does not apply in the same way. Analysis of food production in modern London through the lens of von Thünen's picture of furnishing cities makes clear the flaws in the model and the difficulties in its application not only to some modern cities but also to early medieval cities.[18] The case of nineteenth-century London points out the problems clearly. The spaces of agricultural production in London changed over the nineteenth century, in part responding to increasing demands for residential buildings in the centre, investment in permanent agricultural architecture such as greenhouses, and changes in transport systems. Near the city centre was intensive farming of 'expensive, exotic and out-of-season species such as asparagus, artichokes, melons, celery, pineapples, herbs and salads' grown in hothouses over fertilised soils while in the immediate periphery was a wide range of more conventional crops, grown with specialisation by area.[19] Beyond this, less valuable crops were grown on rotation. These included

---

[17] See Chapter 1, Rome, p. 46, and Wilson, 'Villas, horticulture and irrigation infrastructure'. For late antiquity, see Santangeli Valenzani, 'Vecchie e nuove forme'.
[18] Atkins, 'The charmed circle: von Thünen and agriculture'.
[19] 'Here the variety of crops grown was immense, with a concentration upon the most delicate vegetables requiring skilled attention, such as asparagus, sea-kale, French beans,

'cabbage, potatoes, turnips, and carrots. Soft fruit was common in the outer zones and was often combined on frost-free land as an undercrop with a tree crop of hard fruit such as apples, because of the complementary nature of their labour requirements.'[20] These different zones developed in and around the centre of London, along the river Thames in its floodplain (and presumably the River Lea), being pushed outwards in the later nineteenth century by expanding residential zones and demand for industrial sites, and expanding along with the canal and rail system which permitted transport of produce. The changing costs of labour associated with other industrial activities limited small-scale horticulture at the end of the nineteenth century.[21] Atkins' analysis of von Thünen's model in terms of this early modern city shows complexity related to specific geography, and change brought about by different kinds of building, new technology, and changes in economies. Very little of the urban gardening of nineteenth-century London was determined by von Thünen's two factors. Similarly, this model has not been helpful for explaining the locations of urban and suburban cultivation in early medieval cities, because some of the production of fresh food for the city occurred within the city, at household level.

What Did People Do with Gardens?

Urban food production in the early Middle Ages was far from a subsistence-level strategy for survival. Cultivations in cities emerged as one of the results of the major transformations to life and provisioning for household needs in the post-Roman period. Throughout the evolutions of late antiquity and the early Middle Ages, certain ideas, habits, and values of the classical past shaped the new ways of being, just as new concepts and hierarchies reconfigured these traditions. In antiquity, horticulture and agriculture more broadly held an important place among the activities of man and the uses of the land. Significant ancient Roman cultural esteem was placed upon the effective management of rural estates, so that the land was productive, the crops were well-timed and carefully managed, and the workers of the estate were industrious and obedient. In poetry and literature, working the land and eating the fruits of that industry was a highly valued activity.[22] Greek and Latin works providing information and instructions about agriculture were produced

---

celery, radishes, lettuces, and mustard and cress', Atkins, 'The charmed circle: von Thünen and agriculture', p. 131.
[20] Atkins, 'The charmed circle: von Thünen and agriculture', p. 133.
[21] Atkins, 'The charmed circle: von Thünen and agriculture', p. 134.
[22] Purcell, 'Dialectical gardening'.

in the late Republican and imperial periods, and these continued to circulate even into the Middle Ages in condensed excerpted forms. Likewise, works on natural history included guidance about the cultivation of plants for health and also for medicine; these too continued to be used and reproduced in the Middle Ages.

In early medieval Italy there was little interest in decorative gardening, and this marks a significant change from antiquity. While cities often had landscaping of trees, shrubs, and flowering plants, some private houses also had some decorative plantings in peristyle gardens within 'private' parts of the house, where they were closely related to the status and identity of the homeowner and conveyed to guests this social standing. The *uiridarium* in antiquity was a 'green space', as the term suggests, often planted with trees and shrubs, sometimes enclosed by walls, in some high-status residences. This term continued to be used, though very infrequently, to refer to private gardens or orchards in the early Middle Ages in exceptionally high-status places.[23] In antiquity, a good deal of horticultural attention had been dedicated to the growing of flowers for perfumes and for garlands which were used in celebrations and religious events. Depictions of floral garlands are commonplace in monumental architecture as well as in the decorations of some high-status houses; they may have been very commonplace in antiquity. Perhaps because of the abundance of gardens for celebrations, the writings of some early Christian communities in Rome set themselves apart from their traditional neighbours by eschewing floral garlands. The metaphorical and symbolic associations of flowers changed in late antiquity through new Christian ideals and within the changing social and economic patterns: flowers were no longer used for celebrations, and the cultivation of flowers in areas near to cities stopped as the market for flowers declined. Late antique authors developed a strong symbolic association between roses and Christ's suffering, and roses continued to grow in medieval sites, as *Rosa* sp. pollen was recovered from the pits at the tenth- and eleventh-century urban garden at Ferrara, though these may have been wild bushes.[24]

Emerging ideas about the value of self-sufficiency in religious households, such as monasteries where men and women lived together in dedication to a religious life, drew upon ancient models of estate management applied to a new Christian context. Because some of the men associated with the treatises and rules of early monastic life came from

---

[23] Goodson, 'Admirable and delectable gardens'.
[24] Personal communication from Giovanna Bosi. We await the publication of this pollen record.

elite backgrounds, the paideia of traditional knowledge and values around household management, including the running of agricultural estates, informed the shaping of monastic households. Understanding of the role of not only abbots but also bishops emerged from traditional roles of the head of households and the stewards of estates; providing sufficient food for the entire household and allocating it appropriately were part of the job of early religious leaders. Urban gardens provided the means for religious communities in cities, including monasteries, *scolae* for priests, and charitable houses for feeding the poor and pilgrims.

Some urban gardens may have been used for medicinal purposes, though it remains very difficult to know the degree to which certain plants were cultivated specifically for medicine, as many ingredients were the same as those used for everyday meals. Some historians of medicine have argued that Italy, in the early Middle Ages played key roles in the transmission and translation of treatises of medieval knowledge and also the movement of exotic substances used for medicine. My analysis of the wider economic patterns in the Italian peninsula suggests that long-distance trade of high-value items, including medical compounds, was relatively infrequent between the seventh and tenth centuries, but nonetheless it is plausible that there was some movement of high-value items along ecclesiastical networks, in keeping with the movement of imported luxury textiles and other exotica. Churchmen, rulers, and their courtiers may have moved goods from the southern and eastern Mediterranean into Europe through Italy, but there is little evidence that medical substances grown in Italy were particularly sought elsewhere.

Consideration of gardens and the reasons for which they appeared has made clear that what was grown, when we can determine it, tended to be a range of plants somewhat different from the horticultural assemblage of the Roman period. There were more different cereal and legume crops grown than in the past and more wild species which could have been encouraged to grow in the post-Roman urban environment than appear in comparable contexts in the Roman period. This recognition of the change in what people grew (and what people ate) points to the co-productive nature of human cultivation in the post-Roman environment. People grew fresh food that thrived in their environment, drawing upon wild or semi-wild plants as well as garden staples from antiquity. There is scope for more research in this area, as the archaeobotanical record expands. An urban environmental history of early medieval Italy would need to consider not only useful plants, but also those which grew as weeds alongside tilled earth or planted crops, or which invaded and exploited the conditions of the post-Roman city. Archaeobotanists have

234   Conclusions

used ruderal plants to reveal changes in urban ecologies and waterways; when systematically examined these plants may also be able to tell us about land use and disuse, and perhaps even the movement of people, in the ways that modern ecological geography has recorded the twentieth-century movement of troops through Germany and trade connections through the arrival of new weeds in urban landscapes, or growth of matsutake mushrooms in 'disturbance-based ecologies'.[25] Plants took advantage of environments in early medieval cities, and I would hope that we might know more about how not-useful plants, as well as useful plants, interacted with people in cities.

In the cities of early medieval Italy, interventions in the dense urban landscape were the means to show status and social alliances. The urban history of Italy is usually understood through its monuments: the achievements of major building campaigns which united the populace and provided opportunities for structured leisure, commerce, and administration. The model for this understanding is strongly derived from imperial Rome and scholarly understanding of its monumental fabric. A monument such as the Forum of Peace, built by Vespasian in 71 CE, is a testament to the emperor's resources and his architectural sophistication, and its planting with beds of *Rosa gallica*, and perhaps also trees brought from conquered Judea is a statement of territorial domination.[26] New forms of this kind of performance of power emerged in the early Middle Ages. The construction of a new church, new townhouses, or a new garden was highly visible in urban environments, though previous research on the way in which gifts of land worked in the early Middle Ages has never considered the urban context. From late antiquity to the early Middle Ages, a significant change occurred in the ways in which social status was conveyed through donation or patronage; the late Roman pattern of civic euergetism and benefaction for the city as a tool for self-promotion changed to the improvement of urban churches and private households, where power was displayed by the command of building resources. Historians and archaeologists readily accept the expression of power and prestige in the construction of a new building but have hitherto overlooked the ways in which cultivated spaces might also convey wealth, status, and command of resources. By applying ideas about the power of land in the early Middle Ages and the achievement of

[25] Gandy, 'Marginalia: aesthetics, ecology, and urban wastelands'; Tsing, *The mushroom at the end of the world*. For an attentive analysis of medieval weeds (and how one grain ceased to be a 'weed', see Squatriti, 'Rye's rise and Rome's fall'; on ruderals in the Italian city, see Bosi et al., 'The memory of water'.
[26] Meneghini and Santangeli Valenzani, *I Fori imperiali*, pp. 61–70; Rizzo, 'Indagini nei fori imperiali', pp. 238–9; Pollard, 'Pliny's *Natural history*'.

status through the gifting of agricultural land and benefices, I suggest that urban land worked in similar ways to the advantage of the giver and the receiver. The critical difference between urban agricultural land and rural lands, *beneficia*, and rights is that what happened in the city was highly visible among neighbours and visitors too: we can imagine easily how residents of Pavia or Benevento might notice the well-tended vegetable patch that used to be owned by the priest was now owned by a couple; the house and garden in the royal neighbourhood now belonged to the palace official. These changes in ownership and the social status and relationships that they reflected were enacted in daily life within cities. The social bonds between pope and Frankish diplomat, between king and vassal, and even between family church and a widow and unmarried daughter were highly recognisable and prominent proclamations in dense urban environments. The value of land in the early Middle Ages, whether urban or rural, tied as much to the social relationships achieved by the property transaction as they did to the income potential of the property. But when considering the wider picture of the motors of exchange, the value of social relationships in procuring food becomes doubly important.

Questions about the early medieval economy are difficult to answer with the patchy evidence for the period around 500 to 1050 and given the prevailing assumption about Roman-period economies (and their demise) and later medieval commercialism (and its origins). The vexed quality of the matter is highlighted in early medieval Italy, where by some counts there was greater commercial exchange than elsewhere in Europe; there are merchants identified in our documents and some very exotic imports, but by other accounts there was very little commercial exchange; there are comparatively few coins in circulation, and few markets in the documentary or archaeological record before the eleventh century. Recent scholarship has made clear the strongly local nature of exchange in the Italian peninsula in the early Middle Ages. My consideration of the role of household economies as motors of exchange makes clear not only that very small-scale exchanges and transactions along the networks of extended households facilitated the movement of goods and that we can situate urban cultivation into this picture. Given the absence of commercial-scale farming of fresh food, apart from grain and some olives and wine grapes, household-level cultivation was, for the period between about 500 and 1050, the principal means of acquiring fresh food for most city-dwellers. Historical agriculturists have estimated that in 40 sq. m one can grow the fresh vegetables and legumes needed for a person for a year. These figures are based on pre-industrial period standards of urban agriculture in the central European climate, where potatoes were grown – of course, in medieval Eurasia there were no potatoes – but they have nonetheless been used by environmental historians of late medieval Constantinople to calculate the productivity of the green belt between the Constantinian and Theodosian walls, for example.[27] If we used these calculations, Berengar's garden gift to his vassal in 893 could therefore have produced the vegetables for about fourteen people – not enormous, but certainly significant.[28] Crescentius Marcapullo, in early eleventh-century Rome, could have fed eighty-six on half of his urban plot, assuming the rest was used for residential buildings and other things. When considering the religious economy of donations of food and property to ecclesiastical communities for the spiritual benefit of the donor, and including the idea that religious institutions operate within this network on par with large households, social relations based upon land, bonds of obligation, and kinship are clearly fundamental to the movement of goods.

My research on urban gardening draws upon and contributes to our understandings of social interactions facilitated by the property market and reflected in its records. It makes clear the social allegiances formed in neighbourhoods around properties, and the strategies that families devised to preserve their access to cultivated spaces, by trading them, selling them, or giving them to an institution and preserving usufruct. We have seen neighbours joining forces to acquire cultivated urban properties, and in the listings of property boundaries we can see families owning clusters of parcels in proximity to one another, showing that some families worked together to concentrate their properties in one area, building up a territorial presence in the city. We can see the legacies of ownership preserved in documents, whereby sellers noted the means by which they had come to own parcels of land, sometimes through family relationships.

Household growing of fresh food was, for the period under consideration, central to the feeding of cities in Italy as well as it was essential to the construction of the kinds of social relationships of power and peer-polity which animated political interactions. The study of urban gardening as a social practice provides new information about the transition from ancient to medieval and the degree to which Roman cultural systems, practices, and material structures endured or faded in the post-Roman world, and how societies created new systems of value, habits, and interactions. Horden and Purcell's observation about the cultivation of woodlands is apposite to urban gardens in this regard: 'It is noteworthy that this

---

[27] Koder, 'Fresh vegetables for the capital', p. 51.   [28] See Chapter 3, p. 88.

use of the marginal is a sign of sophistication rather than primitiveness'.[29] What has previously been considered a marginal activity, at the lowest end of economic relevance, was an active agent in the reconsideration of early medieval households and a tool in the arsenal of social mobility and performance of power in early medieval societies.

---

[29] Horden and Purcell, *The corrupting sea*, p. 186.

Bibliography

Primary Sources

Ahimaaz ben, Paltiel, *The chronicle of Ahimaaz*, ed. Marcus Salzman, in *Sefer yuḥasin*, Oriental studies (Columbia University) v. 18 (New York, 1924).

Alfabetum Galieni, ed. Nicholas Everett, in *The alphabet of Galen: pharmacy from antiquity to the Middle Ages. A critical edition of the Latin text with English translation and commentary* (Toronto, 2012).

Amatus of Montecassino, *Ystoire de li normant*, ed. Michèle Guéret-Laferté (Paris, 2011), trans. Prescott Dunbar, in *The history of the Normans by Amatus of Montecassino* (Woodbridge, 2004).

Ambrose, bishop of Milan, *Hexameron*, ed. Karl Schenkl, in *Sancti Ambrosii Opera*, Corpus scriptorum ecclesiasticorum latinorum 32.1 (Vienna, 1896), pp. 3–261, trans. as *Saint Ambrose. Hexameron, Paradise, and Cain and Abel*, trans. John Savage, The Fathers of the Church 42 (New York, 1961).

Ambrosiaster, 'Commentarius in Epistulam ad Timotheum prima', in *Commentarius in Epistulas Paulinas*, ed. H. Vogels, Corpus scriptorium ecclesiasticorum latinorum 81 (Vienna, 1966), vol. III, pp. 249–94.

Andrea of Bergamo, 'Historia', ed. Georg Waitz, MGH, SS RL, vol. I (Hanover, 1878), pp. 220–30.

Annales regni Francorum inde ab a. 741 usque ad a. 829, qui dicuntur Annales Laurissenses maiores et Einhardi, ed. F. Kurze, MGH, SS RG 6 (Hanover, 1895).

Anthimus, *De obseruatione ciborum*, ed. Mark Grant, in *On the observance of foods* (Totnes, 1996).

Asmenius, *De laude horti*, ed. Anne Friedrich, in *Das Symposium der XII Sapientes: Kommentar und Verfasserfrage* (Berlin and New York, 2002).

Augustine, *Confessiones*, ed. James Joseph O'Donnell, 3 vols. (Oxford, 2012).

Augustine, *Sancti Aurelii Augustini episcopi De civitate Dei libri XXII*, ed. Bernhard Dombert, 2 vols. (Leipzig, 1863).

Aventinus, Johannes, *Annales ducum Boiariae*, in *Johannes Turmair's genannt Aventinus Sämmtliche Werke*, ed. Sigmund Riezler, 5 vols., vols. II–III. Johannes Turmair's genannt Aventinus Sämmtliche Werke (Munich, 1881).

Bede, *Historia ecclesiastica gentis Anglorum*, eds. B. Colgrave and R. A. B. Mynors, in *Bede's ecclesiastical history of the English people*, rev. ed., Oxford Medieval Texts (Oxford, 1991).

Benedict of Nursia, *Regula*, ed. Jean Neufville, trans. Adalbert de Vogüé, in *La règle de Saint Benoît*, 6 vols., Sources chrétiennes 181–6 (Paris, 1971–2).
Breviarium ecclesiae Ravennatis (Codice Bavaro) secoli vii-x, ed. Giuseppe Rabotti (Rome, 1985).
Capitularia Regum Francorum, vol. I, ed. Alfred Boretius, in MGH, Leges vol. II (Hanover, 1883).
Cartario di S. Maria in Campo Marzio, ed. Enrico Carusi (Rome, 1948).
Carte del Monastero dei SS. Cosma e Damiano in Mica Aurea, ed. Paola Pavan, Codice diplomatico di Roma e della Regione Romana, 1 (Rome, 1981).
'Carte del monastero dei SS. Cosma e Damiano in Mica Aurea ab an. 982 ad an. 1200, pt 1, X-XI,' ed. Pietro Fedele, *ASRSP* 21 (1898), pp. 459–534; 22 (1899, pp. 25–107, and pp. 383–447).
Cassian, John, *De institutis coenobiorum, De incarnatione contra Nestorium*, ed. Michael Petschenig, in *Cassianus. De Institutis Coenobiorum, De Incarnatione Contra Nestorium*, Corpus scriptorum ecclesiasticorum latinorum 17 (Vienna, 2004).
Cassiodorus, *Institutiones*, ed. R. A. B. Mynors (Oxford, 1937), trans. as *Institutions of divine and secular learning and on the soul*, trans. J. Halporn, Translated texts for historians 42 (Liverpool, 2004).
Cassiodorus, *Variae*, eds. Åke Josefsson Fridh and James W. Halporn, in *Magni Aurelii Cassiodori Senatoris Opera, Pars I*, Corpus Christianorum, Series Latina, 96 (Turnhout, 1973), trans. S. J. B. Barnish, Translated texts for historians 12 (Liverpool, 1992).
Cassiodorus, *Variarum libri duodecim*, ed. Theodor Mommsen, in *Cassiodori senatoris variae*, MGH, AA (Berlin, 1894).
Cato maior, Marcus Porcius, *De agri cultura*, eds. W. D. Hooper and Harrison Boyd Ash, in *On agriculture*, Loeb Classical Library 283 (Cambridge, MA, 1934).
Chartae Latinae Antiquiores. Facsimile editions of Latin charters, First Series, eds. A. Bruckner, R. Marichal, Second Series, eds. G. Cavallo and G. Nicolaj, 118 vols. (Olten and Lausanne, 1954–2019).
Chisholm, Michael, *Rural settlement and land use. An essay in location*, revised ed. (London, 1979).
Chrétien de Troyes, *Cligés*, eds. Stewart Gregory and Claude Luttrell, in *Chrétien de Troyes. Cligés*, Arthurian Studies 28 (Cambridge, 1993).
Chronicon Salernitanum, ed. Ulla Westerbergh, in *Chronicon Salernitanum. A critical edition with studies on literary and historical sources and on language* (Stockholm/Lund, 1956).
Chronicon Sanctae Sophiae: cod. Vat. Lat. 4939, ed. Jean-Marie Martin, 2 vols., Rerum Italicarum scriptores 3 (Rome, 2000).
Cicero, *De officiis*, trans. P. G. Walsh, in *Cicero. On obligations*, Loeb Classical Library 30 (Oxford, 2000).
Clement of Alexandria, *Paedagogus*, eds. Miroslav Marcovich and J. C. M. van Winden, in *Clementis Alexandrini Paedagogus*, Supplements to Vigiliae Christianae 61 (Leiden, 2002).

Codex Carolinus, ed. Wilhelm Gundlach, MGH EE, vol. III (Berlin, 1892), pp. 469–657.
Codex diplomaticus amiatinus: Urkundenbuch der Abtei S. Salvatore am Montamiata von den Anfängen bis zum Regierungsantritt Papst Innozenz III. (736–1198), ed. Wilhelm Kurze, in *Codex diplomaticus Amiatinus: Urkundenbuch der Abtei S. Salvatore am Montamiata von den Anfängen bis zum Regierungsantritt Papst Innozenz III. (736–1198)*, 4 vols. (Tübingen, 1974).
Codex diplomaticus cavensis, ed. Michele Morcaldi, Mauro Schiani, and Silvano De Stefano, 8 vols. (Naples, 1873–93).
Codex diplomaticus langobardiae, ed. Giulio Porro Lambertenghi, Historiae patriae monumenta 13 (Turin, 1878).
Codex Theodosianus, eds. Paul M. Meyer and Theodor Mommsen, in *Theodosiani libri XVI cum constitutionibus Sirmondianis et leges novellae ad Theodosianum pertinentes*, 2 vols. (Berlin, 1905).
Codice diplomatico barese, 19 vols. (Bari, 1897–1971).
Codice diplomatico del monastero di S. Colombano di Bobbio fino all'anno 1208, ed. Carlo Cipolla, Fonti per la storia d'Italia (Torino, 1918).
Codice diplomatico longobardo, I–II, ed. Luigi Schiaparelli, Fonti per la storia d'Italia 62–3 (Rome, 1929–33); III, IV.1, ed. C. Brühl, Fonti per la storia d'Italia 64–5, IV.2 ed. H. Zielinski (Rome, 1973–83), V, ed. H. Zielinski, Fonti per la storia d'Italia 65bis (Rome, 1986).
Codice diplomatico parmense, ed. Umberto Benassi, 2 vols. (Parma, 1910).
Codice diplomatico veronese, ed. Vittorio Fainelli, 2 vols., Monumenti storici ns 1, 17 (Venice, 1940).
Codices latini antiquiores: A palaeographical guide to Latin manuscripts prior to the ninth century, ed. Elias Avery Lowe, 11 vols. (Oxford, 1934).
Columella, Lucius Junius Moderatus, *De arboribus*, eds. E. S. Forster and Edward Heffner, in *On agriculture and trees vol. 3: Res rustica 10–12*, Loeb Classical Library 408 (Cambridge, MA, 1979).
Columella, Lucius Junius Moderatus, *De re rustica*, ed. and trans. Harrison Boyd Ash, Loeb Classical Library 361, 407, 408, 3 vols.
Corpus Inscriptionum Latinarum, ed. Theodor Mommsen et al., 17 vols. (Berlin: 1842–)
De incarnatione contra Nestorium, ed. Michael Petschenig, in *Cassianus. De Institutis Coenobiorum, De Incarnatione Contra Nestorium*, Corpus scriptorum ecclesiasticorum latinorum 17 (Vienna, 2004).
Deusdedit, *Deusdedit presbyteri cardinalis tituli Apolstolorum in Eudoxia Collectio Canonum*, ed. Pio Martinucci (Venice, 1867).
Dictionary of medieval Latin from British sources, ed. Ronald Edward Latham (Oxford, 1975–2013).
Die nichtliterarischen lateinischen Papyri Italiens aus der Zeit 445–700, ed. Jan Olof Tjäder, Skrifter utgivna av Svenska Institutet i Rom, 8o XIX, 1, 2, 3, 3 vols. (Lund and Stockholm, 1954–82).
Dionisi, Giovanni, *De duobus episcopis Aldone et Notingo Veronensi ecclesiae assertis et vindicatis* (Verona, 1758).
Dionysius Exiguus, *Collectio decretorum pontificum romanorum*, ed. J-P Migne, in *PL*, vol. 67 (Paris, 1848), coll 229–345.

Dioscorides, Pedanius, *De materia medica libri quinque*, ed. M. Wellmann, 3 vols. (Berlin, 1907–14), trans. Lily Beck, in *De materia medica. Pedanius Dioscorides of Anazarbus*, rev. ed. (Hildesheim and New York, 2011).

Diplomatum Karolinorum I, Pippini, Carlomanni, Caroli Magni Diplomata, ed. E. Mühlbacher, MGH, Diplomata (Hanover, 1906).

Diplomatum Karolinorum II, Lothari I. et Lothari II. Diplomata, ed. T. Schieffer, MGH, Diplomata (Berlin, 1966).

Donatus, *Regula*, ed. Victoria Zimmerl-Panagl, in *Monastica 1, Donati Regula, Pseudo-Columbani Regula monialium* (Berlin and Boston, 2015).

du Cange, et al., *Glossarium mediae et infimae latinitatis*, rev. ed. (1883–87) (consultable online: http://ducange.enc.sorbonne.fr/EN).

Eberhard of Friuli and Gisela *Testamentum (867)*, ed. Ignace de Coussemakers, in *Cartulaire de l'abbaye de Cysoing, no. 1* (Lille, 1884), pp. 1–5.

Ecclesiae s. Mariae in Via Lata tabularium: partem vetustiorem quae complectitur chartas inde ab anno 921 usque ad a. 1045, ed. Ludo Moritz Hartmann, 2 vols. (Vienna, 1895); ed. Margaret Merores, vol. III (Vienna, 1913).

Ennodius, Magnus Felix, 'Vita beatissimi Epiphani episcopi Ticinensis ecclesiae', in F. Vogel (ed.), *Magni Felicis Ennodi opera*, MGH, AA 7 (Berlin, 1885), pp. 84–109.

Form., ed. Karl Zeumer, MGH, *Leges*, vol. V (Hanover, 1886).

Gargilius Martialis, Quintus, *De hortis*, ed. Innocenzo Mazzini, in *Q. Gargilii Martialis. De hortis*, 2nd rev. ed., Opuscula philologa 1 (Bologna, 1988).

Gargilius Martialis, Quintus, *Gargilii Martialis quae exstant. Collegit disposuit recensuit Sebastianus Condorelli. Vol. 1, Fragmenta ad holera arboresque pomiferas pertinentia* (Rome, 1978).

Gregory I, *Dialogues*, ed. Adalbert de Vogüé, in *Dialogues*, 3 vols., Sources Chrétiennes 251, 260, 265 (Paris, 1978–80).

Gregory I, Pope, *Registrum Epistularum*, ed. Dag Ludvig Norberg, in *S. Gregorii Magni Opera: Registrum Epistularum*, Corpus Christianorum, Series Latina 140, 140A (Turnholt, 1982), trans. John R. C. Martyn, in *The letters of Gregory the Great*, 3 vols., Mediaeval sources in translation 40 (Toronto, 2004).

Gregory of Tours, *Historia Francorum*, eds. Bruno Krusch and Wilhelm Levison, in *Gregorii Episcopi Turonensis Opera. Teil 1: Libri historiarum X*, MGH, SS RM 1,1 (Hanover, 1951).

Gregory of Tours, *Liber in Gloria Confessorum*, ed. Bruno Krusch, in *Gregorii Episcopi Turonensis Opera, Teil 2: Miracula et opera minora*, MGH, SS RM 1, 2 (Hanover, 1885), pp. 294–370.

Gregory of Tours, *Liber vitae patrum*, ed. Bruno Krusch, in *Gregorii Turonensis Opera, Teil 2: Miracula et opera minora*, MGH, SS, RM 1, 2 (Hanover, 1885), pp. 211–94.

I diplomi di Berengario I, ed. Luigi Schiaparelli, Fonti per la storia d'Italia 35 (Rome, 1903).

I diplomi di Guido e di Lamberto, ed. Luigi Schiaparelli, Fonti per la storia d'Italia 36 (Rome, 1906).

I diplomi di Ugo e di Lotario, di Berengario II e Adalberto, ed. Luigi Schiaparelli, Fonti per la storia d'Italia 38 (Rome, 1924).

I placiti del Regnum Italiae, ed. Cesare Manaresi, 3 vols., Fonti per la storia d'Italia 91, 96, 97 (Rome: 1955–60).

Ibn Ḥawqal, *Kitāb ṣūrat al-arḍ*, ed. Johan Kramers and Gaston Wiet, in *Configuration de la terre* (Beirut-Paris, 1964).
Il Codice Perris: Cartulario Amalfitano, ed. Jole Mazzoleni and Renata Orefice, 5 vols. (Amalfi, 1985–9).
Il museo diplomatico dell'Archivio di Stato di Milano, ed. Alfio Rosario Natale (Milan, 1970).
Il Regesto del monastero dei SS. Andrea e Gregorio ad clivum scauri, ed. Alberto Bartola (Rome, 2003).
Inscriptiones latinae selectae, ed. Hermann Dessau, 3 vols. (Berlin, 1892–1916).
Inventari altomedievali di terre, coloni e redditi, ed. Andrea Castagnetti, Fonti per la storia d'Italia 104 (Rome, 1979).
Isidore, *De agricultura, Liber XVII*, ed. Jacques André, in *Étymologies. Livre XVII, De l'agriculture*, Auteurs latins du Moyen Age (Paris, 1981).
Isidore of Seville, *The Etymologies of Isidore of Seville*, ed. and trans. Stephen A. Barney, J. A. Beach, Oliver Berghof, and W. J. Lewis (Cambridge, 2006).
Jerome, *Commentaria in Evangelium S. Matthaei* in *PL*, vol. XXVI, coll. 15-218D, trans. Thomas P. Scheck, in *St. Jerome. A commentary on Matthew*, The Fathers of the Church 117 (Washington, DC, 2008).
Jerome, *Sancti Eusebii Hieronymi epistulae*, ed. Isidorus Hilberg, Corpus scriptorium ecclesiasticorum latinorum 55 (Vienna 1996).
Jerome, *Tractatus sive Homiliae in Psalmos*, ed. Germain Morin, in *Pars II. Opera homiletica*, 2nd rev. ed., CCSL 78 (Turnhout, 1958), trans. as *Homilies on the Psalms* by Marie Liguori Ewald, in *The homilies of Saint Jerome. Volume 1 (1–59 on the Psalms)*, The Fathers of the Church 48 (Washington, DC, 1964).
Jerome, *Vita Pauli*, in *PL*, XXIII, coll. 17–28c.
John the Deacon, *Vita Gregorii*, in *PL*, vol. LXXV.
Jonas of Bobbio, *Vita S. Columbani abbatis*, ed. Bruno Krusch, in *MGH, SSRM*, vol. 4 (Hanover and Leipzig, 1902), pp. 1–156.
Justin Martyr, *Apologie* ed. Giuseppe Girgenti, in *Apologie: Prima apologia per i cristiani ad Antonino il Pio, Seconda apologia per i cristiani al Senato romano, prologo al Dialogo con Trifone* (Milan, 1995).
Justinian, *Codex Iustinianus*, ed. Paul Kreuger, in *Codex Iustinianus*, Corpus iuris civilis, vol. 2 (Berlin, 1929).
Justinian, *Digest*, eds. Theodor Mommsen, Paul Krueger, and Alan Watson, in *The Digest of Justinian*, 4 vols. (Philadelphia, 1985).
Justinian, *Novellae*, eds. Wilhelm Kroll and Rudolf Schoell, in *Corpus Juris Civilis. vol. 3. Novellae* (Berlin, 1928), trans. as *The novels of Justinian: a complete annotated English translation*, trans. David Miller and Peter Sarris (Cambridge, 2018).
Juvenal (Iuvenalis, Decimus Iunius), *Saturae*, ed. Susanna Morton Braund, in *Juvenal and Persius*, Loeb Classical Library 191 (Cambridge, MA, 2004).
Le carte cremonesi dei secoli VIII–XII, ed. Ettore Falconi, Documenti dei fondi cremonesi (759–1069), vol. I (Cremona, 1979).
Le carte degli archivi parmensi dei secoli X–XI, ed. Giovanni Drei Archivio storico per le province parmensi. Nuova serie, 22 bis-29, 7 vols. (Parma, 1922–9).

Le carte più antiche di S. Antonino di Piacenza (secoli VIII e IX), ed. Ettore Falconi (Parma, 1959).
Le Liber Pontificalis. Texte, introduction et commentaire, ed. Louis-Marie Duchesne, rev. ed., 3 vols. (Paris, 1955–7), trans. as *Book of pontiffs (Liber pontificalis): ancient biographies of the first ninety Roman bishops to AD 715*, trans. Raymond Davis, Translated texts for historians 6, rev. ed. (Liverpool, 2010); *The lives of the eighth-century popes (Liber pontificalis): the ancient biographies of nine popes from AD 715 to AD 817*, trans. Raymond Davis, Translated texts for historians 13, rev. ed. (rev. ed. Liverpool, 2007), *The Lives of the ninth-century popes: the ancient biographies of ten popes from A.D. 817–891*, trans. Raymond Davis, Translated texts for historians 20 (Liverpool, 1996).
Le più antiche carte del capitolo della cattedrale di Benevento: 668–1200, ed. Antonio Ciaralli, Vittorio De Donato, and Vincenzo Matera, Regesta Chartarum 52 (Rome, 2002).
Leontius, *Life of Gregory, Bishop of Agrigento*, ed. Albrecht Berger, in *Das Leben des Heiligen Gregorios von Agrigent, Leontios Presbyteros von Rom; kritische Ausgabe, Übersetzung und Kommentar von Albrecht Berger*, Berliner byzantinische Arbeiten 60 (Berlin, 1995).
Luxorius, *Liber epigrammaton*, ed. Morris Rosenblum, trans. Morris Rosenblum, in *Luxorius. A Latin poet among the Vandals* (New York, 1961).
Marcellinus, Ammianus, *Rerum gestarum libri*, ed. John Carew Rolfe, in *Ammianus Marcellinus*, 3 vols., 2nd rev. ed., Loeb Classical Library 300, 315, 331 (Cambridge, 1940–52).
Mediae Latinitatis lexicon minus, ed. Jan Frederik Niermeyer (Leiden, 2004).
Merobaudes, Flavius, *Carmina*, ed. Frederick Vollmer, in *Fl. Merobaudis reliquiae, MGH, AA* vol. 14 (Berlin, 1905), trans. as 'Flavius Merobaudes: A Translation and Historical Commentary', trans. Frank Clover, *Transactions of the American Philosophical Society* 61 (1971), 1–78.
Monumenta ad neapolitani ducatus historiam pertinentia, ed. Bartolomeo Capasso, 3 vols. (Naples, 1881).
Namatianus, Rutilius, *De reditu suo*, trans. J. Wight Duff and Arnold M. Duff, in *Minor Latin Poets, Volume II. Florus. Hadrian. Nemesianus. Reposianus. Tiberianus. Dicta Catonis. Phoenix. Avianus. Rutilius Namatianus. Others*, 2nd rev. ed. (Cambridge, MA, 1934).
Notker the Stammerer, *Gesta Karoli Magni imperatoris*, ed. Hanse Haefele, in *MGH, SSRG* vol. XII (Berlin, 1959).
Odo of Cluny, *Vita sancti Geraldi aureliacensis*, ed. Anne-Marie Bultot-Verleysen, in *Vita sancti Geraldi Aureliacensis. Édition critique, traduction française, introduction et commentaires*, Subsidia hagiographica 89 (Brussels, 2009).
Palladius, Rutilius Taurus Aemilianus, *De re rustica*, ed. René Martin, trans. René Martin and Charles Guiraud, in *Traité d'agriculture* 2 vols., Collection des universités de France 203, 398 (Paris, 1976–2003).
Papsturkunden, 869–1046, ed. Harald Zimmermann, 3 vols. (Vienna, 1984).
Patrologiae cursus completus: series latina, ed. J. P. Migne (Paris, 1844–55).
Pliny the Elder, *Historia naturalis*, trans. Harris Rackham, David Edward Eichholz, and William Henry Samuel Jones, in *Pliny. Natural history*, 10 vols. (Cambridge, MA, 1938–62).

Prudentius, *Liber cathemerinon*, trans. Nicholas J. Richardson, in *Prudentius' hymns for hours and seasons: liber cathemerinon*, Routledge later Latin poetry (New York, 2015).
Prudentius, *Psychomachia*, ed. H. J. Thompson, in *Preface. Daily Round. Divinity of Christ. Origin of Sin. Fight for Mansoul. Against Symmachus 1*, Loeb Classical Library 387 (Cambridge, MA, 1949), pp. 274–343.
'Regesta Neapolitana,' in *Monumenta ad Neapolitani Ducatus Historiam Pertinentia*, ed. Bartolomeo Capasso, vol. II, I (Naples, 1885).
Regesta pontificum romanorum ab condita ecclesia ad annum post Christum natum MCXCVIII, ed. Ph. Jaffé, 2nd rev. ed. (Leipzig, 1885).
Il Regesto di Farfa, ed. Ignazio Giorgi and Ugo Balzani, 5 vols. (Rome, 1879–1914).
Il Regesto sublacense dell'undecimo secolo, eds. Leone Allodi and Guido Levi Rome, 1885).
Regula Magistri, ed. Adalbert de Vogüé, in *La règle du maître*, Sources chrétiennes 14–16, 3 vols. (Paris, 1964–5).
Regula monasterii tarnatensis, in *PL* vol. LXVI, coll. 975–8. *Regum et Imperatorum Germaniae I. Diplomata Conradis I, Henrici I et Ottonis I*, ed. Theodor Sickel, MGH, Diplomata (Hanover, 1879–84).
Regum et Imperatorum Germaniae II. Diplomata Ottonis II et III, ed. Theodor Sickel, MGH, Diplomata (Hanover, 1893).
Sancti Pachomii vita tertia e codice Patmensi monasterii S. Iohannis, ed. François Halkin, in *Sancti Pachomii Vitae Grecae*, Subsidia Hagiographica 19 (Brussels, 1932), pp. 272–406.
Sidonius, Caius Sollius Apollinaris, *Poems and letters*, trans. W. B. Anderson, in *Sidonius. Poems and letters*, 2 vols., Loeb Classical Library 296, 420 (Boston, MA, 1936).
Statuta Ferrariae, anno MCCLXXXVII, ed. William Montorsi, Deputazione provinciale ferrarese di storia patria. Serie monumenti 3 (Ferrara, 1955).
Syllabus Graecarum Membranarum, ed. Francisco Trinchera, in *Syllabus Graecarum Membranarum* (Naples, 1865).
Symmachus, Quintus Aurelius, *Epistolae*, in *PL* vol. XVIII, trans. Michele Renee Salzman and Michael John Roberts, as *Letters of Symmachus* (Atlanta, 2011).
'Tabularium S. Maria Novae', ed. Pietro Fedele, *ASRSP* 23 (1900), pp. 171–237; 24 (1901), pp. 159–96, 25 (1902), pp. 169–209, 26 (1903), pp. 21–141.
Tertullian, *De corona*, ed. Jacques Fontaine in *Q. Septimi Florentis Tertulliani De Corona. Sur la couronne*, Collection de textes latins commentés 18 (Paris, 1966), trans. as *The chaplet, or De corona*, ed. Alex Cleveland-Coxe, in *The Ante-Nicene fathers: translations of the writings of the fathers down to A.D. 325; vol III. Latin Christianity: its founder, Tertullian* (Grand Rapids, MI, 1885), pp. 93–104.
Translatio Sancti Viti martyris, ed. Irene Schmale-Ott, Provinzialinstitut für Westfälische Landes-und Volksforschung (Münster in Westfalen, 1979).
Varro, Marcus Terentius, *De re rustica*, eds. W. D. Hooper and Harrison Boyd Ash, trans. Harrison Boyd Ash and William Davis Hooper, in *Marcus Porcius Cato on agriculture. Marcus Terentius Varro on agriculture*, Loeb Classical Library 283 (Cambridge, MA, 1934).

Varro, Marcus Terentius, 'De sono vocum', in *Grammaticae romanae fragmenta*, ed. Gino Funaioli (Leipzig, 1907), pp. 296–311.
'Vauxhall City Farm – About Us', www.vauxhallcityfarm.org/about-us.
Venantius Fortunatus, *Carmina*, ed. Frederick Leo, in *MGH, AA, Opera Poetica* (Berlin, 1881).
Vergil, *Georgics*, eds. H. Rushton Fairclough and (rev. by) G. P. Goold, in *Eclogues. Georgics. Aeneid: Books 1–6*, Loeb Classical Library 63 (Cambridge, MA, 1999).
Vitruvius, *Liber X*, trans. Ingrid D. Rowland, in *Vitruvius: ten books on architecture*, rev. ed. (Cambridge, 1999).
Walahfrid Strabo, *De cultura hortorum (Hortulus)*, ed. Walter Berschin (Heidelberg, 2007).

Secondary Sources

Agamben, Giorgio, *The kingdom and the glory: for a theological genealogy of economy and government (Homo Sacer II, 2) / Giorgio Agamben; translated by Lorenzo Chiesa (with Matteo Mandarini)* (Stanford, CA, 2011).
AGRUMED: Archaeology and history of citrus fruit in the Mediterranean: Acclimatization, diversifications, uses (Naples, 2017).
Alföldy, Géza, 'Urban life, inscriptions, and mentality in Late Antique Rome', in Thomas S. Burns and John William Eadie (eds.), *Urban centers and rural contexts in Late Antiquity* (East Lansing, MI, 2001), pp. 3–24.
Amari, Michele, *Biblioteca arabo-sicula ossia Raccolta di testi arabici che toccano la geografia, la storia, le biografie e la bibliografia della Sicilia*, 2 vols. (Turin and Rome, 1880–1).
Amelotti, Mario, and Costamagna, Giorgio, *Alle origini del notariato italiano* (Rome, 1975). Amory, Patrick, *People and identity in Ostrogothic Italy, 489–554* (Cambridge, 2009).
Anderson, Michael A., and Robinson, Damian (eds.), *House of the Surgeon, Pompeii: excavations in the Casa del Chirurgo (VI 1, 9–10.23)* (Oxford, 2018).
Anderson, Michael A., and Robinson, Damian, 'Room by room discussion of stratigraphy and architecture', in Michael A. Anderson and Damian Robinson (eds.), *House of the Surgeon, Pompeii: excavations in the Casa del Chirurgo (VI 1, 9–10.23)* (Oxford, 2018), pp. 122–433.
André, Jacques, *L'alimentation et la cuisine à Rome*, rev. ed., Collection d'études anciennes (Paris, 1981).
Andreolli, Bruno, 'Contratti agrari e trasformazione dell'ambiente', in Giosuè Musca (ed.), *Uomo e ambiente nel Mezzogiorno normanno-svevo. Atti delle ottavo giornate normanno-sveve, Bari 20–23 Ottobre 1987* (Bari, 1989), pp. 111–33.
Andreolli, Bruno, 'I prodotti alimentari nei contratti agrari toscani dell'Alto Medioevo', *Archeologia Medievale* 8 (1981), 117–26.
Andreolli, Bruno, 'Il ruolo dell'orticultura e della frutticultura nelle campagne dell'alto medioevo', in *L'ambiente vegetale nell' alto medioevo*, Settimane di studio del Centro italiano di studi sull'alto medioevo 37 (Spoleto, 1990), pp. 175–211.

Andreolli, Bruno, and Montanari, Massimo, *L'azienda curtense in Italia. Proprietà della terra e lavoro contadino nei secoli VIII-XI*, Biblioteca di storia agraria medievale 1 (Bologna, 1983).

Andreolli, Maria Pia, 'Una pagina di storia longobarda: "Re Ratchis"', *Nuova rivista storica* 50 (1966), 281–327.

Andrews, Margaret, 'The Laetaniae Septiformes of Gregory I, S. Maria Maggiore and Early Marian Cult in Rome', in Ida Östenberg, Simon Malmberg, and Jonas Bjørnebye (eds.), *The moving city: processions, passages and promenades in ancient Rome* (London, 2015), pp. 155–64.

Angenendt, Arnold, 'Mensa Pippini Regis: Zur liturgischen Präsenz der Karolinger in Sankt Peter', in Erwin Gatz (ed.), *Hundert Jahre Deutsches Priesterkolleg beim Campo Santo Teutonico 1876–1976: Beiträge zu seiner Geschichte* (Rome, 1977), pp. 52–68.

Angrisani, Maria Luisa, 'Materiali per uno studio della produzione libraria latina antica e alto medievale in Italia (II)', *Bollettino del Comitato per la preparazione della edizione nazionale dei Classici greci e latini*, n.s. 26 (1978), 111–37.

Anton, Hans Hubert, *Studien zu den Klosterprivilegien der Päpste im frühen Mittelalter: Unter besonderer Berücksichtigung der Privilegierung von St. Maurice d'Agaume*, Beiträge zur Geschichte und Quellenkunde des Mittelalters (Berlin/ New York, 1975).

Arena, Maria Stella (ed.), *Roma dall'antichità al medioevo. Archeologia e storia nel Museo Nazionale Romano Crypta Balbi* (Milan, 2001).

Armstrong, Donna, 'A survey of community gardens in upstate New York: Implications for health promotion and community development', *Health & Place* 6.4 (2000), 319–27.

Arslan, Ermanno A., *Repertorio dei ritrovamenti di moneta altomedievale in Italia (489–1002)*, Testi, studi, strumenti 18 (Spoleto, 2005).

Arthur, Paul, 'Archeologia urbana a Napoli: riflessioni sugli ultimi tre anni', *Archeologia Medievale* 13 (1986), 515–23.

Arthur, Paul, 'La città in Italia meridionale in età tardoantica, riflessioni', in Stefania Ceccoli and Attilio Stazio (eds.), *L'Italia meridionale tardo antica. Atti del 38 Convegno di studi sulla Magna Grecia, Taranto 2–6 ottobre 1998* (Taranto, 1999), pp. 167–200.

Arthur, Paul, 'Naples: a case of urban survival in the early Middle Ages?', *MÉFR* 103.2 (1991), 759–84.

Arthur, Paul, *Naples. From Roman town to city-state: an archaeological perspective*, Archaeological monographs of the British school at Rome 12 (London, 2002).

Arthur, Paul (ed.), *Il complesso archeologico di Carminiello ai Mannesi, Napoli (scavi 1983–1984)*, Collana del Dipartimento: Università di Lecce, Dipartimento di Beni Culturali, Settore Storico-Archeologico 7 (Galatina, 1994).

Atkins, P. J., 'The charmed circle: von Thünen and agriculture around nineteenth-century London', *Geography* 72.2 (1987), 129–39.

Augenti, Andrea, *Il Palatino nel medioevo: archeologia e topografia (secolo VI–XIII)*, Bullettino della Commissione archeologica comunale di Roma, Supplementi 4 (Rome, 1996).

Augenti, Andrea, Bondi, Mila, Carra, Marialetizia, Cirelli, Enrico, Malaguti, Celia, and Rizzi, Maddalena, 'Indagini archeologiche a Classe (scavi 2004): primi risultati sulle fasi di Età Altomedievale e dati archeobotanici', in Riccardo Francovich and Marco Valenti (eds.), *IV Congresso di Archeologia Medievale (Abbazia di San Galgano, 26–30 settembre 2006)* (Florence, 2006), pp. 124–32.

Augspach, Elizabeth, 'Meaning', in Michael Leslie (ed.), *A cultural history of gardens in the medieval age* (London, 2010), pp. 101–15.

Azzara, Claudio, 'La ricezione dei capitolari carolingi nel "Regnum Langobardorum"', in Paolo Chiesa (ed.), *Paolino d'Aquileia e il contributo italiano all'Europa carolingia: Atti del Convegno internazionale di studi, Cividale del Friuli-Premariacco, 10–13 ottobre 2002*, Libri e biblioteche (Udine, 2003), pp. 9–24.

Baader, Gerhard, 'Early medieval Latin adaptations of Byzantine medicine in western Europe', *Dumbarton Oaks Papers* 38 (1984), 251–9.

Baldini Lippolis, Isabella, *La domus tardoantica: forme e rappresentazioni dello spazio domestico nelle città del Mediteraneo*, Studi e scavi (Università di Bologna. Dipartimento di archeologia) 17 (Imola, 2001).

Balzaretti, Ross, 'Cities and markets in the early Middle Ages', in Giorgio Ausenda (ed.), *After empire. Towards an ethnology of Europe's barbarians* (Woodbridge, 1995), pp. 113–42.

Balzaretti, Ross, 'The curtis, the archaeology of sites of power', in Riccardo Francovich and Ghislaine Noyé (eds.), *La storia dell'alto Medioevo italiano (VI–X secolo) alla luce dell'archeologia. Atti del Convegno internazionale (Siena, 1992)*, Biblioteca di archeologia medievale 11 (Florence, 1994), pp. 99–108.

Balzaretti, Ross, *The lands of Saint Ambrose. Monks and society in early medieval Milan*, Studies in the early Middle Ages 44 (Turnhout, 2019).

Balzaretti, Ross, 'The politics of property in ninth-century Milan: Familial motives and monastic strategies in the village of Inzago', in *Les transferts patrimoniaux en Europe occidentale, VIII-Xe siècle. Actes de la table ronde de Rome, 6, 7 et 8 mai 1999* (= *MÉFR* 111.2, pp. 487–987), 747–70.

Balzaretti, Ross, 'The politics of property in ninth-century Milan: Familial motives and monastic strategies in the village of Inzago', *Mélanges de l'école française de Rome* 111.2 (1999), 747–70.

Balzaretti, Ross, 'Women, property and urban space in tenth-century Milan', *Gender & History* 23.3 (November) (2011), 547–75.

Bang-Andreasen, Toke, Nielsen, Jeppe T., Voriskova, Jana, Heise, Janine, Rønn, Regin, Kjøller, Rasmus, Hansen, Hans C. B., and Jacobsen, Carsten S., 'Wood ash induced pH changes strongly affect soil bacterial numbers and community composition', *Frontiers in Microbiology* 8 (2017), 1400.

Barbera, Giuseppe, 'Parchi, frutteti, giardini e orti nella Conca d'oro di Palermo araba e normanna', *Italus Hortus* 14.4 (2007), 14–27.

Barbera, Giuseppe, and Cullotta, Sebastiano, 'The traditional Mediterranean polycultural landscape as cultural heritage: Its origin and historical importance, its agro-silvo-pastoral complexity and the necessity for its identification and inventory', in Mauro Agnoletti and Francesca Emanueli (eds.), *Biocultural diversity in Europe* (Cham, 2016), pp. 21–48.

Barbera, Mariarosaria, and Paris, Rita, *Antiche stanze: un quartiere di Roma imperiale nella zona di Termini: Museo nazionale romano Terme Diocleziano, Roma, dicembre 1996–giugno 1997* (Milan, 1996).

Barney, Stephen A., Lewis, W. J., Beach, J. A., and Berghof, Oliver, 'Introduction', in *The etymologies of Isidore of Seville* (Cambridge, 2006), pp. 3–33.

Barnish, S. J. B., 'Pigs, plebeians and potentes: Rome's economic hinterland, c. 350–600A.D', *Papers of the British School at Rome* 55 (1987), 157–85.

Barnish, S. J. B., 'Transformation and survival in the western senatorial aristocracy, c. 400–700', *Papers of the British School at Rome* 56 (1988), 120–55.

Bartoli Langeli, Attilio, 'Private charters', in Cristina La Rocca (ed.), *Italy in the early Middle Ages 476–1000*, The Short Oxford History of Italy (Oxford, 2002), pp. 205–19.

Bassett, Thomas J., 'Community gardening in America', *Brooklyn Botanic Garden Record, Plants and Gardens* 35 (1979), 4–6.

Beaudry, Mary, 'Why gardens?', in Rebecca Yamin and Karen Bescherer Metheny (eds.), *Landscape archaeology: reading and interpreting the American historical landscape* (Knoxville, 1996), pp. 3–5.

Becatti, Giovanni, *Case ostiensi del tardo impero* (Rome, 1948).

Beccaria, Augusto, *I codici di medicina del periodo presalernitano (secoli IX, X e XI)* (Rome, 1956).

Belli Barsali, Isa, 'La topografia di Lucca nei secoli VIII–XI', in *Lucca e la Tuscia nell'alto medioevo*. (Spoleto, 1973), pp. 461–554.

Belli Barsali, Isa, *Lucca: Guida alla città* (Lucca, 1988).

Benvenuti, Marco, Mariotti-Lippi, Marta, Pallecchi, Pasquino, and Sagri, Mario, 'Late-Holocene catastrophic floods in the terminal Arno River (Pisa, Central Italy) from the story of a Roman riverine harbour', *The Holocene* 16.6 (2006), 863–76.

Bertino, Antonio, 'Monete attestate a Luni dal IV al IX secolo', *Rivista di studi liguri* 49 (1983), 265–300.

Bianchi, Giovanna, 'Building, inhabiting and "perceiving" private houses in early medieval Italy', *Arqueología de la Arquitectura* 9 (2012), 195–212.

Biblolet, Jean-Claude, 'Jardins et vergers dans l'oeuvre de Chrétien de Troyes', in *Vergers et jardins dans l'univers médiéval* (Aix en Provence, 1990), pp. 31–40.

Bijsterveld, Arnoud-Jan, 'The medieval gift as agent of social bonding and political power: A comparative approach', in Esther Cohen and Mayke De Jong (eds.), *Medieval transformations: texts, power, and gifts in context*, Cultures, Beliefs, and Traditions (Leiden, 2001), vol. 11, pp. 123–54.

Blair, Dorothy, Giesecke, Carol C., and Sherman, Sandra, 'A dietary, social and economic evaluation of the Philadelphia urban gardening project', *Journal of Nutrition Education* 23.4 (1991), 161–7.

Blamey, Marjorie, and Grey-Wilson, Christopher, *The illustrated flora of Britain and Northern Europe* (London, 1989).

Bloch, Marc, *Feudal society*, trans. L. A. Manyon (London, 1961).

Blume, Hans-Peter, and Runge, Marlis, 'Genese und Ökologie innerstädtischer Böden aus Bauschutt', *Zeitschrift für Pflanzenernährung und Bodenkunde* 141.vi (1978), 727–40.

Bocchi, Francesca, 'Città e mercati nell'Italia padana', in *Mercati e mercanti nell'Alto Medioevo. L'area euroasiatica e l'area mediterranea*, Settimane di studio del Centro italiano di studi sull'alto medioevo 40 (Spoleto, 1993), pp. 139–85.

Bodel, John P., 'Roman tomb gardens', in Wilhelmina F. Jashemski, Kathryn Gleason, Kim J. Hartswick, and Amina-Aïcha Malek (eds.), *Gardens of the Roman Empire* (Cambridge, 2018), pp. 199–242.

Bognetti, Gian Piero, 'Il problema monetario dell'economia longobarda', in Carlo Cipolla (ed.), *Storia dell'economia italiana, vol. 1* (Torino, 1959), pp. 51–60.

Borgongino, Michele, *Archeobotanica: reperti vegetali da Pompei e dal territorio vesuviano*, Studi della Soprintendenza archeologica di Pompei 16 (Rome, 2006).

Bosi, Giovanna, 'Flora e ambiente vegetale a Ferrara tra il X e il XV secolo attraverso i reperti carpologici dello scavo di corso Porta Reno – via Vaspergolo nell'attuale centro storico. Ph.D. Thesis,' (PhD Thesis, Università di Firenze, 2000).

Bosi, Giovanna, Bandini Mazzanti, Marta, and Mercuri, Anna Maria, 'Plants and Man in urban environment: the history of the city of Ferrara (10th–16th cent. A.D.) through its archaeobotanical records', *Bocconea* 23 (2009), 5–20.

Bosi, Giovanna, Benatti, Alessandra, Rinaldi, Rossella, Dallai, Daniela, Santini, Claudio, Carbognani, Michele, Tomaselli, Marcello, and Bandini Mazzanti, Marta, 'The memory of water: Archaeobotanical evidence of wetland plants from Modena (Emilia-Romagna, northern Italy) and palaeoecological remarks', *Plant Biosystems – An International Journal Dealing with all Aspects of Plant Biology* 149.1 (2015), 144–53.

Bosi, Giovanna, Berti, Patrizia, Maioli, Marco, Costantino, Francesca, and Bandini Mazzanti, Marta, 'Applicazioni morfobiometriche in campo archeocarpologico: primi dati su Papaver somniferum nell'Alto Medioevo di Ferrara', *Atti Soc Nat Mat Modena* 137 (2006), 273–387.

Bosi, Giovanna, Guarrera, P. M., Rinaldi, Rosella, and Bandini Mazzanti, Marta, 'Ethnobotany of purslane (Portulaca oleracea L.) in Italy and morfo-biometric analyses of seeds from archaeological sites of Emilia Romagna (Northern Italy), in J. P. Morel and Anna Maria Mercuri (eds.) *Plants and culture: Seeds of the cultural heritage of Europe* (Bari, 2009), pp. 129–39.

Bosi, Giovanna, Bandini Mazzanti, Marta, Florenzano, Assunta, N'siala, Isabella Massamba, Pederzoli, Aurora, Rinaldi, Rossella, Torri, Paola, and Mercuri, Anna Maria, 'Seeds/fruits, pollen and parasite remains as evidence of site function: piazza Garibaldi – Parma (N Italy) in Roman and Mediaeval times', *Journal of Archaeological Science* 38.7 (2011), 1621–33.

Bosi, Giovanna, Bandini Mazzanti, Marta, Montecchi, Maria Chiara, Torri, Paola, and Rinaldi, Rossella, 'The life of a Roman colony in Northern Italy: Ethnobotanical information from archaeobotanical analysis', *Quaternary International* 460 (2017), 135–56.

Bosi, Giovanna, Mercuri, Anna Maria, Pederzoli, Aurora, Torri, Paola, Florenzano, Assunta, Rinaldi, Rossella, and Bandini Mazzanti, Marta, 'Indagini archeobotaniche sui riempimenti delle buche da rifiuti e del pozzo nero di via Cavestro a Parma (X-XI sec. d.C.)', in Marta Marini Calvani (ed.), *Ventidue secoli a Parma. Lo scavo sotto la sede centrale della Cassa di Risparmio in piazza Garibaldi*, BAR, International 2406 (Oxford, 2012), pp. 269–83.

Bougard, François, 'Actes privés et transferts patrimoniaux en Italie centro-septentrionale (VIIIe-Xe siècle)', in *Les transferts patrimoniaux en Europe occidentale, VIII-Xe siècle. Actes de la table ronde de Rome, 6, 7 et 8 mai 1999* (= *MÉFR* 111.2, pp. 487–987), 539–62.

Bougard, François, 'La cour et le gouvernment de Louis II, 840–875', in Régine Le Jan (ed.), *La royauté et les élites dans l'Europe carolingienne* (Villeneuve d'Ascq, 1998), pp. 249–67.

Bougard, François, 'Le credit dans l'Occident du haut Moyen Age: documentation et pratique', in Jean-Pierre Devroey, Laurent Feller, and Régine Le Jan (eds.), *Les élites et la richesse* (Turnhout, 2010), pp. 439–78.

Bougard, François, La Rocca, Cristina, and Le Jan, Régine (eds.), *Sauver son âme et se perpétuer: transmission du patrimoine et mémoire au haut moyen âge (actes de la table ronde réunie à Padoue les 3, 4 et 5 octobre 2002)*, Collection de l'École française de Rome 351 (Padua, 2002).

Bresc, Henri, 'Les jardins de Palerme (1290–1460)', *MÉFR* 84.1 (1972), 55–127.

Bresc, Henri, 'Palermo in the 14th–15th century: urban economy', in Annliese Nef (ed.), *A companion to medieval Palermo: the history of a Mediterranean city from 600 to 1500* (Leiden, 2013), pp. 235–68.

Brogiolo, Gian Pietro, 'Aspetti economici e sociali delle città longobarde dell'italia settentrionale', in Gian Pietro Brogiolo (ed.), *Early medieval towns in the Western Mediterranean*, Documenti di archeologia 10 (Mantua, 1996), pp. 77–88.

Brogiolo, Gian Pietro, 'A proposito dell'organizzazione urbana nell'altomedioevo', *Archeologia Medievale* 14 (1987), 14–46.

Brogiolo, Gian Pietro, 'Architecture and power at the end of the Lombard Kingdom', in José Sánchez-Pardo and Michael G. Shapland (eds.), *Churches and social power in early medieval Europe: Integrating archaeological and historical approaches* (Turnhout, 2015), pp. 451–72.

Brogiolo, Gian Pietro, 'Architetture, simboli e potere nelle chiese tra seconda metà VIII e IX secolo', in Renata Salvarani and Giancarlo Andenna (eds.), *Alle origini del Romanico: Monasteri, edifici religiosi, committenza tra storia e archeologia (Italia settentrionale, secoli IX–X): Atti delle III Giornate di Studi Medievali Castiglione delle Stiviere, 25–27 Settembre 2003*, Studi e documenti 3 (Brescia, 2005), pp. 71–91.

Brogiolo, Gian Pietro, 'Capitali e residenze regie nell'Italia longobarda', in Gisela Ripoll, Josep María Gurt Esparraguera and Alexandra Chavarría Arnau (eds.), *Sedes regiae (ann. 400–800)* (Barcelona, 2000), pp. 144–51.

Brogiolo, Gian Pietro, 'Conclusions', in Gian Pietro Brogiolo and Bryan Ward-Perkins (eds.), *Idea and ideal of the town between late Antiquity and the early Middle Ages* (Leiden, 1999), pp. 245–54.

Brogiolo, Gian Pietro, 'The control of public space and the transformation of an Early Medieval town: a re-examination of the case of Brescia', in William Bowden, Adam Gutteridge, and Carlos Machado (eds.), *Social and political life in Late Antiquity*, Late Antique archaeology 3.1 (Leiden, 2006), pp. 251–83.

Brogiolo, Gian Pietro, 'Ideas of the town in Italy during the transition from Antiquity to the Middle Ages', in Bryan Ward-Perkins and Gian Pietro Brogiolo (eds.), *The idea and ideal of the town between Late Antiquity and*

the Early Middle Ages, Transformation of the Roman world 4 (Leiden, 1999), pp. 99–126.
Brogiolo, Gian Pietro, 'La città tra tarda antichità e medioevo', in Rolando Bussi and Alberto Molinari (eds.), *Archeologia urbana in Lombardia: Valutazione dei depositi e inventario dei vincoli* (Modena, 1984), pp. 48–55.
Brogiolo, Gian Pietro (ed.), *Le chiese rurali tra VII e VIII secolo in Italia settentrionale: 80 Seminario sul tardo antico e l'alto Medioevo in Italia settentrionale, Garda, 8–10 aprile 2000*, Documenti di archeologia 26 (Mantua, 2001).
Brogiolo, Gian Pietro, and Ward-Perkins, Bryan (eds.), *The idea and ideal of the town between late Antiquity and the early Middle Ages*, Transformation of the Roman world 4 (Leiden, 1999).
Brogiolo, Gian Pietro, Cremaschi, Mauro, and Gelichi, Sauro, 'Processi di stratificazione in centri urbani (dalla stratificazione naturale alla stratificazione archeologica)', in *Archeologia stratigrafica in Italia Settentrionale, Atti del Convegno, (Brescia, 1 marzo 1986)* (Como, 1988), pp. 23–30.
Brogiolo, Gian Pietro, Gauthier, Nancy, and Christie, Neil (eds.), *Towns and their territories between late antiquity and the early Middle Ages*, Transformation of the Roman world 9 (Leiden, 2000).
Brookes, John, *Gardens of paradise: the history and design of the great Islamic gardens* (London, 1987).
Brown, Kate, and Jameton, Andrew, 'Public health implications of urban agriculture', *Journal of Public Health Policy* 21.1 (2000), 20–39.
Brown, Peter, *Poverty and leadership in the later Roman empire*, Menahem Stern Jerusalem lectures (Hanover, University Press of New England, 2002).
Brown, Peter, *Power and persuasion in late antiquity: Towards a Christian empire* (Madison, WI, 1992).
Brown, Peter, *Through the eye of a needle: Wealth, the fall of Rome, and the making of Christianity in the West, 350–550 AD* (Princeton, NJ, 2014).
Brown, Warren, Costambeys, Marios, Innes, Matthew, and Kosto, Adam (eds.), *Documentary culture and the laity in the early Middle Ages*, (Cambridge, 2012).
Browning, Robert, 'Minor figures', in E. J. Kenney and W. V. Clausen (eds.), *The Cambridge history of classical literature. II, Latin literature* (Cambridge, 1982), pp. 770–3.
Brubaker, Leslie, and Littlewood, Anthony R., 'Byzantinische Gärten', in M. Carroll-Spillecke (ed.), *Der Garten von der Antike bis zum Mittelalter*, Kulturgeschichter der antiken Welt 57 (Mainz am Rhein, 1992), pp. 213–48.
Brühl, Carlrichard, *Aus Mittelalter und Diplomatik. Gesammelte Aufsätze*, 3 vols. (Hildesheim, 1989–97).
Brühl, Carlrichard, *Fodrum, gistum, servitium regis; Studien zu den wirtschaftlichen Grundlagen des Königtums im Frankenreich und in den fränkischen Nachfolgestaaten Deutschland, Frankreich und Italien vom 6. bis zur Mitte des 14. Jahrhunderts*, Kölner historische Abhandlungen (Cologne, 1968).
Brun, Jean-Pierre, 'The production of perfumes in antiquity: the cases of Delos and Paestum', *American Journal of Archaeology* 104.2 (2000), 277–308.
Brunner, Karl, 'Continuity and discontinuity of Roman agricultural knowledge in the early Middle Ages', in Del Sweeney (ed.), *Agriculture in the Middle Ages. Technology, practice, and representation* (Philadelphia, 1995), pp. 21–40.

Bruno, Vincent, and Scott, Russell, *Cosa IV: The Houses* (= *Memoirs of the American Academy in Rome* 38) (Ann Arbor, 1993).

Bryant, R. G., and Davidson, Donald A., 'The use of image analysis in the micromorphological study of old cultivated soils: An evaluation based on soils from the Island of Papa Stour, Shetland', *Journal of Archaeological Science* 23.vi (1996), 811–22.

Bullough, Donald, 'Urban change in early medieval Italy: the example of Pavia', *Papers of the British School at Rome* 34 (1966), 82–130.

Büntgen, Ulf, Myglan, Vladimir S., Ljungqvist, Fredrik Charpentier, McCormick, Michael, Di Cosmo, Nicola, Sigl, Michael, Jungclaus, Johann, Wagner, Sebastian, Krusic, Paul J., Esper, Jan, Kaplan, Jed O., de Vaan, Michiel A. C., Luterbacher, Jürg, Wacker, Lukas, Tegel, Willy, and Kirdyanov, Alexander V., 'Cooling and societal change during the Late Antique Little Ice Age from 536 to around 660 AD', *Nature Geoscience* 9.iii (2016), 231–6.

Büntgen, Ulf, Myglan, Vladimir S., Ljungqvist, Fredrik Charpentier, McCormick, Michael, Di Cosmo, Nicola, Sigl, Michael, Jungclaus, Johann, Wagner, Sebastian, Krusic, Paul J., Esper, Jan, Kaplan, Jed O., de Vaan, Michiel A. C., Luterbacher, Jürg, Wacker, Lukas, Tegel, Willy, Solomina, Olga N., Nicolussi, Kurt, Oppenheimer, Clive, Reinig, Frederick, and Kirdyanov, Alexander V., 'Reply to "Limited late antique cooling"', *Nature Geoscience* 10.4 (2017), 242–3.

Büntgen, Ulf, Tegel, Willy, Nicolussi, Kurt, McCormick, Michael, Frank, David, Trouet, Valerie, Kaplan, Jed O., Herzig, Franz, Heussner, Karl-Uwe, Wanner, Heinz, Luterbacher, Jürg, and Esper, Jan, '2500 years of European climate variability and human susceptibility', *Science* 331.6017 (2011), 578–82.

Burridge, Claire, 'An interdisciplinary investigation into Carolingian medical knowledge and practice' (PhD Thesis, University of Cambridge, 2019).

Burridge, Claire, 'Incense in medicine: An early medieval perspective', *Early Medieval Europe* 28.2 (2020) 219–55.

Burström, Nanouschka Myrberg, 'Money, coins, and archaeology', in Rory Naismith (ed.), *Money and coinage in the Middle Ages* (Leiden, 2019), pp. 231–63.

Butzer, Karl W., 'The classical tradition of agronomic science: perspectives on Carolingian agriculture and agronomy', in Paul Butzer and Dietrich Lohrmann (eds.), *Science in Western and Eastern civilization in Carolingian times* (Basel, Boston, Berlin, 1993), pp. 439–596.

Butzer, Karl W., 'The Islamic traditions of agroecology: Crosscultural experience, ideas and innovations', *Ecumene* 1 (1994), 7–50.

Cagiano de Azevedo, Michelangelo, 'Aspetti urbanistici delle citta altomedievali', in *Topografia urbana e vita cittadina nell'altomedioevo in Occidente*, Settimane di studio sull'alto medioevo 21 (Spoleto, 1974), pp. 653–78.

Cagnana, Aurora, 'La transizione al medioevo attraverso la storia delle tecniche murarie: dall'analisi di un territorio a un problema sovraregionale', in Sauro Gelichi (ed.), *I Congresso Nazionale di Archeologia Medievale (Pisa 29–31 maggio 1997)* (Florence, 1997), pp. 445–8.

Caillet, Jean-Pierre, *L'évergétisme monumental chrétien en Italie et à ses marges d'après l'épigraphie des pavements de mosaïque (IVe- VIIe siècles)*, Collection de l'École française de Rome 175 (Rome, 1993).
Calvani, Mirella Marini, 'Iuxta Sanctum Petrum', in Mirella Marini Calvani (ed.), *Ventidue secoli a Parma Lo scavo sotto la sede centrale della Cassa di Risparmio in piazza Garibaldi*, BAR international series 2406 (London, 2012), pp. 209–11.
Calza, Guido, Becatti, Giovanni, Squarciapino, Maria Floriani, Calza, Raissa, Pensabene, Patrizio, Pietrogrande, A. L., Baccini, Paola, Paroli, Lidia, Pavolini, Carlo (eds.), *Scavi di Ostia I: Topografia generale*, Scavi di Ostia 1 (Rome, 1953).
Cammarosano Paolo, *Italia medievale: Struttura e geografia delle fonti scritte* (Rome, 1991).
Campbell, Darryl, 'The Capitulare de Villis, the Brevium exempla, and the Carolingian court at Aachen', *Early Medieval Europe* 18.3 (2010), 243–64.
Campbell, Gill, Moffett, Lisa, and Straker, Vanessa, *Environmental archaeology: a guide to the theory and practice of methods from sampling and recovery to post-excavation*, Second edition (Portsmouth, 2011).
Camuffo, Dario, and Enzi, Silvia, 'The analysis of two bi-millennial series: Tiber and Po river floods', in Philip D. Jones, Raymond S. Bradley, and Jean Jouzel (eds.), *Climatic variations and forcing mechanisms of the last 2000 years*, NATO ASI Series I, Global Environmental Change 41 (New York, 1996), pp. 433–50.
Cantini, Federico, and Grassi, Francesca, 'Produzione, circolazione e consume di ceramica in Toscana tra la fine del X e il XIII secolo', in Sauro Gelichi (ed.), *Atti del IX Congresso internazionale sulla ceramica medievale nel Mediterraneo: Venezia, Scuola grande dei Carmini, Auditorium Santa Margherita, 23–27 novembre 2009* (Florence, 2012), pp. 131–9.
Cantino Wataghin, Gisella, 'Quadri urbani nell'Italia settentrionale: tarda Antichità e alto Medioevo', in Claude Lepelley (ed.), *La fin de la cité antique et le début de la cité medievale de la fin du IIIe siècle a l'avènement de Charlemagne. Actes du colloque tenu à l'Université de Paris X-Nanterre les 1, 2 et 3 avril 1993*, Munera: Studi storici sulla Tarda Antichità 8 (Bari, 1996), pp. 239–71.
Capasso, Bartolomeo, 'Pianta della città di Napoli nel secolo XI', *Archivio storico per le province napoletane* 17 (1892), 679–726.
Cappiotti, Francesco, and Varanini, Gian Maria, 'Il pons marmoreus e gli edifici ai piedi del castrum', in Antonella Arzone and Ettore Napione (eds.), *La più antica veduta di Verona. L'iconografia rateriana. L'archetipo e l'immagine tramandata, Atti del seminario di studi, 6 maggio 2011, Museo di Castelvecchio* (Verona, 2012), pp. 109–32.
Carandini, Andrea, '"Hortensia": Orti e frutteti intorno a Roma', in Rolando Bussi and Vittorio Vandelli (eds.), *Misurare la terra: centuriazione e coloni nel mondo romano. Città, agricoltura, commercio: materiali da Roma e dal suburbio* (Modena, 1985), pp. 66–74.
Carandini, Andrea, 'L'ultima civiltà sepolta o del massimo oggetto desueto, secondo un archeologo', in Andrea Carandini, Lellia Cracco Ruggini, and Andrea Giardina (eds.), *Storia di Roma III: L'età tardoantica. 2. I luoghi e le culture*, Storia di Roma (Turin, 1993), pp. 11–38.

Carandini, Andrea, *Schiavi in Italia: gli strumenti pensanti dei Romani fra tarda Repubblica e medio Impero* (Rome, 1988).
Cardini, Franco, and Miglio, Massimo, *Nostalgia del paradiso: il giardino medievale* (Rome, 2002).
Carli, Filippo, *Storia del commercio italiano: il mercato nell'Alto Medioevo* (Padua, 1934).
Carroll, Maureen, 'Contextualising art and nature', in Barbara Borg (ed.), *A companion to Roman art* (Oxford, 2015), pp. 533–51.
Carsana, Vittoria, 'Napoli: uno scavo archeologico nell'ala meridionale di Palazzo Giusso. Relazione preliminari', *Annali di archeologia e storia antica* 3 (1996), 141–8.
Carter, Stephen P., and Davidson, Donald A., 'An evaluation of the contribution of soil micromorphology to the study of ancient arable agriculture', *Geoarchaeology* 13.6 (1998), 535–47.
Carter, Stephen P., and Davidson, Donald A., 'A reply to Macphail's comments on "An evaluation of the contribution of soil micromorphology to the study of ancient arable agriculture"', *Geoarchaeology* 15.v (2000), 499–502.
Carver, Martin, *Arguments in stone: archaeological research and the European town in the first millennium*, Oxbow Monographs in Archeology 29 (Oxford, 1993).
Casey, P. J., *Understanding ancient coins. An introduction for archaeologists and historians* (London, 1986).
Cassarino, Mirella, 'Palermo experienced, Palermo imagined. Arabic and Islamic culture between the 9th and 12th century', in Annliese Nef (ed.), *A companion to medieval Palermo: the history of a Mediterranean city from 600 to 1500* (Leiden, 2013), pp. 89–132.
Castelletti, Lanfredo, Castiglioni, Elisabetta, and Rottoli, Mauro, 'L'agricoltura dell'Italia settentrionale dal Neolitico al Medioevo', in Osvaldo Failla and Gaetano Forni (eds.), *Le piante coltivate e la loro storia. Dalle origini al transgenico in Lombardia nel centenario della riscoperta della genetica di Mendel* (Milan, 2001), pp. 33–84.
Castiglioni, Elisabetta, and Rottoli, Mauro, 'Broomcorn millet, foxtail millet and sorghum in north Italian early medieval sites', *Post-Classical Archaeologies* 3 (2013), 131–44.
Catini, Federico, 'Dall'economia complessa al complesso di economie (Tuscia V–X secolo)', *Post-Classical Archaeologies* 1 (2011), 159–94.
Cavalieri Manasse, Giuliana (ed.) *L'area del Capitolium di Verona: ricerche storiche e archeologiche* (Venice, 2008).
Cavalieri Manasse, Giuliana, and Bruno, Brunella, 'Edilizia abitativa a Verona', in Jacopo Ortalli and Michael Heinzelmann (eds.), *La Cisalpina tra impero e medioevo. Leben in der Stadt* (Wiesbaden, 2003), pp. 47–64.
Cébeillac-Gervasoni, Mireille (ed.), *Les élites municipales de l'Italie péninsulaire de la mort de César à la mort de Domitien, entre continuité et rupture: classes sociales dirigeantes et pouvoir central* (Rome, 2000).
Ceresa Mori, Anna, 'Milano via del Lauro 1-via Bioti 3 Sondaggio', *Notiziario Soprintendenza archeologica della Lombardia* 1983 (1984).
Ceresa Mori, Anna, Pagani, C., and White, N., 'Milano. Indagini nell'area del foro. Biblioteca Ambrosiana', *Notiziario Soprintendenza archeologica della Lombardia* (1990), 173–85.

Chavarría, Alexandra, 'Local churches and lordship in late antique and early medieval Northern Italy', in José C. Sánchez-Pardo and Michael G. Shapland (eds.), *Churches and social power in early medieval Europe: Integrating archaeological and historical approaches*, Studies in the Early Middle Ages (Turnhout, 2015), vol. 42.

Cheema, G. Shabbir, Smit, Jac, Ratta, Annu, and Nasr, Joe, *Urban agriculture: Food jobs and sustainable cities* (New York, 1996).

Cheyette, Fredric L., 'The disappearance of the ancient landscape and the climatic anomaly of the early Middle Ages: a question to be pursued', *Early Medieval Europe* 16.2 (2008), 127–65.

Chisholm, Michael, *Rural settlement and land use* (London, 1968).

Christie, Neil, *From Constantine to Charlemagne: An archaeology of Italy AD 300–800* (Aldershot, 2006).

Christie, Neil, 'Popes, pilgrims and peasants. The role of the *domusculta Capracorum* (Santa Cornelia, Rome)', in Ernst Dassmann and Josef Engemann (eds.), *Akten des XII. Internationalen Kongresses für christliche Archäologie* (Rome, 1995), vol. II, pp. 650–7.

Christie, Neil, *Three south Etrurian churches: Santa Cornelia, Santa Rufina and San Liberato*, Archaeological monographs of the British School at Rome 4 (London, 1991).

Christie, Neil, 'War and order: Urban remodelling and defensive strategy in late Roman Italy', in Luke Lavan (ed.), *Recent research on Late Antique urbanism*, Journal of Roman Archaeology Supplementary Series 42 (Portsmouth, 2001), pp. 106–22.

Christie, Neil, and Loseby, Simon (eds.), *Towns in transition: urban evolution in late antiquity and the early Middle Ages* (Aldershot, 1996).

Ciampoltrini, Giulio, 'Città 'frammentate' e città-fortezza. Storie urbane della Toscana centro-Settentrionale da Teodosio a Carlo Magno', in Riccardo Francovich and Ghislaine Noyé (eds.), *La storia dell'alto Medioevo italiano (VI–X secolo) alla luce dell'archeologia. Atti del Convegno internazionale (Siena, 1992)*, Biblioteca di archeologia medievale 11 (Florence, 1994), pp. 615–34.

Ciampoltrini, Giulio, 'Lucca tardoantica e altomedievale: nuovi contributi archeologici', *Archeologia Medievale* XVII (1990), 561–92.

Ciampoltrini, Giulio, 'Ricerche nell'area dell'anfiteatro', *Bollettino di Archeologia* 16–17–18 (1992), 51–5.

Ciampoltrini, Giulio, Notini, Paola, and Rendini, Paolo, 'Materiali tardoantichi ed altomedievali dalla Valle del Serchio', *Archeologia Medievale* XVIII (1991), 699–715.

Ciancio Rossetto, Paolo, 'Portico d'Ottavia - Sant'Angelo in Pescheria: nuove acquisizioni sulle fasi medievali', *Rivista di archeologia Cristiana* 84 (2008), 415–37.

Ciaraldi, Marina, *People and plants in ancient Pompeii: a new approach to urbanism from the microscope room*, Accordia specialist studies on Italy 12 (London, 2007).

Ciarallo, Annamaria, *Flora pompeiana*, Studia archaeologica 134 (Rome, 2004).

Cima, Maddalena, and La Rocca, Eugenio, *Horti Romani: atti del convegno internazionale: Roma, 4–6 Maggio 1995*, Bullettino della Commissione archeologica comunale di Roma: Supplementi 6 (Roma, 1998).

Cipolla, Carlo, 'Attorno a Giovanni cancelliere di Berengario I', *Rendiconti della Reale accademia dei lincei* 5.14 (1895), 191–212 (reprinted in Scritti di Carlo Cipolla, ed. Carlo Guido Mor (Verona, 1978), i).

Clément, Jean-Marie, *Lexique des anciennes règles monastiques occidentales*, 2 vols., Instrumenta patristica 7A-B (Steenbrugis, 1978).

Clifford, Heather Spaulding, Nicole, Kurbato, Andrei, More, Alexander, Korotkikh, Elena, Sneed, Handley, Mike, Maasch, Kirk, Loveluck, Christopher, Chaplin, Joyce, McCormick, Michael, and Mayewski, Paul, 'A 2000 Year Saharan Dust Event Proxy Record from an Ice Core in the European Alps', *Journal of Geophysical Research - Atmospheres* 124. 23 (2019), 12882–12900.

Coates-Stephens, Robert, 'Housing in early medieval Rome, 500–1000 AD', *Papers of the British School at Rome* 64 (1996), 239–59.

Coates-Stephens, Robert, *Porta Maggiore: monument and landscape: archaeology and topography of the southern Esquiline from the Late Republican period to the present*, Bullettino della Commissione archeologica comunale di Roma. Supplementi 12 (Rome, 2004).

Coates-Stephens, Robert, 'The walls and aqueducts of Rome in the early Middle Ages, AD 500–1000', *The Journal of Roman Studies* 88 (1998), 166–78.

Coffee, Neil, 'Intertextuality as viral phrases: Roses and lilies', in Monica Berti (ed.), *Digital classical philology: Ancient Greek and Latin in the digital revolution* (Berlin, 2019), pp. 177–200.

Collins, Minta, *Medieval herbals: The illustrative traditions* (London, 2000).

Contreni, John J., 'Carolingian renaissance: education and literary culture', in Rosamond McKitterick (ed.), *New Cambridge medieval history. Vol. II: c. 700 – c. 900* (Cambridge, 1995), pp. 709–57.

Cooper, Kate, *The fall of the Roman household* (Cambridge, 2007).

Cooper, Kate, 'The household and the desert: Monastic and biological communities in the Lives of Melania the younger', in Anneke B. Mulder-Bakker and Jocelyn Wogan-Browne (eds.), *Household, women, and Christianities: in Late Antiquity and the Middle Ages*, Medieval Women Texts and Contexts 14 (Turnhout, 2005), pp. 11–35.

Costambeys, Marios, 'The laity, the clergy, the scribes and their archives: the documentary record of eighth- and ninth-century Italy', in Warren Brown, Marios Costambeys, Matthew Innes, and Adam Kosto (eds.), *Documentary culture and the laity in the early Middle Ages* (Cambridge, 2013), pp. 231–58.

Costambeys, Marios, *Power and patronage in early medieval Italy: local society, Italian politics and the Abbey of Farfa, c.700–900* (Cambridge, 2007).

Costambeys, Marios, 'Settlement, taxation and the condition of the peasantry in post-Roman central Italy', *Journal of Agrarian Change* 9.1 (2009), 92–119.

Costambeys, Marios, Innes, Matthew, and MacLean, Simon, *The Carolingian world* (Cambridge, 2011).

Coupland, Simon, 'Charlemagne and his coinage', in Rolf Große and Michel Sot (eds.), *Charlemagne: les temps, les espaces, les hommes. Construction et déconstruction d'un règne*, Haut Moyen Âge 34 (Turnhout, 2018), pp. 449–50.

Courtois, Christian, *Les Vandales et l'Afrique* (Paris, 1955).
Cracco Ruggini, Lellia, 'La città nel mondo antico: realtà e idea', in Gerhard Wirth, Johannes Heinrichs, and Karl-Heinz Schwarte (eds.), *'Romanitas – Christianitas': Untersuchungen zur Geschichte und Literatur der römischen Kaiserzeit Johannes Straub zum 70. Geburtstag am 18. Oktober 1982 gewidmet* (Berlin, 1982), pp. 61–81.
Cracco Ruggini, Lellia, *Economia e società nell' 'Italia annonaria': rapporti fra agricoltura e commercio dal IV al VI secolo d.C.*, Studi storici sulla Tarda Antichità (Bari, 1961 [reprint 1995]).
Cracco Ruggini, Lellia, 'Graduatorie fra "utillimae artes" e saperi scientifici aristocratici nell'Italia di Cassiodoro', *Cassiodoro* 6–7 (2000–1), 73–94.
Crawford, Michael H., 'Italy and Rome from Sulla to Augustus', in Alan Bowman, E. Champlin, and A. Lintott (eds.), *The Cambridge ancient history. Volume X. The Augustan Empire, 43 B.C – A.D. 69* (Cambridge, 1996), pp. 414–33.
Crawford, Michael, 'Money and exchange in the Roman world', *Journal of Roman Studies* 60.1 (1970), 40–8.
Cremaschi, Mauro, and Nicosia, Cristiano, 'Corso Porta Reno, Ferrara (northern Italy): A study in the formation processes of urban deposits', *Il Quaternario. Italian Journal of Quaternary Sciences* 23.2 (2010), 373–86.
Crouch, David, and Ward, Colin, *The allotment: its landscape and culture*, 2nd rev. ed., (Nottingham, 1994).
Cumont, Franz, *Lux perpetua*, rev. ed. by B. Rochette, André Motte, and Bastien Toune (Turin, 2009).
Cuoghi, E, 'L'orto alto-medievale di Ferrara: basi carpologiche per la sua ricostruzione' (Laurea Thesis, Università di Modena e Reggio Emilia, 2006–7).
Curtius, Ernst R., *European literature and the Latin Middle Ages*, trans. Willard R. Trask (Princeton, 1990 [1953]).
Cutler, Anthony, 'Significant gifts: Patterns of exchange in late antique, byzantine, and early Islamic diplomacy', *Journal of Medieval and Early Modern Studies* 38.1 (2008), 80–101.
D'Avray, David, 'Half a century of research on the first papal decretals (to c. 440)', *Bulletin of Medieval Canon Law* 35 (2018), 331–74.
David, Elizabeth, *English bread and yeast cookery* (London, 1977).
Davies, Wendy, 'Gardens and gardening in early medieval Spain and Portugal', *Early Medieval Europe* 27.3 (2019), 327–48.
Davies, Wendy, 'Monastic landscapes and society', in John H. Arnold (ed.), *The Oxford handbook of medieval Christianity* (Oxford, 2014), pp. 132–47.
Davies, Wendy, *Small worlds: the village community in early medieval Brittany* (London, 1988).
Davies, Wendy, 'When gift is sale: Reciprocities and commodities in tenth-century Christian Iberia', in Wendy Davies and Paul Fouracre (eds.), *The languages of gift in the early Middle Ages* (New York, 2010), pp. 217–37.
Davies, Wendy, and Fouracre, Paul (eds.), *The languages of gift in the early Middle Ages* (New York, 2010).
Davies, Wendy, and Fouracre, Paul (eds.), *Property and power in the early Middle Ages* (Cambridge, 1995).

Davies, Wendy, and Fouracre, Paul (eds.), *The settlement of disputes in early medieval Europe* (Cambridge, 1986).
Davis, Jennifer R., *Charlemagne's practice of empire* (Cambridge, 2015).
de Blaauw, Sible, *Cultus et decor: Liturgia e architettura nella Roma tardoantica e medievale: Basilica Salvatoris, Sanctae Mariae, Sancti Petri*, Studi e testi (Biblioteca apostolica vaticana) 355–6 (Città del Vaticano, 1994).
de Certeau, Michel, *The practice of everyday life* (Berkeley, 1984).
Deconchat M., and Balent, G., 'Effets des perturbations du sol et de la mise en lumiére occasionnées par l'exploitation forestière sur la flore à une échelle fine', *Annales For. Sci.* 58 (2001), 315–28.
De Conno, Andrea, 'L'insediamento longobardo a Lucca', in Gabriella Garzella (ed.), *Pisa e la Toscana occidentale nel Medioevo. A Cinzio Violante nei suoi 70 anni* (Pisa, 1991), pp. 59–127.
de Jong, Mayke, 'Monasticism and the power of prayer', in Rosamond McKitterick (ed.), *New Cambridge medieval history. Vol. II: c. 700 – c. 900* (Cambridge, UK, 1995), pp. 622–53.
De Rossi, Giovanni Battista, 'Un'insigne epigrafe di donazione di fondi fatta alla chiesa di S. Susanna dal papa Sergio I', *Bullettino di archeologia cristiana s. II* 1 (1870), 89–112.
De Rubeis, Flavia, 'Epigrafi a Roma dall'età classica all'alto medioevo,' in Maria Stella Arena (ed.), *Roma dall'antichità al medioevo. Archeologia e storia nel Museo Nazionale Romano Crypta Balbi* (Milan, 2001), pp. 104–21.
De Simone, Adalgisa, 'Palermo nei geografi e viaggiatori arabi del Medioevo', *Studi magrebini* 2 (1968), 129–89.
De Simone, Antonio, 'Il complesso monumentale di San Lorenzo Maggiore', in *Napoli antica, Mostra, Museo Archeologico Nazionale Napoli* (Naples, 1985), pp. 185–95.
De Simone, Antonio, 'San Lorenzo Maggiore in Napoli: il monumento e l'area', in *Neapolis Atti del XXV covegno di Studi sulla Magna Grecia* (Taranto, 1986), pp. 233–53.
Deliyannis, Deborah Mauskopf, Dey, Hendrik, and Squatriti, Paolo, *Fifty early medieval things: Materials of culture in late antiquity and the early Middle Ages* (Ithaca, 2019).
Delogu, Paolo, *Mito di una città meridionale (Salerno, secoli VIII-XI)*, 1st ed. (Naples, 1977).
Delogu, Paolo, 'Rome in the ninth century: the economic system', in Joachim Henning (ed.), *Post-Roman towns, trade and settlement in Europe and Byzantium. Vol. 1, The heirs of the Roman West* (Berlin/New York, 2007), pp. 105–22.
Demacopoulos, George E., *Five models of spiritual direction in the early church* (Notre Dame, IN, 2007).
Desplanques, Henri, 'Il paesaggio rurale della coltura promiscua in Italia', *Rivista Geografica Italiana* LXVI (1959), 29–64.
Devos, Yannick, Nicosia, Cristiano, Vrydaghs, L., and Modrie, S., 'Studying urban stratigraphy: Dark Earth and a microstratified sequence on the site of the Court of Hoogstraeten (Brussels, Belgium). Integrating archaeopedology and phytolith analysis', *Quaternary International* 315 (2013), 147–66.

Devroey, Jean-Pierre, *Économie rurale et société dans l'Europe franque (VIe-IXe siècles)* (Paris, 2003).
Dey, Hendrik, *The afterlife of the Roman city. Architecture and ceremony in late antiquity and the early Middle Ages* (Cambridge, 2015).
Dey, Hendrik, 'Diaconiae, xenodochia, hospitalia and monasteries: "social security" and the meaning of monasticism in early medieval Rome', *Early Medieval Europe* 16.4 (2008), 398–422.
Dey, Hendrik, and Fentress, Elizabeth (eds.) *Western monasticism ante litteram: The space of monastic observance in late antiquity and the early Middle Ages*, Disciplina Monastica 7 (Turnhout, 2011).
Di Santo, Alberto, *Monumenti antichi, fortezze medievali. Il riutilizzo degli antichi monumenti nell'edilizia aristocratica di Roma (VIII – XIV secolo)* (Rome, 2010).
Diamond, Arlyn, 'Meeting grounds: Gardens in Middle English Romance', in Laura Ashe, Ivana Djordjevic, and Judith Weiss (eds.), *The exploitations of medieval Romance* (Woodbridge, 2010), pp. 125–38.
Diaz, Henry, Trigo, Ricardo, Hughes, Malcom, Mann, Michael, Xoplaki, Elena and Barriopedro, David, 'Spatial and temporal characteristics of climate in medieval times revisited', *Bullettin of the American Meteorological Society* 92 (2011), 1487–1500.
Diem, Albrecht, 'Inventing the Holy Rule: some observations on the history of monastic normative observance in the Early Medieval West', in Hendrik Dey and Elizabeth Fentress (eds.), *Western monasticism ante litteram: the spaces of monastic observance in Late Antiquity and the early Middle Ages*, Disciplina Monastica 7 (Turnhout, 2011).
Ditchfield, Philip, *La culture matérielle médiévale: l'Italie méridionale byzantine et normande*, Collection de l'École française de Rome 373 (Rome, 2007).
Dizionario biografico degli Italiani, ed. Irene Scaravelli, 95 vols. (Rome, 1960–).
Domene, Elena, and Saurí, David, 'Urbanization and water consumption: influencing factors in the Barcelona metropolitan region', *Geoforum* 38 (2006), 287–98.
Dorofeeva, Anna, 'Miscellanies, Christian reform and early medieval encyclopaedism: a reconsideration of the pre-bestiary Latin Physiologus manuscripts', *Historical Research* 90.250 (2017), 665–82.
Draycott, Jane, *Roman domestic medical practice in central Italy: from the middle republic to the early empire* (New York, NY, 2019).
Duby, Georges, *The early growth of European economy*, World Economic History Series (Ithaca, NY, 1973).
Duchesne, Louis, 'Notes sur la topographie de Rome au Moyen-Âge. – XII. Vaticana (Suite)', *Mélanges d'archéologie et d'histoire* 34.1 (1914), 307–56.
Durliat, Jean, *De la ville antique à la ville byzantine: Le problème des subsistances*, Collection de l'École française de Rome 136 (Rome, 1990).
Durliat, Jean, 'Épigraphie chrétienne de langue latine', in Guglielmo Cavallo and Cyril A. Mango (eds.), *Epigrafia medievale greca e latina: Ideologia e funzione: Atti del Seminario di Erice, 12–18 Settembre 1991*, Biblioteca del Centro per il collegamento degli studi medievale e umanistici in Umbria 11 (Spoleto, 1995), p. 321.

El Faïz, Mohammed, 'L'apport des traités agronomiques hispano-arabes à l'histoire économique d'al-Andalus', in Expiración García Sánchez (ed.), *Ciencias de la Naturaleza in al-Andalus. Textos y Estudios. III* (Granada, 1994), pp. 403–33.

Ellis, Simon P., 'The end of the Roman house', *American Journal of Archaeology* 92.4 (1988), 565–76.

Ellis, Simon P., 'Power, architecture and decor: how the late Roman aristocrat appeared to his guests', in Elaine Gazda (ed.), *Roman art in the private sphere* (Ann Arbor, MI, 1991), pp. 117–34.

Ellis, Steven J. R., *The Roman retail revolution: The socio-economic world of the taberna* (Oxford, 2018).

Epstein, Steven, *The medieval discovery of nature* (Cambridge, 2012).

Erdkamp, Paul, 'The food supply of the Capital', in Paul Erdkamp (ed.), *The Cambridge companion to ancient Rome* (Cambridge, 2013), pp. 262–77.

Erdkamp, Paul, 'War, food, climate change, and the decline of the Roman Empire', *Journal of Late Antiquity* 12.2 (2019), 422–65.

Everett, Nicholas, *Literacy in Lombard Italy, c. 568–774*, Cambridge studies in medieval life and thought: Fourth Series 53 (Cambridge, 2003).

Everett, Nicholas, 'The manuscript evidence for pharmacy in the early Middle Ages', in Charles West and Elina Screen (eds.), *Writing the early medieval West* (Cambridge, 2018), pp. 115–30.

Ewig, Eugen, 'Beobachtungen zu den Klosterprivilegien des 7. und frühen 8. Jahrhunderts', in Josef Fleckenstein and Karl Schmid (eds.), *Adel und Kirche. Gerd Tellenbach zum 65. Geburtstag dargebracht von Freunden und Schülern* (Freiburg im Breisgau/Basel/Vienna, 1968), pp. 52–65.

Farrar, Linda, *Gardens of Italy and the western provinces of the Roman Empire: From the 4th century BC to the 4th century AD*, British Archaeological Reports: International Series 650 (Oxford, 1996).

Feller, Laurent, 'L'exercice du pouvoir par Bérenger Ier, roi d'Italie (888–915) et empereur (915–924)', *Médiévales* 58 (2010), 129–49.

Feller, Laurent, and Wickham, Christopher (eds.), *Le marché de la terre au Moyen Âge*, Collection de l'École française de Rome 350 (Rome, 2005).

Feller, Laurent, Gramain, Agnès, and Weber, Florence, *La fortune de Karol: marché de la terre et liens personnels dans les Abruzzes au haut moyen âge*, Collection de l'École française de Rome 347 (Rome, 2005).

Feniello, Amedeo, 'Alle origini di Napoli capitale', *MÉFR* 124.2 (2012), 567–84.

Fentress, Elizabeth, 'Topographic memory', in Ross Balzaretti, Julia Barrow, and Patricia Skinner (eds.), *Italy and early Medieval Europe: Papers for Chris Wickham* (Oxford, 2018), pp. 213–30.

Ferrari, Guy, *Early Roman monasteries; notes for the history of the monasteries and convents at Rome from the V through the X century*, Studi di antichità cristiana 23 (Vatican City, 1957).

Fish, Suzanne K., 'Archaeological palynology of gardens and fields', in Naomi Frances Miller and Kathryn L. Gleason (eds.), *The archaeology of garden and field* (Philadelphia, 1994), pp. 44–69.

Flanigan, C. Clifford, 'Moving subjects: Processional performance in the Middle Ages and the Renaissance', in Kathleen Ashley and Wim Hüsken (eds.), *The moving subject: Medieval liturgical processions in semiotic and cultural perspective*, Ludus (Amsterdam, 2001), vol. 5, pp. 35–51.

Fleckenstein, Josef, 'Fulrad von St. Denis und der fränkische Ausgriff in den süddeutschen Raum', in Gerd Tellenbach (ed.), *Studien und Vorarbeiten zur Geschichte des großfränkischen und frühdeutschen Adels*, Forschungen zur oberrheinischen Landesgeschichte (Freiburg im Breisgau, 1957), pp. 9–39.

Fleming, John V., 'The garden of the Roman de la rose: Vision of landscape or landscape of vision?', in Elisabeth B. MacDougall (ed.), *Medieval gardens*, Dumbarton Oaks Colloquium on the history of landscape architecture 9 (Washington, DC, 1986), pp. 201–34.

Flohr, Miko, and Wilson, Andrew, 'The economy of ordure', in Gemma Jansen, Ann Olga Koloski-Ostrow, and Eric Moormann (eds.), *Roman toilets: Their archeology and cultural history*, Bulletin antieke beschaving: Supplement 19 (Leuven, 2011), pp. 147–56.

Fontaine, Jacques, 'Valeurs antiques et valeurs chrétiennes dans la spiritualité des grands propriétaires terriens à la fin du IVe siècle occidental', in Jacques Fontaine and Charles Kanneengiesser (eds.), *Epektasis, Mélanges patristiques offerts au cardinal Jean Daniélou* (Paris, 1972), pp. 571–82.

Foxhall, Lin, 'Cultures, landscapes, and identities in the Mediterranean world', *Mediterranean Historical Review* 18.2 (2003), 75–92.

Frezouls, Edmond, 'Rome, ville ouverte. Réflexions sur les problèmes de l'expansion urbaine d'Auguste à Aurélien', in *L'Urbs: espace urbain et histoire (Ier siècle av. J.-C. – IIIe siècle ap. J.-C.). Actes du colloque international de Rome (8–12 mai 1985)* (Rome, 1987), pp. 373–92.

Fritsch, Reinhard, 'Zur Samenmorphologie des Kulturmohns (Papaver somniferum L.)', *Die Kulturpflanze* 27.2 (1979), 217–27.

Fronza, Vittorio, 'Edilizia in materiali deperibili nell'alto medioevo italiano: metodologie e casi di studio per un'agenda della ricerca', *Post-Classical Archaeologies* 1 (2011), 95–138.

Fumagalli, Vito, 'Langobardia e Romania: L'occupazione del suolo nella Pentapoli altomedievale', in *Ricerche e studi sul Breviarium ecclesiae Ravennatis (Codice Bavaro)*, Studi Storici 148–9 (Rome, 1985), pp. 95–108.

Fusconi, Giorgio, *Gli antiquiores romani: le monete coniate dalla zecca di Roma da Adriano I (772–795) a Benedetto VI (975–83)* (Pavia, 2012).

Gabba, Emilio, and Coarelli, Filippo, 'Mercati e fiere nell'Italia romana', *Studi Classici e Orientali* 24 (1975), 141–66.

Gadd, Derek, and Ward-Perkins, Bryan, 'The development of urban domestic housing in northern Italy: The evidence of the excavations on the San Romano site, Ferrara, 1981–4', *Accordia Research Papers* 2 (1991), 105–27.

Galasso, Giuseppe, 'Le città campane nell'alto medioevo', in *Mezzogiorno medievale e moderno*, Reprints Einaudi 41 (Turin, 1975), pp. 61–136.

Galetti, Paola, 'Struttura materiale e funzioni negli insediamenti urbani e rurali della Pentapoli', in Augusto Vasina (ed.), *Ricerche e studi sul "Breviarum Ecclesiae Ravennatis" (Codice bavaro)*, Studi storici (Istituto storico italiano per il Medio Evo) (Rome, 1985), pp. 109–24.

Galetti, Paola, 'Tecniche e materiali da costruzione dell'edilizia residenziale', in Andrea Augenti (ed.), *Le città italiane tra la tarda antichità e l'alto Medioevo: Atti* del Convegno, Ravenna, 26–28 febbraio 2004, Biblioteca di archeologia medioevale (Firenze, 2006), pp. 67–79.

Galinié, Henri, 'L'expression terres noires, un concept d'attente', Les petits cahiers d'anatole 15 (2004).

Gandy, Matthew, 'Marginalia: Aesthetics, ecology, and urban wastelands', Annals of the Association of American Geographers 103.6 (2013), 1301–16.

Gandy, Matthew, 'Unintentional landscapes', Landscape Research 41.4 (2016), 433–40.

Ganshof, François Louis, Frankish institutions under Charlemagne, trans. Bryce Lyon and Mary Lyon (Providence, 1968).

Ganshof, François Louis, 'Note sure la concession d'alleux à des vassaux sous le règne de Louis le Pieux', in Storiografia e Storia: Studi in onore di E. Dupré Theseider (Rome, 1974), pp. 589–99.

Ganz, David, 'The ideology of sharing: Apostolic community and ecclesiastical property in the early Middle Ages', in Paul Fouracre and Wendy Davies (eds.), Property and power in the early Middle Ages (Cambridge, 1995), pp. 17–30.

García Sánchez, Expiración, 'Agriculture in Muslim Spain', in Salma Jayyusi (ed.), The legacy of Muslim Spain, Handbook of Oriental Studies. Section 1. The Near and Middle East 12 (Leiden, 1992), pp. 987–99.

García Sánchez, Expiración, 'Cultivos y espacios agrícolas irrigados en Al-Andalus', in L. Cara Barrionuevo and A. Malpica Cuello (eds.), Agricultura y regadío en Al-Andalus (Almería, 1995), pp. 17–38.

García Sánchez, Expiración, 'Utility and aesthetics in the gardens of al-Andalus: Species with multiple uses', in Peter Dendle and Alain Touwaide (eds.), Health and healing from the medieval garden (Woodbridge, 2008), pp. 205–27.

Garnsey, Peter, Famine and food supply in the Graeco-Roman world: Responses to risk and crisis (Cambridge, 1988).

Garnsey, Peter, Food and society in classical antiquity, Key themes in ancient history (Cambridge, 1999).

Garnsey, Peter, 'Mass diet and nutrition', in Peter Garnsey (ed.), Cities, peasants, and food in classical antiquity: Essays in social and economic history, edited with additions by Walter Scheidel (Cambridge, 1998), pp. 226–52.

Garnsey, Peter, 'Non-slave labour in the Roman world', in Peter Garnsey (ed.), Non-slave labour in the Greco-Roman world (Cambridge, 1980), pp. 34–47.

Garnsey, Peter, and Whittaker, C. R., 'Trade, industry and the urban economy', in Averil Cameron and Peter Garnsey (eds.), New Cambridge ancient history: The late empire A.D., 337–425 (Cambridge; New York, 1998), vol. XIII, pp. 312–37.

Gasparri, Stefano, Italia longobarda: Il regno, i Franchi, il papato, Economica Laterza 782 (Bari, 2016).

Gasparri, Stefano, 'I testamenti nell'Italia settentrionale fra VIII e IX secolo', in François Bougard, Cristina La Rocca, and Régine Le Jan (eds.), Sauver son âme et se perpétuer: transmission du patrimoine et mémoire au haut Moyen Âge Collection de l'École française de Rome 351 (Rome, 2005), pp. 97–113.

Gasparri, Stefano, 'L'alto medioevo: da Teodorico a Berengario (secoli VI-X)', in Stefano Agnoletto, Giuseppe Colombo, Federico de Giacomi, and

Enrica Galbiati (eds.), *Monza. La sua storia* (Cinisello Balsamo (Milan), 2002), pp. 66–9.
Gasparri, Stefano, 'Strutture militari e legami di dipendenza in Italia in età longobarda e carolingia', *Rivista storica italiana* 98 (1986), 664–726.
Gasparri, Stefano, and Azzara, Claudio (eds.), *Le leggi dei Longobardi: Storia, Memoria e Diritto di un Popolo Germanico* (Rome, 2011).
Gasparri, Stefano, and La Rocca, Cristina, *Carte di famiglia: Strategie, rappresentazione e memoria del gruppo familiare di Totone di Campione, 721–877*, Altomedioevo 5 (Rome, 2005).
Gaulin, Jean Louis, 'Tradition et pratiques de la litterature', in *L'ambiente vegetale*, Settimane di studio del Centro italiano di studi sull'alto medioevo 37 (Spoleto, 1990), pp. 103–35.
Gauthier, Nancy, 'La topographie chrétienne entre ideologie et pragmatisme', in Gian Pietro Brogiolo and Bryan Ward-Perkins (eds.), *The idea and ideal of the town between late antiquity and the early Middle Ages* (Leidein, The Netherlands, 1999), pp. 195–209.
Géczi, János, *The rose and its symbols in Mediterranean antiquity* (Tübingen, 2011).
Gelichi, Sauro, 'Dal delta del Po alle lagune veneziane: territorio, commerci e insediamento. Ricerche sull'emporio altomedievale di Comacchio', in Silvana Collodo and Giovanni Luigi Fontana (eds.), *Eredità culturali dell'Adriatico. Archeologia, storia, lingua e letteratura* (Rome, 2008), pp. 169–92.
Gelichi, Sauro, 'Note sulle città bizantine dell'esarcato e della pentapoli tra IV e IX secolo', in Gian Pietro Brogiolo (ed.), *Early medieval towns in the western Mediterranean*, Documenti di archeologia 10 (Padua, 1996), pp. 67–76.
Gelichi, Sauro, 'The cities', in Cristina La Rocca (ed.), *Italy in the early Middle Ages, 476–1000*, The short Oxford history of Italy (Oxford, 2002).
Gelichi, Sauro, and Novara, Paola (eds.), *I laterizi nell'alto medioevo italiano* (Ravenna, 2000).
Gelichi, Sauro, Calaon, Diego, Grandi, Elena, and Negrelli, Claudio, 'The history of a forgotten town: Comacchio and its archaeology', in Richard Hodges and Sauro Gelichi (eds.), *From one sea to another. Trading places in the European and Mediterranean Early Middle Ages* (2012), pp. 169–205.
Ghilardi, Massimiliano, Goddard, Christophe J., and Porena, Pierfrancisco, *Les cités de l'Italie tardo-antique (IVe-VIe siècle): Institutions, économie, société, culture et religion*, Collection de l'École française de Rome 369 (Rome, 2006).
Giardina, Andrea, 'Aristocrazie terriere e piccola mercatura. Sui rapporti tra potere politico e formazione dei prezzi nel tardo impero romano', *Quaderni Urbinati di Cultura Classica* 7 (1981), 123–46.
Giardina, Andrea, 'Le due Italie nella forma tarda dell'impero', in Andrea Giardina (ed.), *Società romana e impero tardo antico* (Bari, 1986), vol. 1. Istituzioni, ceti, economie, pp. 1–36.
Gibbon, Edward, *The history of the decline and fall of the Roman Empire*, 8 vols., (London, 1825).
Giraudi, C., 'Late-Holocene alluvial events in the Central Apennines, Italy', *The Holocene* 15.5 (2005), 768–73.
Giuliani, Cairoli Fulvio, 'Una rilettura dell'area centrale del Foro Romano', in Raymond Chevallier (ed.), *Présence de l'architecture et de l'urbanisme romains:*

hommage à Paul Dufournet: actes du colloque des 12, 13 décembre 1981 (Paris, 1983), pp. 83–93. Giuliani, Cairoli Fulvio, and Verduchi, Patrizia, *L'area centrale del Foro romano* (Florence, 1987).

Gladiß, Dietrich von, 'Die Schenkungen der deutschen Könige zu privatem Eigen (800–1137)', *Deutsches Archiv für Geschichte des Mittelalters* 1 (1937), 80–136.

Gleason, Kathryn, 'To bound and to cultivate: An introduction to the archaeology of gardens and fields', in Naomi Miller and Kathryn Gleason (eds.), *The archaeology of garden and field* (Philadelphia, 1994), pp. 1–24.

Goffart, Walter A., *Barbarians and Romans, A.D. 415–584: The techniques of accommodation* (New Jersey, 1980).

Goldberg, Paul, and Macphail, Richard I., *Applied soils and micromorphology in archaeology*, Cambridge Manuals in Archaeology (Cambridge, 2018).

Goldberg, Paul, and Macphail, Richard I., *Practical and theoretical geoarchaeology* (Oxford, 2006).

Goodman, Penelope, 'Agrarian writers, agronomists', in Roger S. Bagnall, Kai Brodersen, Craige B. Champion, Andrew Erskine, and Sabine R. Huebner (eds.), *The encyclopedia of ancient history* (Oxford, 2013), vol. 1, pp. 205–6.

Goodson, Caroline, 'Admirable and delectable gardens: Uiridaria in early medieval Italy', *Early Medieval Europe* 22.3 (2019), 416–40.

Goodson, Caroline, 'Building for bodies: The architecture of saint veneration in early medieval Rome', in Éamonn Ó Carragain and Carol Neuman de Vegvar (eds.), *Felix Roma: The production, experience and reflection of medieval Rome* (Farnham, 2008), pp. 51–80.

Goodson, Caroline, 'Garden cities in early medieval Italy', in Ross Balzaretti, Julia Barrow, and Patricia Skinner (eds.), *Italy and Medieval Europe: Papers for Chris Wickham*, Past and Present Book Series (Oxford, 2018), pp. 339–55.

Goodson, Caroline, *The Rome of Pope Paschal I: Papal power, urban renovation, church rebuilding and relic translation, 817–824* (Cambridge, 2010).

Goodson, Caroline, 'To be the daughter of Saint Peter: S. Petronilla and forging the Franco-Papal Alliance', in Veronica West-Harling (ed.), *Three empires, three cities: Identity, material culture and legitimacy in Venice, Ravenna and Rome, 750–1000* (Turnhout, 2015), pp. 159–82.

Goodson, Caroline, 'Urbanism in the politics of power in early medieval Italy', in Clemens Gantner (ed.), *After Charlemagne: Ninth-century Italy and its rulers* (Cambridge, forthcoming).

Graham, Benjamin, 'Profile of a plant: The olive in early medieval Italy, 400–900 CE' (PhD Thesis, University of Michigan, 2014).

Grant, Mark, 'Introduction', in Anthimus, *On the observance of foods* (Totnes, 1996), 9–45.

Grey, Cam, 'Landowning and labour in the rural economy', in Jonathon J. Arnold, Shane Bjornlie, and Kristina Sessa (eds.), *A companion to Ostrogothic Italy*, Brill's Companions to European History 9 (Leiden, 2016), pp. 263–95.

Grierson, Philip, 'Commerce in the Dark Ages: A critique of the evidence', *Transactions of the Royal Historical Society* 9 (1959), 123–40.

Grierson, Philip, 'Problemi monetari dell'alto medioevo', *Bollettino della Società pavese di Storia patria* 54.2 (1954), 67–82.

Grimal, Pierre, *Les jardins romains*, Collection hier, 2nd edition (Paris, 1969).
Guarnieri, Chiara, 'Un indagine nel centro storico di Ferrara: lo scavo di via Vaspergolo – Corso Porta Reno (1993–94)', in Guy De Boe and Frans Verhaeghe (eds.), *Urbanism in medieval Europe. Papers of the 'Medieval Europe Brugge 1997' Conference* (Zellik, 1997), pp. 237–48.
Guarnieri, Chiara, and Librenti, Mauro, 'Ferrara, sequenza insediativa pluristratificata. via Vaspergolo – corso porta reno (1993–94)', *Archeologia Medievale* 23 (1996), 275–307.
Guidobaldi, Federico, 'Le domus tardoantiche di Roma come "sensori" delle trasformazioni culturali e sociali', in William V. Harris (ed.), *The transformations of Vrbs Roma in late antiquity*, Journal of Roman archaeology. Supplementary series 33 (Portsmouth, 1999), pp. 53–68.
Guidobaldi, Federico, 'L'edilizia abitativa unifamiliare nella Roma tardoantica', in Andrea Giardina (ed.), *Società Romana e Impero tardoantico II – Roma: politica, economia, paesaggio urbano*, Collezione storica (Bari, 1986), vol. 2, pp. 165–237.
Gutiérrez Lloret, Sonia, 'The case of Tudmīr: Archaeological evidence for the introduction of irrigation systems in al-Andalus', *Early Medieval Europe* 27.3 (2019), 394–415.
Guyotjeannin, Olivier, Pycke, Jacques, and Tock, Benoît-Michel, *Diplomatique médiévale*, Atelier du médiéviste (Turnhout, Belgium, 2006).
Haldon, John, Elton, Hugh, Huebner, Sabine R., Izdebski, Adam, Mordechai, Lee, and Newfield, Timothy P., 'Plagues, climate change, and the end of an empire: A response to Kyle Harper's The fate of Rome (1): Climate', *History Compass* 16.12 (2018), e12508.
Haldon, John, Mordechai, Lee, Newfield, Timothy P., Chase, Arlen F., Izdebski, Adam, Guzowski, Piotr, Labuhn, Inga, and Roberts, Neil, 'History meets palaeoscience: Consilience and collaboration in studying past societal responses to environmental change', *Proceedings of the National Academy of Sciences* 115.13 (2018), 3210.
Hallenbeck, Jan T., 'Pavia and Rome: The Lombard monarchy and the papacy in the eighth century', *The American Historical Review* 88.3 (1982), 665–6.
Halphen, Louis, *Études sur l'administration de Rome au Moyen âge (751–1252)*, Bibliotheque de l'École des hautes études, sciences historiques et phillologiques 166 (Paris, 1907).
Hann, C. M., and Hart, Keith, *Market and society: the great transformation today* (Cambridge, 2009).
Harper, Kyle, *The fate of Rome: climate, disease, and the end of an empire*, Princeton history of the ancient world (Princeton, 2017).
Harper, Kyle, *Slavery in the late Roman world, AD 275–425* (Cambridge, 2011).
Hartmann, Ludo Moritz, *Urkunde einer römischen Gärtnergenossenschaft vom Jahre 1030: mit Einleitung und Erlänternungen* (Freiburg im Breslau, 1892).
Hartswick, Kim J., *The gardens of Sallust: A changing landscape* (Austin, 2004).
Harvey, John, *Mediaeval gardens* (London, 1990). 2nd rev. ed.
Hauck, Karl, 'Paderborn, das Zentrum von Karls Sachsen-Mission 777', in Josef Fleckenstein and Karl Schmid (eds.), *Adel und Kirche: Gerd Tellenbach*

zum 65: Geburtstag dargebracht von Freunden und Schülern (Freiburg im Breisgau; Basel; Wien, 1968), pp. 92–140.

Heffernan, Thomas J., *Passio Sanctarum Perpetuae et Felicitatis in the passion of Perpetua and Felicity* (Oxford, 2012).

Helama, Samuli, Jones, Phil, and Briffa, Keith, 'Dark Ages cold period: A literature review and directions for future research', *The Holocene* 27.10 (2017), 1600–6.

Henderson, John, *Hortus. The Roman book of gardening* (London, 2004).

Hendy, Michael F., 'From public to private: The western barbarian coinages as a mirror of the disintegration of late Roman state structures', *Viator* 19 (1988), 29–78.

Hermansen, Gustav, *Ostia: Aspects of Roman city life* (Edmonton, 1982).

Hillier, Bill, and Hanson, Julienne, *The social logic of space* (Cambridge, 1984).

Hillner, Julia, 'Domus, family, and inheritance: The senatorial family house in late antique Rome', *Journal of Roman Studies* 93 (2003), 129–45.

Hlawitschka, Eduard, *Franken, Alemannen, Bayern und Burgunder in Oberitalien (774–962). Zum Verständnis der Fränkischen Königsherrschaft in Italien*, Forschungen zur oberrheinischen Landesgeschichte 8 (Freiburg im Breisgau, 1960).

Hodges, Richard, *Dark age economics: A new audit* (London, 2012).

Hodges, Richard, *Dark age economics: The origins of towns and trade AD 500–1000*, New approaches in archaeology, 2nd ed. (London, 1989).

Hodges, Richard, *Light in the dark ages: The rise and fall of San Vincenzo al Volturno* (Ithaca, NY, 1997).

Hodges, Richard, and Hobley, Brian (eds.), *The rebirth of towns in the West, AD 700–1050*, Research report (Council for British Archaeology) (London, 1988).

Hodges, Richard, and Patterson, Helen, 'San Vincenzo al Volturno and the origins of the medieval pottery industry in Italy', in *La ceramica medievale nel Mediterraneo Occidentale. Atti del III Congresso Internazionale organizzato dal Dipartimento di Archeologia e Storia delle Arti dell'Università degli Studi di Siena e dal Museo delle Ceramiche di Faenza (Siena-Faenza 1984)* (Florence, 1986), pp. 13–26.

Hohenberg, Paul M., and Lees, Lynn Hollen, *The making of urban Europe, 1000–1950* (Cambridge, MA, 1985).

Holleran, Claire, 'Representations of food hawkers in ancient Rome', in Melissa Calaresu and Danielle van den Heuvel (eds.), *Food hawkers: Selling in the street from antiquity to the present* (London, 2016), pp. 37–60.

Holleran, Claire, *Shopping in ancient Rome: The retail trade in the late Republic and the Principate* (Oxford, 2012).

Hopkins, Keith, 'Rents, taxes, trade and the city of Rome', in Elio Lo Cascio (ed.), *Mercati permanenti e mercati periodici nel mondo romano. Atti degli Incontri capresi di storia dell'economia antica (Capri 13–15 ottobre 1997)* Pragmateiai 2 (Bari, 2000), pp. 253–67.

Horden, Peregrine, 'Sickness and healing', in Julia M. H. Smith and Thomas F. X. Noble (eds.), *Early Medieval Christianities, c.600–c.1100*, Cambridge history of Christianity 3 (Cambridge, 2008), pp. 416–32.

Horden, Peregrine, 'The earliest hospitals in Byzantium, western Europe, and Islam', *Journal of Interdisciplinary History* 3 (2005), 361–89.
Horden, Peregrine, 'What's wrong with early medieval medicine?', *Social History of Medicine* 24.1 (2009), 5–25.
Horden, Peregrine, and Purcell, Nicholas, *The corrupting sea: A study of Mediterranean history* (Oxford, 2000).
Horn, Walter William, and Born, Ernest, *The plan of St. Gall: a study of the architecture and economy of and life in a paradigmatic Carolingian monastery*, California studies in the history of art 19 (Berkeley, 1979).
Howes, Laura, 'Use and reception', in Michael Leslie (ed.), *A cultural history of gardens in the medieval age* (London, 2010), pp. 75–100.
Hubert, Étienne, *Espace urbain et habitat à Rome: du Xe siècle à la fin du XIIIe siècle*, Collection de l'École française de Rome 135 (Rome, 1990).
Hubert, Étienne, 'Mobilité de la population et structure des habitations à Rome et dans le Latium (IXe-XIIIe siècles)', in Rinaldo Comba and Irma Naso (eds.), *Demografia e società nell'Italia medievale: secoli IX-XIV* (Cuneo, 1994), pp. 107–24.
Hudson, Peter, *Archeologia urbana e programmazione della ricerca: l'esempio di Pavia* (Florence, 1981).
Hudson, Peter, 'La dinamica dell'insediamento urbano nell'area del cortile del Tribunale di Verona. L'età medievale', *Archeologia Medievale* 12 (1985), 281–302.
Humphrey, Caroline, 'Barter and economic disintegration', *Man* 20.1 (1985), 48–72.
Humphrey, Caroline, *The unmaking of Soviet life: Everyday economies after socialism* (Ithaca, NY, 2002).
Huxley, Anthony (ed.), *The new Royal Horticultural Society dictionary of gardening*, 4 vols. (London, 1999).
Ieraci Bio, Anna Maria, 'Centri di trasmissione della letteratura medical in età tardo antica e bizantina', in Alfonso Leone and Gerardo Sangermano (eds.), *Nel Mediterraneo medievale: La medicina* (Salerno, 2005), pp. 23–44.
Ieraci Bio, Anna Maria, 'La trasmissione della letteratura medica Greca nell'Italia meridionale fra X e XV secolo', in Antonio Garzya (ed.), *Contribuiti alla cultura greca nell'italia meridionale* (Naples, 1989), pp. 133–255.
Innes, Matthew, 'Framing the Carolingian economy', *Journal of Agrarian Change* 9.1 (2009), 42–58.
Innes, Matthew, 'Land, freedom and the making of the medieval West', *Transactions of the Royal Historical Society* 6.16 (2006), 39–74.
Innes, Matthew, *State and society in the early Middle Ages: The Middle Rhine Valley, 400–1000*, Cambridge Studies in Medieval Life and Thought: Fourth Series (Cambridge; New York, 2009).
Izdebski, Adam, and Mulryan, Michael (eds.), *Environment and society in the long late antiquity*, Late antique archaeology 11–12 (Leiden, 2019).
Jacquart, Danielle, and Paravicini Bagliani, Agostino (eds.), *La scuola medica salernitana: gli autori e i testi. Convegno internazionale, Università degli studi di Salerno, 3–5 novembre 2004* (Florence, 2007).
Jarnut, Jörg, and Becher, Matthias, *Der Dynastiewechsel von 751: Vorgeschichte, Legitimationsstrategien und Erinnerung* (Munster, 2004).

Jashemski, Wilhelmina F., 'The discovery of a market-garden orchard at Pompeii: The garden of the "House of the Ship Europa"', *American Journal of Archaeology* 78.iv (1974), 391–404.

Jashemski, Wilhelmina F., 'The garden of Hercules at Pompeii (II.viii.6): The discovery of a commercial flower garden', *American Journal of Archaeology* 83.iv (1979), 403–11.

Jashemski, Wilhelmina F., *The gardens of Pompeii, Herculaneum and the villas destroyed by Vesuvius*, 2 vols. (New York, 1979).

Jashemski, Wilhelmina F., 'Produce gardens', in Wilhelmina F. Jashemski, Kathryn L. Gleason, Kim J. Hartswick, and Amina-Aïcha Malek (eds.), *Gardens of the Roman Empire* (Cambridge, 2017), pp. 121–51.

Jashemski, Wilhelmina F., Gleason, Kathryn L., Hartswick, Kim J., and Malek, Amina-Aïcha (eds.), *Gardens of the Roman Empire* (Cambridge, 2017).

Jenal, Georg, *Italia ascetica atque monastica : das Asketen- und Mönchtum in Italien von den Anfängen bis zur Zeit der Langobarden (ca. 150/250–604)* (Stuttgart, 1995).

Johnson, Paul S., 'Investigating urban change in Late Antique Italy through waste disposal practices', in Gavin Speed and Denis Sami (eds.), *Debating urbanism within and beyond the walls AD 300–700. Proceedings of a conference held at the University of Leicester, 15th November 2008*, Leicester Archaeology Monograph 17 (Leicester, 2010), pp. 167–95.

Jones, Philip D., 'Medieval agrarian society in its prime: Italy', in Michael Postan (ed.), *Cambridge Economic History of Europe*, 2nd rev. ed. (Cambridge, 1966), pp. 340–431.

Jones, Philip D., 'Per la storia agraria italiana nel medio evo, lineamenti e problemi', *Rivista della storia italiana* 86 (1964), 287–348.

Jones, Richard, 'Manure and the medieval social order', in Michael J. Allen, Niall Sharples, and Terry Connor (eds.), *Land and people: Papers in memory of John G. Evans* (Oxford, 2009), vol. 2, pp. 215–25.

Jones, Richard, 'The urbanisation of Insula VI,1 at Pompeii', in P. G. Guzzo and M. P. Guidobaldi (eds.), *Nuove ricerche archeologiche nell'area Vesuviana (Scavi 2003–2006)*, Studi della Soprintendenza Archeologica di Pompei 25 (Rome, 2008), pp. 139–46.

Jones, Rick, and Robinson, Damian, 'Water, wealth, and social status at Pompeii: The House of the Vestals in the first century', *American Journal of Archaeology* 109.4 (2005), 695–710.

Journal of the Common Council of the City of Detroit from Jan 12 1897 to Jan 11 1898 (Detroit, 1898).

Kalas, Gregor A., *The restoration of the Roman Forum in late antiquity: Transforming public space*, Ashley and Peter Larkin series in Greek and Roman culture (Austin, TX, 2015).

Kalas, Gregor A., 'Writing restoration in Rome: Inscriptions, statues, and the late antique preservation of buildings', in Caroline Goodson, Anne E. Lester, and Carol Symes (eds.), *Cities, texts, and social networks, 400–1500* (Farnham, 2010), pp. 21–43.

Kaplan, R., 'Some psychological benefits of gardening', *Environment and Behavior* 5 (1973), 145–61.

Kaster, Robert A., *Guardians of language: The grammarian and society in late antiquity*, The Transformation of the Classical Heritage 11 (Berkeley, 1988).
Keenan-Jones, Duncan, 'Large-scale water management projects in Roman central-southern Italy', in William V. Harris (ed.), *The ancient Mediterranean environment between science and history* (Leiden, 2013), pp. 233–56.
Keller, Hagen, 'Zur Struktur der Königsherrschaft im karolingischen und nachkarolingischen Italien. Der "consiliarius regis" in den italienischen Königsdiplomen des 9. und 10. Jahrhunderts', *Quellen und Forschungen aus italienischen Archiven und Bibliotheken* 47 (1967), 123–223.
Ker, James, '"Nundinae": The culture of the Roman Week', *Phoenix* 64.3/4 (2010), 360–85.
Koder, Johannes, 'Fresh vegetables for the capital', in Cyril Mango and Gilbert Dagron (eds.), *Constantinople and its Hinterland: Papers from the Twenty-Seventh Spring Symposium of Byzantine Studies, Oxford, April 1993* (Aldershot, 1995), pp. 49–56.
Koder, Johannes, *Gemüse in Byzanz: die Versorgung Konstantinopels mit Frischgemüse im Lichte der Geoponika* (Vienna, 1993).
Koziol, Geoffrey, *The politics of memory and identity in Carolingian royal diplomas: The West Frankish Kingdom (840–987)*, Utrecht studies in medieval literacy 19 (Turnhout, 2012).
Krautheimer, Richard, Corbett, Spencer, and Frankl, Volfango, *Corpus basilicarum christianorum Romae*, Monumenti di antichita cristiana (Rome, 1967).
Kreiner, Jamie, *Legions of pigs* (New Haven, 2020).
Kreiner, Jamie, 'Pigs in the flesh and fisc: An early medieval ecology', *Past & Present* 236.1 (2017), 3–42.
Kreutz, Barbara M., *Before the Normans. Southern Italy in the ninth and tenth centuries* (Philadelphia, 1991).
Kuchenbuch, Ludolf, 'Porcus donativus. Language use and gifting in seigniorial records between the eighth and the twelfth centuries', in Gadi Algazi, Valentin Groebner, and Bernhard Jussen (eds.), *Negotiating the gift: Premodern figurations of exchange* (Göttingen, 2003), pp. 193–246.
La Rocca, Cristina, 'An arena of abuses and competing powers. Rome in Cassiodorius's *Variae*', in Ross Balzaretti, Julia Barrow, and Patricia Skinner (eds.), *Italy and early medieval Europe. Papers for Chris Wickham*, Past and Present Book Series (Oxford, 2018), pp. 201–12.
La Rocca, Cristina, 'Le aristocrazie e le loro chiese tra VIII e IX secolo in Italia settentrionale', in Renata Salvarani, Giancarlo Andenna, and Gian Pietro Brogiolo (eds.), *Alle origini del romanico. Monasteri, edifici religiosi, committenza tra storia e archeologia (Italia settentrionale, secoli 9.-10.): atti delle 3. giornate di studi medievali Castiglione delle Stiviere, 25–27 settembre 2003*, Studi e documenti 3 (Brescia, 2005), pp. 57–70.
La Rocca [Hudson], Cristina, 'Città altomedievali, storia e archeologia', *Studi storici* 27.3 (1986), 725–35.
La Rocca [Hudson], Cristina, '"Dark ages" a Verona: edilizia privata, aree aperte e strutture pubbliche in una città dell'Italia settentrionale', *Archeologia Medievale* 13 (1986), 31–78.

La Rocca, Cristina, 'Donare, distribuire, spezzare: Pratiche di conservazione della memoria e dello status in Italia tra VIII e IX secolo', in Gian Pietro Brogiolo and Gisella Wataghin Cantino (eds.), *7° Seminario sul tardo antico e l'alto Medioevo in Italia Centro Settentrionale: Gardone Riviera 24–26 ottobre 1996*, Documenti di archeologia 13 (Mantua, 1998), pp. 77–87.

La Rocca, Cristina, *Pacifico di Verona: il passato carolingio nella costruzione della memoria urbana*, Nuovi studi storici 31 (Rome, 1995).

La Rocca, Cristina, 'Perceptions of an early medieval urban landscape', in Peter Linehan and Janet L. Nelson (eds.), *The medieval world* (New York, 2001), pp. 416–31.

La Rocca, Cristina, 'Public buildings and urban change in northern Italy in the early mediaeval period', in John Rich (ed.), *The city in Late Antiquity*, Leicester-Nottingham Studies in Ancient Society 3 (London, 1992), pp. 161–80.

La Rocca, Cristina, 'La reine et ses liens avec les monastères dans la royaume d'Italia', in Régine Le Jan (ed.), *La royauté et les élites dans l'Europe carolingienne: Début 9e siècle aux environs de 920*, Histoire et littérature du Septentrion (IRHiS) 17 (Lille, 1998), pp. 269–84.

La Rocca, Cristina, 'Lo spazio urbano tra VI e VIII secolo', in *Uomo e spazio nell'alto Medioevo*, Settimane di studio del Centro italiano di studi sull'alto medioevo (Spoleto, 2003), vol. 2, pp. 397–436.

La Rocca, Cristina, and Majocchi, Piero (eds.), *Urban identities in northern Italy, 800–1100 ca*, Seminari internazionali del Centro interuniversitario per la storia e l'archeologia dell'alto medioevo 5 (Turnhout, 2015).

Labuhn, Inga, Finné, Martin, Izdebski, Adam, Roberts, Neil, and Woodbridge, Jessie, 'Climatic changes and their impacts in the Mediterranean during the first Millennium AD', in Adam Izdebski and Michael Mulryan (eds.), *Environment and society in the long late antiquity* Late antique archaeology 11–12 (Leiden, 2019), pp. 247–70.

Lagazzi, Luciano, *Segni sulla terra: determinazione dei confini e percezione dello spazio nell'alto Medioevo* (Bologna, 1991).

Lancelotti, Carla, and Madella, Marco, 'The "invisible" product: Developing markers for identifying dung in archaeological contexts', *Journal of Archaeological Science* 39 (2012), 953–63.

Lanciani, Rodolfo Amedeo, *Forma urbis Romae* (Rome, 1990).

Landgren, Lena, *Lauro, myrto et buxo frequentata: A study of the Roman garden through its plants* (Lund, 2004).

Larsen, Lillian, and Rubenson, Samuel, *Monastic education in late antiquity: The transformation of classical paideia* (Cambridge, 2018).

Laurent, Amélie, and Fondrillon, Mélanie, 'Mesurer la ville par l'évaluation et la caractérisation du sol urbain: l'exemple de Tours', *Revue archéologique du Centre de la France [En ligne]* 49 (2010).

Laurent, Marie-Aline, 'Organisation de l'espace et mobilasation des ressources', in Jean-Pierre Devroey, Laurent Feller, and Régine Le Jan (eds.), *Les élites et la richesse au haut moyen âge*, Collection haut moyen âge 10 (Turnhout).

Lawrence, Ray, and Wallace-Hadrill, Andrew (eds.), *Domestic space in the Roman world: Pompeii and beyond*, JRA Supplementary Series 22 (Portsmouth, RI, 1997).

Lawson, Laura, *City bountiful: A century of community gardening in America* (Berkeley, 2005).
Le Roy Ladurie, Emmanuel, *The peasants of Languedoc*, trans. John Day (Urbana, IL, 1980).
Leclercq, Jean, *The love of learning and the desire for God. A study of monastic culture* (New York, 1961).
Leclercq, Jean, *Otia monastica. Études sur le vocabulaire de la contemplation au moyen âge*, Studia anselmiana 51 (Rome, 1963).
Lenzi, Mauro, 'Forme e funzioni dei trasferimenti patrimoniali dei beni della Chiesa in area romana', in *Les transferts patrimoniaux en Europe occidentale, VIII-Xe siècle. Actes de la table ronde de Rome, 6, 7 et 8 mai 1999* (= MÉFR 111.2, pp. 487–987) (Rome, 1999), 771–859.
Leone, Nicola Giuliano, Mauro, Eliana, Quartarone, Carla, and Sessa, Ettore, 'Royal art in the Norman age. The sollazzi and the royal park', in Nicola Giuliano Leone, Eliana Mauro, Carla Quartarone, and Ettore Sessa (eds.), *Siculo-Norman art. Islamic culture in medieval Sicily* (Vienna, rev. ed. 2013), pp. 67–89.
Lepelley, Claude, 'Le patronat episcopal aux IVe et Ve siècles: Continuités et ruptures avec le patronat classique', in Éric Rebillard and Claire Sotinel (eds.), *L'évêque dans la cité du IVe au Ve siècle: image et autorité: actes de la table ronde organisée par l'Istituto patristico Augustinianum et l'École française de Rome (Rome, 1er et 2 décembre 1995)* Collection de l'École française de Rome (Rome, 1998), vol. 248, pp. 17–33.
Levison, Wilhelm, 'Das Formularbuch von Saint-Denis', *Neues Archiv* 41 (1919), 283–304.
Lexicon Topographicum Urbis Romae, ed. E. Margareta Steinby, 6 vols. (Rome, 1993–2000).
Lexicon Topographicum Urbis Romae, Suburbium, ed. Adriano La Regina, 5 vols. (Rome, 2001–8).
Leyser, Conrad, *Authority and asceticism from Augustine to Gregory the Great*, Oxford Historical Monographs (Oxford, 2000).
Leyser, Conrad, 'Shoring fragments against ruin? Eugippius and the sixth-century culture of the Florilegium', in Walter Pohl and Maximilian Diesenberger (eds.), *Eugippius und Severin: der Autor, der Text und der Heilige*, Denkschriften. Österreichische Akademie der Wissenschaften, Philosophisch-Historische Klasse 297 (Vienna, 2001), pp. 65–75.
Libertini, Giacinto (ed.), *Documenti del regio archivio napoletano: Volume introduttivo Seconda Edizione* (Regii Neapolitani Archivi Monumenta, 2011).
Librenti, Mauro, 'Ricognizione di superficie e insediamento medievale nella pianura emiliano romagnola. Alcune considerazioni', in Gian Pietro Brogiolo (ed.), *Secondo congresso nazionale di archeologia medievale: Musei civici, Chiesa di Santa Giulia, Brescia, 28 settembre-1 ottobre 2000* (Florence, 2000), pp. 170–4.
Ligt, Luuk de, *Fairs and markets in the Roman Empire: Economic and social aspects of periodic trade in a pre-industrial society*, Dutch monographs on ancient history and archaeology v. 11 (Amsterdam, 1993).
Lirer, Fabrizio, Sprovieri, Mario, Vallefuoco, Mattia, Ferraro, Luciana, Pelosi, Nicola, Giordano, Laura, and Capotondi, Lucilla, 'Planktonic

foraminifera as bio-indicators for monitoring the climatic changes that have occurred over the past 2000 years in the southeastern Tyrrhenian Sea', *Integrative Zoology* 9.4 (2014), 542–54.

Littlewood, Antony Robert, Maguire, Henry, and Wolschke-Bulmahn, Joachim, *Byzantine garden culture* (Washington, DC, 2002).

Ljungqvist, Frederik Charpentier, Seim, Andrea, Krusic, Paul, González-Rouco, Jesús, Werner, Johannes, Crook, Edward, Zorita, Eduardo, Luterbacher, Jürg, Xoplaki, Elena, Destouni, Georgia, García-Bustamanta, Elena, Melo Aguilar, Camilo, Seftigen, Kristina, Wang, Jianglin, Gagen, Mary, Esper, Jan, Solomina, Olga, Fleitmann, Dominik and Büntgen, Ulf, 'European warm-season temperature and hydroclimate since 850 CE', Environmental Research Letters 14 (2019).

Lo Cascio, Elio, 'Canon frumentarius, suarius, vinarius: stato e privati nell'approvvigionamento dell' Urbs', in William V. Harris and Javier Arce (eds.), *The transformations of Urbs Roma in late antiquity*, Journal of Roman Archaeology Supplementary Series 33 (University of Rome La Sapienza and at the American Academy in Rome, 1999), pp. 163–82.

Lo Cascio, Elio (ed.), *Mercati permanenti e mercati periodici nel mondo romano: atti degli Incontri capresi di storia dell'economia antica (Capri, 13–15 ottobre 1997)*, Incontri capresi di storia dell'economica, antica (Bari, 2000).

Lomas, Kathryn, 'Introduction', in Kathryn Lomas and Tim Cornell (eds.), *Urban society in Roman Italy* (London, 1995), pp. 1–7.

Lomas, Kathryn, 'Public building, urban renewal and euergetism in early imperial Italy', in Kathryn Lomas and Tim Cornell (eds.), *'Bread and circuses': Euergetism and municipal patronage in Roman Italy* (London, 2002), pp. 28–45.

Lomas, Kathryn, and Cornell, Tim (eds.), *'Bread and circuses': Euergetism and municipal patronage in Roman Italy* (London, 2002).

Lønstrup Dal Santo, Gitte, 'Rite of passage: On ceremonial movements and vicarious memories (fourth century CE)', in Ida Östenberg, Simon Malmberg, and Jonas Bjørnebye (eds.), *The moving city: Processions, passages and promenades in ancient Rome* (London, 2015), pp. 145–54.

Lopez, Robert Sabatino, *The commercial revolution of the Middle Ages, 950–1350* (Cambridge, 1976).

Lorenzi, Brunella, 'Parchi e verzieri nella Sicilia islamica e normana', in Luigi Zangheri, Brunella Lorenzi, and Nausikaa M. Rahmati (eds.), *Il giardino islamico*, Giardini e paesaggio 15 (Florence, 2006), pp. 208–89.

Loseby, Simon, 'Gregory's cities: Urban functions in sixth-century Gaul', in Ian Wood (ed.), *Franks and Alamanni in the Merovingian period: An ethnographic perspective* (Woodbridge, 1998), pp. 239–84.

Loud, Graham A., 'Introduction', in Prescott N. Dunbar and G. A. Loud (eds.), *The history of the Normans by Amatus of Montecassino translated by Prescott N. Dunbar and Graham A. Loud* (Woodbridge, 2004), pp. 1–38.

Lugli, Giuseppe, 'Hortus', in Ettore De Ruggiero (ed.), *Dizionario epigrafico di antichità romane* (Rome, 1962), vol. 3, pp. 1027–44.

MacCormack, Sabine, 'Sin, citizenship, and the salvation of souls: The impact of Christian priorities on late-Roman and post-Roman Society', *Comparative Studies in Society and History* 39.4 (1997), 644–73.

Machado, Carlos, 'The aristocratic domus of late antique Rome: Public and private', in Giovanna Bianchi, Tiziana Lazzari, and Cristina La Rocca (eds.), *Spazio pubblico e spazio privato tra storia e archeologia (secoli VI-XI)* (Turnhout, 2018), pp. 37–58.

Machado, Carlos, 'Aristocratic houses and the making of late antique Rome and Constantinople', in Lucy Grig and Gavin Kelly (eds.), *Two Romes: Rome and Constantinople in late antiquity*, Oxford Studies in Late Antiquity (New York, 2012), pp. 136–58.

Machado, Carlos, 'Between memory and oblivion: The end of the Roman domus', in Ralf Behrwald and Christian Witschel (eds.), *Rom in der Spätantike: Historische Erinnerung im städtischen Raum*, Heidelberger althistorische Beiträge und epigraphische Studien 51 (Stuttgart, 2012), pp. 111–38.

Machado, Carlos, *Urban space and aristocratic power in late Antique Rome AD 270–535* (Oxford, 2019).

MacKinney, Loren C., 'Medical ethics and etiquette in the early Middle Ages: The persistence of Hippocratic ideals', *Bulletin of the History of Medicine* 26.1 (1952), 1–31.

Macphail, Richard I., 'Dark Earth and insights into changing land use of urban areas', in Gavin Speed and Denis Sami (eds.), *Debating urbanism within and beyond the walls AD 300–700. Proceedings of a conference held at the University of Leicester, 15th November 2008*, Leicester Archaeology Monograph 17 (Leicester, 2010), pp. 145–66.

Macphail, Richard I., 'A reply to Carter and Davidson's "An evaluation of the contribution of soil micromorphology to the study of ancient arable agriculture"', *Geoarchaeology* 13.6 (1998), 549–64.

Macphail, Richard I., 'The reworking of urban stratigraphy by human and natural processes', in A. R. Hall and H. K. Kenward (eds.), *Urban-rural connexions: perspectives from environmental archaeology*, Oxbow Monograph 47 (Oxford, 1994), pp. 13–43.

Macphail, Richard I., Galinié, Henri, and Verhaeghe, Frans, 'A future for Dark Earth?', *Antiquity* 77.296 (2003), 349–58.

Maguire, Henry, 'Gardens and parks in Constantinople', *Dumbarton Oaks Papers* 54 (2000), 251–64.

Mailloux, Anne, 'Modalités de constitution du patrimoine épiscopal de Lucques, VIIIe-Xe siècle', in *Les transferts patrimoniaux en Europe occidentale, VIII-Xe siècle. Actes de la table ronde de Rome, 6, 7 et 8 mai 1999* (=*MÉFR* 111.2, pp. 487–987), pp. 701–23.

Maire Vigueur, Jean-Claude, 'Révolution documentaire et révolution scripturaire: le cas de l'Italie médiévale', *Bibliothèque de l'École des chartes* 153 (1995), 177–85.

Manning, Sturt W., 'The Roman world and climate: Context, relevance of climate change, and some issues', in William V. Harris (ed.), *The ancient Mediterranean environment between science and history* (Leiden, 2013), pp. 103–70.

Marazzi, Federico, 'Cadavera urbium, nuove capitali e Roma aeterna: l'identità urbana in Italia fra crisi, rinascita e propaganda (secoli III–V)', in Jens-Uwe Krause and Christian Witschel (eds.), *Die Stadt in der Spätantike – Niedergand oder Wandel?: Akten des internationalen Kolloquiums in München am 30. und 31. Mai 2003*, Historia: Einzelschriften 190 (Stuttgart, 2006), pp. 33–65.

Marazzi, Federico, *I 'Patrimonia Sanctae Romanae Ecclesiae' nel Lazio (secoli IV–X)*. *Struttura amministrativa e prassi gestionali*, Nuovi studi storici 37 (Rome, 1998).

Marazzi, Federico, 'San Vincenzo al Volturno tra VIII e IX secolo: Il percorso della grande crescita. Una indagine comparativa con le altre grandi fondazioni benedettine italiane', in Federico Marazzi (ed.), *San Vincenzo al Volturno – Cultura, Istituzioni, economia* (Montecassino, 1996), pp. 41–92.

Marazzi, Federico, Olivieri, Donatina, and Stanco, Enrico Angelo, 'I ritmi e le stagioni di una città: dati preliminari dalle stratigrafie del Criptoportico romano di Alife (sec. II–XX)', in Giuliano Volpe and Pasquale Favia (eds.), *V congresso nazionale di archeologia medievale: Palazzo della Dogana, Salone de Tribunale (Foggia), Palazzo dei Celestini, Auditorium (Manfredonia), 30 settembre – 3 ottobre 2009* (Florence, 2009), pp. 204–9.

Margaritelli, Giulia, Vallefuoco, Mattia, Di Rita, Federico, Capotondi, Lucilla, Bellucci, Luca Giorgio, Insinga, Donatella, Petrosino, P., Bonomo, Sergio, Cacho, Isabel, Cascella, Antonio, Ferraro, Luciana, Florindo, Fabio, Lubritto, Carmine, Lurcock, Pontus Conrad, Magri, Donatella, Pelosi, Nicola, Rettori, Roberto, and Lirer, Fabrizio, 'Marine response to climate changes during the last five millennia in the central Mediterranean Sea', *Global and Planetary Change* 142 (2016), 53–72.

Markus, Robert A., *Gregory the Great and his world* (Cambridge, 1997).

Marlowe, Elizabeth, 'The multivalence of memory: The tetrarchs, the Senate, and the Vicennalia Monument in the Roman Forum', in Karl Galinsky and Kenneth Lapatin (eds.), *Cultural memories in the Roman Empire* (Los Angeles, CA, 2015), pp. 240–63.

Marrou, Henri Irénée, *Saint Augustin et la fin de la culture antique*. 4th rev. ed. (Paris, 1958).

Martin, Jean-Marie, Cuozzo, Enrico, Gasparri, Stefano, and Villani, Matteo (eds.), *Regesti dei documenti dell'Italia meridionale, 570–899*, Sources et documents d'histoire du Moyen Âge 5 (Rome, 2002).

Martin, Jean-Marie, 'L'espace cultivé', in *Uomo e spazio nell'alto Medioevo*, Settimane di studio del Centro italiano di studi sull'alto medioevo 50 (Spoleto, 2003), vol. 2, pp. 239–98.

Martin, René, 'Introduction', in *Traité d'agriculture*, Collection des universités de France 203, 398 (Paris, 1976–2003), vol. 1, pp. vii–lxvii.

Martyn, John R. C., 'Introduction', in *A translation of Abbot Leontios, Life of Saint Gregory, Bishop of Agrigento*, Texts and studies in religion 105 (Lewiston, 2004), pp. 7–118.

Martyn, John R. C., 'Introduction', in *The letters of Gregory the Great (Books 1–4)*, Mediaeval sources in translation 40 (Toronto, 2004), vol. 1, pp. 1–116.

Marzano, Annalisa, 'Roman gardens, military conquests, and elite self-representation', in Kathleen Coleman (ed.), *Le jardin dans l'antiquité*, Entretiens sur l'antiquité classique (LX) (Geneva, 2014), pp. 195–244.

Masseti, Marco, 'In the gardens of Norman Palermo, Sicily (twelfth century AD)', *Anthropozoologica* 44.2 (2009), 7–34.

Mazzini, Innocenzo, and Palmieri, Nicoletta, 'L'école médicale de Ravenne: Programmes et methods d'enseignement, langue, hommes', in

Philippe Mudry and Jackie Pigeaud (eds.), *Les écoles medicales à Rome* (Geneva, 1991), pp. 285–310.

McCabe, Anna, 'Imported materia medica 4th–12th centuries, and Byzantine pharmacology', in Marlia Mango (ed.), *Byzantine trade, 4th–12th centuries: the archaeology of local, regional and international exchange. Papers of the thirty-eighth Spring Symposium of Byzantine Studies, St John's College, University of Oxford, March 2004*, Publications of the Society for the Promotion of Byzantine Studies 14 (Farnham, 2009), pp. 273–92.

McClendon, Charles B., *The origins of medieval architecture: Building in Europe, A.D. 600–900* (New Haven, 2005).

McClintock, Nathan, 'Cultivation, capital, and contamination: Urban agriculture in Oakland, California' (PhD Thesis, University of California, Berkeley, 2011).

McCormick, Michael, *Origins of the European economy: Communications and commerce, A.D. 300–900* (Cambridge, 2001).

McCormick, Michael, 'What climate science, Ausonius, Nile floods, rye, and thatch tell us about the environmental history of the Roman Empire', in William V. Harris (ed.), *The ancient Mediterranean environment between science and history*. (Leiden, 2013), pp. 61–88.

McCormick, Michael, Büntgen, Ulf, Cane, Mark A., Cook, Edward R., Harper, Kyle, Huybers, Peter, Litt, Thomas, Manning, Sturt W., Mayewski, Paul Andrew, and More, Alexander F. M., 'Climate change during and after the Roman Empire: reconstructing the past from scientific and historical evidence', *Journal of Interdisciplinary History* 43.2 (2012), 169–220.

McGarry, M. G., 'The taboo resource: the use of human excreta in Chinese agriculture', *The Ecologist* 6.iv (1976), 150–4.

McKitterick, Rosamond, *Charlemagne: Formation of a European identity* (Cambridge, 2008).

McKitterick, Rosamond, *History and memory in the Carolingian world* (Cambridge, 2004).

McKitterick, Rosamond, 'The illusion of royal power in the Carolingian Annals', *The English Historical Review* 115.460 (2000), 1–20.

McKitterick, Rosamond, 'The written word and oral communication: Rome's legacy to the Franks', in Richard North and Tette Hofstra (eds.), *Latin culture and medieval Germanic Europe. Proceedings of the First Germania Latina Conference held at the University of Groningen, 26 May 1989* Mediaevalia Groningana 11 (Gronigen, 1992), pp. 89–112.

McLynn, Neil, 'Review of Sessa, The formation of papal authority', *Bryn Mawr Classical Review* 2013.02.18.

Medieval European coinage with a catalogue of coins in the Fitzwilliam Museum, Vol. 1: The early Middle Ages (5th–10th centuries), eds. P. Grierson, M. Blackburn (Cambridge, 1986).

Medieval European coinage with a catalogue of the coins in the Fitzwilliam Museum, Vol. 14: Italy (III) South Italy, Sicily, Sardinia, eds. P. Grierson, L. Travaini (Cambridge, 1998).

Mencacci, Paolo, Zecchini, Michelangelo, Ambrosini, Riccardo, and Riparbelli, Alberto, *Lucca romana* (Lucca, 1982).

Meneghini, Roberto, and Santangeli Valenzani, Riccardo, 'Fasi tarde di occupazione dell'Isolato con domus e balnea', in Mariarosaria Barbera and Rita Paris (eds.), *Antiche stanze: un quartiere di Roma imperiale nella zona di Termini: Museo nazionale romano Terme Diocleziano, Roma, dicembre 1996–giugno 1997* (Milan, 1996), pp. 172–7.

Meneghini, Roberto, and Santangeli-Valenzani, Riccardo, *Roma nell'altomedioevo: Topografia e urbanistica della città dal V al X secolo* (Rome, 2004).

Meneghini, Roberto, Santangeli Valenzani, Riccardo, and Bianchi, Elisabetta, *I Fori Imperiali: gli scavi del comune di Roma (1991–2007)* (Roma, 2007).

Mengozzi, Guido, *La città italiana nell'alto medio evo; il periodo langobardo-franco (2nd rev. ed. by Arrigo Solmi)*, 2nd rev. ed. (Florence, 1931).

Mercuri, Anna Maria, Bandini Mazzanti, M., Florenzano, A., Montecchi, M. C., and Rattighieri, E., 'Olea, Juglans and Castanea: The OJC group as pollen evidence of the development of human-induced environments in the Italian peninsula', *Quaternary International* 303 (2013), 24–42.

Meyvaert, Paul, 'The medieval monastic garden', in Elisabeth B. MacDougall (ed.), *Medieval monastic gardens*, Colloquium on the History of Landscape Architecture 9 (Washington, DC, 1986), pp. 23–54.

Millar, Fergus, 'Italy and the Roman Empire: Augustus to Constantine', *Phoenix* 40.3 1(1986), 295–318.

Miller, Maureen C., *The formation of a medieval church: Ecclesiastical change in Verona, 950–1150* (Ithaca, 1993).

Miller, Naomi Frances, and Gleason, Kathryn L., 'Fertilizer in the identification and analysis of cultivated soil', in Naomi Frances Miller and Kathryn L. Gleason (eds.), *The archaeology of garden and field* (Philadelphia, 1994), pp. 25–43.

Miquel, André, 'Ibn Ḥawḳal', in B. Lewis, V. L. Ménage, Ch. Pellat, and J. Schacht (eds.), *Encyclopedia of Islam Vol. 3, H–Iram* (Leiden, 1971), pp. 786–88.

Mitchell, John, 'The display of script and the uses of painting in Longobard Italy', *Testo e Immagine nell'alto Medioevo – Settimane di studio del Centro Italiano di Studi sull'alto Medioevo (XLI)* II (1993), 887–954.

Monaci, E., 'Per il tabularium ecclesiae S. Mariae in Via Lata', *Archivio della Società Romana di storia patria* 20.1–2 (1897), 489–90.

Monneret de Villard, Ugo, *Catalogo delle iscrizioni cristiane anteriori al secolo XI, Castello Sforzesco in Milano: le sue raccolte storiche e artistiche* (Milan, 1915).

Montanari, Massimo, *L'alimentazione contadina nell'alto Medioevo*, Nuovo Medioevo 11 (Naples, 1979).

Montanari, Massimo, *Food is culture*, trans. Albert Sonnenfeld (New York, 2006).

Montanari, Massimo, 'I prodotti e l'alimentazione', in Antonio Carile (ed.), *Storia di Ravenna, II/2: dall'età bizantina all'età ottoniana. Ecclesiologia, cultura e arte* (Venice, 1992), pp. 85–100.

Montanari, Massimo, 'Structures de production et systèmes alimentaires', in Jean-Louis Flandrin and Massimo Montanari (eds.), *Histoire de l'alimentation* (Paris, 1996), pp. 283–94.

Moormann, Eric, 'Giardini al piede del Vesuvio. Review article of W. Jashemski, *The Gardens of Pompeii*, II', *Journal of Roman Archaeology* 8 (1995), 391–8.

Morley, Neville, *Metropolis and hinterland* (Cambridge, 1996).

Morton, Lois Wright, Bitto, Ella Annette, Oakland, Mary Jane, and Sand, Mary, 'Accessing food resources: Rural and urban patterns of giving and getting food', *Agriculture and Human Values* 25.1 (2008), 107–19.

Morvillez, Eric, 'The garden in the *domus*', in Wilhelmina F. Jashemski, Kathryn L. Gleason, Kim J. Hartswick, and Amina-Aïcha Malek (eds.), *Gardens of the Roman Empire* (Cambridge, 2018), pp. 17–71.

Moscati, Laura, *Alle origini del comune romano*, Quaderni di Clio 1 (Rome, 1980).

Mouton, Jean-Michel, Sourdel, Dominique, and Sourdel-Thomine, Janine, *Propriétés rurales et urbaines à Damas au Moyen Âge: un corpus de 73 documents juridiques entre 310/922 et 669/1271*, Documents relatifs à l'histoire des croisades 23 (Paris, 2018).

Murphy, Charlene, Thompson, Gill, and Fuller, Dorian Q., 'Roman food refuse: Urban archaeobotany in Pompeii, Regio VI, Insula 1', *Vegetation History and Archaeobotany* 22.v (2013), 409–19.

Myers, K. Sara, 'Representations of gardens in Roman literature', in Wilhelmina F. Jashemski, Kathryn Gleason, Kim J. Hartswick, and Amina-Aïcha Malek (eds.), *Gardens of the Roman Empire* (Cambridge, 2018), pp. 258–77.

Natale, Alfio Rosario, 'Chartae saeculi X (901–28)', *Archivio storico lombardo* cxxiv–cxxv (1998–9), 405–86.

Nef, Annliese, 'Islamic Palermo and the Dār al Islām', in Annliese Nef (ed.), *A companion to medieval Palermo: The history of a Mediterranean city from 600 to 1500* (Leiden, 2013), pp. 39–59.

Neil, Bronwen, 'Imperial benefactions to the fifth-century Roman church', in Geoffrey Nathan and Lynda Garland (eds.), *Basileia: Essays on Imperium and culture in honour of EM and MJ Jeffreys* (Leiden, The Netherlands, 2011), pp. 55–66.

Nelson, Janet L., 'The role of the gift in early medieval diplomatic relations', in *Le relazioni internazionali nell'alto medioevo*, Settimane di studio del Centro italiano di studi sull'alto medioevo 58 (Spoleto, 2011), pp. 225–53.

Nelson, Janet L., 'The wary widow', in Wendy Davies and Paul Fouracre (eds.), *Property and power in the early Middle Ages* (Cambridge, 1995), pp. 82–113.

Nibby, A., and Gell, William, *Analisi storico-topografico-antiquaria della carta de' dintorni di Roma*, 2nd ed. (Rome, 1848).

Nicosia, Cristiano, *Geoarcheologia delle stratificazioni urbane post-classiche* (Rome, 2018).

Nicosia, Cristiano, and Devos Yannick, 'Urban Dark Earth', in *Encyclopedia of global archaeology*, ed. C. Smith (New York, 2014), vol. XI, pp. 7532–40.

Nicosia, Cristiano, Devos, Yannick, and Borderie, Quentin, 'The contribution of geosciences to the study of European Dark Earths: A review', *Post-classical Archaeologies* 3 (2013), 145–70.

Nicosia, Cristiano, Langohr, Roger, Mees, Florias, Arnoldus-Huyzendveld, Antonia, Bruttini, Jacopo, and Cantini, Federico, 'Medieval Dark Earth in an active alluvial setting from the Uffizi Gallery complex in Florence, Italy', *Geoarchaeology* 27.2 (2012), 105–22.

Noble, Thomas F. X., *The republic of St. Peter: The birth of the Papal State, 680–825*, The Middle Ages (Philadelphia, 1984).

Nora, Pierre, Ageron, Charles-Robert, Beauvne, Collete, and Agulhon, Maurice, *Les lieux de mémoire*, 3 vols. (Paris, 1984–92).

Norberg, Dag Ludvig, 'Praefatio', in *S. Gregorii Magni Opera: Registrum Epistularum, Libri I–VII*, ed. Dag Ludvig Norberg, Corpus Christianorum, Series Latina 140A (Turnholt, 1982), vol. 1, pp. v–xii.

Noreña, Carlos F., *Imperial ideals in the Roman West: Representation, circulation, power* (New York, 2016).

Norman, Philip, and Readers, Francis W., 'Further discoveries relating to Roman London, 1906–12', *Archaeologia* 63 (1912), 257–344.

Norrie, James, 'Land and cult: Society and Radical Religion in the Diocese of Milan c. 990–1130' (PhD Thesis, University of Oxford, 2017).

Norrie, James, *Urban change and radical religion: Medieval Milan, c.990–1140* (Oxford, forthcoming).

Nutton, Vivian, *Ancient medicine*, 2nd rev. ed. (New York, 2013).

Nutton, Vivian, 'Early-medieval medicine and natural science', in David C. Lindberg and Michael H. Shank (eds.), *Medieval Science*, The Cambridge History of Science 2 (Cambridge, 2013), pp. 323–40.

Opsomer-Halleux, Carmélia, 'The medieval garden and its role in medicine', in Elisabeth B. MacDougall (ed.), *Medieval gardens*, Dumbarton Oaks Colloquium on the History of Landscape Architecture 9 (Washington, DC, 1986), pp. 93–113.

Ortalli, Jacopo, 'Formazione e trasformazioni dell'architettura domestica: una casistica cispadana', in Monika Verzár-Bass (ed.), *Abitare in Cisalpina L'edilizia privata nelle città e nel territorio in età romana: Atti della XXXI settimana di studi aquileiesi, 23–26 maggio 2000*, Antichità altoadriatiche 49.1 (Trieste, 2001), pp. 25–58.

Ortalli, Jacopo, 'L'edilizia abitativa', in Antonio Carile (ed.), *Storia di Ravenna, II/ 2: dall'età bizantina all'età ottoniana. Ecclesiologia, cultura e arte* (Venice, 1992), pp. 167–92.

Pagán, Victoria Emma, *Rome and the literature of gardens* (London, 2007).

Palmer, R. E. A., 'Customs on market goods imported into the city of Rome', in John H. D'Arms and E. C. Kopff (eds.), *The seaborne commerce of ancient Rome: Studies in archaeology and history*, Memoirs of the American Academy in Rome 36 (Rome, 1980), pp. 217–33.

Papi, Emanuele (ed.), *Supplying Rome and the empire: The proceedings of an international seminar held at Siena-Certosa di Pontignano on May 2–4, 2004, on Rome, the provinces, production and distribution*, Journal of Roman archaeology. Supplementary series 69 (Portsmouth, 2007).

Paris, Harry, Jules, Janick, and Daunay, Marie Christine, 'Occidental diffusion of cucumber (Cucumis sativus) 500–1300 CE: two routes to Europe,' *Annals of botany* 109.1, 117–26.

Park, Marion Edwards, and Maxey, Mima, *Two studies on the Roman lower classes* (New York, 1975).

Parkins, Helen, 'The "consumer city" domesticated? The Roman city in élite economic strategies', in Helen Parkins (ed.), *Roman urbanism: Beyond the consumer city* (London, 1997), pp. 83–111.

Patterson, Helen, Di Giuseppe, Helga, and Witcher, Rob, 'Three south Etrurian "crises": First results of the Tiber Valley Project', *Papers of the British School at Rome* 72 (2004), 1–36.

Peduto, Paolo, 'Salerno nell'alto Medioevo', in Andrea Augenti (ed.), *Le città italiane fra la tarda Antichità e l'alto Medioevo, Atti del convegno (Ravenna, 26–28 febbraio 2004)*, (Florence, 2006), pp. 335–44.

Peña-Chocarro, Leonora, and Pérez-Jordà, Guillem, 'Garden plants in medieval Iberia: the archaeobotanical evidence', *Early Medieval Europe* 27 (2019), 374–93.

Perring, D., 'Lo scavo di via Tommaso Grossi', in Donatella Caporusso (ed.), *Scavi MM3: Ricerche di archeologia urbana a Milano durante la costruzione della linea 3 della metropolitana 1982–1990. 1. Gli Scavi* (Milan, 1991), pp. 212–28.

Petracco-Sicardi, Giulia, 'La casa rurale nell'alto medioevo, come insediamento e come costruzione', *Archeologia Medievale* 7.7 (1980), 363–5.

Petrucci, Armando, 'Alfabetismo ed educazione grafica degli scribi altomedievali (secc. VII–X)', in Peter Ganz (ed.), *The role of the book in medieval culture. Proceedings of the Oxford International Symposium 26 Sept.–1 Oct. 1982*, Bibliologia 3–4 (Turnhout, 1986), pp. 109–32.

Petrucci, Armando, *Writers and readers in medieval Italy: Studies in the history of written culture*, trans. Charles M. Radding (New Haven, 1995).

Phillips, C. Robert, 'Rosalia', in Hubert Cancik and Helmuth Schneider (eds.), *Brill's New Pauly* (Leiden, 2001), vol. 12, pp. 734–5.

Pickering, Andrew, 'Material culture and the dance of agency', in Dan Hicks and Mary C. Beaudry (eds.), *The Oxford handbook of material culture studies* (Oxford, 2012), pp. 191–208.

Pilsworth, Clare, 'Beyond the medical text: Health and illness in early medieval Italian sources', *Social History of Medicine* 24.1 (2011), 26–40.

Pilsworth, Clare, 'Could you just sign this for me John? Doctors, charters and occupational identity in early medieval northern and central Italy', *Early Medieval Europe* 17.4 (2009), 363–88.

Pilsworth, Clare, *Healthcare in early medieval Northern Italy: More to life than leeches*, Studies in the Early Middle Ages 26 (Turnhout, 2015).

Platner, Samuel Ball, *A topographical dictionary of ancient Rome* (Cambridge, [1929] 2002).

Pohl, Walter, 'Frontiers in Lombard Italy: The Laws of Ratchis and Aistulf', in Walter Pohl, Helmut Reimitz, and Ian Wood (eds.), *The transformation of frontiers. From late antiquity to the Carolingians*, Transformations of the Roman World 10 (Leiden, 2000), pp. 117–41.

Polanyi, Karl, Arensberg, Conrad M., and Pearson, Harry W., *Trade and market in the early empires: economies in history and theory* (Glencoe, 1957).

Pollard, Elizabeth Ann, 'Pliny's *Natural history* and the Flavian Templum Pacis: Botanical imperialism in first-century C.E. Rome', *Journal of World History* 20.3 (2009), 309–38.

Pomaro, Gabriella, 'Prolegomeni alla "classe carolina"', *Studi medievali Ser. 3* 25.1 (1984), 465–92.
Potter, Jennifer, *The rose: A true history* (London, 2010).
Pradines, Stéphane, and Khan, Sher Rahmat, 'Fāṭimid gardens: Archaeological and historical perspectives', *Bulletin of the School of Oriental and African Studies* 79.3 (2016), 473–502.
Prigent, Vivien, '*Le mythe du mancus et les origines de l'économie européenne*', *Revue Numismatique* (2014), 701–28.
Purcell, Nicholas, 'Dialectical gardening', *Journal of Roman Archaeology* 14.ii (2001), 546–56.
Purcell, Nicholas, 'The *horti* of Rome and the landscape of property', in Anna Leone, Domenico Palombi, and Susan Walker (eds.), *Res bene gestae: ricerche di storia urbana su Roma antica in onore di Eva Margareta Steinby, Festschrift M. Steinby* (Rome, 2007), pp. 361–78.
Purcell, Nicholas, 'The Roman garden as a domestic building', in I. M. Barton (ed.), *Roman domestic buildings*, Exeter studies in history (Exeter, 1996), pp. 121–51.
Purcell, Nicholas, 'The Roman villa and the landscape of production', in Kathryn Lomas and Tim Cornell (eds.), *Urban society in Roman Italy* (London, 1995), pp. 151–79.
Purcell, Nicholas, 'Tomb and suburb', in Henner Von Hesberg and Paul Zanker (eds.), *Römische Gräberstrassen: Selbstdarstellung, Status, Standard: Kolloquium in München vom 28. bis 30. Oktober 1985*, Abhandlungen (Bayerische Akademie der Wissenschaften. Philosophisch-Historische Klasse) 96 (Munich, 1987), pp. 25–42.
Purcell, Nicholas, 'Town in country and country in town', in Elisabeth B. MacDougall (ed.), *Ancient Roman villa gardens* (Washington, DC, 1987), pp. 185–203.
Quirós Castillo, Juan Antonio, *Modi di costruire a Lucca nell'altomedioevo. Una lettura attraverso l'archeologia dell'architettura* (Florence, 2002).
Rapone, Francesca, 'Il mercato nel Regno d'Italia (VIII- metà dell' XI secolo): Archeologia e storia' (PhD Thesis, Ca' Foscari/Ecole des Hautes Etudes en Sciences Sociales, Paris, 2011).
Rauty, Natale, *Storia di Pistoia I: dall'alto medioevo all'età precomunale 406–1105* (Florence, 1985).
Rea, Rosella, 'Archeologia nel suburbio di Roma. La stazione S. Giovanni della Linea C della Metropolitana', in Antonio Ferrandes and Giacomo Pardini (eds.), *Le regole del gioco. Tracce archeologi racconti. Studi in onore di Clementina Panella* (Rome, 2016), pp. 25–42.
Rea, Rosella, and Saviane, Nicoletta, 'At the foot of the Lateran Hill' [forthcoming].
Rebillard, Éric, and Sotinel, Claire (eds.), *L'évêque dans la cité du IVe au Ve siècle: image et autorité: actes de la table ronde organisée par l'Istituto patristico Augustinianum et l'École française de Rome (Rome, 1er et 2 décembre 1995)* Collection de l'École française de Rome 248 (Rome, 1998).
Reynolds, L. D., and Marshall, Peter K., *Texts and transmission: A survey of the Latin classics* (Oxford, 1983).

Richardson, Jane, Thompson, Gill, and Genovese, Angelo, 'New directions in economic and environmental research at Pompeii', in Sara E. Bon and Rick Jones (eds.), *Sequence and space in Pompeii*, Oxbow monograph 77 (Oxford, 1997), pp. 88–101.

Rickman, Geoffrey, *The corn supply of ancient Rome* (Oxford, 1980).

Riddle, John M., 'The introduction and use of eastern drugs in the early Middle Ages', *Sudhoffs Archiv Für Geschichte Der Medizin Und Der Naturwissenschaften* 49.2 (1965), 185–98.

Rio, Alice, *Legal practice and the written word in the early Middle Ages: Frankish formulae, c. 500–1000*, Cambridge studies in medieval life and thought: Fourth series (Cambridge, 2009).

Rio, Alice, *Slavery after Rome, 500–1100*, 1st ed. (Oxford, 2017).

Rizzo, S., 'Indagini nei Fori Imperiali: Oroidrografia, foro di Cesare, foro di Augusto, templum Pacis', *Mitteilungen des Deutschen Archäologischen Instituts, Römische Abteilung* 1002 (2001), 215–44.

Robinson, Gertrude, *History and cartulary of the Greek monastery of St. Elias and St. Anastasius of Carbone*, Orientalia Christiana XI.5; XV.2, XIX.1, 3 vols. (Rome, 1928–30).

Roch, Martin, 'Inenarrabiles odores. Récits et contextes des "odeurs de sainteté"(V-IXe siècles)', in Marie-Françoise Alamichel and Robert Braid (eds.), *Texte et contexte: littérature et histoire de l'Europe médiévale: [actes du colloque, Université Paris-Est Marne-la-Vallée, 23–24 octobre 2009]* (Paris, 2011), pp. 47–72.

Röckelein, Hedwig, *Reliquientranslationen nach Sachsen im 9. Jahrhundert: über Kommunikation, Mobilität und Öffentlichkeit im Frühmittelalter*, Beihefte zu Francia (Stuttgart, 2002).

Rodgers, Robert H., 'The Moore Palladius', *Transactions of the Cambridge Bibliographical Society* 5.3 (1971), 203–16.

Rogers, Adam, *Late Roman towns in Britain: Rethinking change and decline* (Cambridge, 2011).

Rogers, Robert, 'Κηποποΐα: Garden making and garden culture in the Geoponika', in Antony Littlewood, Henry Maguire, and Joachim Wolschke-Bulmahn (eds.), *Byzantine garden culture* (Washington, DC, 2002), pp. 159–75.

Romano, Dennis, *Markets and marketplaces in medieval Italy, c.1100 to c.1440* (New Haven, 2015).

Rosenwein, Barbara H., 'The family politics of Berengar I, King of Italy (888–924)', *Speculum* 71.2 (1996), 247–89.

Rosenwein, Barbara H., 'Friends and family, politics and privilege in the kingship of Berengar I', in Samuel K. Cohn and Steven A. Epstein (eds.), *Portraits of medieval and Renaissance living: Essays in honor of David Herlihy* (Ann Arbor, 1996), pp. 91–106.

Rosenwein, Barbara H., *Negotiating space: Power, restraint, and privileges of immunity in early medieval Europe* (Ithaca, NY, 1999).

Rosenwein, Barbara H., *To be the neighbor of St Peter: The social meaning of Cluny's property, 909–1049* (Ithaca, NY, 1989).

Rossini, Egidio, 'Documenti per un nuovo codice diplomatico veronese (dai fondi di S. Giorgio in Braida e di S. Pietro in Castello (803–994)', *Atti dell'Accademia di Agricoltura Scienze e Lettere di Verona* 18 (1966-7), 1–72.

Rotili, Mario, 'Architettura e scultura dell alto medioevo a Benevento', in *Corso di Cultura sull'Arte Ravennate e Bizantina* (Ravenna, 1967), pp. 293–307.

Rottoli, Mauro, 'Reflections on early medieval resources in northern Italy: The archaeobotanical and archaeozoological data', *Quaternary International* 346 (2014), 20–7.

Rovelli, Alessia, 'Addenda and corrigenda', in *Coins and coin use in medieval Italy* (Farnham, 2012), pp. 1–8.

Rovelli, Alessia, 'Circolazione monetaria e formulari notarili nell'Italia altomedievale', *Bullettino dell'Istituto storico italiano per il medio evo* 98 (1992), 109–44.

Rovelli, Alessia, 'Introduction', in *Coins and coin use in medieval Italy* (Farnham, 2012), pp. ix–xiii.

Rovelli, Alessia, 'La moneta nella documentazione altomedievale di Roma e del Lazio', in Paolo Delogu and Lidia Paroli (eds.), *La storia economica di Roma nell'alto Medioevo alla luce dei recenti scavi archeologici (Roma, 2–3 aprile 1992)* (Florence, 1993), pp. 333–52.

Rovelli, Alessia, 'Monete, tessere e gettoni', in Lucia Saguì and Lidia Paroli (eds.), *Archeologia urbana a Roma: il progetto della Crypta Balbi: 5* (Florence, 1982), pp. 169–94.

Rovelli, Alessia, 'Money and coinage in the Middle Ages', in Rory Naismith (ed.), *From the fall of Rome to Charlemagne (c.400–800)* (Leiden, 2019), pp. 63–92.

Rovelli, Alessia, 'Some considerations on the coinage of Lombard and Carolingian Italy', in Inge Lyse Hansen and Chris Wickham (eds.), *The long eighth century. Production, distribution and demand*, Transformation of the Roman world 11 (Leiden, 2000), pp. 195–224.

Rovelli, Alessia, 'I tesori monetali', in Sauro Gelichi and Cristina La Rocca (eds.), *Tesori. Forme e uso della ricchezza nell'alto medioevo (secoli V-XI)* (Rome, 2004), pp. 241–56.

Ruggles, D. Fairchild, *Islamic gardens and landscapes* (Philadelphia, 2008).

Ruyt, Claire de, *Macellum: marché alimentaire des Romains*, Publications d'histoire de l'art et d'archéologie de l'Université catholique de Louvain 35 (Louvain-La-Neuve, 1983).

Sadori, Laura, and Susanna, Francesca, 'Hints of economic change during the late Roman empire period in central Italy: a study of charred plant remains from "La Fontanaccia," near Rome', *Vegetation History and Archaeobotany* 14.4 (2005), 386–93.

Sadori, Laura, Giraudi, Carlo, Masi, Alessia, Magny, Michel, Ortu, Elena, Zanchetta, Giovanni, and Izdebski, Adam, 'Climate, environment and society in southern Italy during the last 2000 years. A review of the environmental, historical and archaeological evidence', *Quaternary Science Reviews* 136 (2016), 173–88.

Saguì, Lucia, and Rovelli, Alessia, 'Residualità, non residualità, continuità di circolazione. Alcuni esempi dalla Crypta Balbi', in Federico Guidobaldi, Carlo Pavolini, and Philippe Pergola (eds.), *I materiali residui nello scavo archeologico* (Rome, 1998), pp. 173–95.

Saller, Richard P., *Personal patronage under the early empire* (New York, NY, 1982).
Salzman, Michele, 'From a Classical to a Christian city: Civic euergetism and charity in late antique Rome', *Studies in Late Antiquity* 1.1 (2017), 65–85.
Salzman, Michele Renee, *On Roman time: The codex-calendar of 354 and the rhythms of urban life in late antiquity*, Transformation of the classical heritage 17 (Berkeley, 1990).
Santangeli Valenzani, Riccardo, 'Abitare a Roma nell'alto medioevo', in Lidia Paroli and Laura Vendittelli (eds.), *Roma dall'Antichità al Medioevo. II: Contesti tardo antichi e altomedievali* (Milan, 2004), pp. 41–59.
Santangeli Valenzani, Riccardo, *Edilizia residenziale in Italia nell'altomedioevo*, Studi superiori (Rome, 2011).
Santangeli Valenzani, Riccardo, 'I fori imperiali nel medioevo', *Römische Mitteilungen* 108 (2001), 269–83.
Santangeli Valenzani, Riccardo, 'Pellegrini, senatori e papi. Gli xenodochia a Roma tra V e IX secolo', *Rivista dell' istituto nazionale d'archeologia e storia dell'arte*, s. iii 19–20 (1995–1996), 203–26.
Santangeli Valenzani, Riccardo, 'Residential building in early medieval Rome', in Julia M. H. Smith (ed.), *Early medieval Rome and the Christian West. Essays in honour of Donald Bullough* (Leiden, 2000), pp. 101–12.
Santangeli Valenzani, Riccardo, 'Vecchie e nuove forme di insediamento nel territorio', in Philippe Pergola, Riccardo Santangeli Valenzani, and Rita Volpe (eds.), *Suburbium: il suburbio di Roma dalla crisi del sistema delle ville a Gregorio Magno* (Rome, 2003), pp. 607–18.
Sarris, Peter, 'Introduction: Aristocrats, peasants and the transformation of rural society, c.400–800', *Journal of Agrarian Change* 9.1 (2009), 3–22.
Scarborough, John, 'The opium poppy in Hellenistic and Roman medicine', in Mikulas Teich and Roy Porter (eds.), *Drugs and narcotics in history* (Cambridge, 1995), pp. 4–23.
Scheidel, Walter (ed.), *The Cambridge companion to the Roman economy*, Cambridge companions to the ancient world (Cambridge, 2012).
Schmelzkopf, Karen, 'Urban community gardens as contested space', *Geographical Review – New York* 85 (1995), 364–81.
Scholz, Bernhard Walther, and Rogers, Barbara, *Carolingian chronicles: Royal Frankish annals and Nithard's histories*, Ann Arbor Paperbacks (Ann Arbor, 2000).
Schukoske, Jane, 'Community development through gardening: State and local policies transforming urban open space', *NYU Journal of Legislation and Public Policy* 3 (1999), 351–92.
Schwarz, Ulrich, 'Regesta amalfitana: die älteren Urkunden Amalfis in ihrer Überlieferung, Teil I', *Quellen und Forschungen aus italienischen Archiven und Bibliotheken* 58 (1978), 1–136.
Schwarzmaier, Hansmartin, *Lucca und das Reich bis zum Ende des 11. Jahrhunderts: Studien zur Sozialsthruktur einer Herzogstadt in der Toskana* (Tübingen, 1972).
Scobie, Alex, 'Slums, sanitation, and mortality in the Roman world', *Klio* 68.2 (1986), 399–433.

Semmler, Josef, 'Verdient um das karolingische Königtum und den werdenden Kirchenstaat: Fulrad von Saint-Denis', in Oliver Münsch and Thomas L. Zotz (eds.), *Scientia veritatis: Festschrift für Hubert Mordek zum 65. Geburtstag* (Ostfildern, 2004).

Serafini, Camilo, 'Appendice numismatica', in Bruno Maria Appolonj-Ghetti and Antonio Ferrua (eds.), *Esplorazioni sotto la confessione di S. Pietro in Vaticano eseguite negli anni 1940–49* (Vatican City, 1951), vol. 1, pp. 225–44 (II, 89–103).

Sessa, Kristina, *The formation of papal authority in late antique Italy: Roman bishops and the domestic sphere* (Cambridge, 2012).

Sessa, Kristina, 'The new environmental Fall of Rome: A methodological consideration', *Journal of Late Antiquity* 12.1 (2019), 211–55.

Settia, Aldo Angelo, 'Identification et ventilation des informations', in Ghislaine Noyé (ed.), *Castrum 2. Structures de l'habitat et occupation du sol dans le pays méditerranéens: les méthodes et l'apport de l'archeologie extensive (Actes de la rencontre organisée par l'École Française de Rome, Paris, 12–15 novembre 1984)* (Rome, 1988), pp. 263–6.

Settia, Aldo Angelo, 'Pavia carolingia e postcarolingia', in *Storia di Pavia, II, L'alto medioevo* (Pavia, 1987), pp. 69–158.

Settia, Aldo Angelo, '"Per foros Italie." Le aree extraurbane fra Alpi e Apennini', in *Mercati e mercanti nell'Alto Medioevo. L'area euroasiatica e l'area mediterranea*, Settimane di studio del Centro italiano di studi sull'alto medioevo 40 (Spoleto, 1993), pp. 187–237.

Shaw, Brent, 'Rural markets in North Africa and the political economy of the Roman Empire', *Antiquités africaines* 17 (1981), 37–83.

Sheldon, Harvey, 'The 1972–74 excavations: their contribution to Southwark's history', in Joanna Bird, Alan H. Graham, Harvey Sheldon, and Pat Townend (eds.), *Southwark excavations, 1972–1974*, Joint Publication of London & Middlesex Archaeological Society and Surrey Archaeological Society 1 (London, 1978), pp. 11–49.

Shepherd, Elizabeth J., Olivanti, Paola, DeLaine, Janet, Falzone, Stella, and Morard, Thomas, 'Giardini ostiensi', *Bullettino della Commissione Archeologica Comunale di Roma* 109 (2008), 69–98.

Siciliano, Aldo, 'Rinvenimenti monetali a Monte Sant'Angelo. Prime note', in Carlo Carletti and Giorgio Otranto (eds.), *Culto e insediamenti micaelici nell'Italia meridionale fra tarda antichita e medioevo* (Bari, 1994), pp. 261–85.

Sirks, Adriaan Johan Boudewijn, *Food for Rome: The legal structure of transportation and processing of supplies for imperial distributions in Rome and Constantinople* (Amsterdam, 1991).

Skinner, Patricia, *Medieval Amalfi and its diaspora, 800–1250* (Oxford, 2013).

Skinner, Patricia, 'Noble families in the duchy of Gaeta in the tenth century', *Papers of the British School at Rome* 60 (1992), 353–77.

Skinner, Patricia, 'Urban communities in Naples, 900–1050', *Papers of the British School at Rome* 62 (1994), 279–99.

Smith, Daniel, *The spade as mighty than the sword: the story of the Second World War 'dig for victory' campaign* (London, 2011).

Smith, Julia M. H., 'Old saints, new cults: Roman relics in Carolingian Francia', in Julia M. H. Smith (ed.), *Early medieval Rome and the Christian West: Essays in honour of David A Bullough*, The Medieval Mediterranean 28 (Leiden, 2000), pp. 317–39.

Smith, Julie Ann, *Ordering women's lives: Penitentials and nunnery rules in the early medieval West* (London, 2016).

Smith, R. R. R., and Ward-Perkins, Bryan, *The last statues of antiquity* (Oxford, 2016).

Smith, Rowland B. E., "Restored utility, Eternal City': Patronal imagery at Rome in the fourth century AD', in Kathryn Lomas and Tim Cornell (eds.), *'Bread and Circuses': Euergetism and municipal patronage in Roman Italy* (London, 2002), pp. 142–66.

Sommella, Paolo, and Giuliani, Cairoli Fulvio, *La pianta di Lucca romana*, Quaderni dell'Istituto di topografia antica della Università di Roma 7 (Rome, 1974).

Sommer, Robert, Learey, Fred, Summit, Joshua, and Tirrell, Matthew, 'Social benefits of resident involvement in tree planting: Comparison with developer-planted trees', *Journal of Arboriculture* 20 (1994), 323–8.

Sotinel, Claire, 'Le recrutement des évêques en Italie aux IVe et Ve siècles: essai d'enquête prosopographique', in *Vescovi e pastori in epoca Teodosiana: XXV Incontro di studiosi dell'antichità cristiana, Roma, 8–11 maggio 1996* (Rome, 1997), pp. 193–203.

Spencer, Diana, *Roman landscape: Culture and identity* (Cambridge, 2010).

Spufford, Peter, *Money and its use in medieval Europe* (New York, 1988).

Squatriti, Paolo, 'Il clima dei longobardi', in Gian Pietro Brogiolo, Federico Marazzi, and Caterina Giostra (eds.), *Longobardi: un popolo che cambia la storia* (Milan, 2017), pp. 150–7.

Squatriti, Paolo, 'The floods of 589 and climate change at the beginning of the Middle Ages: An Italian microhistory', *Speculum* 85.4 (2010), 799–826.

Squatriti, Paolo, *Landscape and change in early medieval Italy: Chestnuts, economy, and culture* (Cambridge, 2013).

Squatriti, Paolo, 'Rye's rise and Rome's fall: Agriculture and climate in Europe during late antiquity', in Adam Izdebski and Michael Mulryan (eds.), *Environment and society in the long late antiquity*, Late antique archaeology 11–12 (Leiden, 2019), pp. 342–51.

Squatriti, Paolo, 'Trees, nuts, and woods at the end of the first millennium: A case from the Amalfi coast', in Scott Bruce (ed.), *Ecologies and economies in medieval and early modern Europe: Studies in environmental history for Richard C. Hoffmann*, Brill's Series in the History of the Environment (Leiden, 2010), vol. 1, pp. 25–44.

Squatriti, Paolo, *Water and society in late antique and early medieval Italy A.D. 400–1000* (Cambridge; New York, 1998).

Squatriti, Paolo, 'Water, nature, and culture in early medieval Lucca', *Early Medieval Europe* 4.1 (1995), 21–40.

Staffa, Andrea R., 'Scavi nel centro storico di Pescara, I: primi elementi per una ricostruzione dell'assetto antico ed altomedievale dell'abitato di "Ostia Aterni-Aternum"', *Archeologia Medievale* 18 (1991), 201–368.

Stannard, Jerry, 'Marcellus of Bordeaux and the beginnings of medieval Materia Medica', *Pharmacy in History* 15 (1973), 47–53.
Stasolla, Francesca Romana, 'A proposito delle strutture assistenziali ecclesiastiche: gli xenodochi', *ASRSP* 121 (1998), 1–40.
Stoclet, Alain J., *Autour de Fulrad de Saint-Denis, (v. 710–784)* (Geneva, 1993).
Stoclet, Alain J., 'Les établissements francs à Rome au VIIIe siècle: "hospitale intus basilicam beati Petri, domus Nazarii, scola Francorum"', et palais de Charlemagne', in Claude Lepelley, Michel Sot, and Pierre Richél (eds.), *Haut Moyen-Âge: culture, éducation et société: études offertes à Pierre Riché* (La Garenne-Colombes, 1990), pp. 231–47.
Stoclet, Alain J., 'Fulrad de St. Denis (v. 710–84), abbé et archiprêtre de monastères "exempts"', *Le Moyen Age* 88 (1982), 205–35.
Stoffella, Marco, 'Aristocracy and rural churches in the territory of Lucca between Lombards and Carolingians: A case study', in Stefano Gasparri (ed.), *774, ipotesi su una transizione: Atti del seminario di Poggibonsi, 16–18 febbraio 2006* (Turnhout, 2008), pp. 289–311.
Story, Joanna, 'The Carolingians and the oratory of Saint Peter the Shepherd', in Rosamond McKitterick, John Osborne, Carol Richardson, and Joanna Story (eds.), *Old Saint Peter's, Rome* (Cambridge; New York, 2013), pp. 257–73.
Story, Joanna, 'Cathwulf, kingship, and the royal abbey of Saint-Denis', *Speculum* 74.1 (1999), 1–21.
Sudhoff, Karl, 'Eine Verteidigung der Heilkunde aus den Zeiten der "Mönchsmedizin"', *Archiv für Geschichte der Medizin* 7.4 (1913), 223–37.
Tabacco, Giovanni, 'L'allodialità del potere nel medioevo', *Studi Medievali 3a* XI (1970), 565–615. Reprinted in *Dai re ai signori. Forme di trasmissione del potere nel Medioevo* (2000), pp. 15–66.
Tabacco, Giovanni, 'La connessione fra potere e possesso nel Regno franco e nel Regno longobardo', in *I problemi dell'occidente nel secolo VIII*, Settimane di studio del Centro italiano di studi sull'alto medioevo 20 (Spoleto, 1973), pp. 133–68.
Tabacco, Giovanni, *The struggle for power in medieval Italy: Structures of political rule*, trans. Rosalind Brown Jensen, Cambridge Medieval textbooks (Cambridge, 1989).
Taviani-Carozzi, Huguette, *La principauté lombarde de Salerne (IXe-XIe siècle): Pouvoir et société en Italie lombarde méridionale*, Collection de l'École Française de Rome 152 (Rome, 1991).
Tengström, Emin, *Bread for the people: Studies of the corn-supply of Rome during the late empire* (Stockholm, 1974).
Thorpe, Harry, 'The homely allotment: From rural dole to urban amenity: A neglected aspect of urban land use', *Geography* 60.3 (1975), 169–83.
Toubert, Pierre, *Dalla terra ai castelli. Paesaggio, agricoltura e poteri nell'Italia medievale* (Turin, 1995).
Toubert, Pierre, *Les structures du Latium médiéval: le Latium méridional et la Sabine du IXe siècle à la fin du XIIe siècle*, Bibliothèque des écoles françaises d'Athènes et de Rome 221 (Rome, 1973).
Toubert, Pierre, 'La vita agraria nel medioevo', *Studi storici* 8.2 (1967), 359–65.

Touwaide, Alain, 'The legacy of classical antiquity in Byzantium and the West', in Peter Dendle and Alain Touwaide (eds.), *Health and healing from the medieval garden* (Woodbridge, 2007), pp. 15–28.

Touwaide, Alain, 'Quid pro quo: Revisiting the practice of substitution in ancient pharmacy', in Anne Van Arsdall and Timothy Graham (eds.), *Herbs and healers from the ancient Mediterranean through the medieval West. Essays in honor of John M. Riddle* (Surrey, 2012), pp. 19–44.

Toynbee, Jocelyn M. C., *Death and burial in the Roman world*, Johns Hopkins Paperback ed. (Baltimore, 1996).

Tracy, James (ed.), *City walls: The urban enceinte in global perspective*, Studies in comparative early modern history (Cambridge, 2000).

Traina, Giusto, 'Muratori e la "barbarie" palustre: fondamenti e fortuna di un topos', *L'ambiente storico* 8–9 (1987), 13–25.

Les transferts patrimoniaux en Europe occidentale, VIII–Xe siècle. Actes de la table ronde de Rome, 6, 7 et 8 mai 1999 (=MÉFR 111.2, pp. 487–987) (Rome, 1999).

Travaglini, Adriana 'Le monete', in F. D'Andria and David Whitehouse (eds.), *Excavations at Otranto, vol. II. The finds* (Lecce, 1992), pp. 241–80.

Troncarelli, Fabio, 'Una pietà più profonda. Scienza e medicina nella cultura monastica medievale italiana', in Gian Carlo Alessio (ed.), *Dall'eremo al cenobio : la civiltà monastica in Italia dalle origini all'età di Dante* (Milan, 1987), pp. 703–27.

Tronzo, William, *Petrarch's two gardens. Landscape and the image of movement*, Studies in Art & History (New York, 2014).

Tronzo, William, 'Zisa and Cuba in Palermo', in *Petrarch's two gardens. Landscape and the image of movement* (New York, 2014), pp. 25–67.

Tsing, Anna Lowenhaupt, *The mushroom at the end of the world: on the possibility of life in capitalist ruins* (Princeton, 2015).

Uggeri Patitucci, Stella, 'Scavi nella Ferrara medioevale. Il Castrum e la seconda cerchia', *Archeologia Medievale* 1 (1974), 111–47.

Uggeri Patitucci, Stella, 'Sviluppo topografico di Ferrara nell'alto medioevo', in *Cattedrale di Ferrara. Atti del Convegno Ferrara 11–13 maggio 1979* (Ferrara, 1982), pp. 24–58.

Ulrich, R. S., 'Natural versus urban scenes, some psychophysical effects', *Environment and Behavior* 13.5 (1981), 523–56.

Vaes, Jan, ''Nova construere sed amplius vetusta servare': la réutilisation chrétienne d'édifices antiques (en Italie)', in *Actes du XIe Congrès International d'Archéologie Chrétienne*, Collection de l'Ecole française de Rome (1989), vol. 123, pp. 299–321.

Valenti, Marco, 'La formazione dell'insediamento altomedievale in Toscana. Dallo spessore dei numeri alla construzione di modelli', in Gian Pietro Brogiolo, Alexandra Chavarria Arnau, and Marco Valenti (eds.), *Dopo la fine delle ville: le campagne dal VI al IX secolo: 11° Seminario sul tardo antico e làlto Medioevo, Gavi, 8–10 maggio 2004*, Documenti di archeologia 40 (Mantua, 2005), pp. 193–219.

Vázquez Buján, Manuel Enrique, 'Problemas generales de las antiguas traducciones médicas latinas', *Studi medievali Ser. 3* 25 (1984), 641–80.

Vázquez Buján, Manuel Enrique, 'Remarques sur la technique de traduction des anciennes versions latines d'Hippocrate', in Guy Sabbah (ed.), *Textes médicaux latins antiques*, Mémoires 5 (St-Étienne, 1984), pp. 153–63.

Vera, Domenico, 'Forme e funzioni della rendita fondiaria nella tarda antichità', in Andrea Giardina (ed.), *Società romana e impero tardoantico, 3, Le merci, gli insediamenti* (Bari, 1986), pp. 367–447.

Vera, Domenico, 'Strutture agrarie e strutture patrimoniali nella tarda antichità: l'aristocrazia romana fra agricoltura e commercio', *Opus* 2 (1983), 489–533.

Verhulst, Adriaan E., *The Carolingian economy*, Cambridge medieval textbooks (New York, 2002).

Verhulst, Adriaan E., 'Karolingische Agrarpolitik. Das Capitolare de villis und die Hungersnöte von 792/93 und 805/06,' *Zeitschrift für Agrargeschichte und Agrarsoziologie* 13 (1965), 175–89.

Vessey, Mark, 'Introduction', in Cassiodorus, *Institutions of divine and secular learning and on the soul*. Translated texts for historians 42 (Liverpool, 2004), pp. 3–101.

Veyne, Paul, *Le pain et le cirque: Sociologie historique d'un pluralisme politique* (Paris, 1995).

Violante, Cinzio, *La società milanese nell'età precomunale*, 2nd. rev. ed. (Bari, 1974).

Violante, Cinzio, and Fried, Johannes, *Il Secolo XI: una svolta?*, Annali dell'Istituto storico italo-germanico. Quaderno; 35.35 (Bologna, 1993).

Virlouvet, Catherine, *Tessera frumentaria: Les procédés de distribution du blé public à Rome à la fin de la République et au début de l'empire* (Rome, 1995).

Vismara, Giulio, 'I rapporti patrimonali tra coniugi nell'alto medioevo', in *Il matrimonio nella societa altomedievale*, Settimane di studio del Centro italiano di studi sull'alto medioevo 24 (Spoleto, 1977), pp. 633–91.

Vitolo, Giovanni, 'I prodotti della terra: orti e frutteti', in Giosuè Musca (ed.), *Terra e uomini nel Mezzogiorno normanno-svevo: Atti delle settime giornate normanno-sveve, Bari, 15–17 ottobre 1985*, Atti (Università di Bari: Centro di studi normanno-svevi) 7 (Bari, 1987).

Voigts, Linda E., 'Anglo-Saxon plant remedies and the Anglo-Saxons', *Isis* 70.2 (1979), 250–68.

von Stackelberg, Katharine T., *The Roman garden: Space, sense, and society*, Routledge monographs in Classical studies (New York, 2009).

von Thünen, Johann Heinrich, *Der isolierte Staat in Beziehung auf Landwirthschaft und Nationalökonomie: oder Untersuchung über den Einfluß, den die Getreidepreise, der Reichthum des Bodens und die Abgaben auf den Ackerbau ausüben* (Hamburg, 1826).

von Thünen, Johann Heinrich, *Der isolierte Staat in Beziehung auf Landwirthschaft und Nationalökonomie: oder Untersuchung über den Einfluß, den die Getreidepreise, der Reichthum des Bodens und die Abgaben auf den Ackerbau ausüben*, 2nd ed. rev. (Rostock, 1842).

von Thünen, Johann Heinrich, *Der isolierte Staat in Beziehung auf Landwirthschaft und Nationalökonomie*, 3 vols. (Berlin, 1875).

von Thünen, Johann Heinrich, *Von Thünen's 'Isolated state'*, trans. Carla M. Wartenberg (Oxford, 1966).

Wallace-Hadrill, Andrew (ed.), *Patronage in ancient society*, Leicester-Nottingham studies in ancient society (London, 1990).

Wallace-Hadrill, John Michael, *The long-haired kings*, Medieval Academy reprints for teaching 11 (Toronto, 1993).

Wallis, Faith, 'The experience of the book: Manuscripts, texts, and the role of epistemology in early medieval medicine', in David G. Bates (ed.), *Knowledge and the scholarly medical traditions* (Cambridge, 1995), pp. 105–43.

Ward-Perkins, Bryan, 'Continuitists, catastrophists, and the towns of post-Roman northern Italy', *Papers of the British School at Rome* 65 (1997), 157–76.

Ward-Perkins, Bryan, *From classical antiquity to the Middle Ages: Urban public building in northern and central Italy, AD 300–850* (Oxford, 1984).

Ward-Perkins, Bryan, 'Re-using the architectural legacy of the past: "entre idéologie et pragmatisme"', in Gian Pietro Brogiolo and Bryan Ward-Perkins (eds.), *Idea and ideal of the town between late Antiquity and the early Middle Ages*, Transformation of the Roman world 4 (Leiden, 1999), pp. 225–44.

Weisweiler, John, 'Making masters, making subjects: Imperial ideology and memory policy in the early Roman Empire and in the later Roman state', in Karl Galinsky and Kenneth Lapatin (eds.), *Cultural memories in the Roman Empire* (Los Angeles, CA, 2015), pp. 66–85.

Whittaker, C. R., 'Late Roman trade and traders', in Peter Garnsey, Keith Hopkins, and C. R. Whittaker (eds.), *Trade in the ancient economy* (London, 1983), pp. 163–80.

Wickersheimer, Ernest, *Les manuscrits latins de médecine du haut Moyen âge dans les bibliothèques de France* (Paris, 1966).

Wickham, Chris, 'Aristocratic power in eighth-century Lombard Italy', in Walter A. Goffart and Alexander C. Murray (eds.), *After Rome's fall: Narrators and sources of early medieval history, essays presented to Walter Goffart* (Toronto, 1998), pp. 153–70.

Wickham, Chris, 'Bounding the city', in *Città e campagna nei secoli altomedievali*, Settimane di studio del Centro italiano di studi sull'alto medioevo 54 (Spoleto, 2009), pp. 61–80.

Wickham, Chris, 'La città altomedievale: una nota sul dibattito in corso', *Archeologia Medievale* 15 (1988), 649–56.

Wickham, Chris, 'Conclusions', in Laurent Feller and Christopher Wickham (eds.), *Le marché de la terre au Moyen Âge*, Collection de l'École française de Rome 350 (Rome, 2005).

Wickham, Chris, '*The donkey and the boat: Rethinking Mediterranean economic expansion in the eleventh century*' (public lecture: Padua, Kalamazoo, Birmingham, publication forthcoming).

Wickham, Chris, *Early medieval Italy: Central power and local society 400–1000*, New Studies in Medieval History (London, 1981).

Wickham, Chris, 'Economic and social institutions in northern Tuscany in the 8th century', in Chris Wickham, Mauro Ronzani, Yoram Milo, and Amleto Spicciani (eds.), *Istituzioni ecclesiastiche della Toscana medioevale* (Lecce, 1980), pp. 7–34.

Wickham, Chris, *Framing the early Middle Ages: Europe and the Mediterranean 400–800* (Oxford, 2005).

Wickham, Chris, 'Land sales and land market in Tuscany in the eleventh century', in Chris Wickham (ed.), *Land and power: Studies in Italian and European social history, 400–1200* (London, 1994), pp. 257–74.

Wickham, Chris, *Medieval Rome: Stability and crisis of a city, 900–1150*, Oxford Studies in Medieval European History (Oxford, 2015).

Wickham, Chris, 'Monastic lands and monastic patrons', in Richard Hodges (ed.), *San Vincenzo al Volturno 2: the 1980–86 excavations, part II*, Archaeological monographs of the British School at Rome 9 (London, 1995).

Wickham, Chris, *The mountains and the city: The Tuscan Appennines in the early Middle Ages* (Oxford, 1988).

Wickham, Chris, 'Rural society and economy', in Cristina La Rocca (ed.), *Italy in the Early Middle Ages, 476–1000*, The short Oxford history of Italy (Oxford, 2002), pp. 118–43.

Wickham, Chris, 'La struttura della proprietà fondiaria nell'Agro Romano, 900–1150', *Archivio della Società Romana di storia patria* 132 (2009), 181–239.

Wickham, Chris, 'The Tivoli breve of 945,' in Alain Dierkens, Nicolas Schroeder, and Alexis Wilkin (eds.), *Penser la paysannerie médiévale, un défi impossible ?* (Paris, 2017) [online: http://books.openedition.org/psorbonne/27926]

Wickham, Chris, and Reuter, Tim, 'Introduction', in Wendy Davies and Paul Fouracre (eds.), *Property and power in the early Middle Ages* (Cambridge, 1995).

Wilson, Andrew, 'Villas, horticulture and irrigation infrastructure in the Tiber Valley', in Filippo Coarelli and Helen Patterson (eds.), *Mercator placidissimus: the Tiber Valley in antiquity: New research in the upper and middle river valley: Rome, 27–28 February 2004* (Rome, 2008), pp. 731–68.

Wolf, Kenneth Baxter, *Making history: The Normans and their historians in eleventh-century Italy* (Philadelphia, 1995).

Wood, Ian, 'Teutsind, Witlaic and the history of Merovingian precaria', in Wendy Davies and Paul Fouracre (eds.), *Property and power in the early Middle Ages* (Cambridge, 1995), pp. 31–52.

Xoplaki, Elena, Fleitmann, Dominik, Diaz, Henry, von Gunten, Lucien, and Kiefer, Thorsten (eds), 'Medieval climate anomaly', *PAGES News*, 19(1) (2011), 1–32.

Yule, Brian, 'The "dark earth" and late Roman London', *Antiquity* 64.244 (1990), 620–8.

Zanini, Enrico, *Le Italie bizantine: territorio, insediamenti ed economia nella provincia bizantina d'Italia (VI–VIII secolo)*, Munera: Studi storici sulla Tarda Antichità 10 (Bari, 1998).

Zupko, Ronald Edward, *Italian weights and measures from the Middle Ages to the nineteenth century*, Memoirs of the American Philosophical Society (Philadelphia, PA, 1981).

Index

acorn, 7, 149
Actor-Network theory, 26
Adalbertus, marquis, 216
Adaloald (d. 628), king, 196
Adeodatus (d. 618), pope, 211
Agilulf (d. 616), king, 196
agriculture
    Medieval period, 74, 96–7, 103, 110, 112, 136, 138, 155
    Roman period, 22, 41, 45, 47, 112, 124, 157, 160
    and charity, 30
    and cultural values, 158, 161, 172
Agro Romano, 91, *See also* Rome, food supply
agronomic literature, 102–3, 158, *See also* Columella, Gargilius Martialis, Palladius
Aistulf (d. 756), king, 207, 210
al-Andalus, 101, 103, 177
Alife, 57
allotments, 34, 45, 153
    squatter occupation, 153
almonds, 41
aloe, 183, 184
Alphabet of Galen, 177, 181, 183–5, 187
Amalfi, 19, 80–1, 138, 139
    geography, 80
Amalfitans
    Johannis, 80
    Sergius, *dux*, 80
Amatus of Montecassino, 98–9
Ambrose (d. 397), bishop of Milan, 164, 171
Ambrosiaster, 172
amiscere, 152
Ammianus Marcellinus, 49
aniseed, 108, 113
annona, xiv, 23, 45, 125, 193
    role in late Roman economy, 118, 119, 125
Anthimus (d. 525), 180

apple, 22, 28, 149, 151, 181, 227, 231
aqueducts, 60, 67, 86, 88, 92, 146, 198, *See also* Rome:aqueducts
Arabia, 182, 182
archaeobotany, 23, 28, 58, 103–7
architecture
    preserving memory, 196, 201, 206
    reuse of ancient buildings, 55, 198, 199, 200, 213
    specialist artisans, 70, 211, 234, 200
    status, 199, 200
    in Roman period, 191
Arechis II (d. 787), king, 197, 199
Arezzo, 126
Arno, 72, 82
Arsenius, bishop of Orte, 134
Arthur, Paul, 16, 54–5, 63
artichoke, 230
asparagus, 45, 187, 230
Augustine (d. 430), bishop of Hippo, 162, 164, 169

Balzaretti, Ross, 85, 206
Banaji, Jairus, 122
Baresi
    Caloiohannes, 80
    Falco, *iudex*, 80
    Gualprandus, a priest, 80
    Tamfinita, 80
Bari, 19, 80, 195
    cathedral pavement donors, 195
    geography, 80
barley, 7, 91, 104–6, 110
Barnish, Sam, 125
basil, 112, 183, 184
baths, bathing facilities, 35, 51, 148, 174, 184, 197
    gardens nearby, 37, 86, 94
bay (*Laurus nobilis*), 40
beans, 7, 45, 81, 95, 106, 146, 148, 149–51
    fava, 7, 41, 106

291

Index

beet, 113
Benedict of Nursia (d. 547), 166, 168, 170
benefices, 190, 202–3, 235
Beneventans
  Iohannes, gastald and *iudex*, 229
Benevento, 11, 19, 137, 141, 197, 199, 204
  churches, S. Bartolomeo and
    S. Gennaro, 229
  churches, S. Modesto, 229
  late antique civic euergetism, 194
  property documents, 18
  suburban agriculture, 229
Berengar I (d. 924), king and emperor, 123, 127
  gifts of land, 206, 212–18
berries, 28, 45, 107, *See also* blackberry, raspberry, strawberry
Bertilla, consort of Berengar, 213, 216
Billongo, bishop of Verona, 146
blackberry, 28, 107, 112
blackberry/raspberry, 227
blackthorn, 112
Bobbio, monastery, 121, 130, 148, 159, 211
Bologna
  marketing rights, 127
Boniface, saint of Ferentino, 168
Bosi, Giovanna, 110, 232
box (*Buxus*), 97, 227
bread, 46, 143, 149, 150, 151, 166, 172, 193, 228
  charitable distribution, 91, 146, 174
Brebion of Reggio, 19
Brescia, 46, 55, 62, 195
  churches, S. Giulia, 104–6, 141
  churches, S. Salvatore, 216
  late antique houses, 53
Brogiolo, Gian Pietro, 12, 198, 201
Brown, Peter R. L., 225
Brussels
  Dark Earth, 67
bustard, 181

cabbage, 41, 45, 108, 168, 227, 231
Cagiano de Azevedo, Michelangelo, 15, 16
Capasso, Bartolomeo, 20
Capitulare de Villis, 177–8, 181
Capri, 80–1, 138
Carandini, Andrea, 12, 47
cardamom, 182, 183, 184
Carolingian capitularies, 145, 198, *See also* *Capitulare de Villis*
Carolingian court, 203, 207
Carolingian rulers, 202
  governance of Italy, 126

carrot, 112–3, 231
cartularies, 17, 20
Cassiodorus (Flavius Magnus Aurelius Cassiodorus Senator) (d. *c*. 585), 60–1, 125, 159, 166, 170, 177, 180
Castelletto di Brenzone, 65
Cato the Elder (d. 149 BCE), 46, 157
celery, 161, 230
centuriation, 82
chamomile, 188
charitable institutions, 147, 233
  diaconiae, 88, 90, 91, 173
  xenodochia, 91, 173, 174, 176, 189, 217
charity for the poor, 20, 91, 146, 174
Christian values, 193
  in late antiquity, 193
Charlemagne (d. 814), king and emperor, 130, 210, *See also* Carolingian rulers
Charles III (the Fat) (d. 888), king and emperor, 215
cheese, 174, 180
cherry, 22, 108, 112, 113
chestnut, 7, 22, 27, 107, 121, 149, 150, 184, 285
chestnut groves, 27, 83, 116
chicken, 149, 184
chicory, 112–3
Chrètien de Troyes, 99
Chronicle of Ahimaaz, 139
chrysocolla, 182
Ciaraldi, Marina, 39, 41
citrus
  citron, 7–8, 22, 41
city, *See* urbanism
city walls, 14, 65, 83, 92, 109, 224
Cividale, 197
Classe, 181
Clement of Alexandria (d. *c*. 215), 162
clerical landowners, 96, 218
client–patron relations, 147
  in antiquity, 49–50, 190
climate change (historical), 71–4, 107
Codex Justinianus, 47, 50
coin hoards, 142
  in Alpine passes, 142
  in Italy, 140
  in Rhine-Meuse, 142
coins and coin use, 140–4
  Byzantine, 140, 141
  in charters, 140
  Islamicate, 140–1, 204
  Italian coins in circulation outside of Italy, 142
  Lombard, 140
colonus (Roman agricultural worker), 158

Index

coltura promiscua, 22
Columella, Lucius Junius Moderatus (d. 70 CE), 158, 159, 160, 161
Comacchio, 130
Constantinople, 50, 179, 236
  coins from, 140
  gardens in, 236
coriander, 95, 108, 181
corniolo/dogberry, 28, 107, 112
Corteleona, 197
Cosa, 32
Costambeys, Marios, 123
costus root, 182, 183, 184
courtyard, 16, 33, 36, 80, 81, 83–4, 94, 113, 132, 174, 175, 204, 224
Crawford, Michael, 143
Cremona, 62, 126, 130
crocus, 162, 184–5
crop diversification, 233
  in late antiquity, 107
cucurbits, 94–5, 162
cumin, 130, 182, 182
cypress, 40, 162

Dagibertus, bishop of Novara, 127
damson, 113, *See* plum
Dark Earth, 10, 23–4, 29, 53, 55, 57, 58, 79, 226
  history of the idea, 61–64
  micromorphological analysis, 64
date palm, 41
Davies, Wendy, 103, 176
Delogu, Paolo, 6, 16, 92
Desiderius (d. 786), king, 207
Deusdedit, subdeacon (Ravenna), 36
Deusdedit, cardinal (d. 1097/1100), canonical collection, 37
'Dig for Victory', 153
dill, 112–3
dinar, 142, *See also* coins, Islamicate
Dioscurides, (d. 90 CE), 183, 187
Djemila (Cuicul), 23
donation of land
  as social ties, 204, 219
  to churches, 36, 77, 91
donation 'pro anima', 82, 196, 212

economy
  changes in late antiquity, 70–2, 125
  Early Medieval, 21, 92, 118–20, 125–6, 136, 205
  Roman, 23, 44–5, 199
eggs, 148, 151, 152
einkorn, 105–6
elderberry, 107, 112

elite patronage, *See* euergetism
emmer wheat, 110
environmental history, 27
estate management
  Medieval, 83, 90–1, 120–1, 172
  paterfamilas, head of household, 171
  Roman, 45–7
Ethiopia, 182
euergetism, 196
  bishops, 194
  in late antiquity, 191–5
  inscriptions, 195
European commercial revolution, 119, 128, 137
exotic goods in Italy, 130, 178, 181, 187

Farfa, monastery, 123, 141
fennel, 184
Ferrara, 29, 188
  Corso Porta Reno, 65, 109–13
  statutes, 113
fertilizer, 46, 67, *See also* manure
fig, 22, 113
flax, 100, 113, 144
Flexo, 77
Florence, 195
  excavations at the Uffizi, 66, 67
flowers, ancient Rome, 45, 116, *See also* garlands rose, violet
food sellers
  Roman period, 116
forget-me-not, 40
Formia, 91
Formula Augiensis, 181
formulae in diplomatics, 18, 19, 77, 205, 224
Frankish politics, 18, 19, 77, 171, 205, 224
  centrality of Rome, 207
Fulrad, abbot of St-Denis (d. 784), 207–12

galbanum, 183, 184
gardeners, professional, 138
gardens, *See also uiridaria*
  ancient Roman, 23, 44, 192
  animals in, 101
  archaeobotanical evidence, 103–7
  cultural value, 176, 191
  in courtly literature, 98, 99
  in suburban Roman tomb plots, 161
  vocabulary of, 15–16
  worked collectively, 152–3
Gargilius Martialis, 159, 167
garlands, 41, 161, 162, 232
garlic, 45

Index

Gaudiosus, *defensor* (Ravenna), 36
Genoa, 121
Gisulf II (d. after 1089), prince, 139
gladiolus, 97
gourd, *See* curcurbits
Gozzano, 127
grain, 21, 46, 81, 106, 110, 181, 227, 235,
  See also annona
grape, 5, 7, 20, 39, 41, 108, 112, 235
grass pea, 81, 106
greens, 148
Gregory I (d. 604, pope), 32–9, 71,
    137, 170
  Dialogues, 167–9
  Register, 33–6, 166
Gregory of Tours (d. 594), 71

Hadrian (d. 798), pope, 89, 91, 212
hazelnut, 22, 108, 112
hemp, 113
Herdonia, 43
honey, 184, 187
Honorius I (d. 638), pope, 173, 211
  Register, 37
Horden, Peregrine, 178, 236
hortulanus as surname, 137
house types, 16
  2-storey, 173
  courtyards, 16
  late Roman townhouses, 10, 225
  roofs, 16
  tiled roof, 6
  tower houses, 113
  townhouse, 6, 7, 113, 176, 217
household-level economic activity, 24, 126,
    136, 147, 235
households
  as centres of charity, 172, 176
  religious, 166, 232
Hudson, Peter, 12
hyssop, 112, 113

Iberia, 103, 176
Ibn Ḥawqal, 100
immunity, royal, 126, 209, 211, 221
imports to Italy, *See* exotic goods
  absence of pottery, 131
inscriptions, 190–4, 195, 196, 199
Iohannes, Bishop of Palermo, 35
Isidore, bishop of Seville, 21
  Libri etymologiarum, 160
Italy
  agricultural estates comprising small
    parcels, 120
  differences between North and South, 21

geography, 225
land ownership in the early middle
  ages, 120
Ostrogothic kingdom, 225

jannāt, 103
Jashemski, Wilhelmina, 39, 41
Jerome of Stridon (d. 420), 163, 173
John Chrysostom (d. 407), 163
John the Deacon (Hymmonides)
  (d. *c*. 882), 133
Johnson, Paul, 57
Jones, Philip, 136
juniper berry, 183–4
Justin Martyr, *Apologia*, 162

kinship networks and movement of goods,
    143, 146
Kreiner, Jaimie, 27

La Rocca, Cristina, 12, 15, 20, 217
La Roy Ladurie, Emmanuel, 154
land ownership, 121
  and social ties, 120, 202
lard, 187
late antiquity, 119, 225
  economic declines, 69–70
latifundia, 60, *See also* estate management
Lazio
  statutes on manuring, 67
leeks, 7, 148, 181
legumes, 81, 91, 106, 181
lentil, 105–6, 112
Leo III (d. 816), pope, 91
lettuce, 45, 108, 112–3
Leyser, Conrad, 166
Liber Pontificalis, 71, 89, 90, 159
Life of Gregory, Bishop of Agrigento, 169
lily, 97, 162, 163, 177
Liutprand (d. 744), king, 196, 197
Lombard kingdom, 196
  patronage, 197
  royal court at Pavia, 84
London
  Dark Earth, 61, 62
  food production in the nineteenth
    century, 230–1
Lothar I (d. 855), king and emperor, 126
Louis II (d. 875), king and emperor, 126,
    130, 198
Louis the Pious (d. 840), king and
    emperor, 130
Lucca, 4, 18, 19, 29, 57, 76, 78, 81, 173,
    178, 199, 223
  churches, S. Giorgio, now S. Paolo, 76

Index

churches, S. Michael the Archangel, 81
churches, SS. Gemignano, Paolo
  e Andrea, 173
city walls, 83
coin use, 143, 144
Roman period, 83
urban landscape in the early Middle
  Ages, 83
xenodochium, 174
Lucchesi
  Aurepert, a cleric, 76
  Berucionus Belongonus, 76
  Filipert, a cleric, 83
  Gaidualdo, *uir magnificus*, 83–5
  Grasolf, *munitario*, 144
  Iordanus, *uir uenerabilis*, priest, 76
  Pertuald, *uir deuotus*, 81–2

macellum, 57, 116, 139
Machado, Carlos, 49
Mantua, 62
manure, 66–67, 75, 225
Marano, 7, 148
markets
  as places of social interaction, 124
  as sources of income for the state, 124
  market structures, Milan, 131
  market structures, Pavia, 132
  market structures, Rome, 132–4
  regulations, in ninth century, 126
  rights for urban entities, 128
Martialis, Quintus Gargilius, 158
Martin, Jean-Marie, 12
McCormick, Michael, 118, 142, 182
medicinal garden (*pigmentarium*), 81
medicine
  Galenic principles, 180
  garden products in, 176–188
  recipes for remedies, 180
  translation of texts, 179
melon, 113, 177, 230
Meneghini, Roberto, 52–3
merchants, 127, 145
  of Milan, 132
  of Rome, 134
  of Venice, 130
Metz, 181
Mezzocorona, 104
Milan, 1, 11, 14, 18, 19, 23, 57, 141,
  223, 224
  church properties, 36
  churches, S. Ambrogio, 132, 224
  churches, S. Maria alla Porta, 53
  churches, S. Simpliciano, 196
  coins recovered, 141

late antique houses, 53
lost archiepiscopal archive, 19
market, 131, 139
property documents, 18
Sesto Calende, 127
via Tomasso Grossi, 53
xenodochium, 174
Milanese
  Andreas, archbishop, 174
millet, 7, 104, 106, 110, 146, 148, 149, 150,
  180, 184, 254
mills, 83, 215
mint, 108
Modena, 28
modius, xiv, 81, 89
monasteries
  as centres of consumption, 123, 126
  monastic rules, gardens, 165–7
Montanari, Massimo, 21
Monte Amiata, monastery, 127
Monte S. Angelo, 142
Montecassino, 99, 166, 210,
  223
Monza, 146
  S. Agata, 146
  Thedoaldo, 146
Morgencap, 115
Morley, Neville, 47
Moscow, percentage of families engaged in
  urban agriculture, 153
mustard, 95, 108
Myers, Sara, 158
myrrh, 183, 184

Naples, 7, 11, 16, 19, 23, 32, 57, 79, 104,
  125, 148, 218–20, 223
  churches, S. Eufemia, 218
  churches, S. Gregorio Armeno,
    148
  churches, S. Lorenzo Maggiore, 57
  churches, S. Maria, 204
  churches, SS. Marcellinus and
    Petrus, 148
  churches, SS. Sergius and Bacchus,
    149, 218
  families, 205
  formation of Dark Earth, 57–58
  loss of archival documents, 20
  Palazzo Giusso, 58
  property documents, 7
  regions, Balnei nobi, 137
  regions, Duos Amantes, 218
  regions, Ficariola, 219
  regions, Porta Capuana, 7
  regions, 'Viridario', 218

296   Index

Naples (cont.)
  rise in value of land in 11th century, 138
  Sol et Luna street, 152
  suburban cultivation, 229
  suburbs, Miano, 7
  suburbs, Sede Furcillense, 203
  suburbs, Terzo, 149
  vico Carminiello ai Mannesi, 56
  vico S. Giorgio, 7
Napoletani
  Barbaria, nun, 218–20
  Bonus, *hortulanus*, 137
  Constantinus, *hortulanus*, 137
  Isauri (or Isabri) family, 218–20
  Maria, wife of Peter, 203
  Maru, widow, 218–20
  Pancratius, higumen of SS. Sergius and Bacchus, 149–52
  Peter, *tribunus*, 203
Nicosia, Cristiano, 64, 67
night soil, 66, 67, *See also* fertilizer
Nonantola, abbey, 132, 224
Norman kings of Sicily, 101
North Africa
  role in late Roman economy, 119
nut trees, 20, 22, 44, *See also* chestnut, hazelnut

oat, 110, 112
oikonomia, 170, 171
olive, 22, 39, 83, 89, 107, 235
ollae perforatae, 39
onions, 1, 7, 41, 45, 148
orchards, 22, 41, 76, 88
oregano, 113
ornamental garden plants, 40
ornamental gardens, 97, *See uiridaria*
Ostia, 32, 43, 116
  Garden Houses (Case a Giardino), 43
otium
  Church fathers' view on, 165
Otranto, 141
Otto I (d. 973), emperor, 132
Otto III (d. 1002), 128
Ovid (Publius Ovidius Naso) (d. 17/18 CE), 162

Pachomian rule, 165
Pacificus of Verona, 20
Paestum, 161
paideia, 170
Palermo, 23, 99, 100, 102
Palladius, Rutilius Taurus Aemilianus, 158
  Opus agriculturae in the early Middle Ages, 159

panic (*panicum*), 180
Parma, 130, 145, 195
  Cassa di Risparmio excavations, 134
  Forum, 134
  markets, 134
Parmigiani
  Heripertus, archdeacon, 145
  Rimpertus, priest, 145
  Stephanus, subdeacon, 146
parsley, 112–3, 184
parsnip, 112–3
partible inheritance, 120
pastio villatica, 148
paterfamilias (head of household), 171, 233
patronage of buildings, 196–9, 201–3, 211, 234
Paul the Deacon, 197
Paulinus (d. 431), bishop of Nola, 168
Pavia, 11, 50, 130, 132, 197, 224
  Iohannes, bishop, 175, 206, 217
payment in coin, 140, 141, 144
payment in 'gifts', 148, 151, *See also amiscere*
payment in kind, 147, 148, 151
peach, 113
peach/plum, 22, 227
pear, 22, 28
peasant autonomy in the early Middle Ages, 121
Pippin (d. 810), king of Italy, 198
Pippin (d. 768), king of the Franks, 207
pepper, 130, 182
pergolas, 1, 2, 3, 15, 22, 36, 46, 88
Pesaro, 207
Pescara, 57
phytoliths, 65, 66, 67
Piacenza, 14, 16, 120
Pickering, Andrew, 28
Pilsworth, Claire, 183
pimpernel, 40, 184
pineapple, 230
pinenut, 112–3
Pistoia, 83, 128
  hinterland, 84
  monastery of S. Bartolomeo, 84
Plan of St-Gall, 177
pleasure gardens, *See uiridaria*
  Roman period, 46, 97
Pliny the Elder, 97
  Natural history, 159, 161, 181
plum, 60, 108, 112–3, 227
Polanyi, Karl, 122
'politics of land', 27, 202
Poliziano, antiquarian, 159
Pompeii, 32, 116

Index

damage in 64 CE and modifications to houses, 40–2
House of Hercules's Wedding, 39
House of the Surgeon, 39
House of the Vestals, 39, 40
'Market Garden Orchard', 42
ornamental plants, 39
scale of urban cultivation, 41
poppy, 40, 113, 177, 187, 188
pork, 91, 146, 184, 193
  market in late antiquity, 125
  Merovingian consumption, 27
potato, 231, 235
preservation of memory
  through patronage, 196
privileges, papal, 208–11
privileges, royal, 216
property documents
  Arabic documents from Italy, 19
  boundary clauses, 18, 205
  family relationships, 219
  from Naples, 78
  in Byzantine Italy, 19
Prudentius (Aurelius Prudentius Clemens) (d. c. 413), 163
pumpkin, *See* cucurbits
Purcell, Nicholas, 47, 157, 236
purple gromwell, 40
purslane, 113

Quintus Aurelius Symmachus (d. 402), 194
Quirós Castillo, Juan Antonio, 200

Raduald of Antraccoli, 18
Rapone, Francesca, 128
raspberry, 28, 107, 112
Ratchis, 208, 210
Ratoldus, bishop of Verona, 20, 130
Ravenna, 1, 4, 11, 14, 36, 179, 180, 201, 207
  coins, use in documents, 144
regional markets, 125, 126
  late Roman period, 126
Regnum Italiae, 140
  Carolingian practices around land, 203
  legislating encouraging urban maintenance, 197
Regula (of Benedict), 166
Regula ad virgines, 167
Regula magistri, 166, 172
Regula monasterii tarnatensis, 167
Reichenau, abbey, 177
relics, 211
rents
  obligatory gifts, 151

paid in kind, 149
rice, 181
Riddle, John, 181
Rimini, 207
  Piazza Ferrari, 65
Rio, Alice, 122
river transport, 127
rocket, 113
Roger II (d. 1154), king of Sicily, 101
Romani
  Crescentius Murcapullo, 88–9, 94, 96, 236
  Crescentius, son of Petrus, 6
  Demetria, 94
  Domenicus, swineherd, 94
  Eustacio, dispensator of S. Maria in Cosmedin, 86
  Giorgio, *dux*, 86
  Helena, daughter of Petrus and Ursa, 6
  Iohannes, abbot of SS. Cosma e Damiano, 94
  Iohannes, priest and monk, formerly the duke of Albano, 96
  Jewish merchants, 134
  Leo, a priest of the church of SS. Quattro Coronati, 6
  Leo Protoscrinarius, 92
  Petro, *uir honestus, cervinus*, 94
  Pipino, *vestararius*, 96
  Romano, a subdeacon, 96
Rome, 1, 4, 11, 19, 23, 29, 32, 57, 125, 193, 223
  aqueducts, 59, 92, 198
  aqueducts, Aqua Alessandrina, 94
  aqueducts, Forma Jovia, 94
  aristocratic housing, 212
  artisans, 94
  Baths of Alexander Severus, 94
  Baths of Diocletian, 86
  Campo de' Fiori market (modern), 131
  Carolingian properties, 207
  churches, S. Cecilia, 91
  churches, S. Crisogono, 91
  churches, S. Erasmo, 6, 88, 94
  churches, S. Maria in Domnica, 91
  churches, S. Maria in via Lata, 95
  churches, S. Maria Maggiore, 195
  churches, S. Maria Nova, 3, 6
  churches, S. Martino, 208
  churches, S. Paolo fuori le mura, 35
  churches, S. Prassede, 91
  churches, S. Saba, 169
  churches, S. Stefano, 96
  churches, S. Stefano Maggiore, 91

Rome (cont.)
  churches, S. Stephan cata Galla Patricia, 208
  churches, S. Susanna, 86
  churches, S. Teodoro, 92
  churches, SS. Benedict, Maria, and Biagio, 94
  churches, SS. Ciriaco and Nicola, 229
  churches, SS. Cosma e Damiano in Mica Aurea, 94
  churches, SS. Nereo ed Achilleo, 96
  churches, SS. Sergio e Bacco, 91
  churches, St Peter's, 91, 208
    coins at St Peter's, 144
  churches, St Paul's, 91
  college of gardeners, 95
  Column of Phocas, market stalls nearby, 132
  convents, 34
  Crypta Balbi, 141, 143
  Curia Senatus, 191
  domuscultae, 89, 91–2
  ecclesiastical ownership of property, 146
  evidence of early medieval gardens in documents, 85–97
  food gardening in antiquity, 43–6
  Forum Holitorium, 45
  Forum of Caesar, excavations, 108–9
  Forum of Caesar, medieval houses, 92
  Forum of Nerva, 200
  Forum of Peace, 192, 234
  Forum of Trajan, 108
  Forum Romanum, 132, 200
  hinterland, 91
  hinterland, Campanino, 6
  hinterland, Portuense, 94, 95
  Horrea Piperataria, 45
  Horti, 46
  Imperial Fora, 108
  market structures, 132
  papal household, 147
  Piazza dei Cinquecento, 51, 52
  population, scale, 7, 45
  Porta Maggiore, 92, 93, 95
  Porta Metronia, 88, 89
  Porta Portuense, 95
  professional gardeners, 95, 138
  property documents, 6, 86
  Regio 1, 34, 37, 86, 96
  Regio 2, 6
  Regio 4, 6, 37, 37, 86
  Regio 6, 17
  Regio 9, 37, 92, 229
  regions, ad Scorticlari, 94
  regions, Aventine, 86
  regions, Caelian hill, 6, 88, 90, 94, 96, 227
  regions, Campus Martius, 94
  regions, Capitoline, 139
  regions, *Decenniae*, 6, 89, 90
  regions, Testaccio, 38
  regions, Trastevere, 16, 94
  regions, Viminal Hill, 86
  rise in monetization, 96
  Roman church, 6, 36, 90, 91, 123, 193, 277
  Roman Forum, 191
  scola of gardeners in 1030, 138
  specialised market gardens, 95
  Temple of Venus and Rome, 6
  Theatre of Marcellus, 139
  Tiber, 71
  via Lata, 88
  xenodochia, 91
roof tiles, 83
  stamped with patrons' names, 196
Rosalia, 161
rose, 97, 161, 163, 183, 184, 192, 232, 234
Rosenwein, Barbara, 206, 216
Rovelli, Alessia, 142–4
rue, 177
rye, 106

S. Giovanni di Ruoti, villa, 125
S. Vincenzo al Volturno, 131, 141, 203–4
saccapanna, 7, 184
saffron, 184
sage, 177
Salernitani
  Alfano, archbishop, 139
  Angilpert, priest, 115
  Wiletruda, widow, 115
Salerno, 6, 16, 19, 23, 115–16, 139, 147, 179, 204
  suburban market, 128
salute, 152
Salzman, Michele, 193
Santangeli Valenzani, Riccardo, 92
Saracens, 116
  taking captives, 203
Sarris, Peter, 122
savory, 113, 184
scola, 189
self-sufficiency, 5, 30, 31, 35, 90, 121, 126, 158, 189, 223, 232
Sergius I (d. 701), pope, 37
sesame, 148
Sessa, Kristina, 171
Sicily, *See also* Palermo
  early Middle Ages, 100

Index

Norman court society, 98
Norman gardens, 101
slavery, in the early Middle Ages, 122
sorb, 112
sorghum, 106, 110
sorrel, 113
sour cherry, 113
spolia, *See* architecture: reuse of building materials
squash, 95
Squatriti, Paolo, 27–8, 71, 106, 223
statues, honorific, 192, 194, *See also* euergetism
St-Denis, monastery, 207
  exemptions, 211
Stephen II (d. 757) pope, 207
St-Gall, monastery, 182
St-Martin of Tours, monastery, 211
Story, Joanna, 208
strawberry, 107, 112
Subiaco Register, 88
Syracuse
  coins from, 140

Tabacco, Giovanni, 216
Terres noires, 61, *See also* Dark Earth
Tertullian (Quintus Septimius Florens Tertullianus) (d. c. 220), 163
Theodoric (d. 526), king of Italy, 50, 59, 180
Theodosius (d. 395), emperor, 60
Theuderic I (d. 533/4), king, 181
thyme, 113, 184
Tiber, 72
  markets, proximity to, 139
tobacco, 1
Toto of Campione, 223
Toubert, Pierre, 81, 136
Tours, 27, *See also* St-Martin, monastery
  Prosper-Mérimée Square, 66
Translatio sancti Viti martyris, 211
turnip, 231

uiridaria, 15, 23, 50, 97, 98, 216, 232
urban agriculture, 82
  in London, 230
  in Moscow, 153
  models, 47
  New Deal gardens, 153
urban archaeology, 10
urban economy, 227
urban processions, 14, 126, 134

urban rubbish, 46, 57, 58, 61, 63, 110
urban transformations
  abandonment, 58
  caused by war, 50
  Dark Earth, 63
  in eleventh century, 139
  late antiquity, 38, 51, 55
  townhouses subdivided in late antiquity, 51, 74
urbanism
  as a heuristic, 13
  commercial activity, 128
  context for prestigious gifts of cultivated lands, 217
  early medieval, scholarship of, 11
  elite competition, 206
  Lombard, 14
  of Italy, 9, 11
  of Rome, 11

Val di Serchio, 82
Vandal conquest of North Africa, 193
Varro, Marcus Terentius (d. 27 BCE), 97, 157, 161
Venice, 118, 130
Venosa, 139
Vergil (Publius Vergilius Maro) (d. 19 BCE), 162
  Georgics, 157, 161
Verona, 11, 12, 14, 212–16, 223
  castrum, 206
  churches, S. Pietro in Corte, 212
  churches, S. Siro, 175
  churches, S. Zeno, 130, 217
  Dark Earth, 62
  market, 130
  royal precinct, 213
  property documents, 215
  theatre, 174
  urban transformation under Berengar, 216
  xenodochium, 175
Veronesi
  Atto, 212
  Billongo, bishop, 146
  Dagibert, deacon, 175
  Grimaldus, 213
  Ingelfredus, 217
  Iohannes, bishop of Pavia, 217
  Iohannes, chamberlain, 213
  Iohannes, cleric, 217
  Vualfredus, count, 212
viburnum, 40
villa culture, 44
Vimercate, 127

vineyard, 1, 10, 15, 22, 35, 36, 38, 42, 45, 75, 76, 79, 82, 86, 91, 92, 94, 96, 108, 158, 168, 173, 224, 229
violet, 40, 97, 161, 163, 188
Viper's bugloss, 41
Vitruvius (Marcus Vitruvius Pollio) (d. 15 BCE), 158, 170
Vivarium, 166, 177
vocabulary of horticulture, 15
Volterra, bishop's market, 127
von Thünen, *Der isolierte Staat*, 47, 48, 97, 231

Walahfrid Strabo
 Hortulus, 177
walnut, 227
watermelon, 113

wheat, xiv, 7, 23, 28, 39, 45, 83, 89, 91, 104, 106, 110, 118, 147, 149, 151, 184
Wickham, Chris, 118, 121, 143
William I, king of Sicily, 101
William II, king of Sicily, 101
wills, 146, 174, 175
Wilson, Andrew, 46
wine, 23, 146, 147, 148, 149, 193
 charitable distribution, 91, 174
witnesses, 205

xenodochia, 146, 175, *See* charitable institutions

Zacharias (d. 752), pope, 207, 210

For EU product safety concerns, contact us at Calle de José Abascal, 56–1°,
28003 Madrid, Spain or eugpsr@cambridge.org.

www.ingramcontent.com/pod-product-compliance
Lightning Source LLC
LaVergne TN
LVHW011800060526
838200LV00053B/3641